MAO TSE-TUNG

(Translation of Mao's *Loushan Pass*
February, 1935, during the Long March)

Fierce the west wind,
Wild geese cry under the frosty morning moon.
Under the frosty morning moon
Horses' hooves clattering,
Bugles sobbing low.

Idle boast the strong pass is a wall of iron,
With firm strides we are crossing its summit.
We are crossing its summit,
The rolling hills sea-blue,
The dying sun blood-red.

MAO TSE-TUNG

THE MAN AND THE MYTH

ERIC CHOU

STEIN AND DAY/*Publishers*/New York

To Virginia and my grandchildren

First published in the United States of America in 1982
Copyright © 1980 by Eric Chou
All rights reserved
Printed in the United States of America
Stein and Day/*Publishers*/Scarborough House
Briarcliff Manor, New York 10510

Library of Congress Cataloging in Publication Data

Chou, Eric, 1915-
    Mao Tse-tung, the man and the myth.

    Bibliography: p.
    Includes index.
    1. Mao, Tse-tung, 1893-1976.   2. Heads of state—
China—Biography.
DS778.M3C5353   1981   951.05'092'4 [B]   80-22758
ISBN 0-8128-2769-4

CONTENTS

Introduction: The Making of the Myth   1

1 Early Years and School Days   9
2 The Road to Marxism   30
3 Between Collaboration and Subversion   51
4 The Plunge into Civil War   68
5 The First Taste of Power Struggle   90
6 The Long March and After   113
7 The Land of Promise   139
8 The Decisive Civil War   160
9 The Man in the Forbidden City   175
10 The Addiction to Power   201
11 Mao as an Individual   223
12 The Future of Maoism   243

Chronology   253
Notes on Sources   261
Biographical notes   273
Index   281

ILLUSTRATIONS

Between p 142 and p 143

A youthful-looking Mao Tse-tung
A photo of Mao taken by the author in 1945
Mao arrives in Chungking for peace talks
Mao speech-making and instructing the Red Devils in Yenan, 1942
Mao toasts Chiang Kai-shek in Chungking
Mao speaking at the 7th party congress in Yenan
Mao and Chou En-lai in Yenan, 1945
Mao and Chiang Ching in their ninth year of marriage
Mao declares the establishment of the People's Republic of China
Mao reviews a naval unit off Shanghai in 1953
Mao amidst the harvest in Hunan
Chou En-lai is met by Mao after a visit to Moscow in 1964
Mao, Chou En-lai and Chiang Ching with a group of Red Guards
The official face of Mao

Maps

Central and South China   *80-81*
Red Bases in China 1930-34   *108-9*
Routes of the Long March   *132-3*
Communist Areas of North China before 1947   *168-9*
China's Administrative Divisions   *188-9*

INTRODUCTION
THE MAKING OF THE MYTH

Xerox

The appearance of Mao Tse-tung on the twentieth century world scene is undoubtedly a phenomenon of major importance. He has reshaped the destiny of a quarter of mankind, tipped the balance between democracy and totalitarianism and inspired revolutionary struggles for power all over the world. But as a person he is probably the least known of the modern political leaders. In the eyes of many, he may appear as a mixture of papal infallibility and oriental inscrutability. Yet in reality, he was a man with a deep-rooted sense of insecurity, obsessively suspicious and haunted by fears. Throughout his life, whether in the political wilderness or on the throne of power, he remained in his shell, insular and unfathomable. Even when among his most faithful followers he seldom relaxed his guard, choosing to hide his feelings behind an ever-present smile. To them he was as much a myth as he was to his adversaries. He was feared, respected and worshipped, but never loved.

To have reached the dazzling heights of power, Mao was indeed a most unusual man. But he could only have done it in China in that particular period when the combination of events worked in his favour. Since the humiliating defeat in the second Opium War (1857 – 60), the Manchu Court had lost its prestige as the symbol of an effective imperial rule. Compounded by a protracted series of civil strife and disturbances, notably the Taiping Rebellion (1850 – 64) and the Moslem Rebellion (1862 – 78), the nation's resources were drained by heavy military expenditure. To make matters worse, from time to time droughts and floods caused extensive famine. While the ordinary people starved to death in their thousands, the Manchu rulers in Peking continued to indulge in luxury and corrupt practices. Civil unrest was rife and the Mandate from

1

Heaven, claimed by the Manchus, could no longer be used as a magic wand.

Naturally, not all the court officials were unaware of the grave situation. Realizing that political reform and modernization were needed, the more enlightened ones headed by Li Hung-chang and Chang Chih-tung convinced Emperor Tung Chih of the feasibility of Westernization, by which they meant learning selectively from the West in the hope of strengthening the imperial system. Special envoys were sent to Japan, America and Europe on fact-finding missions and in 1872 the first group of Chinese students went abroad to study. What the Manchu rulers intended to learn from the West was science and technology. They wanted technical knowledge to build railroads, steamships and factories and to produce their own arms and ammunition. They regarded the bold venture as the beginning of a self-strengthening movement.

But by opening up communications with the West they also got some things they had not bargained for. The students going abroad did not restrict themselves to the study of science and technology alone: thrown into a totally different atmosphere of free thinking and independent judgement, they got over the intitial cultural shock and began to doubt the social values and the political system they had known back home. It dawned on them that what was wrong with their country might be more fundamental than they had been given to understand. Inspired by national pride and patriotism, they started to seek answers in Western philosophy and political thought. Constitutional monarchy, republicanism and democracy all had their attractions, and they lost no time in conveying these novel ideas back to China. With Shanghai, under the protective umbrella of extra-territoriality imposed by the Western powers, functioning as the centre of propagation, the intellectuals were soon exposed to political influence from the West in no small way.

In spite of the suppressive measures enforced by the official bureaucracy at all levels, the new tide of political awareness swept along. Meanwhile, the Manchu Court suffered more defeats in resisting the aggressive designs of foreign powers. The Sino-French War (1884 – 5) and the Sino-Japanese War (1894 – 5) ended with more concessions and humiliations on the part of the Middle Kingdom. Between 1896 and 1899, the 'scramble for concessions' caught on. The British, the Germans, the Russians, the Italians and even the Portuguese all got what they demanded. In sheer desperation, Empress Dowager Tzu Hsi staked her forlorn hopes on the Boxer Rising (1899 – 1900) to get rid of the 'foreign devils'. But the fanaticism of the Boxers was no match for cannon-balls and bullets, liberally fired by the invading forces of Western Allies. The outburst of xenophobia entailed large indemnities paid out to the foreign powers and further disgrace for the Imperial rulers.

It was against this background that Mao Tse-tung was born and grew up. Like most of his contemporaries, he cherished the dream of seeing a strong China emerge. But unlike them he wanted to take action and be a force in building up the new country. For a peasant boy who had hardly set foot beyond the limits of his backwater village before the age of fifteen, Mao's ambition owed much to the natural gift of an active mind. He read avidly and was particularly fond of historical novels which never ceased to fire his imagination. While other boys of his age might read these novels for amusement, he relived the lives and adventures of ancient heroes in his reveries over and over again. Of these novels, *The Water Margin* and the *Romance of the Three Kingdoms* influenced him most and became his constant sources of inspiration. The former, the Chinese equivalent of Robin Hood, portrays a group of 108 rebels who were thrown together by various incidents and circumstances. They were the victims of corrupt politics in the Sung Dynasty and were forced to take the law into their own hands, executing the corrupt officials and robbing the rich to give to the poor. *Romance of the Three Kingdoms*, comparable to Tolstoy's *War and Peace*, is a war novel set in the historical period of the Three Kingdoms (A.D. 221 – 265), dealing fully with political intrigues, diplomatic manoeuvres and military strategy and tactics. In China both books had been extremely popular for years, circulating in every corner of the country. They must have been read by millions and millions of people, yet none of these readers could have taken them more seriously than the young Mao did. Their impact on him was so great that later he even rated the *Romance of the Three Kingdoms* higher than Marxist writings when he led the Chinese Communists to fight the Nationalists in the days of the Kiangsi Soviet, years after he had first read it.

With the benefit of hindsight, one can more easily understand why these two novels had been so vital in the shaping of his character. At the turn of the century, Shaoshan was an isolated village and Mao was a lonely child. Rebellious against his unloving father and worn down by the early burden of farm work, he was forced to seek solace from the real world in these works of fiction. Still at a very impressionable age, he gave his fancy a free rein like most children. The difference was, while others could be brought back to the realistic world of parental love and a comfortable home, he found it far more pleasant to live in his imaginary world. With Mao, hatred must have been inborn. In those days, it was not unusual for most fathers to be as severe as his own, though most sons would not have hated their fathers in the way that he did. On his later admission, he really likened his father to the corrupt officials in *The Water Margin* or the treacherous generals in the *Romance of the Three Kingdoms*. For a Chinese son, the harbouring of such thoughts was almost unthinkable.

It was no less strange that, for a boy of his age, he should have identified himself with the character Tsao Tsao in the *Romance of the Three Kingdoms*. A usurper of power, an expert in intrigues and a double dealer, the historical figure portrayed in the novel has always been treated with contempt by readers both old and young. But in the eyes of the young Mao, the universally recognized villain was the hero. How a boy could have reacted so differently from other people after reading the same book defies imagination, unless one is prepared to accept the Chinese Communists' claim that 'Mao is a genius'. Otherwise, it may be explained that he instinctively found himself in the character of Tsao Tsao, with betrayal in his nature.

Aside from these novels, Mao also benefited from his absorption of historical knowledge. Before he started to read Marxist literature in its crudest form, he was already very familiar with the uprisings and rebellions in Chinese history. It impressed him that the peasants were generally the main force behind these events. He also learned about the humble beginnings of many emperors in various dynasties, which must have boosted his confidence and ambition. The rise and fall of the Taiping Rebellion gave him much to ponder over; he knew how its leaders, Hung Hsiu-chuan, Li Hsiu-cheng and Yang Hsiu-ching, failed after their initial success. But it was the tales about Li Tzu-cheng, the leader of the peasant uprising in the seventeenth century, that interested him most. Li swept over the width of the Ming Empire with his peasant forces, captured the Imperial Capital of Peking and drove Emperor Chung Chen to hang himself before the city fell in 1642. The peasant leader started his rebellion against the Ming Court with a handful of ill-equipped men, but it did not take him long to rally more than a million peasants under his command, bringing about the downfall of the Ming Dynasty.

When Mao eventually took up Communism after having toyed with the idea of constitutional monarchy and republicanism, his ambition to rise over the heads of all others remained unchanged. He wanted desperately to reach the top and stay at the top. It was no coincidence that both Chang Kuo-tao and Li Piao, his two rivals in different periods, should have accused him of 'cherishing the dreams of an emperor' and 'being a dictator through and through'. As far as Mao was concerned, political

4

Xerox

theories and systems made little difference to his thirst for power. He might have claimed to be the sole custodian of Marxism and Leninism, but at the same time he thought and behaved like the First Emperor of Chin (221 – 209 B.C.). In spite of what he arguably achieved for China during his lifetime, there is no denying that, like the emperors before him, he ruled by personal decree. It is abundantly clear that in his last years he planned to hand over the reins of power to his wife, Chiang Ching, no matter how the present Chinese leaders now try to dismiss that episode as the Gang of Four's conspiracy to usurp the succession. Since Mao always felt that he owned the whole country, it was only natural for him to try to keep it in the family. With his eldest son, An-ying, killed in the Korean War and the other surviving one, An-ching, mentally unfit, Chiang Ching, in his mind, would have been the logical choice.

If one retraces Mao's rise to power from the very beginning, one can see that it was an uphill struggle against all odds. Compared with the early Chinese Communist leaders, Chen Tu-hsiu, Li Ta-chao and Chang Kuo-tao, Mao was no match for any of them with regard to qualifications or education. Not only did he lack their cultural refinements, he also lagged far behind when it came to a grasp of Marxist theories. He was limited but self-opinionated, with an inclination to argue his head off. On the other hand, his enthusiasm for hard work was boundless and he was always willing to take on additional responsibilities whenever the need arose. These redeeming features doubtless stood him in good stead with his comrades, especially since the party, in its initial stage, consisted of a bunch of intellectuals who preferred pontificating to hard work. They were only too glad to have someone willing to lessen their burden of work. It never occurred to them that Mao was driven more by his personal ambition than altruistic considerations. Gradually but steadily, he strengthened his political muscle and wormed his way up the ladder.

Perhaps it should be pointed out that the stubbornness in Mao was actually his strength. He never conceded defeat. He might lie low for a while when things turned against him, but he was always confident of a comeback. In the art of manoeuvring and manipulating he was quite unequalled. He generally sized up his opponents well and was good at exploiting the weaknesses of human nature, while keeping himself to himself. Even his wife, Chiang Ching, admitted that she never understood him, so how could the other comrades who seldom saw him in his unguarded moments? He was not just ruthless; it was his ability to justify his ruthlessness that counted. He had very little, if any, regard for human lives, and was not afraid of admitting it. Once when the historical records about the First Emperor of Chin were re-examined in China for his benefit, he came out strongly in defence of the ancient tyrant. He was quoted as saying, 'It was nothing that Chin Shih-huang should have buried more than 460 scholars alive . . . In our case we must have at least got rid of 46,000 scholars, one hundred times more'. He spoke of it as though the loss of lives was a very trivial matter, hardly worth bothering about. He held the same harsh attitude towards the heavy casualties China suffered during the Korean War, as well as the cost of millions of lives to the liberation. Yet he had no compunction in attributing all these carnages to the safeguarding of the people's cause. With the expression 'revolution is no garden party', he made light of the price paid for it.

But ruthlessness alone would not have been sufficient, if he had had any moral scruples. With his mind imbued with his hero Tsao Tsao's philosophy of 'betraying them all', he excelled in political intrigue. Like a boxer who makes a habit of hitting below the belt, Mao trapped and stabbed his rivals in the power struggles throughout the years in the most unsavoury manner. The moment he lined up an ally, he was already contemplating how to dispose of him once the job was done. Chen Shao-yu (Wang Ming), one of his victims, came nearest to the mark when he analysed Mao's personality in 1974 from the safe distance of Moscow. Speaking out of personal experience, the one-time protégé of Stalin described the Chinese leader as 'an inhuman dictator, suspicious by nature, thriving on betrayals and massacres . . . ' To prove his point, he cited the persecutions of Lin Piao and Chen Po-ta, Mao's confidential secretary and ghost writer for forty years, as typical examples of the Chairman's way of dealing with his 'closest comrades-in-arms' — without either of them Mao would not have been able to launch the Cultural Revolution to oust Liu Shao-chi, the then Head of State. He also stated that Mao undoubtedly surpassed the historical figure, Tsao Tsao, in pursuing treacheries and devious means, taking into account his actual record.

It is undeniable that Mao showed his ingenuity by transforming the Chinese peasantry into the vital strength of revolution, but few realize that he merely 'adapted historical lessons to present use', as he often stressed. Familiar with the rampaging tactics of the Ming rebel, Li Tzu-cheng, in the seventeenth century, he knew that the Chinese Communists could not hope to stage armed struggles without first gaining control of the agricultural population and the countryside. He was aware of the widespread discontent among the peasants which had been caused by incessant natural disasters and civil wars. With his own peasant background, he understood their plight and spoke their language. Convinced of the wisdom of organizing the massive peasantry into a sizable revolutionary force, he persistently challenged the then leadership for its slavish adherence to the Moscow line of urban uprisings and industrial revolts. He refused to give in, despite repudiations and stiff opposition from the top. In fairness to him, without his foresight and unorthodox approach, the Chinese Communists would not have been able to expand so rapidly and overthrow the Nationalists so easily. But at the time, even Mao could not have foreseen that his bold departure from the accepted Marxist line would have such significance. As for himself, this strengthened his hand in the subsequent power struggles. Meanwhile, the seed of the Sino-Soviet breach was sown. All of a sudden, Mao considered himself the only one who knew how to interpret Marxism and Leninism 'creatively and flexibly', competent enough to lead the World Communist Movement.

In retrospect, one has to agree that there has always been a myth surrounding Mao. He was acclaimed a genius, a revolutionary prophet and the 'creator of New China'. In the remotest corner of the huge country, no household was complete without his portrait on the wall and his works on the table. Even toddlers were taught to thank him for everything — a sweet, a bowl of rice or a toy. If ancient emperors were accepted as Sons of Heaven, Mao was Heaven (God) itself. On the strength of the all-prevailing propaganda apparatus, the Mao cult was firmly established. Fed on the ignorance and superstition of the ordinary people, it became a religion and a way of life. In their eyes, Mao emerged as the symbol of omnipotence, intangible and yet tangible. Like living in a constant state of hallucination, they ceased to question or rationalize.

For obvious reasons, Mao precipitated the cult and perpetuated the myth. An unquestionable megalomaniac, he thrived on adulation and flattery. It satisfied his ego to be glorified and worshipped like a deity, especially since he honestly believed in his own greatness. The belief was not just a reflection of his inherent conceit, it had as much to do with his limitations. In a way, the personality cult could not but have its effects on him, though it was designed for a totally different purpose. Unwittingly he fell a victim to the saturated propaganda of his own making.

Actually, the myth of Mao was not completely engineered by himself. For centuries in China, myths and legends have found their breeding ground among the peasantry. Superstitious and fatalistic, the peasants have always clung to the supernatural for motivation. In Chinese history, rulers and myths went side by side. Some were alleged to have been the reincarnation of ancient gods, while others were believed to have been endowed with superhuman powers. With the peasants as the mainstay of the Communist movement, it was only natural for Mao to explore every avenue to unleash their revolutionary potential. If myths and legends inspired them more than doctrines and slogans did, he might as well perpetuate their circulation. After all, for the sake of the revolution, he would be the last one to be inhibited by other considerations. As far as he was concerned, the superstitions of the peasants should undoubtedly be used to advantage in the light of dialectics.

The myth, of course, did not grow overnight. As the peasants' inborn fatalism and passivity proved to be the main obstacles, systematic measures were taken to combat these inclinations. The propaganda line was geared to convince the peasants that justice was on their side. They were encouraged to believe that the Communist cause was guided by providence, and that the time for change was predestined, though not in so many words. To heighten the psychological effect, mysteries about the background of individual leaders were deliberately intensified. At the same time, anecdotes and tales were allowed to circulate. Gradually, heroic images emerged and illusions abounded, with Mao in the forefront.

Once he reached the top, the myth became even more essential. He used it as a tool to consolidate his control of the Party and rally popular support. It enabled him to identify himself with wisdom and authority, unerring and infallible. His word became law and his deeds were above criticism. Relying on the blind faith he had elaborately woven, he ruled as if with the Mandate of Heaven, responsible to no one but himself. The myth sustained him and he in turn perpetuated the myth.

8

1 EARLY YEARS AND SCHOOL DAYS

Mao Tse-tung was born on 26 December 1893 in the tiny village of Shaoshan Chung in Hunan province, twenty-nine years after the quelling of the Taiping Rebellion and six years before the outbreak of the Boxer Rising. Known as the State of Chu in the Period of the Warring States (481 – 221 B.C.) in Chinese history, Hunan has always been one of the richest provinces in China. With the 'golden' Tungting Lake sprawling across an area of 800 *li* (Chinese miles — about 270 English miles) like a gigantic reservoir, the province is also criss-crossed with several tributaries of the Yangtze river. Mild in winter and not too hot in summer, its status as the granary of Central China remained unchallenged for centuries.

If wealth breeds confidence and independence, the natives of Hunan must be regarded as good examples. They are so confident of themselves that fiery tempers and obstinacy have become their outstanding traits, winning them the nickname of 'Hunan mules' from people in other parts of China. Not surprisingly, more clannish fights have been recorded in Hunan than in any other province while no war can be fought without the participation of Hunanese soldiers.

But on the other hand, Hunan is also noted for having produced, in the old days, a great number of classical scholars. It used to boast of turning out more successful candidates for the state examinations at all levels in the Ching Dynasty than any other province. This would have seemed very logical for, apart from its literary tradition, Hunan had the wealth to afford its natives more educational opportunities. Even when illiteracy was a common feature throughout China in past centuries, most Hunanese were able to read and write.

9

At the time of Mao Tse-tung's birth, the Manchu Court, dominated by Empress Dowager Tzu Hsi, was on the verge of total collapse. Having ruled the whole of China since 1644, the monarchy formed by one of the national minorities was no longer in control of its own destiny. In between the two Opium Wars fought with Britain, both resulting in defeat and humiliation, the Manchus had to spend fourteen long years quelling the Taiping Rebellion led by Hung Hsiu-chuan, an intellectual from Kwangsi province who claimed to be the younger brother of Jesus Christ. And practically in the same period, the protracted rebellions staged by the Nien people in the north-west and the Miao tribe in the south-west, though less serious in nature, constituted worrying aspects which still had to be dealt with. This meant that more Imperial forces were needed and more military expenditure must be met. Naturally, the financial burden fell most heavily on the shoulders of the ordinary people who were already frustrated and angered by the impotence and corruption of their rulers. The seeds of discontent were widely spread and nation-wide unrest was in the offing.

But in the backwater of Shaoshan Chung, the wind of change had not yet blown its way. Tucked away near one of the tributaries of the Hsiang river, this clannish village was a world to itself. Mao Shun-sheng, father of the future Chinese Chairman, was not much different from the average peasant of his time. He wanted to have his own land and worked hard to achieve that aim. While still in his raw youth, he had left the village to join the Imperial army for several years as a foot soldier. His sole purpose was to earn enough money to buy a piece of land so that he would be able to give himself and his family some security. After his return to Shaoshan, he succeeded in acquiring fifteen Chinese acres of farmland and became a smallholder within ten years. This was no mean achievement. Yet he was not satisfied. To open more avenues for income, he started to sell rice and pigs on behalf of the other villagers as an agent.

Industrious and hard-working as ever, he hired only one farmhand to help him. In his thinking, more male offspring in the family meant more pairs of hands to work on the farm. When his eldest son, Tse-tung, was still only six years old, he had no hesitation in making the boy do some light work in the rice fields. As far as he was concerned, this was the way to educate and train his son into becoming a useful man. It never occurred to him that a child of that age should be allowed to play around to his heart's content.

Fortunately for the young Mao Tse-tung, the loving care bestowed on him by his mother, Wen Chi-mei, made his childhood slightly more tolerable. She might not be able to shelter her first-born from her husband's absolute authority, but this kind-hearted woman knew when to dote on the little boy. She covered up for him when his pranks and occasional escapes from farm work were discovered. She also managed to give him an egg or a morsel of pork behind Mao Shun-sheng's back. These small gestures endeared her to Mao Tse-tung in his memory. Years later, Mao still talked about her with his comrades and others in glowing terms. If there was one person who did claim Mao's unreserved love, it was his mother.

When Mao Tse-tung was eight years old, his father, however, sent him to the village school run by an old-fashioned scholar. Not that Shunsheng had any lofty plans for his son's future, he merely wanted the boy to learn to read and write in order to keep books for him later on. To his mind, since his eldest son was going to inherit his properties, a little bit of education would not go amiss. But this did not exempt the boy from his share of the farm work. His day was to be divided into three parts: working on the farm early in the morning and late in the afternoon, and studying in the village school during the day.

From 1901 to 1906, Mao Tse-tung studied under the same teacher, who was extremely severe to his pupils, dealing out punishments like confetti. Like other boys, the young Mao was taught to read Confucian Analects, Mencius, the *Doctrine of the Mean* and the *Great Learning*, all of which he had to memorize by heart from cover to cover. This form of study was definitely no joy at the time, but it did acquaint Mao with the basics of Confucian philosophy which influenced his thinking and writing later on.

Between him and the teacher a great animosity developed. Not particularly good at his studies, Mao was often spanked or slapped in the face by the old schoolmaster. All this was too much for the young boy. Once he simply took off to avoid the corporal punishment, staying away from both home and school for three days until his mother found him. At that time he was just ten years old, and it certainly took some courage to be so rebellious. Mao's hatred for his first teacher lasted a very long time. Thirty-odd years later, when he was interviewed by the American journalist, Edgar Snow, in Paoan in the north-west, he did not forget to call the man who had taught him Confucian classics a 'reactionary and diehard'. To be so unkind and disrespectful to an old teacher would seem to be unthinkable to the Chinese. Then, of course, Mao was nothing less than a revolutionary.

Actually, Mao Tse-tung owed the old village teacher quite a lot. During those years spent under his tutorship, a solid foundation for his future mastery of Chinese letters was laid. It was also then that he came across the two historical novels which eventually formed the basis of his military thinking and revolutionary strategy — the *Romance of the Three Kingdoms* and *The Water Margin*. The former gives a most comprehensive account of military campaigns, political intrigues and power struggles which took place in the historical period of the Three Kingdoms (A.D. 221 – 265) while the latter, set in the twelfth century, is about the gathering of 108 outlaws who decided to take the law into their own hands.

Since in those days novels were regarded as harmful reading matter for youngsters, Mao could not enjoy his favourite books openly. Had he been caught by his teacher while doing so, twenty or thirty stripes of the bamboo stick on his behind would have been the price he would have had to pay. For a boy of twelve or thirteen, the physical pain of the punishment might have been bearable, but the loss of face in front of his schoolmates would have been too much. Resourceful and crafty as Master Mao was, he found his solution. With his father often away at the district town, Hsiangtan, on business, he had no compunction in telling his teacher that he was needed on the farm for some extra work. As these lies were accepted in good faith, the naughty youngster had his way. Finding himself a comfortable spot behind a rock or in the shade of a huge tree, he would spend hours reading one of his favourite novels with great concentration. The world of reality ceased to exist and he gave his imagination free rein.

The images of ancient warriors and folk heroes would rise before his eyes and the surrounding country would be transformed into the various battlegrounds, one after another, vividly described in the two masterpieces. For other boys of his age, the reading of the *Romance of the Three Kingdoms* and *The Water Margin* would, doubtless, offer tremendous pleasure. But Mao took the two novels far more seriously. To him, they were his gospel. He read them over and over again, reliving all the famous battles which are supposed to have occurred in the third and twelfth centuries. Nor did he fail to cram into his memory the political tricks and military plannings narrated by the two ancient novelists Lo Kuan-chung and Shih Nai-an. His obsession was almost inexplicable, especially for a peasant boy like himself. Little did anyone then, including Mao himself, foresee that the lessons learned from the novels would later be used by him to further his revolutionary course, rightly or wrongly.

It would seem that Mao Tse-tung valued these two Chinese novels as much as he valued Marxist and Leninist studies for his entire life. In 1942, when he launched the Cheng Feng Movement (Rectification of the Working Styles) in Yenan, then the Red capital, every single party member was ordered to study the *Romance of the Three Kingdoms* and *The Water Margin* intensively, though from the Marxist angle of course. And even during the worst days of the Cultural Revolution (1966 – 9), these two books were still allowed to circulate, while many living authors were disgraced or imprisoned and their works burned.

Back in Shaoshan in the early 1900s, the young Mao also found the two novels helpful whenever he had a confrontation with his father. Fortified by the arguments and tricks he had learned from these books, he could easily out-argue or out-manoeuvre the poor man. Usually, no Chinese boy in those days would have had the audacity to affront his father, for obedience was accepted as an integral part of filial duty. Talking back to one's parents was simply not done, no matter how right one might be. Of course there was no denying that Mao Shun-sheng was always mean and nasty to his wife and children, yet as a son Tse-tung had no choice. He should have let his father curse and shout at him without showing his own feelings, admitting his errors and even feigning repentance. But this was not the case. For reasons that only made sense to himself, the young boy likened his father to the tyrants and corrupt court officials he had read about, which enabled him to summon enough courage to stage verbal battles against the older man. To his mind, right was on his side.

By the time Mao Tse-tung was thirteen, heated arguments between him and his father practically became a daily occurrence. The older man constantly blamed the boy for his laziness and loitering habits, refusing to give him any meat or eggs. Tse-tung was equally sharp in his retorts. He argued that his father should do more work since he was physically bigger and stronger. Otherwise, he added, it would be blatantly unfair to everybody. He also promised to work harder when he grew older, stating that he would be the one to shoulder the whole burden of work since his father would have to retire before him. Needless to say, Mao Shun-sheng found these arguments repugnant. Yet there was no effective way for him to shut his rebellious son up, unless he was prepared to resort to physical violence.

The worst confrontation took place on a special occasion. That day his father invited a few friends and relatives for dinner. Suddenly he started to call Mao Tse-tung all sorts of names in front of his guests. But the boy of thirteen was not to be frightened. He retorted at the top of his voice in spite of his father's threatening gestures. When the row became more explosive, Tse-tung stalked out of the house, swearing not to come back again. His mother and some of the guests went after him in the hope that he could be persuaded to change his mind, though the youngster was adamant. Perhaps a little worried by now, Shun-sheng joined the chasing party. Meanwhile, he continued to curse his son, if only to save his own face.

Standing on the bank of a small river, Tse-tung was in no mood to give in. He threatened to throw himself into the river and end his life as his father was approaching. The grown-ups could see that the boy meant it. They tried to persuade Shun-sheng to calm down. Eventually, the father agreed to forgive his son, provided the boy would go on his knees to beg for forgiveness.

But Mao Tse-tung refused to oblige. He insisted that he would only bend one knee or else. Even his mother could not make him yield another inch. Thoroughly beaten, his father had to accept this compromising form of apology. Years later, the Chinese Communist leader would still remember this scene with relish. He considered it an early indication of his ability in political negotiations. However, when his poet friend, Hsiao San (alias Emi Siao) wrote about Mao's early life in the 1940s, he regarded this episode as a 'vivid illustration of Mao's revolutionary character', being unafraid to challenge his father's authority against all odds.

The situation soon developed into an armed truce, not completely free from occasional skirmishes which undoubtedly contributed to the tense atmosphere prevailing in the Mao household. Understandably, Mrs Mao was the one who worried most. She knew only too well that the stubborn blood running in the family would make it impossible for either the father or the son to see sense. After many a sleepless night, she came up with a very ingenious idea which had more to do with her feminine instinct than with sound reasoning. As Tse-tung was already a fully-grown young man at the age of fourteen—broad-shouldered and with a husky voice—in 1908 she successfully talked her husband into believing in the feasibility of getting a daughter-in-law. Then a rather fragile woman of forty-one herself, she found it too much to undertake both farm work and household chores unremittingly. Not only had she to cook three big meals every day for five hungry people, but she also had to make their clothes, sandals and cloth socks. Apart from Shun-sheng, Tse-tung and the farm hand, she had two younger sons, Tse-min and Tse-tan, to look after as well.

Once the idea of an arranged marriage for Tse-tung was approved by the family head, Mrs Mao went into action. She did not have to cast her net far. In her native village some miles away in Hsianghsiang District, she found a peasant girl of twenty believed to be named Li. In those days in China, especially in the countryside, it was not an unusual practice to get the son an older wife. In this case, it was not just for the future

14

Chinese leader to get a wife, the Mao family also needed an additional worker.

Furthermore, Mrs Mao seemed to cherish other hopes about this marriage too. It was then generally believed that an unruly young hot-head could be tamed or even completely transformed through an early marriage. The kind woman would have had such thoughts in her mind when she persuaded her husband to give his approval for their son's marital venture, though she was far too tactful to mention anything about it. But sadly, things did not work out as she had expected.

Mao Shun-sheng might not have been convinced by his wife if he had not recently acquired seven more Chinese acres of land. Tight-fisted and hard as he was, the hiring of another farmhand to take on the additional workload was out of the question. He knew he could turn his eldest son into a full-time worker after getting him a wife. According to custom, Tse-tung should be treated as an adult member of the family, in spite of his age, once he married. This meant he should share his father's responsibility to provide for the family by becoming an unpaid farmhand. Then, of course, the new daughter-in-law would also have to work for the family without any form of remuneration. Financially, the shrewd family head would stand to gain.

The marriage by parental arrangement was obviously accepted by Mao Tse-tung without objection, even though he insisted that it had never been consummated. He did not object mainly because all marriages in the world he knew were conducted in the same way. The thought that, as a married man, he would cease to suffer from the humiliation of corporal punishment could have struck him too. Besides, he would have formed some curiosity about the opposite sex at that point, to say the least.

After the wedding Mao started to work full time on his father's farm. Other than physical labour, he did the inventories and kept the books as well. But long hours of work did not seem to wear him down, for he still had the energy to pursue his studies. In the village he became acquainted with a law student who had come back from Shanghai, and studied under the latter for six or seven months. The young tutor was more like a friend to Mao, but he did make him more aware of the outside world. Before then, the district town of Hsiangtan was all that the young peasant had heard of and known about.

But it was the next tutor whose influence on Mao was considerable. He was Mao Lu-chung, a respected scholar in the village in his fifties. Going to him after his working hours, Tse-tung studied more classics and learned to write articles under the old master's guidance. He found to his pleasant surprise that Mr Mao was not an ordinary village pedant. Natu-

15

rally well-versed in Chinese classics, the old man was equally familiar with the works of contemporary authors. He introduced the young Mao to the writings of Kang Yu-wei and Liang Chi-chao, the two leading constitutional monarchists who had inspired the abortive 'Hundred Days' Reform' during Emperor Kuang Hsu's reign in 1898.

These readings opened Mao Tse-tung's eyes. For the first time in his life he began to be interested in political issues and current affairs. He suddenly realized that he had more important tasks to undertake than to oppose his autocratic father. It also occurred to him that for his own good he must leave the backwater of Shaoshan. He tried to persuade Shun-sheng to send him to one of the modernized schools either in Hsiangtan or his mother's native town, Hsianghsiang. His words appear to have fallen on deaf ears for his father refused to release him from the farm work. The older man insisted that he could not afford to hire an additional farmhand. He also believed that those 'new-fashioned schools were for the rich boys'. But those arguments did not put off the stubborn young Mao.

By hook or by crook, he managed to raise small loans from some of his relatives and gave the money to his father for the wages of a hired hand. In a sense, he was paying the ransom for his freedom. Shun-sheng might not be too pleased, but he had to let him go. His change of heart in 1910 marked the first turning point in Tse-tung's life. Otherwise the potential revolutionary might have ended up as a small landlord and rice merchant in his native village, raising children and pigs with equal enthusiasm.

At first, Mao Tse-tung applied for a place in a primary school in Hsiangtan. He was rejected on account of his height. Almost six foot tall at the age of sixteen, he would look incongruous in the midst of school-boys who were no older than twelve or thirteen, explained the school authorities. As a result, possibly through the help of his mother's family in Hsianghsiang, he enrolled at the Tungshan (East Hill) Primary School there as a boarder. Like many other similar schools at that time, Tungshan only provided two classes, the fifth and sixth grades.

Life at the school was not a happy experience for a country bumpkin like Mao. Clad in long Chinese gowns made of coarse cloth, he looked out of place among his younger schoolmates in silk or satin. Neither did his abrupt manners and awkward movements help. The only boy who did not make fun of him was the future poet, Hsiao San, and their friendship lasted for a long time to come. Many years later, when Hsiao went to join Mao's revolution in Yenan in the early 1940s, he was one of the few who survived the Rectification Campaign scot-free. Mao's favouritism could not be ruled out.

Even though several years older than the other boys, Mao did not do very well with his lessons at the Tungshan Primary School. He was good at Chinese classics and composition, but geography and mathematics constantly confounded him. As far as history was concerned, he was frequently at odds with the teacher. Armed with the knowledge of the *Romance of the Three Kingdoms* and *The Water Margin*, he challenged the teacher about historical facts and events. No matter how hard the teacher tried to convince him that novels were not history, the over-aged pupil refused to pay any heed. Incessant heated arguments in the classroom soon sparked off Mao's hostile feelings for the history teacher. He went on to organize his classmates, petitioning the principal to have the poor man sacked. Not unexpectedly, the request was turned down. But as the teacher happened to be a distant cousin of the principal, Mao regarded the refusal as the outcome of nepotism. Affected by his defiant mood, he decided to go further by driving the principal to resign. He started to collect signatures for another petition. However, his persuasion and coercion failed to gain him the necessary support of his schoolmates. They were too timid to rise against the head of the school, not to mention the fact that they did not share Mao's point of view.

Understandably, the unsuccessful attempt did not go unnoticed. The school board had no difficulty in spotting Mao as the trouble-maker. Although no disciplinary action was taken, the watchful eyes were everywhere. Under constant surveillance, the young rebel could hardly find the situation comfortable. Perhaps this is why he left the Tungshan Primary School after spending less than one year there, and without graduating.

On the other hand, he did not really waste his time in the school. He might not have benefited much from his formal lessons, but his outside readings enlightened his mind. He read the biographies of George Washington, Peter the Great and Napoleon Bonaparte avidly, and learned more about Kang Yu-wei and Liang Chi-chao by reading more of their works. Ambitious by nature, he would have been inspired, though he had yet to find his own direction.

In the spring of 1911, Mao Tse-tung embarked on a new adventure. After leaving the Tungshan Primary School, there was no way that he could put up with his father's authority back home. With some financial aid from his cousin Wang Chi-fan, he set out for Changsha, the provincial capital of Hunan. He planned to enter one of the secondary schools there, without any real preference. On his arrival he was dazzled by the prosperous atmosphere of Changsha. The streets were crowded with well-dressed people and the shops displayed all kinds of luxury goods which he could not even name. And on the Hsiang river running along the city wall, he caught his first glimpse of foreign gunboats with a feeling of wonder.

Having attended school in Hsianghsiang district, he had no trouble in being admitted to the Changsha Branch of Hsianghsiang Middle School. But he was compelled to discontinue his studies after six months when his money ran out. The brief spell at that school was, however, very memorable for him. In April that year, he had the chance to read a newspaper published by the Tungmenghui, the predecessor of the Kuomintang (Nationalist Party), in Shanghai. The news about Dr Sun Yat-sen and his revolutionary activities gave him endless excitement. As the *Min Li Pao*, the newspaper, carried an editorial encouraging people to cut off their pigtails to rebel against the Manchu government, Mao immediately did so and persuaded his schoolmates to follow suit. With Hunan then still under the control of the Manchus, such a gesture must be attributed to his tremendous courage, as well as his revolutionary fervour.

But this was not all. Having read through the Revolutionary Programme of the Tungmenghui published by the paper, his admiration for Dr Sun Yat-sen knew no bounds. He was so carried away that he wrote an article which was transcribed on a wall poster. In the article he argued that Dr Sun Yat-sen should be invited back from Japan to be the first President of the country, with Kang Yu-wei and Liang Chi-chao, the two constitutional monarchists, as his Premier and Foreign Minister. The extraordinary combination he suggested certainly indicated his confused political thinking; but then he was only an immature youth of eighteen who thought he knew more than he really did. The interesting point is, this could have been the very first wall poster of its kind, heralding the deluge of wall posters during the Cultural Revolution decades later. In the field of political propaganda, Mao was already ahead of his time.

Perhaps subconsciously influenced by his father, the next step Mao took was to become a soldier. One day, after listening to a stirring speech by a Nationalist emissary, he joined the revolutionary army. With a monthly pay of eight dollars (about US$2.00), he was financially better off than before. He could afford to subscribe to a newspaper and buy books and magazines. The basic training and military drill did not worry him, for he was used to physical exertion after the experience on his father's farm. As the other recruits were mainly of peasant stock, Mao felt very much at home with them. He would read, write letters and fill in forms for these illiterates, enjoying their gratitude and admiration. Before long, he was accepted as their leader and spokesman, which gave him his first taste of power and glory, though on a very small scale.

Since Mao had no intention of making the army his career, he quit his regiment several months later. By that time the Republic had already been established after the overthrow of the Manchu Dynasty in October 1911. Determined to give himself more education, the ex-soldier enrolled at the First Middle School of Hunan, a new institution set up by the provincial government. His original plan was to complete the four-year course there. But, unfortunately, he found the tuition fees too high and the teachers less than competent. As soon as the spring term of 1912 ended, he left the school.

After careful consideration, he figured out that his meagre savings would last him longer if he educated himself. Resourceful as always, he moved into the dormitory of the Changsha Branch of Hsianghsiang Middle School sharing a room with some of his former schoolmates. Although he was not entitled to do so, the students there were too embarrassed to report him to the school authorities. Paying three dollars a month for his board and lodging, he had no immediate money worries. Early in the morning, he would walk to the provincial library which was about one mile away. He soon became a permanent fixture in the main reading room, spending all his waking hours there. He would be the first to arrive and the last to leave. He read extensively and avidly, though apparently without any definite plan. Like most of his contemporaries, he believed that any published work would be useful.

For almost one year he persevered with this form of self-education, going through scores of books new to him. It was in this period that he read Charles Darwin's *The Origin of Species*, T. H. Huxley's *Ethics and Evolution* and *The Social Contract* by J. J. Rousseau, which had all been translated into Chinese by the prominent scholar, Yen Fu. He also enjoyed some masterpieces of Roman and Greek literature, in their Chinese versions of course. The impact of these European thinkers on Mao is hard to assess, but if his own admission is anything to go by, he considered them the 'progressive force' of western civilization, according to one of his official biographers who quoted him.

But when word about his new pattern of life reached the village of Shaoshan some thirty miles away, his father was furious. He insisted that Tse-tung must go back to school to earn a diploma. By now a fairly well-off landowner in the eyes of the villagers, he would not want his son to stain the family name by being branded as a layabout. And, to young Mao's surprise, his father even promised to contribute towards the school expenses.

This unusually generous gesture could have been one of the factors which persuaded the son to oblige. Meanwhile, he was also facing the problem of being evicted from the dormitory of the Hsianghsiang school in Changsha, which was going to admit more new students. Then, the monotonous and lonely existence of the past year would have helped make him opt for a change. After all, it would be unnatural for a young man of nineteen not to mix with people and seek company, especially when Mao's restless nature is considered.

In the spring of 1913, Mao started the search for a new school. Uncertain of what he wanted to do in the future, he took the entrance examinations of a junior law school and a business academy, both successfully. But, after discussing it with some friends, he abandoned the idea of becoming either a lawyer or an accountant. Having now decided to train as a teacher, he tried the First Normal School of Hunan and was accepted. From his point of view, this must be seen as a stroke of luck, for, unknowingly, he was about to shape his political direction in the five and a half years he was to spend there.

With Hunan ranked among the foremost provinces in modernization and progress at that time, its capital city, Changsha, emerged as one of the centres of westernized education. Although the First Normal School was only a secondary school according to rules and regulations, it maintained a very high academic standard. The teaching staff consisted of eminent classical scholars as well as returned students from England and Japan. The students were selected strictly on merit and school discipline was upheld with considerable success.

It did not take Mao Tse-tung long to find the new surroundings congenial to his taste. With the school programme emphasizing social sciences and Chinese classics and literature, he coped with his studies very well. Equipped with an extensive knowledge of current affairs and a mastery of classical Chinese, he distinguished himself in essay writing. Hardly a week went by without one of his articles being selected by the composition teacher and pinned on the notice board, together with the best writings of other schoolmates, for public appreciation. Encouraged by the special honour, he wrote better and better. Always anxious to express himself and find an audience, he was glad that he was given the forum through his writing. Undeniably, even at this stage, he could put forward his arguments forcefully and convincingly, a gift that was to be fully developed as he grew older.

Of all the teachers, Mao admired Yang Chang-chi most. A Confucian scholar, Yang had the additional advantage of having studied in England. With a disdain for officialdom and the establishment, he had turned down a vice-ministerial post in Peking, only to come back to Changsha to teach ethics at the First Normal School. Being an idealist, as Mao later mentioned about him to the American journalist Edgar Snow in the north-west after the Long March, Chang-chi believed in self-discipline, self-denial and self-examination—the guidelines for the Sung school of Confucian scholars led by Chu Hsi in the twelfth century. More often than not, the ethics teacher would impress on his students the importance of finding one's direction in life. He would also expound his belief that society could not be reformed until the individuals were educated and made aware of their moral obligations. Still without his own political philosophy, Mao would have probably absorbed these ideas unconsciously.

Yang Chang-chi's influence could have been the cornerstone of some of Mao's arguably un-Marxist approaches to revolutionary issues, as seen by his Russian comrades. Years afterwards, when the Chinese leader demanded that his followers achieve puritanical and stoical communism through the process of permanent revolution, it would seem that he had inadvertently abandoned materialism for idealism, if the substance of his arguments were closely scrutinized. As to his persistent emphasis on the employment of self-criticism as the ultimate weapon to improve the political qualities of individual party members, he could have seen fit to expand the Confucian idea of self-examination for his political purposes. The difference is: whereas the ancient Confucian philosophers aimed at perfection of character for themselves, Mao demanded this of all other people, but not of himself.

Apart from Yang Chang-chi, Hsu Teh-li was another teacher at the First Normal School whom Mao came to like. Generally regarded as a radical, Hsu, having passed the state examination at the provincial level, pursued further studies in Japan for a few years. Not yet a communist when he and Mao first met, the two of them soon struck up a friendship. Hsu's status as a teacher enabled him to help the younger man on several occasions. In 1915, Mao was almost expelled after his attempt to organize a students' strike (over the increase of school fees) had been discovered. It was Hsu and Yang Chang-chi who appealed to the principal for Mao's reprieve. And, whenever Mao had a clash with the school authorities, which was not infrequent, both or either of them would get him off the hook, though never forgetting to give him a gentle reprimand afterwards. At the time, Hsu certainly could not have foreseen that in the early 1940s he would serve under Mao Tse-tung's leadership in Yenan as his education minister.

As the school was not short of good students, Mao found the intellectual atmosphere there quite invigorating. He made a few friends, often getting together with them to discuss current affairs and national events with great zeal. With Yuan Shih-kai in Peking making moves to restore the monarchy and civil wars being fought everywhere in China, it was natural that these young men became deeply concerned. Patriotic blood ran high in their veins and they decided that they must do their utmost for the country. Among his friends Mao was particularly close to Tsai Ho-shen, another favourite student of Yang Chang-chi's. A native of Hsianghsiang like Mao's mother, Tsai was as articulate as Mao, if not more. But he was less impatient and less impulsive than Mao. Irrefutably, he had a profound influence on Mao's conversion to communism. When in 1919 he went to France as a worker-student, Tsai, in his steady flow of letters, gradually led his friend to believe that communism was the sole solution for China.

Another unlikely friend, judged by later developments, was Hsiao Yu, the older brother of Hsiao San, the poet who had been close to Mao at the Tungshan Primary School. Already in his third school year when the Chinese leader arrived on the scene, Hsiao Yu at first tended to adopt a condescending attitude towards the crude newcomer. But they soon formed a friendship after Mao had made Yang Chang-chi's shortlist of good students. The two of them could not have seen things eye to eye, mainly because Hsiao was a conformist by nature, and came from a middle-class family background. However, this did not stop them from enjoying each other's company. In the summer of 1916, they hiked through several districts around the Tungting Lake, without a penny between them. Placing much faith in the generosity and hospitality of the farmers and peasants in that area, they had set out deliberately with only the clothes on their backs. All along the way, they were fed, put up for the night and even given spending money. And, at the end of their roaming journey, they returned to Changsha several weeks later and forty-four coppers richer. They split the pecuniary gain and cherished the wonderful experience, especially thinking of the warm welcome accorded to them by everyone they had met. As a meal for one person then cost about two coppers, even the insignificant amount of money they had made was quite something.

Latterly, the Chinese Communist historians often interpreted this episode as Mao's early effort of 'conducting social investigation', trying to create the image of a 'revolutionary genius' whose social consciousness was inborn. But on the Chinese leader's own admission, it was a newspaper account about two students' journey across the Chinese inland on foot that inspired him to do so. He meant to undertake a similar adventure initially on a smaller scale, as he put it, with every intention of going further some other time. It is not altogether impossible that he might have thought of the Chinese saying: 'To become an accomplished scholar, one has to read 10,000 volumes of books and walk the distance of 10,000 *li*.'

Mao, however, enjoyed the adventure so much that in the following summer he and Tsai Ho-shen did it again. This time they covered roughly the same area, with Mao more or less as a guide. It seemed that they took the road in a very leisurely manner, for the future chairman managed to write a few travel sketches during the journey and sent them to a Changsha paper for publication. According to Mao's good friend, Hsiao San, this trip was quite a fruitful one, for it enabled the Chinese leader to observe peasant life with his own eyes and gain a better understanding of social customs and superstitions. But one thing is sure, in view of his own background, Mao would have established an instant rapport with villagers and peasants in the countryside fairly easily. He spoke their language and understood their feelings.

But if Mao Tse-tung and Hsiao Yu went their separate ways after they left the school, there was another schoolmate whose name Mao chose to omit. According to Hsiao Yu, that student was Tan Wu-peng. Not particularly good at his studies, Tan was a great talker. He and Mao frequently engaged in long discussions. For hours and hours they would discuss the emperors and kings in Chinese history, examining their successes and failures with all seriousness. The son of a high official, Tan seemed to know more about history, politics and the nature of government than the rest of his schoolmates. This may have won him Mao's admiration. In one of their sessions the latter brought up the subject of the presidency. Tan argued that one did not need to be educated to become a ruler, citing Emperor Kao Tsu of the Han Dynasty (206 – 194 B.C.), Emperor Tai Tsu of the Sung (A.D. 960 – 976) and Emperor Tai Tsu of the Ming (A.D. 1368 – 99) to prove his point. He went on to say that if one wanted to rule the country, one must organize a political party and build an army under one's firm control. While others present dismissed Tan's words with a laugh, Mao voiced his agreement whole-heartedly, not forgetting to praise his friend's insight.

It would be wrong to over-emphasize the kind of influence Mao had been under in his early life; yet to overlook it completely would not be right either. However, as a man of action he lost no time in trying his hand as an organizer at the First Normal School. Between 1915 and 1917, he played an important role in the Students' Association, either as its secretary or its executive. When the school had a new principal, Mao and some of the active students obtained his permission to organize the

23

Student Self-Government which had considerable say in the school administration. No new teachers could be engaged without the consent of the students who were represented on the school board. As regards their welfare and school facilities, the students were also consulted before any decision could be made. With Hunan then dominated by conservative politicians and educators, this was indeed no mean achievement on the part of the students.

Invariably, Mao's leadership was soon accepted by his schoolmates and he became very popular with them. In June 1917, when the students of the First Normal School voted for the most outstanding figure in their midst, Mao won the title with an overwhelming majority, heading a list of thirty-four. The success gave him a great deal of satisfaction, and his reputation as a student leader went beyond the confines of the school itself. But as ambition knows no limits, Mao now realized that he could set higher aims and achieve even greater successes.

Through the recommendation of Yang Chang-chi, Mao had been a faithful reader of the *New Youth Magazine* (*Hsin Ching Nien*) since its inception in 1915. Highly popular with the young people, the magazine was edited by Chen Tu-hsiu who was later to be the first General Secretary of the Chinese Communist Party when it was founded in 1921. Until then, Chen merely regarded himself as a radical, advocating new culture and new ideas in his magazine. He placed much faith in total westernization and science. Unable to read English or any other foreign language, Mao relied on the *New Youth Magazine* as an important source of information about the Western world. It was from the various articles published in this magazine that he vaguely learned something about democracy, socialism, political parties and individual freedoms in an indirect way.

Inspired by these ideas and encouraged by his mentor, Yang Chang-chi, he decided to form a society to absorb people of like mind for the promotion of new culture and political progress which, he believed, would be good for the country. Actually, he had entertained such an idea for a long time. As early as 1915, he and Hsiao Yu, together with a few schoolmates, had already set up a study group under the name of the New People Study Society (*Hsin Min Hsueh Hui*). But unfortunately, it never worked, partly due to the lack of enthusiasm. Now, two years later, Mao deemed it feasible to revive and expand the group by broadening its foundation. In the autumn of 1917, he sent circular letters to all the schools in Changsha, asking to have them displayed on notice boards or walls to attract attention. Expressing the desire to seek friends for mutual encouragement to achieve higher aims, he signed these letters with his pseudonym which was only known to his friends. When one of the letters reached a girls' school, the principal was greatly disturbed. With women's emancipation still unheard of, he suspected that the letter contained mean and unspeakable motives. It was not until he was reassured by one of Mao's friends, a primary school teacher, that he heaved a sigh of relief.

To Mao's disappointment, the response was negligible. He received only a total of four replies indicating support. But he refused to be discouraged. He wrote back arranging to meet these correspondents at the Provincial Library for a preliminary exchange of ideas. At the first meeting Mao did all the talking while his new acquaintances occasionally said a few words. It seemed ironic that one of them happened to be Li Li-san, the man who later engaged Mao in the power struggle within the Chinese Communist Party in its initial stage, for no less than twelve years. To Mao's recollection, his future rival sat there, his arms folded, without uttering a single word.

In the next few months, several more meetings were held in the library. Even with the disappearance of the disinterested Li Li-san, Mao failed to convince the remaining three of the significance of the proposed organization. Realizing that his recruiting campaign should take a new direction, he discussed the matter with Tsai Ho-shen and a few friends who shared similar convictions and aspirations. After getting together a few times, they agreed on the aims and regulations of the New People Study Society. With the reformation of China as its ultimate goal, the society offered a forum for the angry young men to express their discontent and voice their opinions. The first formal meeting was held in Tsai Ho-shen's home, a farm house at the foot of the Hengshan Mountain on the other side of the Hsiang river. As regards the date, even the Chinese official historians and biographers differ; two of them make it one Sunday in 1917 while another two state that it was 18 April 1918, also a Sunday. However, fourteen people attended the meeting and automatically became the founder members. Mao was in the chair for the discussions and consequently was elected vice-president of the society, with Hsiao Yu as president. It is believed that he deferred to Hsiao because the latter was then already a school teacher and had wider contacts.

The regulations passed at the meeting were drafted by Mao, full of moral flavour and rather didactic in tone. It was stipulated that the members must be virtuous youths with sublime aims, prepared to serve the country and the people, and that they must not gamble, visit prostitutes or take a concubine. Nor should they be lazy, greedy or accept bribes, it added. New members must be sponsored by the existing members for the society's consideration and election. A resolution was also passed that, in order to extend its influence, the society must make every effort to absorb as many new members as possible. Obviously, Mao wanted to build up his personal following through the New People Study Society, though his ambition was well concealed from the other members. It was years later that Hsiao Yu, with the benefit of hindsight, pointed out that the society was, in fact, Mao's first power base which he eventually turned into a communist cell in Changsha. But to be fair to Mao, at the time the society was founded, he hardly knew anything about communism. Although he had political ambitions, he had yet to find an outlet. As to later developments, his practical instinct would have made him see the advantage of using the society as the rallying point for his comrades. Shrewd as he was, it would have been very unnatural of him not to manipulate events to suit his own purposes.

Incidentally, Mao's ability for organizational work did not restrict itself to the founding of the New People Study Society. In November 1917, he earned another feather in his cap by organizing the defence of the First Normal School against the possible invasion of a group of routed soldiers. These troops, previously under the command of a northern warlord, were defeated by the Kwangsi army which opposed the restoration of the monarchy, in a battlefield south of Changsha. As the provincial governor had taken flight and the city of Changsha was defenceless, the defeated troops dragged themselves northward, gathering in the vicinity of the First Normal School, with either looting or occupying the school buildings as their objective. In his capacity as an executive of the Student Self-Government, Mao was entrusted with the task of fending off the oncoming invaders.

Seeing this as an opportunity to demonstrate his military talent, he immediately took command. He negotiated with the police station in the neighbourhood and secured the help of a dozen or so armed policemen who agreed to guard the small hill overlooking the school, ready to open fire at the invaders, if necessary. Then he picked a couple of hundred of those schoolmates who had taken the course in military training in the school, arming them with mock rifles and strings of firecrackers. As soon as the routed soldiers were in sight, the policemen on the hilltop fired warning shots into the air while the students set off the firecrackers. Amid all these noises, Mao and a few others shouted to the soldiers, who were now frightened and confused, ordering them to surrender their arms. The ingenious plan worked and even the teachers praised Mao lavishly, not to mention the admiration expressed by the other students.

Naturally, Mao always thought of this episode with immense pride. In the 1940s, many senior cadres in Yenan often heard him referring to it as a typical example of psychological warfare. What he did not mention was that he had put his intimate knowledge of the *Romance of the Three Kingdoms* into practice. Those who have read the novel would remember the vivid account of how General Chu-ke Liang outmanoeuvred his enemy, Ssu-ma Yi, with the aid of a defenceless fortress. When the Wei troops led by the latter laid siege to Mienyang, Chu-ke Liang did not have any fighting force to defend the city. But instead of fleeing in a panic, he ordered all the city gates to be opened, with himself playing a Chinese harp (*ching*) on top of the city wall. Catching sight of him from afar, Ssu-ma Yi decided that there must be troops lying in ambush within the city walls and hastily withdrew. Mao's employment of mock rifles and firecrackers for the defence of his school would seem to have been inspired by this ancient tale. Under the same circumstances, many people with less courage would have chosen to give personal safety more consideration. But Mao was different. He did not hesitate to tackle the difficult situation against heavy odds, positively and resourcefully, even at the risk of his own life and many other lives. Maybe this had something to do with his aspirations for leadership, or simply because he was a gambler by instinct.

With his reputation enhanced by this incident, Mao started to widen his contacts outside the school. Gradually but systematically, he was able to recruit more members for the New People Study Society, including a few school teachers and local journalists.

In the meantime, these hectic activities did not affect his continuing involvement with the night school for workers which was set up by him and two primary school teachers. From Monday to Friday, they spent two hours each night teaching some workers to read and do sums, free of charge. In the past, night schools of similar nature had been formed and discontinued. But Mao saw that his night school would be a success. Before each class, he would repeatedly remind the workers of the importance of being literate, emphasizing the fact that they did not have to pay a single penny for such a benefit. Compared with his colleagues, he seemed to have much greater powers of persuasion.

In early 1918, when Changsha was again caught in the clashes of two rival armies, Mao Tse-tung had another chance to impress people with his military talent. He organized the student army of the First Normal School into a form of voluntary police force, taking to the streets to maintain law and order. Joined by the students of other schools, they carried out their mission successfully, to the gratitude of the townsfolk. Furthermore, Mao also formed relief teams, handing out food and money to the

27

refugees, with women and children as their main beneficiaries.

These eventful years in Changsha apparently did Mao much good in the shaping of his character. He had the chance to embrace new ideas, to meet people with ideals and develop himself into a man of many parts. But politically, he had yet to grow out of immaturity and confusion. Like most of his fellow natives, he subscribed to the 'Great Hunan' concept, a form of narrow-minded provincialism which was later to contribute much to the internal conflicts of the Chinese Communist Party. In his mind, anything connected with Hunan must be good. He admired Tseng Kuo-fan, the Ching general who suppressed the Taiping Rebellion, because the latter was a native of Hsianghsiang, his mother's birthplace. Two other Hunanese, Tan Ssu-tung the constitutional monarchist and Huang Hsing the Tungmenghui leader, were also high in his esteem. It goes without saying that these heroes in his youth ceased to be mentioned on any condition after his accession to power, since ideological considerations had to come first. Even as a young man, the leader of the Chinese Communist Party was not supposed to have admired people of different political beliefs, especially a man like Tseng Kuo-fan who would be defined as a reactionary or counter-revolutionary in the communist context.

But in a country as big as China, provincialism or regionalism is bound to find its expression one way or another. The special feeling about one's origin or roots is inborn while personal ties are often determined by one's background and surroundings. In spite of Mao's constant denunciations of all kinds of political deviations in his party throughout his life, he could hardly have claimed to be above blame himself. It is highly doubtful that he ever succeeded in overcoming the 'Great Hunan' mentality even in his old age. Naturally, sometimes he might not have been aware of it himself. When Prime Minister Tanaka of Japan called on him in Peking in 1972, he gave his visitor a copy of *Li Shao*, the masterpiece of the ancient Chinese poet Chu Yuan, as a parting gift. At the time, the unusual gesture puzzled many people and gave rise to a variety of interpretations. Perhaps it would not be totally irrelevant to add a comment here. While it is beyond any doubt that Chu Yuan must rank among the greats in Chinese literature, he happened to be a Hunanese like Mao himself. He was born in the ancient state of Chu and served as a court official.

All told, his school days in Changsha seemed to have a special place in Mao's heart. In the autumn of 1925, on the eve of his departure for Canton to help the Kuomintang (Nationalists) organize the peasants, he recalled those happy years in a long poem entitled 'Changsha':

Alone I stand in the autumn cold
On the tip of Orange Island,
The Hsiang flowing northward;
I see a thousand hills crimsoned through
By their serried woods deep-dyed,
And a hundred barges vying
Over crystal blue waters.
Eagles cleave the air,
Fish glide in the limpid deep;
Under freezing skies a million creatures contend to freedom.
Brooding over this immensity,
I ask, on this boundless land
Who rules over man's destiny?

I was here with a throng of companions,
Vivid yet those crowded months and years.
Young we were, schoolmates,
At life's full flowering;
Filled with student enthusiasm
Boldly we cast all restraints aside.
Pointing to our mountains and rivers,
Setting people afire with our words,
We counted the mighty no more than muck,
Remember still
How, venturing midstream, we struck the waters
And waves stayed the speeding boats?

2 THE ROAD TO MARXISM

In June 1918, Mao Tse-tung graduated from the First Normal School with honours, only to join the long queue of unemployed teachers. Nor did he have any luck in finding a different job. Frustrated and broke, he often had to scrape for one meagre meal each day. His close friend, Tsai Ho-shen, was even more hapless, counting himself lucky if he did not have to go hungry for more than two or three days. To stave off his hunger, he would take books to read in a pavilion at the foot of the Hengshan Mountain near his home, partly because he did not have the heart to face his equally hungry mother and sister. The two friends put their heads together, deciding that they must leave Changsha for good. It was at this point that they thought of their esteemed teacher Yang Chang-chi, who had left earlier in the year to take up the appointment as a professor at Peking University. Together with a few other classmates, they wrote their former teacher a long letter, exploring the possibility of finding work in Peking.

At about the same time, they received some brochures about the Worker-Student Programme for going to France, which was under the auspice of renowned educators such as Tsai Yuan-pei and Li Shih-tseng, the presidents of Peking University and the Sino-French University in Peking. To Mao and his friends, the need to go to the national capital became even more obvious. The optimism of youth made them believe that once they got to Peking they could either find a job or go to France to pursue advanced studies.

But unknown to his friends, Mao wanted to go to Peking with another ambitious plan in mind. Having been a faithful reader of the *New Youth Magazine*, he was eager to meet the people behind the magazine.

Confident of his own writing ability, he secretly entertained the hope of being appreciated by the people associated with the *New Youth Magazine*. He was under the illusion that he would impress the cultural circles in Peking with his knowledge and eloquence. Like a big fish in a small pond, he could not conceive that his success in Changsha was less than adequate to open the doors in Peking.

If they still had some lingering doubts about the wisdom of making the long journey, the postcard from Yang Chang-chi decided the issue. The old professor promised to give them his help whenever they needed it. Absolutely delighted, they immediately made their travel plans. Tsai Ho-shen left for Peking first, with Mao staying behind to organize those students who definitely wanted to go to France. It was not an easy matter. Each of them had to raise a few hundred dollars for the fare, and it was also necessary for them to approach the provincial authorities for grants. When things dragged on, Mao lost his patience. In September, however, he and more than twenty students set out for Peking by train. This was the first time he had set foot beyond the boundaries of Hunan province, and he was twenty-five years old.

Peking was not exactly what Mao would have wished it to be. His arrival did not raise a ripple in the multitudes of the ancient city. Fortunately, Yang Chang-chi was as good as his word. The professor took Mao and a few others in under his roof, until they could find some cheap lodgings.

Meanwhile, realizing Mao's desperate need of money, he recommended his former student to Li Ta-chao, Peking University's chief librarian who later turned out to be one of the two principal founders of the Chinese Communist Party. (The other was Chen Tu-hsiu, the editor of the *New Youth Magazine*.) But at the time when Mao first saw him, Li had yet to accept Marxism. Being a friend of Yang Chang-chi's, he hired Mao to work in the library of Peking University. The title of library assistant conferred on him was deceptive, for he merely did menial work and earned a monthly wage of eight dollars, slightly more than a servant would get. Conceivably, his ego was injured.

But sustained by his stubbornness, Mao tried to make the best of it. He was always very respectful to Li, particularly in the presence of others, and he managed not to show any disdain for the work he really disliked. He knew the chief librarian could be used for his own purposes, since Li Ta-chao was a big name in the cultural circles of Peking. In no time Li was duly impressed. To show his appreciation, he introduced Mao to join the Young China Society which consisted of a group of student leaders and cultural workers. (The society was the predecessor of the

Young China Party which took part in Chiang Kai-shek's coalition government in Nanking in the late 1940s.)

According to Li Huang, one of the founders of the Young China Society, Mao did not really impress him as a man of great intellectual capacity, though he was extremely persuasive and full of pragmatism. In the society meetings, Li recalled, the Worker-Student Programme for going to France was frequently discussed. Impetuous and impatient, Mao tended to dismiss the other participants' remarks as irrelevant. His master plan for the France-bound students was to practise laundry work to perfection before their departure. To prove the validity of his argument, he laundered the clothes of another member for demonstration. Anyway, he did manage to convince some of the members. When the Worker-Student Mutual Aid Group was subsequently formed, the opening of a laundry shop in France was one of its main projects.

Li believes that in those days Mao was still under the influence of Chu Hsi's school of Confucian philosophy, with the conviction that the endurance of hardships would make one better equipped to cope with greater responsibility and the more important tasks in one's life. It seems that Li's observation is quite an authentic one. But on the other hand, Mao's contempt for the intellectuals could have been at work too when he suggested the laundry work. With his peasant background, he would have harboured some resentment for the city folks in the Young China Society. He wanted to impress on them that deeds and actions should take precedence over words and ideas. In fact, he had hardly any appetite for physical labour himself. During his short spell with the revolutionary army in 1911, according to Hsiao San, he spent two dollars each month to buy water so that his share of the water-carrying job, as required by the army, could be fulfilled. And, in his talks at the Yenan Forum on Literature and Art in May 1942, he freely admitted that he used to regard physical labour as something beneath his dignity. Taking all this into consideration, Mao's laundering performance at the Young China Society could be seen as his effort to achieve a dramatic effect. As far as he was concerned, he would have done anything to persuade the other members there. This is consistent with his 'revolutionary utilitarianism'.

If Mao Tse-tung's association with the Young China Society was but a passing phase in his political search, the guidance he received from Li Ta-chao during this short period in Peking shaped his future destiny. Again, it was through Li's patronage that he was allowed to join the Marxist Study Group, an informal gathering of intellectuals with Li playing the leading role. As for Mao, this meant he would be able to know more people and, hopefully, make himself better known in the cultural circles. His motive, though more practical than idealistic, was understandable. In Peking University he was nobody. In spite of his attempts to make friends with some student leaders such as Lo Chia-lun and Tuan Hsi-peng (who both later figured prominently in Chiang Kai-shek's government), they snubbed him. These unhappy experiences might have been shrugged off by most people, but Mao was not a man who would forgive and forget. The urge to win some form of recognition burned in him. The participation in the Marxist Study Group, in his reckoning, could at least give him a status symbol, if nothing else. At this juncture, he had not yet acquainted himself with information about socialist movements in the West, let alone Marx and his philosophy. Naturally, neither he nor his official biographers would like to dwell too much on his relationships with Li Ta-chao. Otherwise, his claim as the custodian of orthodox Marxism and Leninism may sound a little lame.

Introduced either by Yang Chang-chi or Li Ta-chao, Mao saw Chen Tu-hsiu several times between late 1918 and early 1919. It is believed that Chen was less than impressed by the lanky and talkative youth from Hunan then, especially in view of the former's established position and intellectual arrogance. Although Mao did tell Edgar Snow later in 1936 of Chen's influence on him quite genuinely, he could have meant those writings in the *New Youth Magazine*. In a lengthy interview conducted with the aid of an interpreter, some subtle points could have been missed unintentionally or through language difficulties.

However, if Mao did not succeed in widening his contacts through the Marxist Study Group, he did come round to read the Chinese version of the *Communist Manifesto* which, he later claimed, inspired him to become a Marxist almost instantly. Such a statement may sound exceedingly simplistic and incredible, but then as a romantic revolutionary, Mao was not immune from exaggerations and fanaticism. With him, anything could happen.

But life in Peking was still an uphill struggle for Mao Tse-tung. No matter how hard he tried, his lowly position in the library of Peking University remained a drawback, excluding him from the élite of the academic community. Even Yang Chang-chi could not be of any great assistance to him. After all, there were thousands and thousands of secondary school graduates in Peking, and Mao was merely one of them.

In the spring of 1919, when Tsai Ho-shen and other students from Hunan were ready to sail for France from Shanghai, Mao decided to return to Changsha. He could not find the money to go abroad with them, not to mention the fact that he had not taken any French lessons in the past months. But, to save the loss of face, he told the others that there were a lot of things to be done back in Hunan. Of course, it was also possible that he realized the futility of continuing to struggle in Peking on subsistence level. He knew when to beat a retreat and was quick at making up his mind.

After borrowing ten dollars for his fare to Shanghai to see his friends off, Mao left Peking with a deflated ego. He broke his train journey at Chufu in Shantung to visit the Confucius Temple, as well as the birthplace of Mencius, presumably with the reverence of a disciple. While sauntering there, he could hardly have anticipated that, half a century later, he would launch the mammoth anti-Confucius movement throughout China. In retrospect, he must have wished that he had never made this side trip.

He ran out of money near Nanking and lost his only pair of shoes on the train. It was a stroke of luck that an old friend from Hunan suddenly appeared, giving him a small loan so that he could continue his unfinished journey. While in Shanghai another friend offered to find him the necessary financial means if he would join the others to go to France; again Mao refused. He insisted that by staying behind, he would be in a position to study the problems of China from within whereas his friends could acquire new knowledge in France for their solution.

Shortly after the departure of his friends for France, Mao headed for Changsha, full of ideas and plans as usual. The few months spent in Peking seemed to pay off, for he now had no trouble in finding a teaching post at Hsiu Yeh Primary School through the help of some old friends at the First Normal School, his former hunting ground. In the eyes of those that mattered, having worked in a university library, especially in Peking, was a very good qualification.

In the school Mao was only required to teach six periods of Chinese history. This enabled him to devote most of his time to political activities. His first priority was to reactivate the New People Study Society which had become dormant during his absence. As someone who had met Chen Tu-hsiu and Li Ta-chao in person, he now appeared to the other members as a celebrity himself. Whenever they gathered, Mao was always the one to talk, to motivate and to dictate. Adroitly but firmly, he led the society to the left, more or less modelling it on Li Ta-chao's Marxist Study Group. With the May 4th Movement in Peking swaying the minds of the whole country and the appeal of patriotism in full cry, anything 'new and radical' went. In Shanghai and Peking, books on Marxism and other forms of socialism were hastily translated and printed, not excluding propaganda pamphlets of dubious sources. Anxious to find the solutions to the myriad problems faced by their country, the Chinese intellectuals began to embrace political theories and ideologies indiscriminately. National confidence was at its lowest ebb and total westernization was advocated by some eminent scholars in all seriousness. In a sense, this confusion of thought was to Mao's advantage. He knew the time was ripe for him to go further.

In the name of the New People Study Society, he and some of its members contacted a number of school teachers, student leaders and local journalists, convincing them of the need to organize a patriotic movement in Hunan province, in response to the May 4th Movement for the sake of the national good. The idea gained sufficient support and the Provincial Association of Hunan Students was set up in June, with Mao and his society in the background. The association immediately called a strike of all students in the province and passed resolutions demanding the abrogation of the humiliating treaty of twenty-one articles concluded between the Peking Warlord Government and Japan, the boycott of Japanese goods and the dismissal of the three senior officials responsible for the signing of the treaty. The patriotic movement in Hunan thus started.

But Mao had more ideas. He suggested to the leaders of students' associations that to consolidate its role in the patriotic movement, the association should have its own mouthpiece. They must propagate revolutionary theories to stimulate the masses, he argued. The proposal was accepted and the student leaders entrusted Mao with the editing of the association's weekly publication, the *Hsiangchiang Review* (*Hsiangchiang Ping Lun*). Needless to say, he was only too happy to grab the editorship.

In less than two weeks, Mao brought out the first issue of the *Hsiangchiang Review*, after hectic activities and hard work, on 14 July 1919. It was quite possible that he had deliberately chosen that day to coincide with the French Revolution. In the inaugural editorial, however, Mao stated the aims of the publication, stressing the importance of 'spreading revolutionary thoughts' in order to catch up with the 'tide of world revolution'. As the publication could not afford to pay its contributors, Mao wrote most of the pieces himself under a variety of pen names.

Actually, this brainchild of Mao Tse-tung's was not that original. It bore great resemblance to *The Weekly Review* (*Mei Chou Ping Lun*), first published by Chen Tu-hsiu and Li Ta-chao in Peking in December 1918, either in its format or its contents. But this did not seem to affect the popularity of the new publication. The 2,000 copies of its first issue sold out within one day, and the reprint of another 2,000 in three days. Encouraged by the initial success, Mao had 5,000 copies printed for the second issue. Meanwhile, Chen Tu-hsiu extended a helping hand from

Peking. In the thirty-sixth issue of *The Weekly Review*, he hailed Mao's publication as a 'good brother of ours' springing up under the nose of the warlord in Hunan, particularly praising the long article on 'Great Unity of the People' which was written by none other than Mao himself. As a result, the *Hsiangchiang Review* became increasingly popular. It even found readers in Hankow, Canton and Chengtu, and was highly applauded by the radicals and leftists.

However, it was inevitable that Chang Ching-yao, the warlord who controlled Hunan, would resort to suppressive measures. He disbanded the Provincial Association of Hunan Students and banned the *Hsiangchiang Review* simultaneously. The fifth issue of the publication never saw the light of day and Mao's editorship lasted barely five weeks. But the set-back failed to discourage Mao and he immediately bounced back. He approached the students of the Hsiangya Medical College, offering to edit their magazine the *New Hunan*.

The acquisition of the editorship of the school magazine gave him new ideas. With the help of some female members of the New People Study Society, he influenced a girls' school to launch its own periodical, with himself as editorial consultant. Likewise, the primary school where he taught also started a publication under his guidance. He wrote for all three of them with one singular aim. Believing that Hunan should lead the country towards a revolutionary course, he had been organizing secret activities to oust the warlord, Chiang Ching-yao, since the suppression of the *Hsiangchiang Review*. With a membership now totalling more than seventy in number, the New People Study Society had steadily extended its influence on many schools and some newspapers. Using the society as the nerve centre, Mao helped revive the Provincial Association of Hunan Students as an underground organization to ensure the support of the students.

Mao's strategy was both ingenious and sensible. Since Chang Ching-yao was a northerner appointed by the Warlord Government in Peking, he could easily convince his fellow natives that Hunan should be governed by a Hunanese. The emphasis on this point gained him support even from people who would normally shy away from any form of anti-establishment activity. Moreover, Chang's notoriety for his corrupt practices and brutality was a great help too. But to win nation-wide sympathy, Mao realized that a demonstration of solidarity and strength was needed. With nationalism and patriotism sweeping over the whole country, he saw the feasibility of confronting Chang Ching-yao with an anti-Japanese movement, rather than exposing his corruption and misbehaviour.

The students in Changsha were duly organized into small teams. They raided shops and stores, searching for Japanese goods and then set them alight in public squares. Chang Ching-yao interfered by sending his troops to restrain the students, presumably in the name of law and order. His action backfired and the students branded him a traitor.

The biggest confrontation took place on 2 December 1919. That Sunday morning, more than 5,000 school teachers and students marched through the main streets of Changsha. They took Japanese textiles and other manufactured goods from the shops and carried them to a huge playground in the town centre, getting ready to burn them. Just then, a whole battalion of Chang's troops arrived on the scene. They molested and dispersed the students with their fixed bayonets, before the eyes of the onlooking crowds.

Later that night, Mao Tse-tung and the student leaders called an emergency meeting of the students' representatives, to discuss ways to speed up the ousting of Chang. It was resolved that a students' strike in the province should be called, while efforts should also be made to enlist support from all possible quarters. The strike started a few days later and most schools in Changsha joined in. A public statement was issued, demanding the removal of Chang Ching-yao.

But as the strike apparently failed to achieve its objective, the organizers decided to send a delegation to Peking to appeal for Chang's dismissal, since he took orders from the Warlord Government there. Headed by Mao, the small delegation left Changsha towards the end of December and reached Peking in early January 1920. This trip was also of some significance in Mao's personal life. His mentor, Yang Chang-chi, had just died in Peking, and he wanted to be near Yang Kai-hui, the daughter whom he had courted assiduously during his last sojourn in the capital. After the death of his own mother in 1918, Mao considered himself entirely free from the marital bond she had arranged for him.

In Peking, Mao and the other representatives called on government officials and congressmen of Hunan origin or with Hunan connections, urging them to lend their weight to the anti-Chang campaign. Having collected sufficient signatures for the petition, they went to the prime minister's office to state their case. To their frustration they were kept waiting at the main entrance for hours on end; the prime minister had no time for them.

When it became obviously pointless to remain in Peking any longer, Mao and his colleagues agreed to resort to other means. Two of them went to Hengyang to approach General Wu Pei-fu who was known to be against Chang Ching-yao. Another two left for Chenchow in western Hunan to appeal to General Tan Yen-kai, who was a Hunanese and owed his allegiance to the revolutionary government in Canton. The plan was to persuade both generals to drive Chang out of Hunan by force. And to mobilize public opinion behind the whole campaign, Mao was to go to Shanghai on his own. But it was not until April that he finally left Peking.

However, for Mao the months spent in Peking were far from fruitless. It was during this period that he had the chance to read some serious works on Marxism and Leninism, recently translated into Chinese. He was also able to see Li Ta-chao, by now a confirmed Marxist, frequently and between them a close relationship was formed. Through Li he met Teng Chung-hsia, another Marxist for whom he had high regard. Both of them played a great part in clarifying the confusion of political thought in Mao's mind, a fact he later preferred not to talk about, for no particular reason. But it was quite clear that he left Peking for Shanghai under Li's instruction.

At that time, Chen Tu-hsiu, co-founder of the Chinese Communist Party, was living under the jurisdiction of the International Settlement in Shanghai, which offered ample protection for his personal safety. Due to his involvement in the May 4th Movement, he had lost his post as Dean of the School of Liberal Arts at Peking University after being imprisoned for six months. Shanghai would seem the right place for him to carry on his political activities, far beyond the reach of the Warlord Government in Peking. Furthermore, this cosmopolitan town was rapidly becoming a hotbed of radical ideas and clandestine movements.

Different from his previous experiences in Peking, Mao Tse-tung found Chen Tu-hsiu far more amicable than before. They had long sessions together, discussing the books on Marxism and the Russian Revolution Mao had read during his brief stay in Peking. These discussions benefited the younger man a great deal, for Chen really knew these subjects well, apart from being a firm believer. Many years after, Mao still talked of Chen's influence on him in glowing terms, frankly admitting that he became a Marxist 'in theory and in action' as a result of his Shanghai visit in 1920. But because of the eventual expulsion of Chen Tu-hsiu from the party, these frank remarks have been carefully altered by Mao's official biographers.

If Mao cherished this visit to Shanghai as a milestone on his road to Marxism, he could not deny the failure of his other mission. He never succeeded in getting the anti-Chang Ching-yao campaign off the ground. Indeed, there were quite a few Hunanese personalities in Shanghai; yet they did not share his enthusiasm for getting rid of the brutal Chang. Not that Mao was unpersuasive, but people tended to turn a deaf ear to his arguments. Financially, he was even worse off. Probably thinking of his advice to the members of the Young China Society, he worked as a laundryman in his spare time. But the money he earned barely covered his tram fares, as he told a friend in Changsha in one of his letters.

Fortunately, in June his luck changed. The two friends who had gone to Hengyang succeeded in persuading General Wu Pei-fu to attack Chang Ching-yao with his troops. Chang took flight and General Tan Yen-kai, with General Wu's understanding, moved into Changsha to exert his control. This enabled Mao to go back to his province as one of the heroes, even though he did not really accomplish his part of the work in Shanghai.

Back in Changsha he received his reward. As I Shun-ting, one of his former teachers at the First Normal School, was on General Tan Yen-kai's staff, he recommended Mao to be the principal of the primary school attached to his old school. This elevation pleased Mao in many ways. He knew that he would not have got the position, even with his former teacher's backing, if he had not made a name for himself. The *Hsiangchiang Review*, though short-lived, had contributed to his new distinction. He was not just one of the qualified teachers, but an intrepid editor who had fought the brutish Chang Ching-yao determinedly. His association with Li Ta-chao and Chen Tu-hsiu may also have helped since they were both giant figures in the cultural world. And from the materialistic point of view, Mao was glad that he would now have a decent income. As a school principal, he was entitled to his expenses in addition to his monthly salary. With this improved financial situation, he could afford to marry Yang Kai-hui in July that year, when she was still in mourning for her father. This must have raised a few eyebrows, for, according to Chinese custom, the mourning period for one's parent lasts three years in which wedding and birthday celebrations are strictly forbidden. Obviously, Mao was unconcerned about the reactions.

His stable personal life by no means blunted his appetite for revolutionary action. Before Mao returned to Changsha in June, Chen Tu-hsiu had in May formed the Provisional Central Committee of the Chinese Communist Party in Shanghai, with himself as secretary. It was during one of their long sessions that Chen at least accepted Mao as a fellow traveller, if nothing more. He was then entrusted with the secret mission of organizing communist activities in Hunan, with recruitment of potential members a high priority. As a committed Marxist, Mao Tse-tung did his best to carry out Chen's instructions. With the New People Study Society already under his domination, he set out to convert some of its members first. In his reckoning, such a move involved less risk since they were his friends who would never give him away, even if they might not accept communism. For the same reason he worked on his new wife, Yang Kai-hui.

To meet the ideological needs, he and some of his trusted friends formed the Marxist Study Group, the first of its kind in Changsha. It aimed at a number of young radicals who had been seeking leadership and identification. But as such a group could not be expected to observe strict discipline, Mao set up the Socialist Youth Corps as a parallel organization. He preferred smaller groups because they could be more easily controlled, not to mention the need to avoid the watchful eyes of the provincial authorities. It was also possible that he would like to restrict the membership of the New Study Society to a group of closer friends, if only to consolidate his position as its president. He always knew how to gain and use power.

Since his involvement with these three groups still left him with some time and energy to spare, Mao and a couple of friends formed The Cultural Bookstore. It soon became another gathering place for the radicals, giving him more satisfaction than custom. The development was not exactly what he had hoped for, although the main interest of the bookstore certainly did not lie in anything as mundane as making money. To expand his sphere of influence, he needed a wider audience and a bigger following. The stream of customers frequenting the bookstore, in his eyes, might yield some new converts to his Marxist cause.

But amid these activities, Mao Tse-tung did not forget to do something for the revolutionary masses either. He lent a hand in setting up two night schools, one for the workers and another for the peasants. Though no longer able to teach them himself, he would still appear at these night schools from time to time to make his presence felt.

It must be noted that Mao did not have everything his own way in this period, as some of his hagiographers have dutifully claimed. Between 1920 and 1921, Changsha was also rife with anarchism and nihilism. In many schools, the students were particularly interested in anarchism, seeing it as the ultimate solution to the problems faced by their country. To make full use of the situation, the anarchists, mostly intellectuals with a middle-class background, lost no time in stepping up their activities. They organized a youth society and a youth club to recruit students into their movement. As for the workers, they established the Hunan Labour Union. And, not to be outdone by Mao, they owned The Health Bookstore. In some aspects, they were more successful than most people realized.

To Mao this was a challenge he could not afford to ignore. He had to strike back. For it was clear to him that the spread of anarchism would nullify his efforts in promoting Marxism. To ensure success, he decided to employ infiltration tactics. As he now also taught Chinese at the First Normal School, he took some of his older students into his confidence. They were helped by him to form the Chung Hsin Study Group, with the study of Marxism and the abolition of anarchism as its main aims. These students were also instructed to make friends with schoolmates with anarchist inclinations, so that they could be dissuaded from taking the wrong path. Meanwhile, Mao himself undertook the more difficult task of breaking up the anarchist domination of the Hunan Labour Union. With patience and perseverance, he finally won over a few important officials of the union who agreed to denounce anarchism as unacceptable to the workers, though rather tentatively.

To complement these measures, Mao decided that some lighter touches might be more effective. He organized literary gatherings and Sunday excursions, ostensibly without any political aim. With scores of members hand-picked from the New People Study Group, the Marxist Study Group and the Socialist Youth Corps as the backbone, he set up the Sunday Club as a new centre to handle these seemingly friendly activities. They got together practically every Sunday, roaming the scenic spots around Changsha. In the relaxed atmosphere they were able to mix informal chats with serious discussions, with no temperatures raised and no recriminations exchanged. On these occasions they would take turns to host the party, providing food and drinks to wind up the outings on a high note. Through the strengthening of personal ties, Mao eventually turned the club into the headquarters for the anti-anarchist campaign, with great success.

But meanwhile, he did not really devote himself to the Marxist cause alone. Against the advice of some of his comrades, he suddenly threw himself into another political movement of a totally different nature. He shocked them by the display of his Great Hunan mentality once again. On 6 July 1920, in a joint statement published by a leading local newspaper, he and seventy-six people demanded the autonomy of Hunan. Judging by the style of writing, the statement was obviously Mao's masterpiece. It pointed out that since the outsiders had made a mess in this province, it was time for the Hunanese people to run their own affairs. To implement autonomy, the article went on to suggest the abolition of military governorship, the reduction of forces and the election of a new provincial congress of 600 deputies to represent the Hunanese people. But the military governor, Tan Yen-kai himself, did not come under any attack, apparently because he was a Hunanese. In spite of its strong denial of 'tribalism' or 'regionalism', the astounding statement was heartily welcomed by the natives of Hunan.

Encouraged by the local support, Mao wrote a series of ten articles, published by the same paper between 3 September and 3 October. The autonomy movement now really took off. On 19 October Mao and his associates, with the assistance of the Provincial Association of Hunan Students, organized a mass rally of over 10,000 people, demanding a new constitution for the province. A representation was sent to call on Tan Yen-kai, who promised to consider their demands in a sympathetic manner. In fact, he was merely trying to stall them.

However, the movement fizzled out when the local people failed to sustain the momentum. But this did not seem to bother Mao. It was possible that he had by now recognized his own folly in deviating from the Marxist line. Or simply because he was too busily involved in his other activities to pursue the autonomy issue. One of his main concerns was that the financial foundation of his political ventures had yet to be established.

Before the Cultural Bookstore was opened in September, he had intended it to be both financially viable and politically useful. To give it a status symbol, he had asked Tan Yen-kai to inscribe the signboard with his famous calligraphy. This was a very shrewd move. For it would also give the bookstore a protective colour since Tan was the military governor. In the Chinese sense, it was comparable to the sign By Royal Appointment. The running capital of the bookstore had been raised in a very peculiar way, with a view to the control of the whole business. While Mao and some members of the New People Study Society contributed 400 dollars, another 600 were made up of small donations, with no strings attached. In this manner, Mao and his associates had no difficulty in making the bookstore the centre of left-wing culture in Changsha. But the initial months were an endless struggle. With some 200 titles and forty-odd magazines on sale, the bookstore merely attracted curious youths who preferred browsing to purchasing. Commercially, the outlook was bleak.

Reality had to be faced. More titles, especially popular novels, were stocked to appeal to a wider readership. Meanwhile, Mao made himself a negotiator for special deals. He arranged to employ sales agents from among the students in those schools which were either directly or indirectly connected with him, using them to sell books and magazines to their schoolmates. He gave concessions to small book shops in the remote districts outside Changsha, so that they could be claimed as branches of The Cultural Bookstore to boost its image. In an old society hitherto unexposed to this type of sales drive, the business of the bookstore began to pick up. If Mao's approach contained an element of capitalism, he compromised for revolution's sake.

On the other hand, some of Mao's friends believed that he wanted to make the bookstore a success for an entirely different reason. According to Hsiao Yu, the young revolutionary then appeared to be very keen to impress his partner at The Cultural Bookstore. She was Tao Ssu-yung, one of the few women members of the New People Study Society. Like Mao, she was a native of Hsiangtang and had studied under Yang Chang-chi. She was described by Hsiao as a most gentle and elegant lady, and she and Mao had been deeply in love for quite some time. If Hsiao's memory did not fail him, he seemed to think that Mao was not yet married to Yang Kai-hui when The Cultural Bookstore was set up. But Tao left the bookstore quite abruptly several months later, when she and Mao broke up over political differences. She went to Shanghai and founded her own school there. She died in 1932. Her unyielding political stand has, however, caused the official historians and biographers to tread carefully around this stage of Mao's revolutionary activities. Her significant contribution to the forming of The Cultural Bookstore, both financially and spiritually, has been deliberately ignored, for fear that the mere mention of her name would lead people to associate her with Mao romantically.

But Mao was far from being able to adhere to the Marxist theories firmly and consistently in 1920. He might have then considered himself to be a confirmed Marxist, but there was no denying that his knowledge of Marxism was still very sketchy and fragmentary. Not knowing any foreign language, he could only read bits and pieces of Marxist literature available in Chinese. He was not entirely to blame, since Karl Marx's major work *Das Kapital* was not translated into Chinese until many years later. The guidance he had came mainly from Li Ta-chao in Peking. Chen Tu-hsiu seemed to have some reservations about him as a party organizer; he could not endorse Mao's involvement in the autonomy movement of Hunan and yet had no way of stopping him. A big fish in a small pond, Mao was too sure of himself to listen to any advice with which he happened to disagree. Once back in Changsha, he wanted to be his own master, Marxism or no Marxism.

One of his diversified moves in the summer of 1920 was the organizing of the Society for the Study of Russia. With a few local educators, he set it up that August. Other than the promotion of Russian studies, the society was to sponsor a worker-student programme for sending some Hunanese students to the Soviet Union. This must be seen as Mao's own initiative, since neither Li nor Chen took similar measures in Peking or Shanghai. But the society did not make much impact and its worker-student programme for the Soviet Union never went beyond the stage of empty talks. The failure could be chalked up as an experience, though the more alarming aspect was Mao's total ignorance of the Russian situation. Undoubtedly, he seemed unable to tell the difference between France and the Soviet Union, which indicated the level of his understanding of world affairs. Perhaps this was forgivable. Since he first discovered the existence of many other countries on the world map in the Provincial Library in 1912, they remained vague names in his mind.

Incidentally, Mao's interest in the Soviet Union was inspired by his close friend Tsai Ho-shen, then in France. From Tsai's long letters, Mao read more about the Russian Revolution than from any other source. Full of admiration, he began to believe that China must take the Russian path. The Society for the Study of Russia was, as he saw it, a step in the right direction. It was also under Tsai's influence that he saw the armed struggle of the proletariat as the sole means to grasp political power in a country like China. In one of his letters Tsai said in part, 'Ever since the tremendous success of the Russian Revolution, the world revolutionary movement has turned to a new direction. This means: stage the proletarian revolution to grasp political power and establish the proletariat dictatorship to reform the society.' These words were accepted by Mao as gospel. He immediately wrote back to express his whole-hearted support, elated and full of praise. And, whenever the members of the New People Study Society gathered, he would pass Tsai's letters around for everyone to read and discuss.

But at times Mao seemed to dissipate his energy without a sense of priority. His rationale was not always matched by his enthusiasm. In the instance of the Marxist Study Group, its lack of success was partly due to his inability to pay more attention to it. The group was formed about the same time as The Cultural Bookstore in September 1920. From the party's point of view, it should take precedence over the bookstore. But Mao's priority appeared to be the other way round. He worked much harder at the promotion of book sales than at preparing the ideological groundwork for the party. For a very long period, the membership of the group numbered no more than eleven or twelve.

Even the organizing of the Socialist Youth Corps was not off the ground as smoothly as Chen Tu-hsiu would have liked. Mao received the go-ahead signal from Chen as early as October 1920, but it was not until January 1921 that the Hunan branch of the Socialist Youth Corps was formally established. Among the very few members Mao had successfully recruited, was his wife, Yang Kai-hui, who had been attending the Marxist Study Group regularly. This was a natural thing for Mao to do, for he could count on her unquestionable loyalty, to say the least. It was also his belief that revolution should begin in the family.

Actually, Mao's constant deviation from the Marxist course at this stage was hardly surprising, for in Changsha he could not really look to anyone for ideological guidance. In his confused mind, he was simply unable to make the right judgement. His dithering and dallying over the set up of the Socialist Youth Corps could be attributed to his lack of confidence, even though he would be the last man to admit it. According to his authorized biographer, Li Jui, he 'began to understand Marxism and Leninism only after reading *The Communist*', the organ of the Provisional Central Committee of the Chinese Communist Party, which was first published on 7 November 1920 in Shanghai. This explains everything.

The Hunan Branch of the Chinese Communist Party was formed in the spring of 1921, after Peking, Kwangtung and Hupei. Its ten members were entirely recruited from the New People Study Society and this enabled Mao to achieve a tight control from the very beginning. The relative success of The Cultural Bookstore, his commercial venture, gave him an additional advantage. As the bookstore had by now expanded its business by having seven branches in the districts outside of Changsha, Mao could easily finance the new party branch with some of his profits, thus enhancing his leadership among a handful of Hunanese intellectuals who turned to communism almost at random. It was beyond any doubt that most of them even knew less about Marxism and Leninism than Mao did. They merely succumbed to his persuasion and revolutionary zeal.

The First National Congress of the Chinese Communist Party was, in fact, engineered by the Third International. In June 1921, the Comintern sent Maring, accompanied by Nikonsky of the Red Labour Union International, to China. They first approached Li Ta-chao and Chang Kuo-tao, who was to be Mao Tse-tung's arch-enemy during the Long March and afterwards, in Peking, advising them to hold a formal meeting to found the party. Chang then took them to Shanghai to discuss the matter with the Provisional Central Committee of the Chinese Communist Party. With Chen Tu-hsiu away in Canton heading the education board of the Kuomintang government, they were received by Chen's deputy, Li Han-chun, who accepted the proposal. He immediately notified various branches to send their representatives to Shanghai in July to attend the congress.

Representing Hunan, Mao was one of the thirteen delegates from seven regions, including Hupei, Shanghai, Canton, Peking, Tsinan and Tokyo. At that time, there were only fifty-seven party members altogether. Without either Chen Tu-hsiu or Li Ta-chao present, the congress was held in four sessions, not lacking its dramatic side. The first three sessions took place in a modest terraced house, where Li Han-chun and his brother lived, in Shanghai's French Concession, presided over by Chang Kuo-tao. The two men from Moscow, Maring and Nikonsky, were there too, presumably in their advisory capacity. But the fourth and final session had to be hastily dispersed before it could get down to serious business. The sudden appearance of an intruder, who pretended to have come to a wrong address, made them sense danger. The house was searched by the French detectives immediately after. With all the others gone, Li Han-chun was able to fend them off without giving any secrets away.

For the sake of security, the final session was postponed for a few days. Instead of Li's place, it was held in the form of a boat picnic on the South Lake of Chiahsing, a small town near Shanghai. To avoid arousing unnecessary curiosity among the local people, Maring and Nikonsky were excluded. The party constitution was passed and the Central Bureau elected. On account of the small membership, the delegates decided not to adopt the name 'Central Committee' which, in their opinion, would sound incongruous or even preposterous under existing conditions. Chen Tu-hsiu was, as expected, elected Secretary and a member of the Central Bureau, the other two being Chang Kuo-tao and Li Ta, responsible for organization and propaganda, respectively. Not overlooked because of his absence, Li Ta-chao was made the only alternative member of the bureau.

But as for Mao, the role he played at the congress was rather insignificant. He merely kept the meeting records in coordination with another participant, contributing very little to the discussions. To glorify him, the Chinese Communist historians have blatantly changed his role as a recorder into 'secretary of the congress'. However, he was confirmed by the congress as Secretary of the Hunan Party Branch, no more than he had expected.

Returning to Changsha after the congress, Mao again plunged himself into the thick of activities. Together with Ho Shu-heng and a few others, he set up the Self-Study University that August in an old school building on the outskirts of Changsha. By no means a university in its ordinary sense or structure, it was more like a forum for discussion with teachers and students playing an equally important part. In spite of Mao's claim that the university combined the best of the ancient Chinese college system and the modern school concept, it failed to attract a significant number of students. Academically, the so-called university had very little to offer. In addition to some reading matter in social science, the curriculum consisted of free discussions and essay writing. The only novelty was that the teachers and the students were supposed to learn from each other, an idea Mao revived many years later during the Cultural Revolution.

On the other hand though, the Self-Study University did serve some of Mao's political purposes. Using it as a front organization, he could shield his underground activities with comparative ease. From time to time, he would hold seminars on Marxist studies in the university on the pretext of academic interest. It seemed that the provincial authorities did not quite realize the true nature of Mao's new establishment, for it was not until twenty-seven months later that Governor Chao Heng-ti ordered the Self-Study University to be shut down, mainly because of Mao's involvement in the labour movement.

The university also offered Mao the satisfaction of converting his second brother, Tse-min, into a communist. Since the death of their father in 1920, the younger brother had been looking after the family farm in Shaoshan, contented with the life of a landowner. Anxious to save his brother's soul, Mao frequently gave him advice in vain. With the establishment of the university, he eventually succeeded in getting Tse-min to come to Changsha by offering him a post as a teacher. To a young peasant of twenty-four, without any qualifications to speak of, the offer was too tempting to resist. Once he came to join his elder brother at the Self-Study University, the die was cast. Living on the same premises, he had little resistance to Mao's gentle persuasions. Before long, he willingly joined the party, following the footsteps of his sister-in-law, Yang Kai-hui. Needless to say, Mao was delighted. At this time, he had already cultivated his youngest brother, Tse-tan, as a member of the Socialist Youth Corps, at the tender age of fourteen. And three years later, in 1924, the boy became a fully-fledged party member as well.

If the Self-Study University did not fulfil all Mao's hopes, he compensated for it with his success in the labour movement. Between 1922 and 1923, in a spell of ten months, he effectively organized no less than twelve strikes, ranging from coal miners, railroad workers, textile workers and tailors to barbers. But it was the building workers' strike which turned out to be the most tenacious, lasting twenty days until a satisfactory settlement was reached. The provincial governor, Chao Heng-ti, was so harassed that he confessed to one of his aides, 'I will not be able to survive if we have to deal with a second Mao Tse-tung—one of him has already given the whole province so much trouble'. As Mao never exceeded the legal limits, there was little Chao could do to stop him. It must, however, be pointed out that Mao did not undertake every task by himself during this period. The Central Bureau in Shanghai had sent Li Li-san and Liu Shao-chi, recently returned from France and Russia, to assist him in organizing the workers in Hunan. This was verified by Li Jui in his book published in 1957, long before Liu was branded 'China's Khruschev' and fell into disgrace. When Mao told Edgar Snow in 1936 that by May 1922, he had organized more than twenty trade unions in Hunan, he did not exaggerate at all. What he omitted to mention was the assistance of Li and Liu.

As a party organizer, Mao was equally successful. Between 1921 and 1923, he set up party units in eleven different districts other than Changsha. In view of the lack of communication facilities and the geographical distance, this was certainly no mean achievement. Not surprisingly, when the total number of party members reached 950 in 1925, Hunan accounted for 400 of them, including, of course, his wife and two brothers.

But in spite of his undeniable success in Hunan, Mao was still underrated by the Central leadership in Shanghai. In July 1922, when the Second National Congress of the Chinese Communist Party was held in Hangchow by the West Lake, he failed to make the list of twenty delegates, representing a total membership of 123. The Central Committee elected at the congress consisted of Chen Tu-hsiu, Li Ta-chao, Chang Kuo-tao, Kao Chun-yu and Mao's close friend, Tsai Ho-shen, who had just returned from France. On the instruction of the Third International, the congress adopted the resolution on the United Front line. It had been decided in Moscow that the Communist Movement in China could not be successful without entering some form of alliance with the far more powerful and popular Kuomintang, since nationalism definitely had greater appeal to the Chinese people. The idea was first rejected by Chen Tu-hsiu and his comrades. But as the Chinese Communist Party owed its financial existence to the Comintern, having received more than 200,000 dollars (about US$50,000) through G. Marin and other agents since the spring of 1920, they had to give in. To carry out the new line, it was resolved that all party members would be permitted to join the Kuomintang as individuals, while retaining their membership of the Chinese Communist Party. Apparently, this must be seen as a design to infiltrate the Kuomintang, which eventually led to the great purge conducted by the latter in 1927 on a national scale.

If Mao had some reservations about the new United Front line, he was too busily involved in his multiple activities in Hunan province to express his own view. Realizing that the Party work should be conducted in absolute secrecy, he had used a pseudonym to rent an unobtrusive farm cottage on the fringe of a small village called Chingshuitang or the Clear Water Pond. Living there with his wife, Yang Kai-hui, like an ordinary couple, he turned it into a command post. Secret meetings were held at night and the comings and goings were hardly noticed. It was also convenient for him to burn the midnight oil or get back at daybreak, since the cottage was surrounded by shrubs and trees through which no human eye could see. He often worked into the small hours for he really had so much on his plate. Unable to trust others and reluctant to delegate, he continued to exert his control over everything. Busy as he was, he did not even spare himself the less important work such as the running of the Cultural Bookstore. But on the other hand, his concern about the bookstore was not totally irrelevant. To consolidate his control of the local party, he must hold the strings of the money bag. In many aspects, the Cultural Bookstore was the local party's treasury.

Towards the end of 1922, Mao found it imperative to obtain legal status for the trade unions. Earlier, two labour leaders had been secretly executed by Governor Chao Heng-ti. As a result, many workers shied away from the labour movement for the sake of their personal safety. The situation worried Mao and his comrades. After discussing the matter, they decided to confront the governor with the aid of the provincial constitution, in which freedom of association was listed as one of the civic rights. Together with twenty-three representatives of various trade unions, Mao called on the governor and his police chief, demanding the legalization of their organizations. This shrewd move took Chao Heng-ti by surprise. Since he could not refute the constitution, he had to resort to delaying tactics. He promised to consider their demands in due course, though without meaning to do so.

To submit Chao to the pressures of public opinion, Mao wrote several articles for some Shanghai papers accusing him of violating the provincial constitution. He also attacked the secret executions and other high-handed measures enforced by the governor. As news travels fast, Chao soon learned of the contents of these articles. He was determined to remove the thorn in his side, and patiently waited for the opportune moment.

But he did not have to wait for long. In April 1923, Mao launched the *New Era*, the organ of the Hunan Branch of the Chinese Communist Party. Although it was disguised as the school publication of the Self-Study University, the Marxist approach taken by the periodical was loud and clear. Chao Heng-ti ordered it to be banned after the appearance of a few issues. Meanwhile, he sent some soldiers to Chingshuitang to arrest Mao. What he did not expect was that one of Mao's agents working in the provincial government got wind of this and rushed to warn him in time. Shortly before the arrival of the soldiers at his door, Mao climbed over the back wall and escaped in the dark night.

Cherishing the hope that the storm might soon blow over, he merely went into hiding in other parts of Changsha. He had no intention of relinquishing the power base he had built up with painstaking efforts, if there still were some chance. But Chao Heng-ti was not in a compromising mood. He put a price on Mao's head and posters for his arrest were prominently displayed in all public places. It now became clear to Mao that he had to flee the town. After handing over his responsibilities to his trusted comrade Hsia Hsi, a member of the New People Study Society, he left for Shanghai to work for the party there, playing a comparatively minor role under the leadership of Chen Tu-hsiu. This was not exactly to his liking, but he had no choice.

3 BETWEEN COLLABORATION AND SUBVERSION

Even with Mao's political instinct and shrewdness, he could not have arranged a better time to arrive on the scene. Earlier in Shanghai in January, Dr Sun Yat-sen, leader of the Kuomintang, and Moscow's special envoy, A. A. Joffe, had issued a joint statement to confirm Sun's policy of 'uniting with the Russians and accommodating the Communists'. In fact, this was the United Front line pursued by the Comintern. To be fair to Sun, he did not reach his fateful decision lightly. Having been snubbed by both Britain and the United States, he was in desperate need of foreign support for his revolutionary cause. Naturally, such a situation in China did not go unnoticed by the Soviet Union and the Comintern. As early as 1921, the Comintern representative, G. Marin, approached Dr Sun Yat-sen in Kweilin in South China without success. In May 1922, A. S. Dalin was sent by the Communist Youth International to see the Chinese leader in Canton, again with the proposal for the United Front. Nor did he have any luck. But Moscow persevered. In August 1922, Marin made another effort. After forcing Chen Tu-hsiu and his Central Committee to toe the Comintern's line on the United Front in a conference in Hangchow, he called on Dr Sun in Shanghai to negotiate for the Kuomintang's acceptance of individual Chinese Communists as its members. Against some stiff opposition within his own party, Sun yielded to Marin's request. With the benefit of hindsight, one could see Dr Sun Yat-sen's point better. In his reckoning, the Kuomintang, with a membership of 100,000, should have little or no trouble in absorbing less than 200 Communists into its fold, especially on an individual basis. Moreover, he never understood the true nature of a country like the Soviet Union.

In a sense, the failure of the West to assess the situation in China competently and dispassionately was partly to blame. Western diplomats in those days never took Dr Sun Yat-sen and his cause seriously. But in fact, Sun was like a George Washington to the Chinese people. Brought up in Honolulu and educated in Hong Kong, he aspired towards democracy. His political theory, known as The Three People's Principles, is in the spirit of Lincoln's Gettysburg Address, striving to create a government 'of the people, by the people and for the people'. Having overthrown the Manchu rule and established the Republic of China in 1911, he surrendered the presidency to the northern warlord, Yuan Shih-kai, for the sake of peace. Unfortunately, his unselfishness did not work. Without him and his Nationalist Party taking the lead, the country drifted into more spells of political uncertainty. Even though the ambitious Yuan's attempt to restore the monarchy with himself assuming the throne had been defeated, it merely led to endless civil wars when warlords virtually turned the regions and provinces they occupied into individual kingdoms. As the shadow of another national disaster loomed on the horizon, Dr Sun Yat-sen had no alternative but to organize a second revolution, endeavouring to achieve national unification by overthrowing all the warlords either with military force or through political means.

With the West continuing to support the Warlord Government in Peking and Japan stepping up its aggressive designs on China, he was actually forced to take a calculated risk or he would have had to abandon his cause. As he saw it, national interests must be his main consideration even if the path was a thorny one. Like a boxer in a tight corner, he had to punch his way out.

As for Chen Tu-hsiu and the leading Chinese Communists, they seemed to have come to terms with the United Front line imposed upon them by the Comintern after their initial reaction. They began to see the advantage of operating from within the more established Kuomintang. It was obvious to them that the other party, on the strength of its longer history and more moderate political aims, could serve as a protective shield for the Chinese Communist Party. The Chinese people were too conservative to accept a totally alien political philosophy such as Communism. Chen Tu-hsiu and his comrades might not want to admit it, but Moscow was right in saying that its Chinese protégé did not fare very well. Basically, the Chinese Communist Party merely attracted intellectuals of petit bourgeois background, which was not a healthy development. The United Front line was Moscow's prescription for a patient who was constitutionally weak. It was hoped that he would gradually restore his health under the wings of the Kuomintang. At that time, no one could have foreseen that this line would lead to the endless power struggles within the Chinese Communist hierarchy, sowing the first seed of discontent between the mentor and the protégé. A typical Chinese intellectual in spite of his Communist belief, Chen Tu-hsiu hated to be ordered around by the Comintern. More often than not, he would opt for national pride rather than political reality.

When Mao Tse-tung was still in Changsha, he hardly realized that the collaboration course with the Kuomintang was not without its complications and intricacies. As a novice of Marxism, he was unable to understand the basic difference between a nationalist revolution and a socialist revolution. Without direct contacts with the Comintern, he did not have Chen Tu-hsiu's unhappy experiences. Not in a position to dictate the party's policy, he accepted the United Front line quite readily. After the Second Party Congress in Hangchow in July 1922, he and two of his friends formed a Kuomintang branch in Changsha, giving themselves the additional membership in another party. Although his activities as a Kuomintang member in his native province were never recorded, his claim to the Kuomintang membership seemed to be genuine. Anyway, the Kuomintang was a loosely organized political party; it tended to accept new members without being particular about records and details.

With his friend Tsai Ho-shen on the Central Committee, Mao found it less difficult to work under Chen Tu-hsiu in Shanghai. It was also through Tsai's help that his hard work and achievements in building up the party network in Hunan province were duly recognized. In June 1923, the Third Chinese Communist Party Congress was held in the Kuomintang stronghold, Canton, to symbolize the collaboration of the two parties. Mao went along with Chen Tu-hsiu and Tsai Ho-shen. The main task of the congress was to reaffirm the United Front line dictated by the Comintern, which had been faithfully followed by the Central Committee in the past year. Apart from discussing the collaboration issue in full, the congress elected a new Central Committee of nine, and its five alternate members as well. For the first time Mao was elected to the Central Committee, taking over the organizational department from Chang Kuo-tao who objected to the proposed collaboration between the party and the Kuomintang. The elevation came with the power Mao had constantly been seeking. With Tsai Ho-shen heading the propaganda department, the Hunan influence was definitely gaining ascendancy in the party set-up. The new prospects must have been gratifying to Mao, in view of his keen interest in his home province, which always came first.

Actually, Mao did not contribute much to the Third Congress. With Chen Tu-hsiu firmly in control and the Comintern laying down the guidelines, the reaffirmation of seeking collaboration with the Kuomintang was a foregone conclusion. That Chang Kuo-tao should have stood against the explicit instruction of the Third International fully demonstrated his political naiveté. But Mao was far more circumspect and reticent at the congress. Contrary to his usual self, he sat through the discussions without expressing any doubt about Moscow's line. His lack of lustre, however, makes it very difficult for the Chinese Communist historians to glorify him. Writing about the Third Congress many years after, all they could say was that 'Chairman Mao maintained the correct stand'. In ordinary language, this means that he supported Chen Tu-hsiu and won his place on the Central Committee.

At the turn of 1924, the Kuomintang eventually came round to form an alliance with the Chinese Communist Party. Having engaged M. M. Borodin, the Russian representative of the Third International, as his political advisor, Dr Sun Yat-sen started the reorganization of the Kuomintang in October 1923. On 20 January in the following year, the First National Congress of the Kuomintang was summoned in Canton to give a finishing touch to the whole process. The Central Executive Committee of the Kuomintang was duly elected at the congress. Out of its twenty-four members, the three Communists were Li Ta-chao, Tan Ping-shan and Yu Shu-teh. There were seventeen alternate members and six of them were Communists, including Lin Tsu-han, Chu Chiu-pai, Chang Kuo-tao and Mao Tse-tung. Moreover, Tan Ping-shan was made director-general of the Organization Department and Lin Tsu-han the Peasant Department.

Undoubtedly, the outcome of the congress must be seen as a total success by Mao and his senior comrades. With a membership of slightly over 300, their party was a mere dwarf compared with the Kuomintang which had more than 100,000 members. The distribution of power between the two parties indicated that Dr Sun Yat-sen really lent over backwards to accommodate the Chinese Communists, arguably to the extent of absurdity. Of course, one could interpret his generous gesture to the Communists as a reflection of his faith in the Russians. But then, with Chiang Kai-shek just back from a fact-finding tour in the Soviet Union, he should have shared Chiang's reservations about Moscow's true motives.

As for Mao Tse-tung, he had much to thank Dr Sun Yat-sen for. Either in the Communist Party or in the Kuomintang, there were many others who should have been elected to the Central Executive Committee as an alternate member instead of him. Take Chiang Kai-shek for instance. He joined the Kuomintang as early as 1908 and was commandant of the

Whampoa Military Academy, the nucleus of the Kuomintang army. But he did not get elected to the policy-making body of his own party. While in the case of Mao, he merely acquired his membership in the Kuomintang in the summer of 1922. If Sun did not go all out to lend his support to Mao and the other Communists, none of them would have stood the remotest chance. If the recollections of a veteran Kuomintang member were accurate, Mao certainly did not put on an impressive performance at the congress. Instead, he was noticed for 'his rude manners and shrill voice, speaking with a practically incomprehensible accent'.

But Mao's good fortune did not stop here. With his comrade Tan Ping-shan at the head of the Organization Department, he was appointed his secretary to run it. For the purpose of infiltration, he could not have landed in a more strategically vital area. He had access to all the personnel files, and was able to scrutinize the background material of those Kuomintang members who were of interest to the Chinese Communists.

His return to Shanghai coincided with the setting up of the Kuomintang's Executive Headquarters in that cosmopolitan city in March. The new organization was under the joint control of two Kuomintang leaders, Hu Han-min and Wang Ching-wei. (Hu headed the right wing while Wang was then firmly on the left, long before he collaborated with Japan in the Sino-Japanese War between 1937 and 1945.) Again Mao took up the organizational work in the capacity of secretary. In the meantime, he was also responsible for the organization of his own party. For a young man of thirty-one, these heady days must have boosted his ego.

For several months he seemed to have played his double role fairly competently. His colleagues in the Kuomintang Executive Headquarters were quite satisfied with his work. Because of their faith in the collaboration, they were totally unaware of the hidden designs of the Communists. But it was Mao's own comrades who pulled no punches in criticizing him. Some of them accused him of being over-zealous in the Kuomintang's work while others said things to the contrary. Either way he was in the wrong. Quite unaccustomed to being at the receiving end of criticism, Mao was exasperated. On top of this, he fell out with Chen Tu-hsiu over some party issues.

Fed up with the whole situation, he abruptly left Shanghai to go back to his native town Hsiangtang that December, ostensibly on sick leave. In fact, his claim of poor health was a tactical move. While unwilling to tender his resignation to give his opponents that satisfaction, he still hoped to resume his work in Shanghai under more favourable conditions. Like all politicians, he always kept his options open.

Once back in Hsiangtang he did not pretend to be unwell any more.

But with Governor Chao Heng-ti still after him, he stayed clear of the provincial capital, Changsha. Using his village Shaoshan as a base, he made sorties into a few rural districts to motivate the peasants for the revolutionary cause. His faith in the peasant power was a deep-rooted one, deriving from both his instinct and historical knowledge. For centuries in China, peasant rebellions precipitated the downfall of practically every single imperial dynasty. On the other hand, no conqueror achieved victory without the support of the peasantry. As the Chinese population, at all times, contains no less than eighty per cent of peasants, they are like human ants spreading all over the country. To the politically ambitious Mao, the thought of building up a military force of numerous peasants had been clinging to him since the days when he avidly read *Romance of the Three Kingdoms* and *The Water Margin* to the displeasure of his father. In his imagination, he saw no reason why the events in the Han and Sung dynasties could not be made to re-occur in his own time.

Unfortunately, his comrades in the Chinese Communist Party were far less imaginative than he. Indiscriminately westernized and sedulously pro-Moscow, they shut their eyes to anything Chinese, either in history or in real life. When Mao tried to expound his theory on peasant power in relation to revolution, as his rival Chang Kuo-tao recalled in his memoirs, at the Third Party Congress in Canton, all he got in return was a few sneers. Their slavish adherence to the Comintern line made them regard Mao as a revolutionary heretic, if nothing more.

Though definitely frustrated, Mao was not a man who needed a receptive audience. So long as he knew he was right, nothing could stop him from pursuing his original idea. Having encountered some setbacks in Shanghai, it was only natural for him to seek compensation somewhere else. In his mind, going back to his familiar surroundings offered him the ideal opportunity to practise what he believed. The steps he took to organize the peasants around Shaoshan were cautious but effective. He called at their homes from door to door, having a chat here and there. Being a native, he was readily accepted by the peasants as one of their own. He listened to their problems and offered some advice only when they asked for it. With enormous energy and inexhaustible patience, he walked miles each day to make these personal contacts, gradually building up a following. Knowing that the peasants were always anxious to overcome their illiteracy, he set up a night school in the village shrine for them, leaving it in the charge of his wife, Yang Kai-hui. In this way he was able to absorb the women and children as well. Staying behind the scenes himself, he sent for some of his comrades who had been working among the coal miners at Anyuan some miles away. With them to assist

Yang Kai-hui, the night school was rapidly expanded into a secret centre of the peasant movement. Those who attended the night school were not only taught to read and write, they were also subjected to the rudimentary form of political indoctrination. Mao was constantly there to speak against the local officialdom, the landed gentry and the money lenders, explaining to them the need for the peasants to stick together for their own good. As he spoke their language, his words went down well with them. It must be admitted that Mao was always at his best in the midst of workers and peasants, taking to them like a duck to water.

As it was equally important to him to extend the party network to his own village, Mao was determined to see it done this time. After careful observation, he picked four village youths to work around him. For several months he carefully taught them the basic concepts of Marxism, to the best of his rather limited ability. However, these youths seemed to respond well. On a June night in 1925, they were led to his headquarters in an attic room, and under the candlelight he swore them in as the first four Communist Party members in Shaoshan. As a matter of interest, two of them were his cousins.

With the work at Shaoshan well under control, Mao began to spread his activities into other villages. He helped the peasants to form their own night schools and taught them to organize themselves into small units. Between January and August that year, he was supposed to have organized 'more than twenty peasants' night schools and as many peasants' associations' in the Hsiangtang area, according to the official records published during the Cultural Revolution in the late 1960s. While one has no reason to doubt Mao's considerable success in those short months, these figures do not necessarily have to be accepted without reservations.

But in 1925 Mao was not allowed to expand his peasant movement for long. In spite of his concealed identity, word had got around that a radical movement was gaining in volume around Hsiangtang district. Towards the end of August, Chao Heng-ti issued an order to have the 'organizer of the radical movement' arrested, though not knowing who it was. But before the garrison force of Hsiangtang received the governor's order, Mao was already warned of his imminent danger by his contacts in Changsha. It allowed him time to borrow some money and make necessary arrangements for his wife. When the local troops came to Shaoshan to arrest him, he had just gone.

Relying on his political instinct, he went south to Canton instead of rejoining Chen Tu-hsiu in Shanghai. With the Kuomintang-Communist alliance in full swing, he sensed that the nerve-centre of the Kuomintang would offer ample scope for his ability. Of course he was right. In Canton his Kuomintang friends received him with open arms, in accordance with Dr Sun Yat-sen's policy. They placed so much trust in him that he was immediately made Deputy Director of the Central Propaganda Department, which was then headed by Wang Ching-wei, leader of the Kuomintang left wing. Since the Chinese Communists aimed at creating disharmony and conflicts within the Kuomintang for their own benefit, Mao found himself in a most manoeuvrable position. Besides, Wang Ching-wei did not hesitate to demonstrate his pro-Communist sympathy in a very helpful way. He let Mao run the whole show.

This exceeded Mao's wildest dreams, and he was no slow customer. Fully realizing the importance of a political party's ideological forum, he took over the editorship of the Kuomintang's organ the *Political Weekly*. In the name of the alliance, he gave the periodical a disguised Marxist slant. It is impossible to estimate the extent of ideological influence he succeeded in exerting on the Kuomintang members during that period, but there is no denying that he did manage to pull off a *coup de maître* under the very nose of the Kuomintang leaders who were either too trusting or too náíve. To suit his own purposes, Mao wrote many pieces for the *Political Weekly* in the form of editor's comments. He even wrote from time to time to sing Chiang Kai-shek's praises applauding his unquestionable 'love and care for the people'.

But from Mao's point of view, his most significant task during his Canton sojourn (October 1925 – July 1926) must be his involvement with the Peasant Movement Training Institute. As the Kuomintang forces had earlier enjoyed considerable support from the peasants in the Tungkiang area in Kwangtung province, the institute was subsequently set up in Canton with the aim of exploring the revolutionary potential of the peasantry. With his experience in organizing the peasants' associations in Hunan, Mao did not have to do anything to be included in the institute as one of the lecturers. Naturally, he took this post more seriously than many others. Not unlike the Chinese Communist leadership, the Kuomintang did not really regard the organizing of peasants as a task of primary importance. Such an attitude suited Mao fine. Without too much trouble, he was able to take over the actual control of the institute unopposed. His job was made easier, for the director of the institute was Peng Pai, another Communist who had to spend more time in the Tungkiang area to lead the peasant movement there. Peng's absence enabled him to have a completely free hand, while the Kuomintang people were too indifferent to interfere.

The training course lasted about eighteen weeks, offering some twenty-five subjects on various aspects of the peasant movement. As Wang Shou-tao, a member of the Tenth Central Committee of the Chinese Communist Party, described in an article in 1977, Mao did not become the director of the institute until the spring of 1926. But before then, he was already very much in charge. When the institute was first formed in 1924, it merely offered training to the natives of Kwangtung province. Between the summer of 1924 and the autumn of 1925, the three training classes produced some 400 rural workers who were sent to different parts of the province. It was no sheer coincidence that the institute started to recruit cadets on a nationwide scale after Mao's participation. Secret emissaries were dispatched to all the provinces in China to conduct the recruiting campaign. The enrolment of each training class was trebled, no less than 300 cadets at a time. As usual, Mao paid special attention to his native province Hunan. For each training class, he saw that plenty of Hunanese cadets were included. His brother Tse-min and some of his villagers were among them. It was, therefore, no surprise that there were at least thirty to forty Hunanese in each class when he ran the institute.

According to Wang Shou-tao, Mao taught Chinese Geography, Rural Education and the Problems of Chinese Peasants at the institute. But his main concern was obviously the secret expansion of Communist influence inside the Kuomintang. And he seemed to have been very successful in this respect. Quietly but firmly, he turned the Peasant Movement Training Institute into a breeding ground for Communist cadres. Hundreds of high school students like Wang were converted and indoctrinated in the spell of a few months, and they later became the backbone of Mao's following in the party.

But it was his ability to attend to details that put him in good stead with the cadets at the institute. Knowing the different eating habits in various regions, he ensured that the southerners got their rice and the northerners their steamed bread or noodles. To achieve culinary variety, he made the cadets run their own mess. Even the handful of Moslems were allowed to have their particular food, without having to violate their religious beliefs. Unlike most people in his position, Mao understood how to win the hearts of the underlings. He was perceptive enough to realize the need to please them by showing some care and concern. As an ancient Chinese saying goes, a successful politician is one who can pretend most, one who is not to be seen through.

Actually, Mao could not have found a better moment to play his double role in Canton. Since Dr Sun Yat-sen's death in March 1925, the Kuomintang had lost its recognized leader who had been holding the party together. With the left wing led by Wang Ching-wei now dominating the Central Executive Committee, the Kuomintang was extremely vulnerable to Communist infiltration. Manipulated by the Russian adviser, Borodin, Wang was more interested in defeating the right-wing opposition in his own party than checking the Communist activities. Not only had he virtually made Mao the propaganda chief of the Kuomintang, he also left two other vital departments in the hands of the Communists. With Tan Ping-shan continuing to head the Department of Organization and Lin Tsu-han the Department of Peasants, Mao could rely on his two senior comrades to offer the necessary assistance from within the Kuomintang. It was through Lin's recommendation and support that he took over the control of the Peasant Movement Training Institute. This was a favour Mao never forgot. To repay Lin, he made the older man the titular head of the Border Government in Yenan in the 1940s after the Long March.

The institute was important to Mao in many ways. Having acquired sufficient experience in organizing the peasants in Hunan, he needed a forum to consolidate the theoretical basis of his belief in peasant power. It was clear to him that Chen Tu-hsiu and those who mattered in the party refused to be convinced. The fact that he failed to be re-elected to the Central Committee at the Fourth Party Congress in January 1925 was self-evident. In his reckoning, he saw his successful performance in the Kuomintang set-up in Canton as a stepping stone to return to the seat of power on the Central Committee. Elusive though such an opportunity might appear to be, Mao always saw 'the possibility in the most impossible situation', as the veteran Communist leader Tung Pi-wu said to me in Nanking in the spring of 1946, when he expounded the value of 'revolutionary optimism'.

But in March 1926, Mao encountered his first set-back in Canton. After the abortive attempt to kidnap Chiang Kai-shek by a Communist officer named Li Chih-lung, known as the Chungshan Gunboat Incident, the Kuomintang was forced to tighten its internal security. Tan Ping-shan and Lin Tsu-han were no longer allowed to take charge of the Department of Organization and the Department of Peasants, while Mao was removed from the Department of Propaganda. However, this did not seem to worry Mao too much. For he was appointed Director of the Peasant Movement Training Institute instead, probably as a face-saving formula. The new development gave him the chance to concentrate on the institute, giving it his undivided attention. Apart from taking practical measures for its expansion, he used the institute as the hotbed of his revolutionary theory. He stepped up the military training for the cadets, with the idea of enabling them to organize the militia when the need arose. Since his party had decided to 'arm the people' at the Fourth Congress held in Shanghai in January 1925, he was even more sure that his idea of mobilizing the multitude of poor peasants would sooner or later be adopted by the Central Committee. A man of common sense, he could not agree with most of his comrades that political power could be grasped by enlisting the support of industrial workers alone. He knew he was 'against the tide', but it was not in his nature to budge an inch once his mind was made up.

The comparative seclusion of the institute did him another good. After lecturing on the problems of Chinese peasants systematically for a period of time, he was able to collect his thoughts to start some serious writing along the Marxist line. By now it was clear to him that he had to stake his claim as a theoretician before he could advance his party career. No matter what he thought of Chen Tu-hsiu, Chu Chiu-pai and those Russian-trained comrades, they were superior to him in Marxist theories. Based on his lecture notes and drawing from his experiences in Hunan, he wrote an Analysis of the Classes in Chinese Society, which was later to be included in his Selected Works after his accession to power. In this article he tried to establish Chinese peasants as the 'rural proletariat', advocating their usefulness to the revolution. It marked the beginning of his ceaseless efforts to convert the Chinese Communist Party into his own mode.

If he succeeded in achieving quite a lot during these months in Canton, it was due to the oversight of his Kuomintang colleagues. In the eyes of the Nationalists, he could not even compare with Chou En-lai, who was then heading the Political Department of the Whampoa Military Academy. But on the other hand, it seemed that Mao was cautious enough to keep a low profile. According to Kuo Mo-jo, the late President of the Chinese Academy of Sciences, his first impression of Mao at that time was his modesty and low voice, coupled with his rather effeminate looks. Hard of hearing, Kuo expressed his surprise at finding a revolutionary who spoke so softly. As the Chinese author made these remarks as early as 1933, when Mao was still struggling for his political ascendancy in the Kiangsi Soviet, the picture he constructed must be a fairly accurate one.

Actually, Mao's modesty could have something to do with his failure to impress Borodin, the Russian overlord who forged the Nationalist-Communist alliance. Not once did the arrogant Russian bother to see someone of lesser consequence such as Mao, since he already had Tan Ping-shan, Lin Tsu-han and Chou En-lai at his beck and call. Mao was not only unimpressive in appearance, he also had the disadvantage of knowing no foreign language. Like most foreigners in China, Borodin tended to equate the language aptitude of a Chinese to his political brain. This could have been a key factor for him to ignore Mao completely. Not a man to be slighted, Mao would have harboured deep resentment towards Borodin in return. In his subconsciousness, the anti-Russian feeling could have then started its fermentation.

But Mao was not to carry on his political work in Canton for long. In July 1926, shortly after Chiang Kai-shek had launched the Northward Expedition to overthrow the Warlord Regime in Peking, Mao was summoned to Shanghai by the Central Committee of his party. Although the Chinese Communists were against the military campaign, they could not afford to disagree with Borodin who was in favour of it. Meanwhile, they had to prepare themselves to claim their share of success if the Northward Expedition turned out to be victorious. These considerations persuaded Chen Tu-hsiu and his associates to accept Mao's argument about organizing peasant power. As an instant measure, the Advisory Committee for the Peasant Movement was set up with Mao as its secretary, under the guidance of the Central Committee. Since the Chungshan Gunboat Incident in Canton in that March, Chen Tu-hsiu and those Communist leaders in Kwangtung province had been at odds with each other. He could not appreciate the need for Tan Ping-shan and Lin Tsu-han to lose their foothold in the Central Headquarters of the Kuomintang by giving up the two departments. But little did he know that under the cloud of suspicion, they really had no choice. Even the Nationalist leader, Wang Ching-wei, was compelled to take off to Paris to avoid the accusing fingers, while Borodin rushed back from Moscow to make a peace offer to the enraged Kuomintang. In a way Mao was lucky to be caught in the conflict. To strengthen the central command, Chen reluctantly chose to put up with him at this point.

Naturally, Shanghai would be the least likely base for anyone to direct the peasant movement. In December 1926 Mao had the chance to return to Changsha to attend the Hunan Peasants' Assembly after the National Revolutionary Army under Chiang Kai-shek had pushed forward along the Yangtze river. For him the warm reception did not come as a surprise. With most peasant associations in the province controlled by the people he had trained in Canton, he would not have settled for less.

Basking in glory, he went ahead with the preliminary plans to organize the peasants into para-military units, with various peasant associations as a front to distract the Nationalists. This fully demonstrated his insubordinate nature, for he had yet to seek the Central Committee's approval. According to the authorized version of Chinese Communist history, the then General-Secretary, Chen Tu-hsiu, was not perceptive enough to concur with Mao's views. In fact, Mao had long decided to go his own way. Earlier that year, when he took charge of the Peasant Movement Training Institute in Canton, he emphatically told his cadets that they were to lead the armed peasants in the revolutionary struggle. As Wang Shou-tao remembered vividly in 1977, Mao made it clear to them that they must immediately organize the peasants into the 'lance and spear units' to fight the feudal landlords once they went back to their own areas. At that time, the Central Committee of his party did not even consider the feasibility of organizing the peasants in any form.

Fortunately for Mao, the split in the Kuomintang, engineered by Borodin, enabled him to further his efforts in arming the peasants. With the Wuhan Nationalist Government established in Wuchang and Hankow towards the end of 1926, Wang Ching-wei hastened back from France and the left-wing elements in the Kuomintang were firmly in control. Dictated to by Borodin, the Wuhan set-up was the ideal hunting ground for the Communists. Since aligning with the Kuomintang left was the strategy of the Chinese Communist party, Chen Tu-hsiu sent Mao to Wuhan to strengthen the United Front, in the hope of controlling the Kuomintang by means of intensified subversion. Bathed in the congenial atmosphere of the new nerve-centre of the Kuomintang, the ubiquitous Mao sensed that he could play his game with a free hand. After consulting his Kuomintang colleagues, he was allowed to remove the Peasant Movement Training Institute from Canton to Wuchang, so that he could continue to be its head. As his secret designs concerning the institute were largely unknown to the others, he was able to run it as a para-military organization, transforming the cadets into his faithful pawns.

The Wuchang Institute was much bigger than its predecessor in Canton. It took in more than 800 cadets at its inception in March 1927, according to veteran Communist, Liu Chen, who was one among them. In his recollections, the institute was run on a strictly military basis. The cadets received four hours of military drill every single day, including target practice, quick march and mock battles. All the instructors were Communists, Liu added, and Mao was addressed as 'political commissar'. Obviously, Mao intended to turn the institute into the cradle of his military cadres, increasing his political capital in the power game. With the Chinese Communist Party now rapidly expanding into a 'party of the masses', he felt that he should strive to regain his standing in the central leadership. This was by no means an easy task. Apart from coping with Chen Tu-hsiu whom he intensely disliked, he was also at odds with Chang Kuo-tao who was a rising star in the party. Then there were Chu Chiu-pai and Li Li-san, the favourites of Moscow, waiting in the wings. To understand Mao's political struggle during this brief period, one can be illuminated by the succinct accounts made by the Chinese Communist historians who stated that he had to 'fight against Chen Tu-hsiu's rightist opportunism on one hand and Chang Kuo-tao's leftist adventurism on the other'.

But in fact, it was Mao who committed the blunder of carrying the peasant movement too far. When he went to Changsha from Shanghai in December 1926, he virtually undermined the foundation of the peasant movement by solely relying on the poor peasants. They were encouraged to create disorder in the rural areas, grasping land from the landlords, the rich peasants and even the middle peasants. As a result, numerous lives were lost in bloody battles and farm products destroyed. When information about these excesses reached the Central Committee, Mao was on the spot. However, he was given another chance. In January 1927, he hurried to Hunan under the orders of the Central Committee on a fact-finding tour. His mission was to investigate the grievances and rectify the deviations as well as to pacify the discontented rural population in those countries which had suffered heavy losses. Fully aware of his own responsibility in causing the chaos, Mao was more anxious to defend himself than to seek a solution. He knew only too well that any form of recognizing the errors committed by the peasant organizers would reflect his incompetence and misjudgement. Nor did his obstinate nature allow him to admit his inability to grasp the real situation in the countryside. And above all, he was not about to jeopardize his political future in the party by offering his rivals the weapons to attack him.

Weighed down with these considerations, he set out to whitewash everything. In thirty-two days he flitted across Hsiangtang and the other four trouble-ridden counties like Gogol's inspector-general, summoning those he wanted to see and hearing them out. As imagined, he surrounded himself with the poor peasants and readily accepted their explanations and stories. The injured and the wronged were never given a chance to air their grievances, since Mao had no time for them. Back in Wuchang he immediately started to write his Report on an Investigation of the Peasant Movement in Hunan, which was later published in the *Guide Weekly*, the party's organ. In the lengthy report he employed every possible argument to justify himself, dismissing the unfortunate happenings in Hunan at one stroke. But his painstaking effort did not save his skin.

In early April Chen Tu-hsiu arrived at Wuhan with Wang Ching-wei, a few days before Chiang Kai-shek took action to purge the Kuomintang of its Communist elements in Shanghai. In May the Fifth Congress of the Chinese Communist Party was held in Wuhan, mainly to reaffirm its alliance with the Kuomintang left under the leadership of Wang Ching-wei. But when the issue of the excessive peasant movement was brought up for discussion, Chen Tu-hsiu put the blame squarely on Mao. To indicate his displeasure and distrust, he deprived the latter of his voting right at the congress. As if this extraordinary measure were not humiliating enough for Mao to bear, the then party leader effectively stopped him from being elected to the Central Committee. The disgrace would have been too much for anyone else in a similar position to stomach, but Mao did not lose his composure. The opportunist in him suggested that he should pretend to accept Chen's authority without complaint. Meanwhile, as a last resort he approached his close friend, Tsai Ho-shen, for help.

He was not entirely disappointed. As obliging as ever, Tsai spoke to Chen on his behalf and proposed a face-saving formula. With Chen's concurrence, Mao was made an alternate member of the Central Committee instead. Though better than nothing, this hardly satisfied his ego. His hatred for Chen reached a new high, but he forced himself to express deep gratitude. Confident that his time would come, he knew he had to be patient.

Actually, Mao must be held partially responsible for the collapse of the Wuhan Nationalist Government as well, if one examines the events in that period dispassionately. When the regime under the Kuomintang left was first established in Wuhan, it commanded far more support from the National Revolutionary Army than the Nanking Government under Chiang Kai-shek. But as the peasant movement in the provinces of Hunan, Kiangsi and Hupei was allowed to run amok under Mao's guidance, the morale of the army was badly hit. Since most officers and men came from the families of the middle peasants, they refused to let their parents and relatives fall victims to the so-called land reform. Division after division, the army switched its allegiance to the Nanking Government, enabling Chiang Kai-shek to gain the upper hand. To stop the rot, the Wuhan Government had no alternative but to sever its connection with the Communists, in a peaceful manner. This took place in July 1927, barely two months after the Fifth Congress of the Chinese Communist Party had branded much hope on the Kuomintang left. But it was already too late. The Wuhan Government still went under.

The rapid deterioration of the prospects for the Chinese Communist Party shocked the Comintern. But Stalin was not slow in finding a scapegoat. He decided that Chen Tu-hsiu must go, to be replaced by a three-man team headed by Chu Chiu-pai. Before the transition of power, however, a standing committee of the Political Bureau, headed by Chang Kuo-tao, stood in for a brief spell. Chen was conveniently condemned for his 'erroneous opportunism in surrendering to the Kuomintang', since the prestige of the Third International must be preserved. In his own defence, Chen pointed out that he had merely been carrying out the orders of the Comintern, though reluctantly admitting his own error. If the other responsible Communists were sympathetic to Chen, none of them had the courage and integrity to speak up against their masters. Between an arrogant leader such as Chen and the money-bag of Moscow, they obviously knew how to make their choice.

The sacking of Chen Tu-hsiu certainly did not cause Mao a sleepless night, since there was no love lost between them. But ironically, his falling out with the deposed leader, in fact, spared him from sharing the political disgrace. During the short period of the Nationalist-Communist alliance, Mao was no less an 'opportunist' than Chen in his approach. On record he agreed that the Communists must rely on the Kuomintang for leadership in the national revolution, simply because the latter could muster much broader support from the Chinese people. He was all for the idea of working from within the Kuomintang and flying the Kuomintang flag to cover their Communist identity, in view of the generally anti-Communist feeling throughout the country. While working alongside the Nationalists either in Canton or Wuhan, there was no proof that he did not compromise his Marxist stand in important issues such as land reform or the distribution of power between the two parties. If Chen Tu-hsiu were guilty of following the opportunist line, Mao was always there to put it into practice, without raising the faintest voice of doubt.

Having been barred from the Central Committee by Chen, Mao had the advantage of emphasizing his dissent with the former. Thus he was able to distract the attention of his comrades from his previous records. The confusion in the party leadership caused by the abrupt action of Moscow also helped. With self-interest coming foremost in everyone's mind, even his future rival, Chang Kuo-tang, was too occupied to find fault with him. As far as the Comintern was concerned, he was still a small fish, not worth bothering about. Although Mao usually hated to be slighted by the masters in Moscow, at this point in time he was only too glad to be. For him it turned out to be a blessing in disguise.

In all fairness, the Comintern was not really competent enough to direct the Chinese Communist movement from the remoteness of

Moscow. Totally ignorant of the rapid developments in China, it compounded its blunder by sending the wrong men to do the liaison work. Neither Borodin nor his colleague, M. R. Roy, was received by the Chinese Communist leadership with respect. Haughty and dogmatic, they treated their Chinese comrades like subordinates. To make the matter worse, the two of them were constantly at odds. They often gave conflicting orders to the Chinese Communists, expecting them to achieve the impossible. While feigning all obedience in their presence, the Chinese comrades frequently ridiculed and criticized the two Comintern agents among themselves. They were disdainfully referred to as the 'hairy barbarians', and sometimes the 'hunchback foreign devil' in the case of Roy. Their inability to come to grips with the revolutionary realities in China was bitterly attacked, with enthusiasm and in the best proletarian tradition. Naturally, the masters in Moscow could not have realized these frictions and tensions, even if they had the most fertile imaginations. To heighten its folly, the Comintern ordered the Chinese Communists to remain inside the Kuomintang after the Wuhan Government had publicly severed its relations with the Chinese Communist Party. If the Chinese comrades then still reserved some respect for the Comintern, such a directive would have wiped out the last bit of it.

But amid all the confusion, Mao Tse-tung found the path for himself. As he was then well down on the bottom rung of the Central leadership, he decided that he would fare better by seeking regional power. When the Central Political Bureau under Chang Kuo-tao made arrangements to disperse the responsible comrades after the Wuhan break-up, he was instructed to proceed to the comparative safety of Szechuan province to organize the peasants. But he had other ideas. He offered to go back to Hunan instead. His courageous gesture impressed the members of the Political Bureau, as Chang Kuo-tai later recounted. It was clear to them that, being a wanted man in his native province, he was running an enormous risk. What they could not see was Mao's immense confidence in the solid work he had done in Hunan. He knew he could count on the loyal support of his fellow natives, not to mention his intimate knowledge of local circumstances. To fulfil his ambition, he was quite prepared to take a gamble, especially when he felt that he had a winning hand. Judging by later developments, he certainly made a crucial decision. Had he not volunteered to return to his native province, his fate would have taken a different turn.

4 THE PLUNGE INTO
CIVIL WAR

Towards the end of July 1927, the Chinese Communist Party was in great disarray. Hardly having time to recover from the heavy toll of the Shanghai massacre in April, it now lost the last hope of clinging to the Kuomintang left to stage a comeback. Although claiming a membership of over 59,000 in May at the Fifth Congress, the party was as demoralized as it was disunited. After the 'resignation' of the party leader Chen Tu-hsiu, the provisional Political Bureau headed by Chang Kuo-tao failed to come up with a clearly defined policy because of its precarious future. Nor did the Comintern help. Sometime in July, its new representatives, Besso Lominadze and Heinz Neumann, descended on Hankow like overlords, condemning Chen Tu-hsiu and reprimanding Chang Kuo-tao and the other leaders in the same breath. Having humiliated the Chinese comrades to their hearts' content, they declared their intention to reorganize the Central leadership. To facilitate the reorganization, they sent Chang Kuo-tao, Chou En-lai and Li Li-san off to Nanchang in late July to plot the August 1st Uprising against the Nationalists. Meanwhile, one of the two foreigners went to Hunan to expose the error of opportunism committed by the Central leadership and announce the forthcoming reorganization, obviously to forestall any possible resistance conceived or put up by Chang Kuo-tao and his colleagues. It is fair to say that the two Comintern representatives virtually set the Chinese Communists on the path of armed uprisings, which was to cost millions of Chinese lives in the ensuing years.

Ironically, at that time the Chinese Communists really resorted to military means out of desperation rather than conviction. It is true that before the arrival of Lominadze and Neumann, they had contemplated the possibility of launching military adventures in Kwangtung, Kiangsi, Hunan and Hupei. But the idea was dropped by Chen Tu-hsiu and his colleagues when they could still hang on under the shelter of the Wuhan Government. Even with the Nanchang Uprising on 1 August the Chinese Communists were far from confident about their own cause. To confuse the people, they continued to disguise themselves as the left-wing elements of the Kuomintang. As for the organization to direct the uprising, they formed the Kuomintang Revolutionary Committee, ostensibly including Madame Sun Yat-sen and a few Nationalists in the midst of an overwhelming number of Communists. By doing so, they hoped to rally more popular support. Strictly speaking, this approach must be regarded as an act of opportunism, the very crime Chen Tu-hsiu was supposed to have committed. But if anybody did have some doubts, no one was prepared to challenge the order from Moscow.

When the Nanchang Uprising was suppressed by the Nationalist troops, Chou En-lai, Chu Teh, Yeh Ting and Ho Lung led the remnants of the routed Communist forces fleeing southward, with the faint hope of reaching Swatow to establish a base there. If the report made by Chang Kuo-tao to the Central Committee in October that year was anything to go by, in less than two months, the Communists lost 13,000 troops through mutinies, desertions and casualties, with barely 8,000 left in strength, scattered and demoralized. This was certainly not a very triumphant beginning for the much heralded 'armed revolt of the workers and peasants', though in their attempt to glorify the Nanchang Uprising, the Chinese Communists have consequently made 1 August the Army Day.

However, the Nanchang setback shocked Lominadze and Neumann. On 7 August, they hastily called an emergency meeting of the Central Committee in Kiukiang, separated from Nanchang by the immense Poyang Lake, to examine the situation. The meeting was only attended by ten of the regular committee members, and Mao Tse-tung was the only alternate member present. As arranged, Chu Chiu-pai, the new favourite of the Comintern, formally denounced Chen Tu-hsiu's 'opportunism' at the meeting and the others joined in. The Central Committee was summarily reorganized and a new Provisional Political Bureau of three was formed, headed by Chu Chiu-pai. He was also made General Secretary of the party, thus completing the disgrace of Chen Tu-hsiu. As the Chinese Communist historians may have every right to refer to this meeting as the 'historic August 7th Conference', they choose not to mention the 'historic' element: the ousting of the founder of the Chinese Communist Party.

Anxious not to repeat Chen Tu-hsiu's errors, Chu Chiu-pai went to the other extreme by plunging into more military adventures. In fact, there was little else he could do. To pursue the 'armed uprising' line to a further extent, Chu and his colleagues decided to organize the revolts of workers and peasants in Hupei, Hunan and Kwangtung, in the hope that they would link up with the Communist forces driven away from Nanchang by the Nationalists. But due to the execution of the 'terrorist line', as the Comintern termed it, these revolts petered out when they encountered the resistance of the people in various regions. Take the Canton Uprising on 11 December 1927, for instance. In spite of its initial success and the establishment of the Canton Soviet, it was demolished by the anti-Communist workers organized by the Kwangtung Trade Union and the Engineering Union within three days. It was another total defeat suffered by the Chinese Communists, and Chang Tai-lei, acting Chairman of the Canton Soviet, lost his life.

Although Mao Tse-tung did not respect Chu Chiu-pai any more than he did Chen Tu-hsiu, Chu's decision to step up military activities appealed to him. It had always been his belief that political power could not be obtained through peaceful means. A worshipper of Tsao Tsao, the Chinese Machiavelli in the Period of the Three Kingdoms (A.D. 221 – 265) who excelled in staging military coups and practising devious statecraft, he felt that his party would not survive without creating a state of confusion and chaos. Not that he was unaware of the superior strength of the Nationalists in purely military terms, but he had the courage to strive for the fulfilment of his political aims, against all calculations, and at all costs. Most important of all, he was confident of his own military talent which had yet to be recognized by his comrades. When the Central Committee sent him to help organize the Autumn Harvest Uprising in his native province Hunan, he accepted the mission with great enthusiasm.

But unfortunately, the Autumn Harvest Uprising encountered the same fate as the other armed revolts in Hupei and Kwangtung. With the Hunan Party Committee led by Peng Kung-ta, Mao operated as the special representative of the Central Committee. He took charge of the area between western Kiangsi and eastern Hunan, covering three counties along the border between the two provinces. The uprising started in Hunan in early September, according to the Chinese Communist records, when the armed units of workers and peasants from Anyuan county occupied Liling. About the same time, the peasants in Liuyang and Pingkiang launched their revolts, sweeping towards Changsha, the provincial capital. They were to join forces with the rebel units from Anyuan, to form a pincer movement against Changsha. This move turned out to be a strategic blunder, for the 'over-emphasis on military operations caused the failure in mobilizing the masses of peasantry, leading to the temporary setback'. Changsha remained intact and the Communist forces were routed.

Actually, to set off the Autumn Harvest Uprising in Hunan, the Chinese Communists had four regiments at their disposal, numbering no less than 9,000 men. But the trouble was, the majority of these troops had not been politically indoctrinated. They turned against the Communists when the chips were down. As Mao later recalled not without bitterness, even the 'commander of the First Division betrayed the Red Army to join the Nationalists' after the unsuccessful Pingkiang campaign. The campaign marked Mao's first military defeat, and he was severely punished by the Central Committee for his 'failure to mobilize the peasants'. In the enlarged meeting of the Provincial Central Political Bureau in Shanghai on 14 November 1927, he was sacked as its alternate member. He also lost his seat on the Hunan Party Committee.

The disciplinary action taken by the Central leadership made no difference to Mao, for he had something much more important to worry about. After the disastrous defeat in the vicinity of Pingkiang, the menace of extinction loomed over his head like a dark cloud. Earlier on in Tungku, he had been captured by the local militia when he tried to sneak past their sentry-boxes. But as he was clad in the garments of an average peasant, a pyjama suit made of white coarse cloth, his captors did not discover his true identity. By offering a few silver dollars and pretending ignorance, he regained his freedom some twenty days later. He had barely recovered from that frightening experience as he managed to reach the rebel units near Pingkiang, only to throw himself into the midst of demoralized bands of men. It was clear to him that he must act immediately.

Too stubborn to accept defeat, he was determined to regroup and reshape the battered troops to carry on the armed struggle. Instead of renewing the futile attempt to close on Changsha, as the Central Political Bureau had specified, Mao gathered about 1,000 men from the various routed regiments at Wenchiashih on the Kiangsi border. On 19 September he called an enlarged meeting of the army cadres there. In the meeting the decision to march towards the Chingkang Mountains was taken. As the secretary of the Front Committee, Mao had no trouble in persuading the cadres to support his idea about this strategic retreat. He set his mind on the Chingkang Mountains for a variety of reasons. Geographically, the whole area sprawls on the Hunan-Kiangsi border, consisting of a few mountainous towns which were beyond the effective control of either provincial government. Although the Nationalists had by now established themselves in the big cities and coastal towns, they lacked the numerical strength to extend their authority into remote areas such as the Chingkang Mountains. The Northward Expedition led by Chiang Kai-shek owed its success more to the swift surrender of local warlords rather than genuine military conquests. These warlords were accepted into the Nationalist camp without having to know anything about the political ideals of Dr Sun Yat-sen. Except for the flags and uniforms, they did not really have a change of heart. They continued to rule their own regions more or less in the same manner. As far as they were concerned, personal interests must come first. Between them splits and conflicts were unavoidable. It was under these conditions that the Chingkang Mountains and areas of similar nature became the haven of bandits and outlaws, in the tradition of *The Water Margin*.

To Mao's credit, he was perceptive enough to see the advantage in exploiting the situation. In his mind, there was no doubt that he must do all he could to hold these 1,000-odd men together, even for his own survival. The directive of the Central Political Bureau might not have escaped his memory, but he believed that he had to take his own initiative. Not impossibly, he could have thought of the familiar Chinese saying: 'When a general is on a mission, he may reject some of the monarch's orders.' With the Central Committee too far away to breathe down his neck, he would like to stake his life on his own judgement, reckless though it might seem. As Tung Ping-wu, the late Vice-Chairman of the People's Republic of China, said to me in Nanking during the Nationalist-Communist peace talks in 1946, Mao's decision to lead the defeated troops to the Chingkang Mountains 'was of vital importance to the future of the Chinese Communist Party, for it enabled him to establish the first revolutionary base in the middle of hostile forces, setting the pattern for the party's military strategy'. But he became evasive when I asked him whether the then Central Committee did repudiate Mao for going it alone. Then he looked thoughtful, stroking his moustache and saying, 'A daring move is often seen as a reckless deed by people who are less perceptive and creative'. In not so many words, he confirmed what I sought to know without giving a direct answer.

But in 1927, Chu Chiu-pai and his associates would have reacted as they did for the sake of party discipline. Rightly or wrongly, they could not afford to tolerate any form of challenge to their authority. Judged by the accounts and recollections of some seasoned Communists who served under Mao at that time, his decision to march to the Chingkang Mountains must be regarded as a last throw by the gambler in him, having more to do with his instinct than his judgement. The desperate need to find a foothold for his demoralized and embittered men forced him to take a less than even chance. Though reorganized into a division at Wenchiashih, the 1,000-odd men were in tatters and rags, underfed and badly equipped. Mao himself was a sorrier sight. With his feet injured after escaping from the captivity at Tungku, he could hardly walk. To carry him, the men fastened two bamboo poles to a chair. As the autumn chill set in near the end of September, his peasant suit of white coarse cloth was too light for the weather. To keep warm, he had to wrap himself in a double-layer bedcloth, while being carried in the chair. But these seemingly insurmountable hardships did not diminish Mao's 'revolutionary optimism', as one of his aides Chen Po-chun wrote about this episode many years later; he told the men historical anecdotes and extolled revolutionary virtues all the time, keeping them from feeling downcast and depressed. Even if Chen tended to exaggerate Mao's influence to a certain extent, this would have been his way to maintain the men's morale. He believed in the power of words, and never ran short of them. This was particularly true when he was among the workers and peasants who were intellectually inferior to him.

On the way to the Chingkang Mountains, the depleted division under Mao was ambushed and attacked by the local troops at several stages. Despite his ceaseless effort to exhort the men, he found it impossible to stop the increasing number of deserters. On 29 September they dragged their weary bodies to a tiny town called Sanwan for a brief rest. Mao realized that he must take another drastic step. He called the men together, giving them the choice of leaving or remaining under his command. Each of those who decided to leave was handed five silver dollars for his homeward-bound fares. About 600 or 700 men indicated their wish to follow him anywhere, and they became known as the 'Sanwan Men' who formed the backbone of Mao's most trusted cadres for many more years to come. He reorganized them into a regiment and continued to head for the Chingkang Mountains. His brother, Tse-min, was in this group.

When they moved nearer to their destination, Mao was faced with another dilemma. As had been rumoured, the whole area around the Chingkang Mountains was ruled by the two bandit leaders, Wang Tso and Yuan Wen-tsai, with the aid of a few hundred outlaws. They collected taxes and enforced their own laws, which did not preclude their occasional plunderings and kidnappings when they felt so inclined. To take over control of the area, Mao either had to get rid of Wang and Yuan or seek their cooperation. On ideological grounds he should have had no hesitation, for the obvious choice was to fight it out with them. But Mao was too pragmatic to think in Marxist terms. He knew he could not risk another defeat at the hands of these bandits, since their strength was an unknown factor. After some deliberation, he decided to join up with Wang Tso and Yuan Wen-tsai and sent an emissary to make the necessary approach.

As Yuan was the brain of the bandit group, the emissary approached him first, profferring a couple of nice hand guns as a gift from Mao himself. The friendly gesture appealed to Yuan and he agreed to meet Mao for a talk. The meeting turned out to be a success, for an instant rapport was established between the two of them. Through Yuan's arrangements, Mao met Wang Tso to discuss the terms of cooperation. With Yuan already convinced by Mao's eloquence and arguments, Wang was an easy prey. Over tumblers of wine and heaps of food, he accepted Mao's 'commission' as a battalion commander, and so did Yuan. To impress the two bandit leaders with his sincerity, Mao and they became sworn brothers, taking an oath before the eyes of their men. This was a very shrewd move on Mao's part, because this special relationship would forestall them from betraying him under any circumstances. He knew very well that in the world of bandits, the oath of sworn brothers was not to be broken. As for himself, it was another matter. To keep an eye on Wang and Yuan, he made Ho Chang-kung, one of his confidants, their political commissar, presumably to give these newly converted revolutionaries some political guidance in the interest of the Marxist cause.

Doubtless, there was an element of luck that Wang Tso and Yuan Wen-tsai should find Mao congenial and trustworthy. But then, compared with them, he had the advantage of having handled more difficult people such as his superiors and rivals in the party. As Wang and Yuan were still peasants at heart, he knew how to work on them and win their confidence. Cut off from the Central leadership, he had every pretext to be more independent and flexible in executing the party line. Chu Chiu-pai, being an adherent to the Comintern directives, would not have approved of Mao's earthy approach of linking up with the bandits had he been consulted. But as for Mao, he never held Moscow in high esteem.

The Chingkang Mountains covered an area of about 550 *li* lying on the junction of four extremely poor counties—Ningkang, Linghsien, Suichuan and Yunghsin. The main mountain, steep and rocky, was inaccessible except for several winding paths which could be easily guarded. It was both the stronghold and hideout for Wang Tso and Yuan Wen-tsai before the arrival of Mao and his weary troops. Initially, the two bandit leaders refused their new 'commander', as Mao was known in that area, access to the mountain itself. They preferred to keep him at arm's length for the sake of precaution. But this did not worry Mao. He was quite happy to have the use of the flat terrain shielded by the small hills. Without the imminent danger of being attacked by the Nationalist forces, he could have the breathing space to carry out further reorganization and rebuild the fighting strength.

Formally adopting the name of the Workers and Peasants Revolutionary Army, Mao committed his men to raiding the nearby Chaling county for a start. But the encounter with the Nationalist troops there turned out to be a disaster. He was roundly defeated, and his regiment commander defected to the Nationalists. Hastily beating his retreat, he feigned heading for Yunghsin before moving back to the direction of the Chingkang Mountains. He covered his tracks well, for the Nationalist troops were led to chase the shadows. The defeat made him more aware of the importance of strengthening party organization in the army. Determined to achieve effective control of all military units, he deemed it necessary to form party organization at the company level. Between the winter of 1927 and early 1928, he was personally involved in this task. In his faded grey uniform, he moved about freely among the ordinary soldiers, like one of them. The dishevelled hair and the tall, stooping figure became a familiar sight in every company, platoon and squad. Probably owing to his experience as a school teacher, he was good at explaining things in very simple words, sparing his audience the ordeal of digesting Marxist jargon. The men felt drawn to him because he never talked down to them, always patient and full of understanding. They were particularly flattered as he knew each of them by name. Before long, Mao was able to command their affection and loyalty almost naturally. This marked the beginning of his 'reliance of the masses', extending his influence to the grass roots level.

In the meantime, he did not overlook the men's material needs. He had new uniforms made and issued to them. The uniforms were still made of grey cloth, in conformity with the military tradition. But to distinguish his men from the Nationalist troops, the caps were of a different shape, resembling those worn by the Russian workers. They also had to wear red armbands for easy identification. More significantly, he introduced the unified ration system so that the men and the officers would eat the same kind of food. As he saw it, hardships had to be shared and fairness would make scarcity more tolerable. When several veteran Communists wrote about their experiences at the Chingkang Mountains years later, none of them failed to single out the revolutionized ration system as Mao's most popular measure, with the issuing of the new uniforms running a close second. What they did not see was that he merely emulated his heroes in

The Water Margin, sharing wine and meat among the men in equal portions.

But understandably, Mao never felt safe until he could turn the main mountain into a fortified command post. It was all very well that he could roam the adjoining areas. Yet there was no way for him to entrench himself in the event of a determined Nationalist attack. Fortunately, Ho Chang-kung proved to be a great help. Having worked on Wang Tso for some time without much success, he found out that the bandit happened to be a very obedient son. With Mao's approval, he spent hours showing attention to Wang's mother, almost like a courtier. Immensely pleased, the old woman ordered her son to treat his new 'commander' with greater trust and respect. Influenced by his mother, Wang allowed Mao and his men to station themselves on the main mountain, a concession the latter had been dreaming of. This enabled him to proceed with the setting up of a political and military base for his party, in his own interest, of course.

Having established his headquarters on the mountain itself, Mao set out to enlarge the surrounding areas by means of launching surprise attacks and instigating local poor peasants to stage isolated revolts. He would unleash his troops to raid the nearby county towns, ransacking the houses of the landlords and the rich with unquestionable revolutionary zeal. These raids were absolutely necessary, since there was no other way to obtain provisions for his Workers and Peasants Revolutionary Army, now expanded into three regiments once again. On the other hand, these military movements were essential to the men's morale, keeping them at the ready all the time. As the ancient Chinese strategist, Sun Wu, asserted, an army must not be allowed to stay idle. Mao certainly knew how to put this theory into practice. Naturally, to lend respectability to these raids, red flags were waved and political slogans shouted. According to Lai Yi, a senior army officer who wrote in 1976 to laud Mao's achievement during the Chingkangshan period, the Chinese leader used to motivate his men in not so many words. Before each raid, Mao would, he recalled, tell the men the importance of 'acquiring food-stuffs, resources and cash for the base', encouraging them to force their way into the big houses belonging to the 'wicked gentry'. He went on to quote Mao as saying, 'To mobilize and organize the masses, we must rob the rich and give it to the poor. Since the poor people may not dare to accept the things taken away from the landlords and the gentry at first, we should only go to them after nightfall.'

Of these raids, Lai Yi seemed to remember the one on Suichuan parti-cularly well. As the first Chinese New Year (sometime in January 1928) since the establishment of the Chingkangshan base, he said, was approaching, Mao summoned all the units together. In his usual manner, the 'commander' briefed his men about their immediate mission. He told them that they were to raid Suichuan this time, for the local armed force was too weak to put up any form of resistance. 'The gentry and the land-lords are stinkingly rich there,' he said, 'piles of silver dollars lie asleep under the floorboards, waiting for us to make good use of them. When we get there, we must deal the wicked gentry heavy blows, take the money and mobilize the masses.' These words produced immediate effects on the men, as Lai recalled.

In a vivid account, he described how Mao led the troops marching down the mountain road. 'Fully inspired, we charged towards Suichuan in the cutting winter wind. Though still clad in our tattered uniforms, we were no longer bothered by the recent setbacks. Chests out and chins up, we looked forward to taking on the important mission ahead of us.' Like everyone else, Lai obviously carried out Mao's orders to the letter. When his squad broke into the heavily locked house of a local bigwig, he was dazzled by its rich contents. But having fed on pumpkins and sweet potatoes for months in the Chingkang Mountains, he found it difficult not to remark on the abundance of foodstuffs, his mouth watering. He noted that some hundred pounds of cured pork, cured chickens and cured fish were soaking in huge barrels of tea oil for preservation, to be consumed in the forthcoming Chinese New Year.

From Mao's point of view, the operation was a great success. For Lai went on to describe the New Year celebrations they held in Suichuan. 'When all units returned to the town after collecting funds and material supplies from the villages within a radius of twenty *li*, Commissar Mao was greatly pleased. He announced a three-day holiday on the New Year's Eve, and gave each of us a few silver dollars. That evening, we all had a big dinner. My company used an ancient temple for the occasion, the officers and the men ate and drank together. Firecrackers were set off amid the merry sound of gongs and drums; all the streets were brightly lit up throughout the night.'

But this was not all. After the New Year celebrations, Mao imme-diately resumed his 'fund-raising' campaign. The men were organized into small groups, moving out in all directions to comb the villages further away. Again Lai Yi described how his group did its job, matter-of-factly. 'On reaching Tsoan, we were divided into several groups, each covering a specified route. We waved the red flags of a propaganda team, shouting slogans to urge the poor to follow us. We promised to share out with them the money we would get from the wicked gentry and the crooked landlords. At first, the people wavered. Then suddenly, a human stream gathered behind us, cheering and shouting. We simply put notices on the doors of the wicked gentry and the crooked landlords, demanding that they pay fines for having exploited the poor. Scared, they handed over the sums we demanded without fail.' If these accounts were reasonably accurate, it would seem that Mao's way of practising Marxism in those days was rather unorthodox, to say the least. Obviously, he was more inspired by what he had read in *The Water Margin* than in Lenin's teachings.

However, the pursuance of these marauding tactics might have relieved Mao's base in the Chingkang Mountains of its acute shortage of food and other supplies, it also led the Nationalists to step up military operations in this area. Although Mao, with topographical advantage, managed to stave off a few small-scale attacks, he realized that the Nationalists were bound to launch more military campaigns against the Chingkang Mountains. In order to hold out, it was imperative for him to have reinforcements. To his delight Ho Chang-kung came back with some good news. Earlier on, Mao had sent him to Changsha to report to the Provincial Party Committee on the establishment of the Chingkang-shan base. Having accomplished his mission, the able aide had to find a roundabout way to return to this area. To avoid being intercepted by the Nationalist troops deployed between Changsha and the Hunan-Kiangsi border, he drifted into the northern part of Kwangtung, by way of Canton. Due to the tightened security measures enforced by the Kuomintang, he did not manage to reach Shaokuan till the end of December in 1927. After spending several months on the road, he needed a bath badly. As he dipped himself in the public bath, he happened to overhear the conversation between two junior Nationalist officers, apparently under the command of the former Yunnan warlord, Fan Shih-sheng. By sheer chance they talked about none other than Chu Teh, revealing that he now served in Fan's army under the pseudonym of Wang Kai, as well as the location of his unit. Overjoyed, Ho hurried to the small town where Chu's troops were stationed. There he not only saw Chu Teh, but also ran into Chen Yi whom he had known in France. On behalf of Mao, he invited them to lead their troops to the Chingkang Mountains to strengthen the revolutionary struggle. But Chu needed no persuasion, for he had been of like mind. He had already sent Mao Tse-tan, Mao's younger brother, to the Chingkang Mountains with the same proposal.

Since the abortive Nanchang Uprising in August, Chu Teh had been ceaselessly pursued by the Nationalist forces. With some 900 men left, he had no alternative but to seek the shelter of Fan Shih-sheng, his old colleague in the Yunnan Army prior to the Northward Expedition. By no means loyal to the Kuomintang, Fan made him change his name to Wang Kai to serve as a regiment commander under his command. He was allowed to keep his own men together and given a free hand to absorb new recruits. The arrangement suited Chu Teh perfectly, for he could have time to re-establish contacts with other Communist units to resume the armed struggle. Having read about the Chingkang Mountains in the newspapers, he was all set to head that way to join forces with Mao when the time was ripe. The unexpected visit of Ho Chang-kung gave him the additional stimulus.

In February 1928, Chu Teh went into action. He led his men to attack his benefactor Fan Shih-sheng's other units before breaking away to push towards Southern Hunan. It was not until March that Mao received an order from the Party Committee of that area requesting him to give Chu the necessary assistance. The committee also formally recognized Mao as the commander of the First Division of the Workers' and Peasants' Army. To link up with Chu's operation, he deployed two understrength regiments to launch feint attacks on the Nationalist units in pursuit of his prospective partner. Several weeks later, Chu Teh and Chen Yi eventually shook off the chasing Nationalists to reach the Chingkangshan area, when Mao was still leading one regiment to cover their rear. On 28 April Mao returned. He and Chu formally met for the first time in the disused Lungchiang College in Lungshih, a market town of Ningtu county. To commemorate the occasion, a mass meeting was held on 4 May in the town square. As expected, both Chu and Mao spoke of the significance of the unification of 'two revolutionary forces' cheered and applauded by some 10,000 peasants and soldiers who had been summoned from towns and villages in the whole area.

But behind the closed doors there was a different scene. To establish a unified command, the two revolutionary forces had to be reorganized into a single military unit. Numerically, Chu Teh's Red Fourth Army consisted of 1,700 men while Mao's First Division of the Workers and Peasants Revolutionary Army totalled less than 800. As regards quality, Chu's men were regular soldiers, better equipped and battle-hardened. With due respect to Mao, he had to contend with an assortment of workers, peasants and bandits without formal military training. But he had the advantage of being the 'host', as Chu Teh called him in his conversation with Chen Yi and other cadres of the Red Fourth Army. Although his subordinates complained to him about Mao's arrogance and aggressiveness in no uncertain terms, Chu remained his modest self, caring more for revolutionary solidarity than personal power. He was

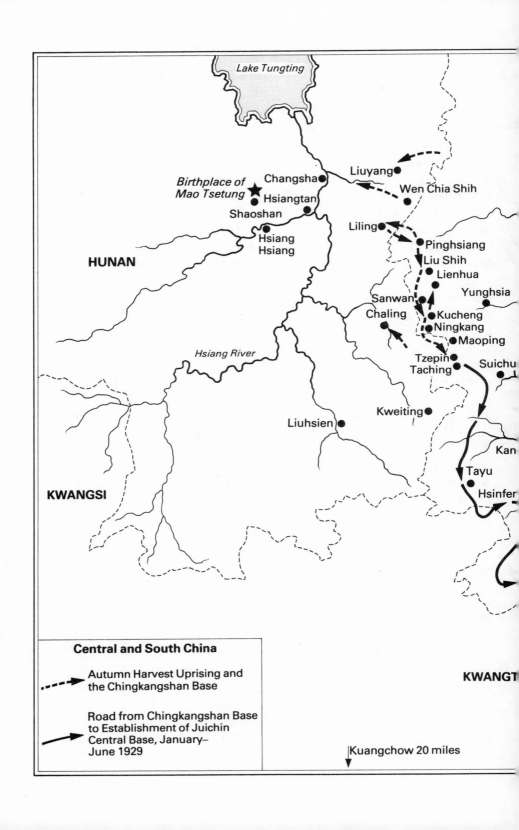

Lake Tungting

Liuyang

Changsha

Birthplace of Mao Tsetung

Wen Chia Shih

Hsiangtan

Shaoshan

Liling

Pinghsiang

Hsiang Hsiang

Liu Shih

Lienhua

HUNAN

Yunghsia

Sanwan

Kucheng

Chaling

Ningkang

Maoping

Hsiang River

Tzepin

Taching

Suichu

Kweiting

Kan

Liuhsien

Tayu

KWANGSI

Hsinfer

Central and South China

- - - → Autumn Harvest Uprising and the Chingkangshan Base

——→ Road from Chingkangshan Base to Establishment of Juichin Central Base, January– June 1929

KWANGT

|Kuangchow 20 miles

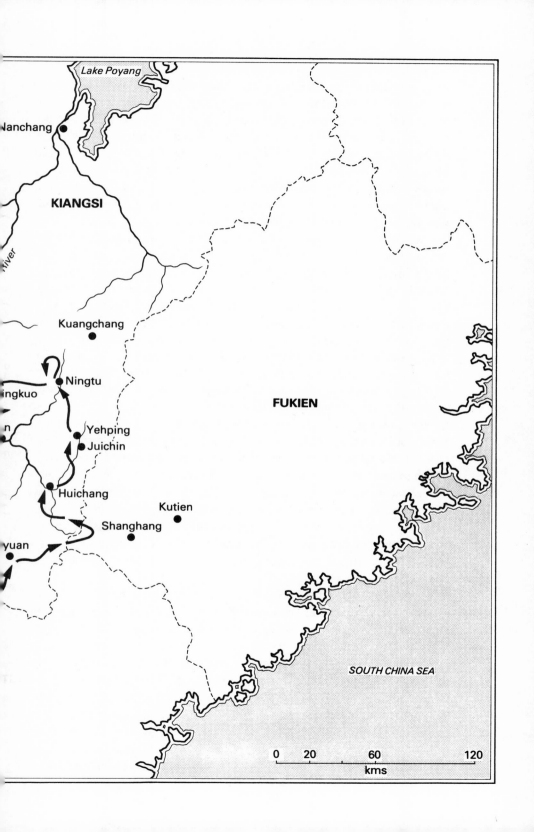

willing to give Mao a slight edge in their negotiations about the reorganization. Anyway, Mao was shrewd enough to back down on unimportant points. They agreed to use the name of the Red Fourth Army in preference to that of the Workers and Peasants Revolutionary Army coined by Mao in his creative mood. When it came to the issue that mattered, Mao stuck to his ground. Chu's troops were reorganized into two regiments and Mao's men made up the third. The post of the army commander naturally went to Chu and Mao became the army's political commissar, which seemed to be the logical development.

It would be too arbitrary to interpret all this as Mao's insatiable appetite for power. He might be less aggressive if the Central Committee, now safely installed in the International Settlement of Shanghai, had not treated him so harshly after the collapse of the Autumn Harvest Uprising, which was not entirely his fault. Dismissed from both the Central Political Bureau and the Hunan Provincial Party Committee, he even had to take orders from the Special Committee of Southern Hunan, a disgrace he found hard to live with. Having successfully occupied the Chingkang Mountains to set up the first military base for the party, he felt that he was in a position to challenge the authority of the Central Committee 'consisting of a bunch of foreign-trained students'. The idea 'power grows out of the barrel of a gun' gradually took shape in his mind. He seriously considered the possibility of developing the Chingkangshan base, as Ho Chang-kung later disclosed, into the pivot of power from which to lead the nation-wide Communist revolution. Impossible though it might seem to most of his comrades, Mao was nothing if not a dreamer. His conviction was strengthened when he took into account the disharmony and conflicts among various units of the Nationalist forces. Even within the Kuomintang, he could still count on its left wing as a potential ally. But to his annoyance, Chu Teh did not think along the same line.

A typical soldier, Chu Teh saw military victories as the sole means to advance the revolutionary cause. After moving into the Chingkangshan area, he fought against the Nationalist troops more successfully than Mao had done. But unlike the latter, he did not bother to organize the people or emphasize the propaganda work. This led Mao to critize his 'sheer military viewpoint' and 'roving rebel mentality'. What he meant was that Chu should try to consolidate his military successes by winning popular support through political work. He also wanted Chu to consider the Chingkang Mountains as a base of a permanent nature. Nevertheless, they never allowed their differences to surface in view of the circumstances. They could not afford to have an open split when the Nationalist forces were still encircling the whole area.

On the other hand, the difference did spur Mao to step up the political control of the army with increasing firmness. He set the aim of absorbing two out of every three soldiers into the party, so that he, as political commissar, would be able to exert greater influence than the commander. No matter how busy he was, he made a point of mixing with the soldiers, always full of concern. He chatted with them and was not afraid of using vulgar expressions for their benefit. To impress the soldiers with the importance of defending the base at all costs, as the veteran Communist Chu Liang-tsai quoted him years after, he likened it to 'a man's backside without which he cannot sit down for a rest'. He then went on to say that they must protect the base as vigorously as they would their own backside. His words brought the house down, but the point was driven home. According to Chu Liang-tsai, everyone present 'instantly recognized the significance of the base to the revolution', convinced that 'Commissar Mao's political thought was always correct'.

In order to undermine Chu Teh's popularity with the men who had served under him since the Nanching Uprising, Mao often went out of his way to please them. He had the gift of creating a favourable first impression, able to hide his feelings behind the smokescreen of ready smiles and gentle manners. He was also good at judging the character of a man, which enabled him to spot the ambitious and the potential leaders. Of Chu's junior officers, he lost no time in showing interest in Chen Yi, later to be his Foreign Minister, and Lin Piao, his future Defence Minister and heir-apparent who eventually emerged as his greatest enemy in 1971. With Chen he did not have much luck. Having known Chu since the days in France and coming from the same province Szechuan, Chen had no doubt where his loyalty lay. In meetings and discussions, he continued to side with Chu unwaveringly. But Lin Piao was very responsive. A mere company commander, he was overwhelmed by Mao's attention and concern. With his assistance, Mao inched his way into more platoons and squads of the original Red Fourth Army, making sure that 'politics takes command'. To reward Lin, he eventually persuaded Chu to give him the command of a regiment. Since Lin was a graduate of the Whampoa Military Academy, the undoubting Chu obliged, totally unaware of Mao's real motive. He even thanked Mao for being so observant and straightforward, taking the trouble to remind him of his oversight.

As a matter of fact, it was hard for most of those cadres not to be impressed by Mao during the Chingkangshan period, especially when they first met him. He might be arrogant to his equals and disdainful to his superiors, but with those who were junior to him in status he was all modesty. In his book *The Red Army and I*, Kung Chu vividly wrote about his first meeting with Mao. Then a political commissar with one of Chu Teh's regiments, he reached the Chingkang Mountains with the advance unit. 'When Hu Shao-hai and I entered the town of Shuiko', he recalled, 'I ordered the men to sit resting by the roadside. Just as I was about to call on Mao Tse-tung, four guards of the Workers and Peasants Revolutionary Army escorted someone towards my direction. Tallish, broad in the shoulders and long in the arms, he was in a faded grey uniform. His hair was extremely long and untidy, and he appeared to have not shaved for days. It was only when we exchanged our names that I found him to be Mao Tse-tung. Despite his casual manners, he was so gentle and friendly that one could not help warming to him.' Obviously impressed, Kung further recalled Mao's hospitality with relish. 'At that moment, one of his guards reported to him that the supper was ready. He immediately told the guard to invite Regiment Commander Hu over to join us. The three of us ate and chatted with much pleasure. It was a gorgeous meal. Before our arrival, he had already taken the trouble to send someone to buy a big, fat chicken. There were also plenty of eggs and cured pork, as well as an enormous jug of rice wine. In the course of our retreat after the defeat, such an elaborate supper was memorable and heartening—a rare treat!' Since Kung later deserted the Red Army, that he should still write glowingly about Mao after his defection indicates the Chairman's artfulness in dealing with people, an asset most of his rivals found wanting.

With the arrival of Chu Teh, the military strength of the Chingkangshan base was more than doubled, soon developing into a fighting force of 3,000 strong. Mao freely attributed the expansion and progress to his successful mobilization of the masses, as he would say. But in fact, Chu should take the credit. Better known and well liked by the rank and file, he would have attracted a greater following than Mao could have hoped for. Between April and July in 1928, it was Chu who repulsed the two large-scale attacks staged by the Nationalists from Hunan and Kiangsi, though at considerable cost. Before then, all Mao had done was to raid undefended towns and fight local militia instead of regular forces. It was during these two campaigns, according to Kung Chu, that Chu Teh introduced the basic concepts of guerrilla tactics which Mao claimed to be his creation:

'The enemy advances, we retreat; the enemy camps, we harass; the enemy tires, we attack; the enemy retreats, we pursue.'

Possibly, Chu explained these notions verbally while Mao put them down in writing, not forgetting to alter one or two words here and there.

To be fair to Mao, he did then have the urge to improve his military knowledge. For this purpose, he never hesitated to pick the brains of professional soldiers. He would discuss all aspects of each victory or defeat with them, down to the most minute detail and at great length. Undoubtedly, he was good at absorbing other people's ideas and summing them up in his own words. If one is well versed in Chinese classics, one would have no difficulty in detecting that his strategic thought is basically a hotchpotch of General Sun Wu's Military Strategy, *Romance of the Three Kingdoms* and *The Water Margin*. During the civil war in the early 1930s, the Communist general Liu Po-cheng bitterly attacked him for learning his strategy from these novels. And so did many other cadres in the Red Army. But Mao managed to survive these criticisms eventually, without yielding an inch. Stubborn as always, he could not see why he should concur with the others. He knew he would have the last laugh when things turned out in his favour.

Despite his painstaking efforts to woo the junior officers and men. Mao did not really succeed in undercutting Chu Teh's position in their hearts. The latter might not be very good with words, but he shared their hardships and acted like one of them, as if it were the most natural thing for him to do. To the ordinary soldiers, he was the father-figure rather than the commander. As the Chingkang Mountains were so barren and poor, the men had to come down to the dales and valleys to chop firewood. Like pack animals, they would then climb up the steep mountain paths with heavy loads on their shoulders. Not once did Chu Teh fail to join them in doing this chore. He did what everyone had to do, disregarding his age and seniority. The other officers soon followed suit, and the men were greatly inspired. But Mao was the only exception. To defend himself, he argued that the revolution called for the division of labour instead of having everyone engaged in the same kind of work. Although no one bothered to refute him, his attitude could have hardly enhanced his popularity with the men. However, the incident deepened his dislike for Chu, for he felt that the commander deliberately took on physical labour to show him up. When he later summed up the experiences in the Chingkang Mountains, he vigorously criticized the practice of 'absolute egalitarianism', obviously with Chu Teh as his target.

But during the Chingkangshan period there was some change in Mao's personal life for which he could not hold anyone responsible. Before the Autumn Harvest Uprising, he had sent his wife Yang Kai-hui, together with their three young boys, back to her mother's home in Changsha, and for months they had been without any form of contact. For the sake of the revolution, Mao might be willing to sacrifice anything; yet a life without a woman was hard for him to put up with. The yearning had as much to do with his mentality as his physical desire. Since he regarded himself as a hero, albeit a revolutionary one, it was unthinkable that he should be without a beauty at his side. Luckily for him, the beauty appeared in the form of Ho Tzu-chen, a young girl student of eighteen. In July 1928, Mao was with a unit of the Red Fourth Army entering the town of Yunghsin. Full of revolutionary fervour, Ho came to see him for some political enlightenment. Mao fell for the pretty young girl at first sight and made her feel very much at home. They discussed revolutionary problems enthusiastically and passionately, from some time in the afternoon into the small hours until Mao unceremoniously bedded her. The following morning he introduced her to the men around him, saying that they had decided to become man and wife to work together for the revolution. To celebrate the happy event, he forked out some money to give a small party for the well-wishers. When Kung Chu heard about it, he went along to offer his congratulations the day after. Mao could not conceal his joy, beaming and laughing incessantly. He asked Kung to stay for lunch and told his orderly to prepare special dishes, promising his guest that he would treat him to another formal dinner. But this time Kung did not meet the bride, for Ho had gone to the neighbouring town Ningtu, Mao said, to carry out some propaganda work. Typical of Mao, he was anxious to impress his comrades with his new woman's usefulness to the party. He did not appear to feel uneasy about having committed bigamy. Since Yang Kai-hui was trapped miles away in Changsha, he could not see why he should not take another wife.

While Mao began to find life in the Chingkang Mountains more tolerable now that he had Ho Tzu-chen to cater for his needs, he and Chu Teh committed another military blunder. Under the delusion that they had sufficient military strength to occupy larger towns, they launched an attack in August on Panghsien county in Southern Hunan. With Mao holding the fort in the Chingkang Mountains, Chu led 2,500 troops into the campaign. Unexpectedly, one of his battalion commanders defected to the Nationalist side in the first encounter. To make matters worse, the regiment commander he trusted most was killed in action. Hastily beating a retreat, Chu fled back to the Chingkangshan base with his remaining units, much depleted in number. At this point, Mao could have easily put the blame squarely on Chu's shoulders. But he had another target to aim at. For some time he had been at odds with the Hunan Party Committee, whose authority over him was like a thorn in his side. Insubordinate and self-righteous, he resented the fact that he had to take orders from the committee operating underground in Changsha, remote from the battlefront. Between Chu Teh and himself there might have been conflicts and contradictions, but for the time being they, as he reasoned, should be shelved. In his report to the Central Committee in Shanghai, he vaguely termed the defeat as the 'August Incident', giving a brief account of the campaign. Chu Teh was completely exonerated, for in his conclusion he attributed the military setback to the 'inability of some members on the Hunan Party Committee to grasp the situation'. If the Central Committee had some doubts about his explanation, they were never made known. After all, it was Mao and Chu who controlled a sizable military force, not the Hunan Committee.

Following Chu Teh's defeat near Panghsien, the Nationalist forces closed in from all directions to lay siege to the Chingkangshan area, gradually tightening the ring. Aware of the Communists' acute shortage of food supplies, the Nationalists chose to bide their time. Starting in September, they moved towards the Chingkang Mountains at a measured pace. Contrary to most of his comrades, Mao predicted that the siege would be lifted within three months in view of the 'unavoidable conflicts between various units of the Kuomintang Army'. He decided to hold out. Storing up provisions to last three months, the Red Fourth Army entrenched itself in the mountains after abandoning the surrounding counties, in anticipation of the Nationalists' eventual withdrawal. But Mao's prediction failed to materialize. The Nationalists continued to push forward, and there were signs that they would stay for the winter. About the siege, General Chen Yi, the late Chinese Foreign Minister, had vivid recollections. In *A Brief History of the Red Army's Development*, he stressed the men's heroic quality in facing up to hardships when he referred to this episode. 'At that time,' he said, 'the troops did have some gold which they confiscated from the wicked landlords. But in the Chingkang Mountains, you could not buy anything even with the gold. The snowy weather was bitterly cold. Some of the men wore flimsy summer clothes in the winter; those who did not have cloth sandals had to go barefoot. There were no quilts at all. Everybody was given a bundle of hay to sleep in. For daily meals cooked pumpkin was the only dish.' But in passing, he did touch on Mao's miscalculation of the length of the siege, saying that 'as it was estimated that the siege would definitely not last long, we merely prepared to store up foodstuffs, oil and salt for three months' consumption'.

In November, the defence was strengthened with the arrival of the Red Fifth Army led by Peng Teh-huai. Previously a regiment commander in the Nationalist forces, Peng staged a military uprising in Pingkiang in July to join the Communist side. The Hunan Party Committee immediately reorganized his regiment into the Red Fifth Army and made him its commander. Having engaged the Nationalists in a few battles, he lost almost a half of his original 1,500 men. He was then ordered by the Hunan Committee to move to the Chingkang Mountains to join up with the Red Fourth Army in defending the base. But for Mao and Chu, although the reinforcement of more than 800 men was most welcome it, however, aggravated the shortage of food and other provisions. The situation worsened with each day. Towards the end of December, the three of them held a military conference to decide the next move. It was resolved that the Red Fourth Army would fight its way through the encirclement to Western Fukien, while the Red Fifth Army would remain behind to defend the base. In early January 1929, Mao and Chu managed to break through, heading for the Fukien-Kiangsi border to seek a new base. As both Wang Tso and Yuan Wen-tsai refused to leave their own area, Mao left them in the hands of Peng Teh-huai. With their assistance, Peng was able to hold out for another three months. But in April, he had to abandon the Chingkangshan base as well. Before fighting his way through the Nationalist siege, however, he killed Wang and Yuan, the men who had offered Mao the shelter he desperately needed some eighteen months ago.

Although the Chingkangshan base fell short of Mao's expectations to become the power centre of the Communist revolution, it did give him the chance to strengthen his theories on military occupation and rural uprisings, which was to lead to his party's departure from the Comintern line. It also made him realize the importance of securing the control of the army in order to achieve personal dominance in the party hierarchy. As regards his conflicts with Chu Teh, these experiences served to sharpen his combative instincts and improve his art of manoeuvring and manipulating, much to his benefit. But most important of all, this brief period marked the beginning of his determined efforts to challenge the party leadership, ruthlessly and aggressively. His strength, if it can be said so, stemmed from his unsurpassable ego, having no regard for anyone else but himself. Just like his spiritual mentor, Tsao Tsao, he had no hesitation to 'betray all the people in the world' when it was necessary. In dealing with him, Chu Teh was often so exasperated that he called Mao 'the dictator' behind his back. Chu was not alone, for the Hunan Party Committee was equally persistent in criticizing Mao's 'individual heroism' and 'total lack of democratic approaches'.

But it was Kung Chu who seemed able to look at Mao in this period from a detached angle. The author of *The Red Army and I* admired Mao for his ability, and had a few kind words to say about him. Commenting on Mao, he said: 'He may not be a professional soldier, but his strategy and tactics for the Red Army are sound and correct. To strive for the initiative and to encircle the cities with the countryside does make sense. He is a talented organizer. He mobilized the people in the areas surrounding the Chingkang Mountains with great efficiency, and led them to support the revolutionary struggle. It was right that the Chingkangshan base should be developed into the command post of the revolution. To stretch out from there for steady expansion was a safe measure, indicating his far-sightedness. He was absolutely right in insisting on armed struggles and relying on the peasants to form the bulwark of revolution.' Since these words came from someone who had taken part in the building up of the Chingkangshan base, they must be regarded as an authentic assessment.

Nevertheless, Kung also analysed the conflicts between Chu Teh and Mao with the benefit of an eyewitness. Unfortunately, he emphasized too much the clash of personalities, not perceptive enough to see through Mao's real ambition. 'The main cause for their conflicts,' he wrote, 'in my view, was the clash between two contrasting personalities. Mao Tsetung was a dictator who took military and political decisions single-handedly, resisting any form of interference. He was also very stubborn and refused to accept second opinions. Chu Teh adopted the democratic style; he consulted the others before taking any decision. Mao regarded himself as the sole leader, heavily tainted by individual heroism. But Chu was always very modest; he wanted to have the jobs done without thinking about his personal gains or losses. When it came to dealing with people, Mao was a hypocrite, going round and about to achieve his aims, whereas Chu was frank and honest, as straight as a rod.' However, Kung went on to say, 'Mao had the ability and the wisdom to lead the Chinese revolution. But as it was so difficult to cope with him, I kept him at a distance with due respect.' He might have had very favourable impressions of Mao when they first met, but by this time he had obviously had second thoughts.

Millions of words have been written by the Chinese historians on the significance of the Chingkangshan stage to the transformation of the Chinese revolution, which cannot be faulted, especially in the light of later developments. But what they have omitted to say is that it was of far greater importance to Mao's political career, providing him with the launching pad he could not have done without in the long process of power struggle. It is also undeniable that this period foreshadowed the splits and conflicts within the Chinese Communist Party for decades to come. As for Mao, it pointed to the way of military communism in confirmation of his beliefs, not that he needed it.

5 THE FIRST TASTE OF POWER STRUGGLE

Little known to Mao and Chu Teh, while they had been endeavouring to hold out in the Chingkangshan area in the past months, the Central Committee in Shanghai had gone through another upheaval. In July 1928, the Sixth Party Congress, under the guardianship of the Comintern, was held in Moscow. Among the eighty-four delegates, differences and conflicts caused them to split into several small cliques, attacking one another ferociously. It was Bukharin, the then head of the Third International, who came to the rescue. Under his guidance, the congress passed its resolutions and re-elected the Central Committee which included Mao, despite his absence. The reinstatement undoubtedly gave him some satisfaction, though it fell short of his expectations. It seemed that he had regarded a seat in the Politburo as a just reward, if what Tung Pi-wu said in Nanking in 1946 reflected Mao's thinking at the time. 'The Sixth Congress failed,' Tung said, 'to recognize the significance of the Chingkangshan base in the Chinese revolution, even though Comrade Mao Tse-tung was elected to the Central Committee.'

In the congress, however, Chu Chiu-pai's military adventurism was unanimously condemned, and so was his policy of staging revolts everywhere without taking objective conditions into consideration. Although he still made the Politburo, the Third International kept him in Moscow under observation. To forestall further conflicts within the Chinese Party leadership, the Comintern also made Chang Kuo-tao—another member of the Politburo—stay, as well as three other members of the Central Committee. But all these precautions did not really work. Once the Chinese comrades returned to Shanghai, they no longer toed the Moscow line as closely as the Third International would have liked. As

Hsiang Chung-fa, the new General Secretary, was, in fact, a worker without much education, he became a figurehead of the Politburo. He left policy decisions in the hands of his two able colleagues Chou En-lai and Li Li-san, who worked together like twins. In place of Chu Chiu-pai's military adventurism, the two of them pursued the line of staging urban uprisings and launching military attacks on the cities to strive for revolutionary victories. This was later to be known as the Li Li-san line, for which Li paid dearly. He was condemned by both the Comintern and his own party, eventually summoned to Moscow in November 1930 to confess his errors. He was then kept there to go through the re-education process, not to return to China until 1945, two years after the dissolution of the Third International.

Like many of his comrades, Mao was not slow to hop on the band-wagon of Li's opposition. The others did so mainly for self-preservation; he also had personal grudges in mind. But in fact, when the Li Li-san line was enforced in 1929 and 1930, he was less than articulate in voicing his doubt and disagreement, even though most Chinese historians have liberally credited him with 'the foresight of repudiating the erroneous Li Li-san line from the very beginning'. There was no way that he could have done so, since Li carried with him the authority of the Politburo. Besides, in the period immediately after the abandoning of the Ching-kangshan base, Mao's main concern was to seize control of the Red Fourth Army under Chu Teh's nose. With the newly promoted Lin Piao firmly on his side, he was gradually gaining the upper hand. To consolidate his following among the rank and file, he took the unusual step of organizing the conference of the party's representatives in the Red Fourth Army. This was virtually done without the authorization of the Central Committee, not to mention the fact that it was completely against the party's system of organizing downward. By manipulating the conference, he was in a better position to set his finger on military matters.

Naturally, Chu Teh could not help feeling the increasing menace to his power and authority. But there was little he could do. Even the Politburo in Shanghai had to put up with Mao's creation of the unlawful set-up, for fear that the common soldiers might react differently if Mao were disciplined. With his influence steadily building up in the Red Fourth Army, Mao decided that he should stamp his authority by harassing Chu whenever possible. After making a few abortive attempts, he realized that he had to be patient. It was not until the December of 1929 that he had his way. Before then, Chu Teh had been successful in a number of military encounters with the Nationalist forces. Between June and December, he led the main strength of the Red Fourth Army into Fukien province no less than three times, occupying the county towns of Shanghang, Lungyen, Yungting, Changting and Wuchung to help establish the Soviet Areas of South-eastern Kiangsi and North-western Fukien. He also expanded his military strength to 7,000 strong. But in early December, he pushed southward into Kwangtung province to attack Meihsien county with some initial success, only to be ambushed by the Nationalist units when he withdrew from there. No sooner had he rejoined Mao in Shanghang than the latter summoned a meeting of the party's representatives in Kutien village, taking him to task. In the meeting Mao severely criticized Chu for sticking to the wrong military strategy. Among other things, he listed 'the purely military viewpoint, subjectivism, individualism and the ideology of roving rebel bands' as Chu's main failings. Since heavy casualties had been suffered during the retreat, Chu could not but accept the criticisms reluctantly. The irony was that he could have easily refuted Mao if he were more eloquent. He only had to point out that all he did was to carry out the directives of the Politburo, challenging his political commissar to submit the whole issue to Shanghai.

Actually, Chu Teh was not alone in disagreeing with Mao on important matters. His right-hand man, Chen Yi, was so fed up with Mao's political tricks that he took a secret trip to Shanghai to report to the Central Committee that autumn. He told the committee of the conflicts between Chu and Mao, asking for its intervention. He did not mince his words in saying who was in the wrong. Apart from Chen's verbal report, the committee had already been receiving complaints about Mao from the local party organizations in Hunan, Kiangsi and Fukien. When it became clear that some action must be taken, the Central Committee ordered Mao to appear before it in Shanghai. In the spring of 1930, he was sent several stern letters to that effect. But he chose to ignore them completely. Fully aware of his untenable situation, he had no intention of facing the music. Nor did he think it was wise for him to leave his power base in the army. Although this amounted to insubordination, there was nothing the Central Committee could do about it. Moreover, the top comrades in Shanghai were then engaged in ideological battles themselves. The Moscow-trained Wang Ming, alias Chen Shao-yu, had just started his criticisms of the Li Li-san line, condemning Li for having deviated from Leninism and the Comintern policies. The leader of the 'Twenty-eight Bolsheviks', more widely known as the 'International Faction', Wang was regarded by Moscow as the most trustworthy Chinese comrade who should be groomed and assisted to take charge of the Communist movement in China. Deeply involved in their own disputes and infights, none of the members on the Central Committee could perceive the serious nature of Mao's challenge to the party discipline. Otherwise, he would not have been able to get off the hook. In politics one needs luck, and it was obviously on Mao's side this time.

But more important than luck was the strength of his character. He had the courage and the will to fight against all odds. Even his limitations and prejudices turned out to be to his advantage. After his successful venture in the Chingkang Mountains, he made no secret of his contempt for the party leadership in Shanghai. In his eyes, Chu Chiu-pai, Li Li-san and Chou En-lai were but a bunch of useless intellectuals unfit to lead the Chinese revolution. When he first met Chu Teh in 1928, according to Kung Chu, he did not hesitate to use foul language in attacking the Central Committee, calling its members the 'rotten eggs who knew nothing better than talking nonsense and making stupid decisions'. To emphasize his disdain for them, he banged the table and mouthed more four-letter words. While Chu Teh and Chen Yi merely smiled, the others present were shocked.

It was his disrespect for the Central Committee that caused him to tamper with its directives. In the instance of the land revolution in the Chingkangshan area, he shifted from one extreme to the other, completely at variance with the Central Committee. At first he confiscated the land indiscriminately for redistribution, and when it backfired, he tended to be too lenient with the rich peasants. Doubtless, acts like this led to his constant clashes with the Hunan Party Committee or the Special Committee of Southern Hunan at that time. In terms of organization, both committees had authority over him. But since Mao had the military muscle, he could afford to contradict or ignore them. Frustrated, some members of the Hunan Committee openly criticized Mao's 'undemocratic attitude'. They even went further by calling him the 'new warlord'.

Unlike most people, Mao seemed to thrive on controversies and contradictions. As far as he was concerned, he must always have the final say. No matter how illogical his case might be, he refused to yield an inch, for he honestly believed that nobody else could possibly be right. Whereas such an egotistic attitude would have destroyed any other political leader, Mao was saved by the unique circumstances in China during that period. Illiterate, ignorant and hungry, the overwhelming majority of the Chinese people were still living in the feudal age. A roof over their heads and three bowls of rice each day were all that they dreamed of. Except for the privileged few, they were consumed with discontent and hatred. This was particularly true among the peasants in the countryside. Mao was not only perceptive enough to draw revolutionary strength from the peasantry, he also knew how to mobilize and organize the peasants into fighting units. When the Red Fourth Army roamed in Western Fukien, he was most efficient in organizing the local populace despite the barriers of dialects, as Chang Ting-cheng, at one time Attorney-General of China, recalled in 1976. Having attended the Peasant Movement Training Institute in Canton, Chang, a native of Yungting in Western Fukien, immediately became Mao's right-hand man in that area. He did not only act as the latter's interpreter, but was also instrumental in pacifying the natives' fears and suspicions about the outsiders. By making him Chairman of the Yungting Soviet, Mao won the hearts of the local people overnight. They might not understand anything about Marxism or the Red Army, but it was very easy for them to identify with Chang, the primary school teacher who had grown up among them.

In Chang's recollections, Mao in those days seemed to be extremely good at arousing and agitating crowds. He knew how to appeal to their emotions. Instead of expounding the theories and aims of Communism, he simply told them that it would enable everyone to have food and clothes according to his needs. He emphatically stated that the poor were the 'goodies' and the rich the 'baddies', without bothering to mention the class struggle or exploitation. Perhaps his definition of 'imperialism' was most original, for he described it as the 'foreigners who make the rich even richer'. Evidently, all this went down very well with the labourers and peasants, who started to swell the ranks of the Red Fourth Army, hitherto mainly consisting of the natives from Hunan and Kiangsi. The most important development was that these new recruits played a major part in rallying the local support, without which Mao would not have been able to form the secret party cells down to the village level. As he saw it, such a step was absolutely vital, since the Red Fourth Army was still fighting a guerrilla war, unable to hold towns or cities for long.

It seemed that Mao again made good use of his intimate knowledge of his favourite novel *Romance of the Three Kingdoms* on some occasions, judging by what another veteran Communist, Lai Chuang-chu, wrote about this period in 1977. He remembered vividly how Mao succeeded in convincing the propaganda teams of the importance of their work, only after he had told them an anecdote about the ancient general, Chu-ke Liang. 'Commissar Mao impressed us,' Lai said, 'that by doing the propaganda work we were actually emulating the ancient hero Chu-ke Liang in the best possible way. Since he was so good at motivating his officers and men, we must be able to do the same with our warriors and the people. Every one of us should aim at becoming another Chu-ke

Liang.' Conceivably, these words would have had great impact on his audience. At that time, Chu-ke Liang was the legendary hero of every Chinese male, breaching all class barriers. To use him as a model, Mao certainly struck the right note in everybody's heart. Unlike his Moscow-trained comrades, he had the knack of saying the right things to the right people.

But as usual, he could not get along with the local party organization of Western Fukien. While he had been gleefully forming the secret party cells in that area, the Western Fukien Party Committee denounced him for stepping over the line and reported the whole matter to the Central Committee in Shanghai. Fortunately for Mao, his military muscle was by now getting stronger. In June 1930 the Red Fourth Army, after absorbing defecting Nationalist units and scattered bands of bandits in Western Fukien, had grown threefold in strength. It was reorganized into the Red First Army Corps, ordered by Li Li-san to attack the cities in Hunan. Two months later, it joined up with Peng Teh-huai's newly formed Red Third Army Corps in Liuyang to become the Red First Front Army. With Chu Teh as its commander-in-chief and Mao as its chief political commissar, the First Front Army was the kingpin of the Communist forces which now totalled some 70,000, spreading in the pockets of Honan, Anhwei, Hupei, Hunan, Kiangsi, Fukien, Kwangsi and Kwangtung. The rapid expansion of the Red Army was mainly due to the outbreak of wars between Chiang Kai-shek and Yen Hsi-shan and Feng Yu-hsiang, and then between Chiang and Li Tsung-jen.

Fully realizing that he should consolidate his political control of the much enlarged Red First Front Army, Mao was not happy with the limited power of a political commissar. Again he called a meeting of the party's representatives from all units to elect himself as the secretary of the General Front Committee, giving him the power to overrule the strategic and tactical decisions made by Chu Teh or Peng Teh-huai. In this manner he extended his influence to various units of the six armies which made up the First Front Army. To introduce his form of 'democratic resolutions' to the whole army, he formed the Joint Conference of the Party's Representatives from All Units which had a say in all matters. Although the military commanders loathed it, they could do nothing since Mao represented the party. They had no way of knowing that he, in fact, had not been authorized by the Central Committee to create these organs.

That September, however, the Central Committee in Shanghai finally took firm steps to purge Li Li-san from the leadership, immediately after the big defeat suffered by Chu Teh and Mao in attacking Nanchang, the provincial capital of Kiangsi. The defeat was seen as another result of the execution of the Li Li-san line. Anxious to dissociate himself from Li's political errors, Mao was most articulate in voicing his support of the Central Committee's decisions regarding Li, partly because of the long-standing feud between them. Since there were still a number of followers of the Li Li-san line in the Kiangsi area, Mao took on the purging task with great enthusiasm. His primary target was the Kiangsi Provincial Soviet in Futien, a small town in that province. But for some puzzling reason, he turned the purge into a massive slaughter. Many members of the Kiangsi Soviet were executed without trial or investigation, and no less than 4,400 people lost their lives that December, including some 700 proven party members. The Action Committee of the Kiangsi Soviet managed to write to Chu Teh and Peng Teh-huai, condemning Mao for his 'ruthless conspiracy in slaughtering comrades' without finding out the truth. The letter further accused Mao of his personal ambitions in jockeying for power; with it a copy of Mao's secret order was enclosed. In the order Mao demanded the arrest of Chu Teh, Peng Teh-huai and two other military commanders, who were supposedly involved in 'secret negotiations with the White Army'. The authenticity of this secret order was hard to prove, though the style of writing bore some resemblance to Mao's. It was also doubtful whether the letter ever reached Peng or Chu, in view of the widespread confusion around Futien. In all probability they would have intervened to restrain Mao from indulging in indiscriminate persecutions and executions, if they had received the appeal from the Kiangsi Provincial Soviet.

In perspective, Mao could have done better without the Futien incident, which really forced the Central Committee to establish its presence in the Soviet area. To Wang Ming, Chou En-lai and some other leaders, it was quite obvious that the purge of the Li Li-san line had been carried out by Mao to excess, if not deliberately distorted. In January 1931, the Central Politburo of the Soviet Area was set up in Kiangsi, with Chou En-lai as its secretary. But as Chou could not leave Shanghai yet, Hsiang Ying, later to be the commander of the New Fourth Army during the brief Nationalist-Communist alliance after the outbreak of the Sino-Japanese War in 1937, was sent to the Soviet area to act for him. Upon Hsiang's arrival, the General Front Committee was immediately disbanded and Mao lost his post as its secretary. He was also dismissed from the position of Chief Political Commissar. Without his power base, he was no longer in a position to handle the party and administrative affairs in the Soviet area. His wings were clipped and the shadow of further decline was looming. Bitter as he was, the worst had yet to come.

Ironically, it was the Nationalists who did him a favour by launching the First Campaign of Encirclement against the Soviet area in Kiangsi. While Hsiang Ying was about to start investigating the Futien incident, the Nationalist troops closed in from all directions. In his capacity as political commissar of the First Front Army, Mao persuaded Chu Teh to adopt his strategy of 'luring the enemy deep' before they staged their counter-attacks. The strategy was successfully executed and the Nationalists were repulsed. Naturally Mao took the credit. But what was more important was that he succeeded in impressing Hsiang Ying with his military talent. Meanwhile, the lapse of time made the Futien incident look less important and even insignificant. When the acting secretary of the Central Politburo of the Soviet Area eventually proceeded with the investigation, evidence had been destroyed and witnesses were either dead or silenced. The findings were as inconclusive as Mao could have hoped for. Several months later, however, the Central Committee in Shanghai did issue a circular summing up the Futien incident. While Mao was not named for his deviations in carrying out the purge, the Central Committee criticized the 'exaggeration about the number of counter-revolutionaries' existing in the Soviet Area. This would seem to be the subtle way to condemn Mao for his excessive measures in handling the whole matter.

There is little doubt that Mao must take the blame for the loss of so many innocent lives in the incident, since he was the one who gave the orders. As expected, the official sources have chosen to dismiss the massive slaughter rather lightly. When Mao told the American journalist, Edgar Snow, about the Futien incident during his interview in 1936, he casually cited it as an effort to root out the Li Li-san line, as if it were a rather boring routine. He did not even vaguely mention its repercussions or the extent of his involvement. Since the American knew practically nothing about the Chinese Communist Party, that Mao should have voluntarily touched on the Futien incident was quite strange. The logical explanation seems to be that he must have borne the mental burden of the whole matter for some time so that talking about it would have given him a sense of relief. With Snow he could say what he liked, without the worry of showing himself in a bad light. But this was not all. In April 1945, when Mao was firmly in control of the whole party in Yenan, he made another attempt to shift the blame for the Futien incident onto the shoulders of other comrades. In the statement on the Resolutions on Some Historical Issues, he vaguely referred to the incident as the result of following Wang Ming's 'new leftist line', causing 'many outstanding comrades to lose their lives, to the great pain of the party'.

Compared with later developments in the relentless power struggle, the loss of human lives in the Futien incident appeared to be minimal; what bothered Mao was that he was then still a new hand in ruthless killings. He had to live with the conscience of a first-time executioner. Undeniably, there were scores of counter-revolutionaries among the dead. But Mao seemed to resort to the massive slaughter for the sake of self-preservation. With the imminent setting up of the Central Politburo in the Soviet Area, he was worried about those enemies of his in the Kiangsi Provincial Soviet. He had to take precautions against their possible moves to expose his political errors when the man responsible for the Politburo arrived on the scene. The Central Committee's directive to purge the Li Li-san line could not have come at a better time. In its name he could easily cover up his designs to get rid of his enemies. Once it started, there was no way to exert any restraint.

But in fact, Mao merely won a temporary reprieve. Unknown to him, the Central Committee in its Shanghai meeting in January 1931 had decided to hold him responsible for the practice of 'right-wing opportunism' in the Soviet Area. His methods of 'fund-raising', taking from the rich to give to the poor, and dispersing cadres to motivate the masses were all called into question. He was condemned for having confined himself to the narrow experiences gained in the Chingkang Mountains, as well as his peasant mentality. Since the meeting was held after Hsiang Ying's departure for Kiangsi, Mao did not even have the chance of getting some hints from the new arrival's mouth. In September that year, the Third International summoned Wang Ming to Moscow for consultation, and he was kept there to succeed Chang Kuo-tao as the party's representative to the Comintern. Chin Pang-hsien, alias Po Ku, became the General Secretary of the Central Politburo and the Central Committee. Like Wang Ming, he did not think kindly of Mao. To comply with Moscow's instructions, Chin started to move the Central Committee to Kiangsi, in gradual steps, that very month.

On 7 November the date specially picked to coincide with Russia's October Revolution, the First All China Soviet Congress was held in Juichin in Southern Kiangsi to proclaim the establishment of the Chinese Soviet Republic and elect a Central Executive Committee of sixty-three members. Three weeks later, the Central Executive Committee in turn elected Mao to be its Chairman, the equivalent of Head of the Central Soviet Government. He was also made Chairman of the Council of People's Commissars, the administrative body of the government. In both set-ups, he had Hsiang Ying and Chang Kuo-tao as the two Deputy Chairmen. Impressive though his new positions might sound, he was, in fact, kicked upstairs. In a Communist regime, both the party and the army come before the government. He was excluded from the reorganized Central Politburo which consisted of Chin Pang-hsien, Chou En-lai, Chang Wen-tien (also known as Lo Fu), Hsiang Ying and Chen Yun, later to be the chief economic planner in the Yenan days, with Chin as General Secretary. And when the Central Military Committee was formed, Chu Teh was made its chairman, which was an additional disappointment to Mao. Although he was appointed a secretary of the newly created Central Secretariat to save his face, it did not entitle him to have any say in policy decisions. With his power greatly curbed and his pride deeply wounded, he always looked back at this period of political decline in anger. Fourteen years later, he still talked about it in Yenan with venom, describing it as the period when 'the correct party and military leadership was altered'. He was a man who could neither forget nor forgive.

Chou En-lai arrived at Juichin in December 1931, shortly after the convening of the All China Soviet Congress. With the full backing of the International Faction led by Wang Ming and Chin Pang-hsien, he became the most powerful figure in the Kiangsi Soviet Area. As Secretary of the Central Politburo of the Soviet Area and Chief Political Commissar of the entire Red Army, he took complete control of both party and military affairs. Smooth, sophisticated and cunning, he was more than Mao's equal in the art of manoeuvring and manipulating. Before long Mao found himself in an even worse situation, neglected and isolated. Actually, Hsiang Ying was the one to fire the first shot at Mao in the Soviet Area. After receiving the September directive from the Central Committee, he called the First Party Congress of the Soviet Area on 1 November in Juichin, conveying the party leadership's resolutions regarding Mao's 'right-wing opportunism' for discussion. Though not named, Mao was obviously the target for fierce criticisms. He was attacked for building his personal influence in the army, forming small cliques, interfering with the work of local party organizations and a variety of other political errors. Realizing that there was nothing he could do to alter the situation, he could not but admit his mistakes. Perhaps the only compensation was, all his enemies had to come out into the open, enabling him to avoid unnecessary risks and reassess the strength of his own side.

Under these circumstances, he knew that he must keep a low profile. It required him to swallow his pride and watch every step. After his election to the chairmanship of the Central Soviet Government and the Council of People's Commissars, he was even more careful. As it was apparent to him that he had been made into a figurehead, he decided to play the game accordingly. Always deferring to Hsiang Ying's opinions and decisions, he made himself scarce in the public eye. Pleading ill-health, he lived in a shabby cottage miles from the hubbub of Juichin. With Ho Tzu-chen constantly at his side, he amused himself by re-reading his favourite novels the *Romance of the Three Kingdoms* and *The Water Margin* countless times. For serious reading, he chose to pore over the *Military Strategy of Sun Wu*, the ancient strategist in the period of the Warring States (481 – 221 B.C.), with the eagerness of a devoted disciple. Though no longer having any say in military matters, he still believed that his recall would come once the Red Army encountered setbacks. He also read the works of General Tseng Kuo-fan, the conqueror of the Taiping Rebellion, probably because Chiang Kai-shek was reputed to be Tseng's great admirer. As General Sun Wu pointed out many centuries ago, 'Know yourself and your opponent equally well; then you can achieve one hundred victories out of one hundred battles'. This could have been in Mao's mind when he became interested in 'the enemy of the people' such as Tseng Kuo-fan.

But curiously, he did not bother to improve his knowledge of Marxist studies, it seemed, when he had all the time he needed. Nor did he write anything on revolutionary theories in this period. The scarcity of Marxist literature in Chinese in the Soviet Area could have contributed to this seeming failure of his, since he knew no other language. It was also possible that he did not want to attract undue attention from his enemies, who would jump on him at the first instance if he touched off more controversies in the field of revolutionary philosophy. When I discussed the Kiangsi Soviet period with Yang I-chih, a party theoretician and Chou En-lai's confidant, in Peking in the winter of 1956, the French-trained Marxist scholar naturally avoided breathing a word about Mao's political wilderness in Juichin. But he did say that 'Chairman Mao's illness did not stop him doing a lot of thinking about the correct course for the Chinese revolution, for a number of comrades tended to accept the Comintern's directives too literally, without taking objective circumstances into consideration'. However, he insisted that during this period Mao did write a lot of long letters discussing problems with some comrades. 'But unfortunately, these letters got lost or destroyed before the Long March, otherwise they would have been included in his selected works for our benefit.' He never mentioned the names of the recipients of Mao's letters, but Teng Hsiao-ping could have been one of them. Then involved with the local party organization the Kiangsi Provincial Soviet, the diminutive Teng was very close to Mao. Working away from Juichin and having no stake in the power struggle, he would have been considered by Mao as a safe man on whom to vent his feelings. This special relationship was to last for many years to come, partly to account for Teng's nine political lives even after his siding with Liu Shao-chi against Mao in 1959. Ruthless though Mao was, he could not forget that in the Juichin days Teng had been one of the very few who 'sent him some charcoal in the snow', as the Chinese saying goes, when he seemed down and out.

According to Yang I-chih, it was about this time that Mao learned about the execution of his first wife Yang Kai-hui, who had been imprisoned in Changsha by the Nationalist authorities since the brief Communist occupation in the summer of 1930. His two older boys An-ying and An-ching, aged ten and nine, were smuggled to Shanghai by the Communist underground in Changsha, but he was unable to find out more about them. Without Ho Tzu-chen, who had just given him a baby, it would have been inconceivable for him to survive this personal tragedy, compounded with his political misfortune. Even as a figurehead, he was not accorded the minimum courtesy. When Dr Fu Lien-chang, the Communist expert on public health, came to Juichin on official business in 1932, to his surprise he found that in the Central Soviet Government Mao was the only one who did not have an office. And after he reported to the Chairman of the Central Soviet Government in his humble abode on some relatively unimportant matters, Mao kept reminding him that he must go to Hsiang Ying for final approval. Fu wrote about this in 1959 to portray Mao's humility and thoroughness, but unintentionally he revealed his far from enviable position as well. It was Kung Chu, author of *The Red Army and I*, however, who caught Mao in one of his weaker moments. In 1934, Mao went to live in Yutu which was the seat of Kung's military region. On a summer evening he went to see Mao. Over a few cups of rice wine the latter suddenly broke down. 'One tends to be sentimental after a few drinks,' Kung recalled, 'Mao and I exchanged reminiscences about the struggle in the Chingkang Mountains. "Comrade Kung", he suddenly sighed, "since I joined the revolution, I have been dismissed from the Central Committee three times and reprimanded eight times. And now they are going to make me shoulder the blame for the present setbacks. There is certainly no room for the veteran comrades from the Chingkangshan days." While speaking he shed tears and coughed. In the flickering light of the bean oil lamp, he looked particularly depressed, his face drawn and gaunt.'

But his momentary weakness was not uncalled for. Having been grilled for three or four years, a lesser man would have been completely crushed. Between 1932 and 1934, his political errors were constantly criticized in conferences and meetings. People closely associated with him had their share of punishment. Teng Hsiao-ping lost his post in the Kiangsi Provincial Soviet for having followed his 'luring the enemy deep' strategy, thus failing to bring the war to the 'White Areas' to harass the Nationalists. Under the same charge Mao's youngest brother, Tse-tan, was dismissed from the aforesaid organ, and so was Chang Ting-chen in Western Fukien. Although his other brother, Tse-min, was allowed to continue as the Director of the Soviet National Bank, he shied away from Mao to avoid possible trouble. But for Tse-tan the worst was yet to come. He was forbidden to have any contact with his eldest brother pending further investigation. As he was married to Ho Tzu-chen's younger sister, Ho Yi, the two women occassionally exchanged messages through a third party to cheer each other up. Sometimes Tzu-chen would send some fried chilis and eggs to the younger couple, a subtle way to tell them of Mao's unaltered material well-being. If Tse-tan had been less adamant in protesting his innocence, the opponents of his brother might have treated him differently after making him 'confess his errors'. Unfortunately things did not turn out this way. Equally obstinate but less circumspect when compared with his eldest brother, he could not hold his tongue. While still under investigation, he lashed out at the International Faction bitterly and unrelentingly, either among his friends or in front of some informants. For three years he was assigned to work with the Anti-Imperialism League, a fringe organization without any significance. And he was killed in 1935 during the Long March, still in disgrace. It was not until 1942 that Mao got round to clear his name in Yenan, too late to give him any comfort.

In retrospect, the Ningtu Military Conference in August, 1932 must have been a nightmare for Mao. The conference discussed the strategy to deal with the imminent Nationalists' Fourth Encirclement Campaign which was very much in the air. Had he kept his mouth shut, he would not have become the target for concerted attacks since it was not on the cards. But having played no part in the victories over the two previous campaigns launched by the Kuomintang forces, he was obviously aching for action. The urge was so great that he momentarily forgot his caution. Still considering himself the foremost military strategist, he spoke enthusiastically of the advantage of 'luring the enemy deep', as if the different strategy pursued by his comrades in the two previous campaigns should be rescrutinized. But as the Central Politburo of the Soviet Area led by

Chou En-lai had already decided on the 'Strike first' strategy, no one at the conference was supposed to air a different view. Mao's unwitting remarks immediately drew a barrage of firepower on himself. One after another, those present at the conference rose to refute him. Chou En-lai, Hsiang Ying, Chu Teh, Peng Teh-huai, Chen Yi and Liu Po-cheng—the one-eyed general trained in Moscow—all had a field day. They criticized Mao for his obsession with the limited experiences of the Chingkangshan days, his insistence on guerrilla tactics and his inability to absorb the teachings of the Russian Red Army. Some of them even attacked his strategy as the symbol of defeatism, with retreat as its sole aim. Liu Po-cheng was most satirical when he uttered his criticisms. He said that 'some comrade' possessed the mentality of a 'village pedant', totally unable to understand modern warfare. He pointed out that one could not hope to learn all about strategy and tactics from *Romance of the Three Kingdoms* or *The Water Margin*. He also questioned the wisdom of reading the writings of General Tseng Kuo-fan, tartly adding that they should be left for people like Chiang Kai-shek to study. As to the ancient strategist, Sun Wu, he dismissed his concepts about war as outdated and reactionary. Outnumbered and outargued, Mao was forced to eat humble pie.

But the matter did not end there. Mao's unsuccessful attempt to revive his military strategy made the Central Politburo worry about the extent of his harmful influence on the military cadres who had accepted his wisdom regarding revolutionary warfare in the past couple of years. *Romance of the Three Kingdoms* and *The Water Margin* had been avidly read by a vast number of junior commanders and officers to seek guidance. The craze did not die with Mao's removal from his post in the Red Army. The abandonment of positions and outposts in the face of the advancing Nationalists was justified as the need for 'making a strategic retreat' while the avoidance of frontal engagements was regarded as the sensible way to 'conserve the revolutionary strength'. Clearly, as far as most military officers were concerned, Mao's principle of 'luring the enemy deep' and theory on guerrilla war never ceased to work at the back of their minds. Since the expansion of the Soviet Area was Moscow's explicit wish, Chou En-lai and his colleagues could not very well let the lethargic mood in the Red Army continue to prevail. In his capacity as Chief-of-Staff, Liu Po-cheng wrote on the Red Army's strategy and tactics in the first issue of *Revolution and War* (November 1932), the organ of the Central Military Committee, in the hope of rooting out Mao's military philosophy once and for all. The arguments at the Ningtu Military Conference were repeated, stressing the importance of learning from the valuable experiences of the Russian Red Army. In no uncertain terms the one-eyed general criticized those commanders who looked upon *Romance of the Three Kingdoms* and *The Water Margin* as military classics, at the cost of ignoring the basics of modern warfare and damaging the revolution. He did not mention Mao by name. But every reader of the article knew only too well who the 'poisonous weed' was. In the preface Hsiang Ying reinforced Liu's point of view. He pointed out the absurdity of learning the strategy of Tseng Kuo-fan and other Hunanese generals during the Taiping Rebellion, giving Mao another slap in the face. For several months, the article was made compulsive reading matter for military personnel at all levels, to be followed by discussions. As the target for this campaign, Mao had to sit it out. Although he never accepted the judgement passed by the Central Politburo on him, he could not afford to speak up again. Between survival and pride, he knew which to choose. His fortitude seemed to pay off, for no more charges were brought against him after the campaign was over. Preoccupied with the preparations for another large-scale war with the surrounding Kuomintang forces, the Central Politburo decided to give the matter a rest.

But Mao thought otherwise. When he reached Pao-an in Northern Shensi in 1936 after the Long March, he finally was in a position to state his case. In his manual entitled 'Problems of Strategy in China's Revolutionary War' he reiterated the 'correctness' of his military philosophy and strategic concepts, summing up the errors committed in past campaigns. Naturally, Chou En-lai, Hsiang Ying and Liu Po-cheng were all to carry the can. Vaguely referring to them as 'some people', he exposed their slavish attitude in copying the experiences of the Soviet Union. 'They say that it is enough merely to study the experience of revolutionary war in Russia', he wrote in part, 'or merely to follow the laws by which the civil war in the Soviet Union was directed. But they do not see that if we copy and apply them without allowing any change, we shall also be "cutting the feet to fit the shoes" and be defeated.... They fail to see that while we should set special store by the war experience of the Soviet Union, we should likewise cherish the experience of China's revolutionary war, because there are many factors that are specific to the Chinese revolution and the Chinese Red Army.' To be able to establish his authority on military matters must have been extremely gratifying for him, especially after having waited in desperation for several years.

If the exclusion from the top command of the Red Army in the Juichin days hurt Mao most, there were other accusations and denunciations he did not really deserve. When Chin Pang-hsien reached Juichin in 1933, Mao's position was in the state of a sinking boat. Having been criticized, condemned and ostracized in the past two years, he was sustained by vengeance alone. By now his men such as Teng Hsiao-ping, Chang Ting-cheng, Tan Chen-lin (later to be Governor of Chekiang after the establishment of the People's Republic) and a host of others were all in disgrace, the chance for him to rebuild his power and influence seemed very remote. But since in political struggle there is no room for mercy, Chin decided to tighten the screw even further. Not that he did it out of personal animosity; it was clear to him that Moscow wanted to have firm control of the revolutionary development in China, no longer prepared to tolerate deviationists or heretics in the mode of Mao. As a leading member of the International Faction in the party, Chin also had his own political stake to think of. With Wang Ming sitting in Moscow to receive orders from the Comintern, it was up to him to carry them out effectively. Even if he had the slightest sympathy for Mao's plight, he could not afford to allow his sentiment to cloud his judgement as a Moscow-trained Communist.

Being a cautious man, Chin did not want to underestimate Mao's dormant influence in the Soviet Area covering parts of Hunan, Fukien and Kiangsi. He was aware of the fact that Mao had spared no effort in placing his men in local party organizations to hold key positions, as well as infiltrating the army units with the aid of the party cells he had previously formed. To break up the pro-Mao cliques, Chin and his associates in the Central Politburo agreed that they must continue to expose Mao's deviations and departures from the orthodox Marxist line, as determined by the Comintern. The opportune moment came when the Nationalists' Fourth Encirclement Campaign petered out due to Japan's aggressive military moves in North China. Some of Chiang Kai-shek's crack units had to be diverted to the north for any eventuality. The temporary lull enabled the Communist leadership to concentrate on internal problems, of which the liquidation of Mao's ideological hold was high in the order. In official publications and authorized articles, backward peasant mentality, narrow-minded experimentalism, archaic military thought, persistent employment of guerrilla tactics, and incorrect land policy were again brought up for severe criticisms. From April 1933 onward, millions of words were churned out in the space of a few months.

If there were any relief for Mao during this period, it was because he happened to be away from Juichin to supervise the land investigation programme, after he had been accused of committing 'rich peasant deviations', allowing the rich peasants to retain too much land and gain too much profit. But it seemed that he must still have been under tremendous mental pressures, for he ended up in the Central Nursing Hospital with a nervous breakdown that September. During his hospitalization, Tung Pi-wu was probably one of the very few visitors. Then the principal of the Marxist Communism School in Juichin, Tung was not involved in the power struggle. Judging by what he told me in Nanking in 1946, he seemed to have been sympathetic to Mao in those difficult days. This could have been why Mao always treated him with respect after regaining power in Yenan, entrusting him, together with Chou En-lai, with the task of negotiating with the Kuomintang. Of course Tung did not admit anything about Mao's nervous breakdown; he chose to describe him as one of those 'constantly bothered by malaria which sapped his otherwise limitless energy'.

But, back in 1933, the Central Politburo took a different approach in purging Mao. Instead of making him the sole target, the emphasis was to clip his wings first. In anticipation of further Nationalist offensives, it picked several military commanders of known association with Mao as the objects of criticism, under the veil of 'strengthening Marxist military thought in the Red Army'. Lin Piao was one of them, but he was shrewd enough to admit his past errors before the heat was on. Tan Chen-lin, the then commander of Fukien Military Region, was less fortunate. Regarded as Mao's true disciple since the Chingkangshan period, he had no escape. Authorized by the Central Politburo, Peng Teh-huai and his Third Red Army Corps launched the attack in a scathing article, which was published in the official Red China Magazine. Tan was accused of pursuing the 'opportunist strategy and tactics of Chu-ke Liang's in *Romance of the Three Kingdoms*, obstructing the progress of our military skills'. His failure to annihilate the retreating Nationalist units in recent battles was cited as the typical example of his reluctance to incur casualties on his own troops, thus endangering the positions held by other units. He was also attacked for his indecision and wavering attitude 'in the best tradition of guerrilla-ism', which resulted in unnecessary retreats and quick flights in the face of the enemy. Since Tan was then holed up with a considerable military force in the remote Western Fukien, he was, however, spared the humiliation of being relieved of his command.

But it was Mao's other protégé, Hsiao Ching-kuan, later to be the Commander of the Chinese Navy after the establishment of the Peking regime, who suffered the worst disgrace. Graduating after Mao from the First Normal School in Changsha, he followed his old school-mate to the Chingkang Mountains and was sworn in as a party member by Mao himself. As a member of Mao's inner group, he rapidly climbed to the post of Commander of Fukien-Kiangsi Military Region in 1932. After he abandoned Lichuan county that year, he was transferred to the Seventh Red

Army Corps as its Political Commissar, presumably with Mao's help. In 1933, however, he was court-martialled by Chou En-lai on the charge of abandoning his duties as a commander. He was expelled from the party and sentenced to five years' imprisonment, doubtlessly a move to humiliate Mao as well. Though unable to intervene at the time, Mao reinstated him into the party immediately after his own success in grasping the military command from Chou during the Long March.

As Kiangsi was the most important part of the Soviet Area, Chin Pang-hsien had to deal with the Provincial Party Committee, the Provincial Soviet and the Kiangsi Military Region with particular care. Dominated by Mao's men down to the village level, the base of the Central Soviet Government was no haven for the Central Politburo controlled by the International Faction. To eliminate Mao's influence, Chin must at the same time avoid stirring up widespread fear and unnecessary resentment. He decided to narrow down the struggle by singling out those at the helm. Needless to say, Teng Hsiao-ping, Mao Tse-tan and a couple of others bore the brunt. Both Teng and the younger Mao came under criticism for forming small cliques and practising favouritism. They were even more vigorously attacked for their part in pursuing Mao's military strategy such as 'luring the enemy deep' and 'avoiding to bring the war into the White Areas'. They were also held responsible for the spread of pessimism and defeatism throughout the Kiangsi Soviet Area, which caused serious concern to the Central Politburo. Teng was dismissed from his post as Secretary of the Kiangsi Provincial Party Committee and Tse-tan was removed from the Kiangsi Military Region, as well as from their positions in the Provincial Soviet. But as the latter happened to be Mao's brother, he was further denounced by *The Red China Magazine* in a lengthy article. He was called 'a maniac of *Romance of the Three King-doms*, copying from it the strategies and tactics which have caused damaging results'. His enthusiasm in encouraging his subordinates to read the aforesaid novel and his habit of reading a certain newspaper published in Shanghai also came under attack, for 'it shapes his line of pessimistic and wavering opportunism.' All these charges would have been very fitting for Mao himself, but the Central Politburo obviously preferred to use his brother as a scapegoat.

Although Mao was not named in these struggles since Chin Pang-hsien's arrival in Juichin at the turn of 1933, the International Faction had been planning to suppress him with finesse and thoroughness. Having dealt with the army and the local party organizations, Chin Pang-hsien turned his attention to the Central Soviet Government. In the name of 'wiping off bureaucratic practice and right-wing opportunism', he

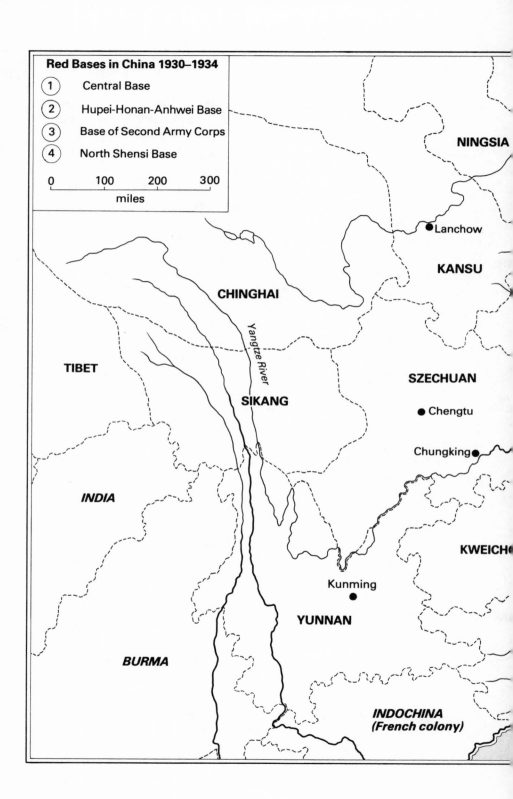

Red Bases in China 1930–1934

1. Central Base
2. Hupei-Honan-Anhwei Base
3. Base of Second Army Corps
4. North Shensi Base

0   100   200   300
miles

NINGSIA

●Lanchow

KANSU

CHINGHAI

TIBET

Yangtze River

SZECHUAN

SIKANG

● Chengtu

Chungking●

INDIA

KWEICHO

Kunming
●

YUNNAN

BURMA

INDOCHINA
(French colony)

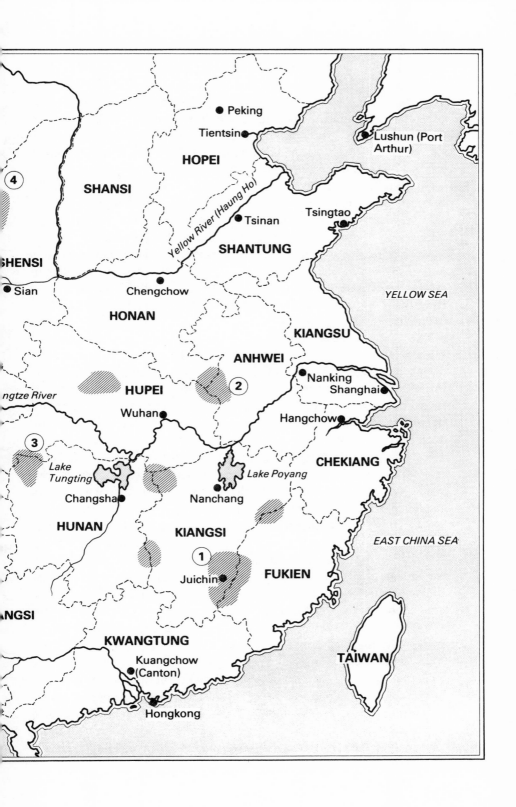

sacked Ho Shu-heng, Mao's closest comrade since the Changsha days in 1921, as People's Commissar for the Supervision of Workers and Peasants. Teng Tzu-hui, a noted follower of Mao who was later to be one of China's economic planners in the 1950s, was demoted from his post as People's Commissar for Financial Affairs. Being no fool, Mao clearly knew that the International Faction had yet to get at him to complete its list. But he would not give up so easily even when the writing was on the wall. To indicate his support for the decisions made by the Central Polit-buro, he undertook to supervise the land reinvestigation programme in person. The work took him to several counties outside of Juichin, at least temporarily away from the hot seat. It was also possible that he was anxious to find out whether his 'rich peasant deviations' had harmed the land revolution as claimed by his rivals. Or he simply wanted to demon-strate his revolutionary zeal by doing the dirty work while Chin Pang-hsien and his associates talked their heads off in the comparative comfort of Juichin.

The crunch came when the Central Committee held its fifth session in January 1934. In the air of inevitability, the committee gathered to discuss the counter-moves as Chiang Kai-shek was about to launch his Fifth Encirclement Campaign which had been put off due to the coup staged by the Nationalist 19th Route Army in Fukien two months before. In conformity with the usual practice, the chair decided that past errors must be re-examined before the discussion of new plans could proceed. It was at this juncture that Mao again came under fire. The same old criti-cisms were readily mouthed by his rivals and the same charges were made. But from his point of view, the most ridiculous charge was that he had failed to show enthusiasm in supporting the policy of aiding the 19th Route Army in its recent coup. Indeed he did express some doubt about the feasibility of allying with 'the reformist counter-revolutionary forces in Fukien', but then he was not in a suitably responsible position to affect the execution of such a policy. Besides, it was Peng Teh-huai who dragged his feet when he was sent to Fukien to aid the 19th Route Army, and yet not a harsh word was thrown in his direction. Conceivably, Mao would not have bothered to defend himself under these conditions, no matter how angry he might have been.

His defeat was complete when he was again excluded from the expanded Central Politburo of which Chu Teh became a new member. To rub salt in the wound, the Second All China Soviet Congress held in the same month elected Chang Wen-tien to succeed him as Chairman of the Council of People's Commissars, leaving him the empty title of Chairman of the Central Soviet Government which was under Hsiang

Ying's control. These decisions were naturally pre-arranged by the Central Politburo, to be made public through the medium of the congress for the sake of respectability. The congress also elected its Central Executive Committee of 175, and none of Mao's men made the list, not even Teng Hsiao-ping who had by now moved over to Chou En-lai's side to indicate his repentance.

To make life more tolerable, Mao left Juichin shortly after the dust of the All China Soviet Congress had settled down. He resumed his work in the land reinvestigation, a more soothing way to lick his wounds. For several months he moved from one place to another, often on one night stands. The work might be boring and trivial, but at least he found himself safe among the guileless peasants and obliging junior cadres who had no knowledge of the power struggle at the top. No longer had he to be on guard all the time. Whenever he wanted someone to share his inner thoughts, Ho Tzu-chen was close at hand. She was not just a devoted wife, but also a staunch supporter of his political line who made the best listener. With enormous will power and unflagging faith in him, she never failed to offer a few words of encouragement, subtly and tactfully, at the right moment. Her loyalty to her husband was even admired by his rivals, especially when his future was extremely bleak. As Kung Chu, the author of *The Red Army and I*, recalled in 1954, she seemed to be the stronger of the two. When Kung frequently called on them during their brief stay in Yutu in September 1934, she always 'wore a slight smile on her face about the room' while Mao moaned and groaned. No wonder when Mao turned his affections to the Shanghai movie actress Lan Ping (Chiang Ching) four years later in Yenan, he was condemned for his infidelity by friends and foes alike.

It is beyond any doubt that the last two years, 1933 and 1934, of the Kiangsi Soviet registered the rapid decline of Mao's political fortune, which was at its nadir in the summer months of 1934 when Chiang Kai-shek's iron ring around the whole area was steadily tightening. Excluded from all top level meetings, Mao had no access to any vital information. Although the Chinese official historians have rewritten the party history, they have found the Kiangsi period a stumbling block. Not unimaginably, they would portray Mao as the one who made all the decisions and directed all the military campaigns, but they have not authenticated it with any form of documentation. However, some of them have shyly mentioned that all the relevant documents had been destroyed in the revolutionary war, as if to justify their inadequacy.

When I discussed this period with Yang I-chih in Peking in December 1956, he remarked that 'the Kiangsi situation would have been totally different if Chairman Mao had held the reins'. The confidant of Chou En-lai also hinted that the Sino-Soviet split was already in the air. 'In the recently held Eighth Party Congress', he said, 'the Chairman stated that there are two pillars in the socialist world. While the Soviet Union has a great party, we have a mature one. After Stalin's death, our Chairman has become the sole interpreter of Marxism and Leninism.' But he refused to answer my questions about the struggle between the International Faction and Mao during the Kiangsi period. 'It's now a part of history,' he smiled.

6 THE LONG MARCH AND AFTER

But fate smiled again on Mao just when he seemed doomed to political oblivion. To counter the Fifth Encirclement Campaign conducted by Chiang Kai-shek around the Central Soviet Area in Kiangsi, the Red Army had adopted the strategy dictated by the Comintern military adviser Otto Braun, who assumed the Chinese name of Li Teh for security reasons. Unfamiliar with the Chinese situation but enjoying the full support of Chin Pang-hsien and Chou En-lai, the German agent decided that, to nullify the block-house tactics of the Nationalists, the Red Army must stage close-range short attacks within the confines of the Soviet Area, with the aim of wiping out various Nationalist units in small pockets where they could not be covered by the supreme firepower from the block-houses they had systematically built along their advance. He also emphasized the need for an 'all-line mobile defence', which meant that under no circumstances should any position or point be abandoned. To be fair to him, his rigid thinking must have been greatly influenced by the Central Politburo's decision that 'not an inch of the Soviet territory should be lost to the enemy'. That Chin Pang-hsien and Chou En-lai should have placed so much faith in Braun's judgement, as Yang I-chih explained to me in Peking in 1956, was not entirely due to their respect for the Comintern. As it was known to them that Chiang Kai-shek had German military advisers on his staff, Yang said, the two Communist leaders regarded Braun as the ideal man to penetrate the German mentality in Chiang's military moves. What Yang omitted to say was that since the Central Politburo had then denounced Mao's 'luring the enemy deep' strategy and guerrilla tactics, it was only natural for Chin and Chou to look for a completely different approach in conducting the war.

Braun's ideas would have appealed to them since they were diametrically opposite to Mao's. Besides, all the military commanders concurred.

While Mao had been busying himself with the mundane work of land reinvestigation in remote villages and hamlets, the military situation worsened considerably. Unfortunately, Braun's strategy backfired. Neither close-range short attacks nor mobile defence stood a chance in the face of Chiang Kai-shek's combined air-land offensive. Meanwhile, the economic blockade enforced by the Nationalists began to bite. The Kiangsi Soviet Area had always heavily relied on material resources smuggled in from the Nationalist region; now the people could not even get salt. As for the Red Army, both provisions and ammunitions reached rock bottom and morale was extremely worrying.

In the early part of April 1934, one column of the Nationalist forces approached Chienning in Western Fukien while another column pressed towards the outskirts of Kwangchang, about sixty miles north of Juichin, the seat of the Central Soviet Government. Under Otto Braun's influence, Chin Pang-hsien and Chou En-lai decided to fight a decisive battle at Kwangchang to push back the oncoming Nationalist forces. In mid-April, Chin Pang-hsien, Chou En-lai, Chu Teh, Braun, Peng Teh-huai and Liu Po-cheng all gathered in the walled city of Kwangchang to discuss the battle plans; they also went to the front line to inspect positions and supervise the campaign. Meanwhile, the Central Committee and the Council of People's Commissars issued a joint directive to party organizations and local soviets in the combat zone, demanding their unqualified support for the defence of Kwangchang, Chienning and Juichang, a town lying to the south of Juichin which was also under pressure.

The Kwangchang campaign started on 10 April. The Chinese Communists deployed the crack units of their First, Third, Fifth and Ninth Army Corps north of Kwangchang, as well as east and west of its satellite town, Yuchiang. Between Kanchu and Kwangchang, fortifications were constructed along the hilly parts of the countryside, forming the strategic points for mobile defence. Braun's new strategy and tactics were submitted to the most severe test.

Having sought to fight a major battle with the Communists all along, the Nationalists threw nine divisions and three special columns into this particular campaign. For almost twenty days both sides engaged in fierce battles and hand-to-hand fighting; every inch of road between Kanchu and Kwangchang was covered with blood. Although the Communists ceaselessly launched close-range short attacks on the flanks of the invading forces, the Nationalists kept pushing forward. With the aid of bombers and heavy artillery, they demolished the strong fortifications meticulously planned by Otto Braun. On 28 April the Nationalists captured Kwangchang. Casualties suffered by both sides were equally heavy, each in the region of 4,500 or more.

In early May, the Central Politburo held an emergency meeting in Juichin, and some members of the Central Committee were included. The Kwangchang campaign was critically examined, with Chin Pang-hsien anxiously explaining that the defeat had not been caused by either strategic or tactical error. He stressed the superiority of the Nationalists' strength and firepower, and blamed the other units of the Red Army in Fukien, Chekiang and Hunan for failing to harass the enemy on the flanks. To defend Braun, he pointed out that the new tactics had not been correctly and flexibly employed in action, as if the military commanders were largely to blame. Dismayed though they were, none of the military men had the courage to speak up against the Comintern military adviser. It was Chang Wen-tien who, after listening to the military cadres in private, tactfully expressed some doubt about the soundness of close-range short attacks. But Braun would not hear of it. He insisted that his new tactics had been distorted and misused, refusing to accept any responsibility.

Mao Tse-tung was at the meeting. But he did not make any attempt to criticize the Kwangchang campaign, according to one of those present. He waited until the future war plans were being discussed. At that point, he suggested that the Red Army in the Central Soviet Area should be divided into four groups pushing towards Fukien, Chekiang, Kiangsu and Hunan to divert the Nationalist forces, before they were pulled back into Kiangsi to defend the Central Soviet Area. His idea was dismissed by Braun as far-fetched and impractical; it was also vigorously opposed by Hsiang Ying.

As the discussion went on, more conflicting opinions were expressed. Some suggested abandoning the Central Soviet Area while others advocated defending it to the last man. In his capacity as Chairman of the Central Military Committee, Chou En-lai summed up various ideas to draw up a comprehensive plan. To carry out Braun's strategy and tactics, strong fortifications were to be built north of Shihcheng to stop the southward drive of the Nationalists. For mobile defence and close-range short attacks, crack units would be employed. Mao's suggestion was partly accepted. The Red Seventh Army Corps and the Red Tenth Army in north-eastern Kiangsi would be sent deep into Fukien and Chekiang, using the name of 'Japan-resisting Vanguards' to confuse the people. The Red Sixth Army Corps along the Hunan-Kiangsi border would be sent into Hunan to join up with Ho Lung's Red Second Army Corps to distract the Nationalist forces from the west, in order to facilitate the counter-attacks of the main force of the Red Army. Nor did Chou En-lai completely refute the idea of abandoning the Central Soviet Area. He admitted that preparations must be made to break through the encirclement if the situation continued to deteriorate.

As it was most important not to affect the morale of the Red Army and the local populace, the plans for the strategic retreat were carried out under the wrap of secrecy. Ostensibly to strengthen the defence of the Central Soviet Area, reduced to the six counties of Ningtu, Hsinkuo, Shihcheng, Juichin, Yutu and Changting in July, a new recruiting campaign was conducted and food supplies were 'borrowed' from the peasants with great vigour. Only a handful of people at the top knew that the Central Soviet Area would be abandoned in good time to avoid total annihilation. But in all honesty, nobody had the ingenuity of coining the heroic term 'Long March' yet.

To hold out against the advancing Nationalists, Hsiang Ying remained in the Central Soviet Area as an overlord. He had the unenviable mission of covering the retreat of the Central authorities and the main force of the Red Army at all costs, as well as maintaining guerrilla warfare in the whole area. Of those who stayed to assist him, Chen Yi became his right-hand man, serving as Commander of the Central Soviet Military Region. But what concerned Mao most was that his youngest brother, Tse-tan, had been ordered to remain behind too. In one of his rare emotional moments, he went to call on Hsiang Ying, asking him to look after Tse-tan whenever possible. And Ho Tzu-chen and himself were also faced with the sad but inevitable decision of leaving their three young children in the care of some peasant families. Despite Mao's political setbacks in the past years, Ho had not been deterred from producing him a baby practically every year.

On 18 October 1934, the great exodus began. The Central Column consisting of the leading cadres of various organizations was under Chou En-lai's personal command, escorted by the First, Third, Fifth, Eighth and Ninth Army Corps, commanded respectively by Lin Piao, Peng Teh-huai, Tung Chen-tang, Chou Kun and Lo Ping-hui, making up the Red First Front Army. The total strength was claimed to be 100,000, including drafted coolies and packhorse grooms. With Western Hunan as the tentative destination, Chou En-lai hoped to re-establish the Central Soviet Government in that mountainous region with the aid of Ho Lung's forces which seemed to have secured a foothold there. In view of the difficult journey ahead, only thirty or forty women, mostly wives of the high-level comrades, were allowed to join the historic retreat. At the outset Mao appeared to be very low in spirits. He did not even bother to take his precious briefcase, which had never left his side since the Ching-kangshan days. When his bodyguard, Chen Chang-feng, reminded him to take it along, he shook his head dejectedly. He had no important documents or military maps to fill the briefcase, he said. He started the journey on horseback, while Ho Tzu-chen walked.

To avoid head-on clashes with the stronger units of the Nationalist army, they moved southward to break through the defence line of the Kwangtung forces and then head west for Southern Hunan. Towards the end of November, after a forced march for five days and five nights, they crossed the Hsiang river and made their way into the Miao tribe's region in Kwangsi province, continuing to push north-westward in the direction of Western Hunan. But before contact could be established with Ho Lung, the Red Second Army Corps under him suffered a heavy defeat, and Western Hunan ceased to be safe enough for the Central Soviet Government to make a stand there. In early December, after the advance units had captured Tungtao county in Western Hunan, the main force turned back to Kweichow province to occupy Liping, a tiny county town defended by a few hundred local troops possessing more opium pipes than rifles. Actually, Kweichow would seem to be the ideal place for the Chinese Communists to rebuild their power centre. Enveloped in mountains, the province was extremely poor. For centuries it has been described as an area where 'the sun never shines for more than three days, not one yard of the ground is flat and not a single soul owns three *feng* [Chinese grams] of silver'. Pestered by corruption and malpractices, the local population was ripe for any form of rebellion. The warlords merely kept their troops to suck the blood of the people, not really prepared to cope with invasion from outside. Not surprisingly, the Red Army encountered practically no resistance in taking one town after another.

After occupying Tsunyi on 5 January 1935, however, the Central Politburo decided to call a brief halt for necessary rest and reorganization. It was almost three months since the breakthrough, with the chasing Nationalist forces now some distance away. To discuss future moves, Chin Pang-hsien summoned an enlarged meeting of the Central Politburo in Tsunyi, later to be known as the Tsunyi Conference. But he had not the slightest inkling that he was about to meet his downfall. The meeting was held in the old city of Tsunyi, from 6 to 8 January. Apart from the Politburo members Chin Pang-hsien, Chang Wen-tien, Chou En-lai, Chen Yun and Chu Teh, it was attended by the Central Committee members including Mao Tse-tung, Liu Shao-chi, Li Wei-han (Lo

Mai) and Peng Teh-huai. Of those specially invited to have their say, Liu Po-cheng, Lin Piao and Nieh Jung-chen represented the military. Otto Braun was present as an observer, accompanied by his interpreter.

Unknown to Chin, in the past weeks Mao had been incessantly working on the military commanders who generally disapproved of Chou En-lai's cumbersome way of organizing the strategic retreat. Reluctant to leave material resources behind, Chou had ordered the Red Army not to discard anything. Even printing presses and other heavy machines were loaded for the march, greatly impeding the mobility of the fighting forces. As Liu Po-cheng later in 1959 wrote about the Long March, he pointed out the error committed by Chou En-lai, though not by name, in very sharp words. 'Assuming the permanent role of the rearguard, the then Fifth Army Corps of the Red Army had to escort the train of heavy machines, mules and packhorses, moving westward along the Kwang-tung-Kwangsi-Hunan border', he recalled. 'The whole army of more than 80,000 men could only inch their way along the winding, narrow mountain paths, often spending a whole night to negotiate a small ravine, frustrated and exhausted. It was impossible for us to shake off the chasing enemy forces, who advanced swiftly along the main roads gaining on us.' But he was even more critical when it came to the crossing of the Hsiang river. 'Faced with the heavily concentrated enemy forces, the leftist leadership was completely helpless. It merely ordered various units to force a breakthrough by means of hard fights, in the vague hope of joining up with the Second and the Sixth Army Corps. After a week of fierce battles on the east bank of the Hsiang river near Chuanhsien in Kwangsi, we finally made the crossing. But we paid a very heavy price. We lost more than one-half of our fighting strength.' If Liu felt so bitter after the lapse of a quarter of a century, it would not be difficult to imagine his reactions at the Tsunyi Conference. Usually critical of Mao, the complete change of his position must have affected the attitude of those sitting on the fence.

But in the conference it was Peng Teh-huai who spoke up first. Immediately after Chou En-lai's military report, the heated debate began. Not known for his refined language, Peng bluntly blamed the Central Politburo for its error in turning the strategic retreat into a huge removal exercise. The slowness of movement, he pointed out, had caused the Red Army extremely heavy losses. When Mao rose to speak, he sharply criticized the leadership's mistake in pursuing Braun's defensively oriented strategy and tactics, which, he said, necessitated the abandonment of the Central Soviet Area and the strategic retreat. He insisted that the heavy losses suffered by the Red Army would otherwise have been avoided. Liu

Shao-chi attacked the Central Politburo from a different angle. He exposed the failures and defections of the underground workers in the Nationalist area. According to him, the intelligence network had virtually collapsed as a result. He accused the leadership of having pursued the line of leftist opportunism which jeopardized the revolution.

In his own defence Otto Braun refuted Mao's argument vigorously. He refused to admit that his strategy and tactics could have caused the irreversible defeat. And to the annoyance of the military commanders present, he blamed them for their inability to carry out close-range short attacks and mobile defence effectively. When someone pointed out that he did not really understand the revolutionary situation in China, he retorted that in the past both Chen Tu-hsiu and Li Li-san had criticized the then Comintern representative in the same breath, wondering why no Chinese comrade had bothered to tell him so before the setback. He was as arrogant as ever.

With equal vigour Chen Yun defended the Communist underground led by him in the Nationalist area. He argued that since the Mukden Incident in 1931 the underground workers had successfully organized the anti-Japanese struggle and the volunteer movement throughout the country, at the cost of the precious lives of many cadres. To dismiss such heroic acts as adventurism, he said, was an insult to the party itself.

In his reply Chin Pang-hsien adamantly defended the correctness of the general line pursued by the Central Politburo. To refute Liu Shao-chi, he referred to the Comintern's directives since the Shanghai meeting of the Central Committee in January 1931. He stated that the leadership, with international assistance, had overcome the crisis created by the right-wing elements to split the party. It had crushed, he said, the first four encirclement campaigns staged by the Kuomintang, established control of the immense Soviet Area, formed the Soviet Republic, organized the Red Army of 300,000 and carried out the land revolution in the Soviet Area. He asked whether all these achievements should be regarded as the outcome of leftist adventurism. Unyielding, he insisted that the failure to crush the Nationalists' Fifth Encirclement Campaign should not be held as a weapon to defame the whole party, to the extent of writing off its past efforts and achievements.

For two days the debate went on. Emotions were high and the atmosphere was explosive. Neither side would like to come round since the stake involved the future direction of the party and the fate of the leadership. Liu Po-cheng—the one-eyed general—eventually tipped the balance. Hitherto a staunch supporter of Chin and his Politburo, he suddenly switched his allegiance to Mao Tse-tung, expressing his faith in

Mao's strategic concept. He was followed by Lin Piao and Nieh Jung-chen, who voiced their doubt about the Central Politburo's judgement on military matters. Realizing that the military had now lined up against him, Chou En-lai began to admit his errors in the Fifth Encirclement Campaign and the ensuing strategic retreat. As always, he knew when to abandon a sinking ship. But Chin still refused to give in.

At this point Chang Wen-tien played his hand. Assuming the role of a peacemaker, he stressed the importance of unity and solidarity. He asked everyone to be rational as a good Marxist ought to be. On one hand, he confirmed the correctness of the general line pursued by the Politburo; but on the other, he pointed out that it had adopted a wrong military strategy either in countering the Nationalists' last offensive or conducting the large-scale retreat. After much theorizing and pontificating, he concluded that Chin Pang-hsien, Chou En-lai and Otto Braun must accept the responsibility for the defeat, in the spirit of a true Communist. Apparently, by dwelling on the military blunders, he absolved himself from blame since he was not involved in that respect. To point an accusing finger at Chin, he certainly had his own interest in mind. Other than Chin, he was the most senior member of the Central Politburo. But this did not stop Mao from regarding him as an ally and a 'good' comrade, as he later indicated to Edgar Snow in an interview in 1936.

With Chang shifting his ground, Chin had to admit defeat. On the third day, the resolution of 'Examining the Erroneous Military Line Pursued by Comrades Po Ku [Chin Pang-hsien], Chou En-lai and Li Teh [Otto Braun]' was passed at the meeting, to be mimeographed for distribution among senior cadres in various army corps. Both the Central Politburo and the Central Military Committee were reorganized. Chang Wen-tien replaced Chin Pang-hsien as General Secretary of the party and Mao Tse-tung succeeded Chou En-lai as Chairman of the Central Military Committee. Mao was also elected to the Central Politburo to fill the vacancy left by Hsiang Ying who did not join the Long March. But as no reorganization of the Central leadership should be carried out without assembling the whole body of the Central Committee, the question of legality arose. To remedy the situation and seek the approval of the Comintern, Chen Yun was sent to Moscow for the mission, travelling incognito. Having discarded the radio equipment during the retreat, there was no other way to communicate with the Comintern. For the same reason Pan Han-nien, an espionage expert who was to be First Deputy Mayor of Shanghai in 1949, was sent to the Nationalist areas to strengthen the underground work, with Shanghai and Hong Kong as his bases. Liu Shao-chi had his share of the rewards. After the disbanding of the Eighth Army Corps, he was transferred to the Third Army Corps to head its Political Department, coining a useful relationship with Peng Teh-huai who had virtually overshadowed Chu Teh.

But actually, Mao seemed to be quite sure of his success even before the Tsunyi Conference. For him, the turning point was the ad hoc meeting of the Central Politburo in Liping towards the end of December in 1934. By then, all the military commanders had become convinced that the Central leadership's plan to re-establish the Central Soviet Government in Western Hunan was unworkable. They were so fed up with Otto Braun that they began to lose faith in the Central Military Committee headed by Chou En-lai. After the catastrophic losses at the Hsiang river, with more than 50,000 troops killed or captured, they were in a state of shell-shock, to put it mildly. All they wanted was to hang on to the remaining military strength of some 30,000, not prepared to risk another major clash with the Nationalist forces. In these circumstances, it was only natural for them to see Mao's idea of retreating into Kweichow to set up a new Soviet Area there as sound and practical. The way they felt was succinctly recorded by Liu Po-cheng when he wrote his article 'Recollections of the Long March', in 1959. 'At this critical moment,' he said, 'Chairman Mao saved the Red Army. He insisted that the attempt to join up with the Second and Sixth Army Corps must be abandoned in favour of advancing to the thinly defended Kweichow, seeking to fight a few victorious battles to give our troops a rest.... His idea was supported by the majority of our comrades. Had he not then insisted on the change of plan, the remaining 30,000-odd men of the Red Army would have faced total destruction.' Until then, Liu had always been at odds with Mao where military strategy was concerned. His admission should, therefore, be. seen as evidence of Mao's successful manoeuvring of the generals during the Long March.

It is beyond any doubt that Mao would not have been able to unseat Chin Pang-hsien in Tsunyi without the assistance of Chang Wen-tien. In the past, he would not have bothered to form a temporary alliance with Chang, who had treated him as badly as Chin had. But the Juichin experience had taught him to be more patient in the game of power struggle. Despite the support of the military commanders, he knew he was no match for the Central Politburo if it remained united. Chang Wen-tien's secret ambition to reach the top was regarded by him as an exploitable factor of the disunited Politburo. It also made him realize that he had the chance to break up the International Faction—a chance he could ill afford to miss. Moreover, with Chang taking over from Chin at the helm, it would be more acceptable to the Comintern since they both belonged to the pro-Moscow group. Not that Mao had any regard for the Comintern; but he was realistic enough to count on further patronage from Moscow without which the Chinese Communist Party could not hope to survive. Although Wang Chia-hsiang, another member of the Central Politburo, did not attend the Tsunyi Conference because of his illness, he was in that town when it took place. Closely associated with the International Faction like Chin and Chang, he begrudgingly admitted that Mao's masterstroke at the Tsunyi Conference was to play Chang off against Chin. After Wang's appointment as China's first ambassador to the Soviet Union in 1949, one of his confidants in Hongkong told me that he would at least have been made Foreign Minister if Chin Pang-hsien had not lost out at the Tsunyi Conference. Sensing something behind these words, I pressed for further explanation. It was then that this confidant of Wang's obliged me with a fairly comprehensive account of the Tsunyi Conference. He said that if Wang Chia-hsiang had not been absent from the conference at that time, he might have been able to dissuade Chang from turning against Chin and Chou En-lai when the chips were down.

But even with his emergence from the Tsunyi Conference as a victor, Mao owed much of his political ascendancy to none other than Chou En-lai. Having been disgraced, a lesser man would have denied Mao any form of assistance, if only for the sake of pride. But not the magnanimous Chou. After handing over the Central Military Committee to Mao, he still retained his post as Vice-Chairman of the Revolutionary Military Commission under the Central Soviet Government. In this capacity he continued to help Mao out in military affairs as if nothing had happened. For all his eloquence and ideas, Chou En-lai found it difficult to cope with the more practical side of leading more than 30,000 battered and demoralized troops. This was when Chou began to impress him with his worth as an outstanding organizer, thorough in plans and good at details. Not infrequently, he would stay up night after night to await dispatches and reports from various units until they were all at hand. He had to study and analyse them, familiarizing himself with the fluid situation. The work was so demanding that it finally wore him down. Carried on a stretcher most of the time, he would not allow his ill health to interfere with his work. If Mao never forgot to encourage the exhausted and underfed warriors with words and gestures, Chou did all his talking with deeds. His influence on morale would seem to be greater in the long run, especially when words tended to lose their meaning.

Apart from working with dedication under Mao himself, Chou also did his best to bring him and Chu Teh together. But most important of all, he succeeded in convincing Mao that Liu Po-cheng was the right man to lead the advance units, in preference to Mao's own choice, Lin Piao. When it became obvious that the Red Army would not stand a chance of establishing a foothold in Kweichow, the new Politburo under Chang Wen-tien decided to continue the march heading for Northern Szechuan where the Red Fourth Front Army under Chang Kuo-tao occupied several counties. To avoid confronting Chiang Kai-shek's main forces, the plan was to move north-westward, entering Southern Szechuan and then crossing the Chinsha river near Yipin and Luhsien to reach Northern Szechuan. But unexpectedly, the local units of Szechuan held their line firmly at several strategic points, inflicting heavy casualties on the advancing Red Army. Meanwhile, two columns of Chiang's Central Army were close at heel. The only alternative was to retreat into Kweichow, trying to dash for Northern Szechuan by route of Yunnan, the province noted for its difficult terrain in the north. Having left Tsunyi in mid-January, the Red Army returned to capture it once more towards the end of February after sustaining several defeats in Southern Szechuan. The setback must have shaken Mao's confidence as a military strategist, for he now readily agreed with Chou on future movements and plans.

After a short spell of rest in Tsunyi, reorganizing, recruiting and requisitioning, the Central Politburo resisted Mao's renewed recommendation of holding out in Northern Kweichow to set up a new base area. Despite the reasons he gave at a meeting, everyone else knew that he did not cherish the prospect of seeking cooperation with Chang Kuo-tao who thought little of him. As far as the others were concerned, internal conflicts must not outweigh the threat from outside. In March, however, with Liu Po-cheng leading the vanguard consisting of military cadets and cadres, the much diminished Red First Front Army resumed its march westward. The next few months marked the most difficult stage of the Long March, and human endurance was put to the severest test. The Communist warriors not only had to fight valiantly against Nationalist forces from all directions, but also had to achieve the seemingly impossible task of crossing the Wu river, the Chinsha river and the Tatu river under the enemy's heavy artillery fire. They marched across swamps, made their way through virgin forests and climbed over pathless mountains, on the strength of sheer determination. For days on end, they lived on the bark of trees, wild plants and anything they could lay their hands on. Many of them died of unattended wounds, and even more died of illness and hunger. The rest simply had to move on.

When the First Front Army eventually struggled to Maokung in North-western Szechuan on 16 June 1935, the Fourth Front Army met it with open arms. Since March, Chang Kuo-tao and his commander Hsu Hsiang-chien, had led their army to fight its way westward with considerable success, in response to the Central Politburo's request to meet the First Front Army halfway. Whereas Mao and Chou En-lai had less than 10,000 survivors with them, Chang Kuo-tao maintained a sizable fighting force of nearly 80,000, well-equipped and full of confidence. In tatters and barefoot, the cadres and soldiers of the First Front Army could not but feel ashamed of their own appearance in front of the luckier comrades from the other army. Although Chang Kuo-tao was very generous in allocating provisions and new weapons to the First Front Army as well as transferring three of his regiments under its command, he had no way of stopping his men from assuming an air of arrogance and disdain. It did not take long for ill feelings to grow between both sides.

Still, what mattered most was the attitude of those at the top. In the opinion of Chang Kuo-tao and his chief associates, the Politburo reshuffle in Tsunyi was 'illegal and unconstitutional'; they backed up their argument with the party constitution. To be fair to Chang, he was perfectly right. He would have succeeded in squeezing Mao out of the Politburo had he adopted a more tactful approach.

On 25 June the Central Politburo held another meeting in Lianghokou, a small town north of Fukien county. The meeting was attended by those Politburo members who were present, including Chang Kuo-tao of course. From the side of the Fourth Front Army, Chen Chang-hao and Hsu Hsiang-chien, in their capacity as members of the Central Committee, were also invited. Originally, being one of the twenty-eight Bolsheviks, Chen had been as much a protégé of the Comintern as Chen Shao-yu (Wang Ming), Chin Pang-hsien or Chang Wen-tien. But since his joining the Fourth Front Army as its political commissar, he had become Chang Kuo-tao's right-hand man. When the meeting started, Chang Wen-tien intended to proceed with the discussion of the future moves for the Red Army as planned. But Chang Kuo-tao immediately brought up the issue of legality of the Tsunyi reorganization of the Central leadership. He was followed by Chen Chang-hao who denounced Chin Pang-hsien, Chang Wen-tien and Mao Tse-tung for their collective part in meddling with the party constitution to suit themselves. By attacking the three of them in the same breath, he made a cardinal error. If he had been more observant, he would have detected the victimization of Chin Pang-hsien and the uneasy alliance between Chang Wen-tien and Mao. He should have tackled them individually and differently, concentrating his firepower on Mao who, after all, had forced the reshuffle. In this way, he could have won the support of Chin Pang-hsien and Chou En-lai, thus enhancing the chance of reversing the Tsunyi resolutions. Chin would have been only too happy to regain his position as General Secretary while Chou would not have objected to the resumption of his control of the Central Military Committee. Chen Chang-hao should also have taken into account the opportunist in Chang Wen-tien, who would have yielded in the wind like a willow. But unfortunately, all these considerations seemed to have escaped his mind. Once again, luck was on Mao's side.

However, Chen Chang-hao's blunder enabled Mao to rally round him Chin Pang-hsien, Chang Wen-tien and Chou En-lai, since none of them had escaped the indiscriminate attack. Together they defended the Tsunyi reshuffle as an absolutely necessary measure to forestall the collapse of the party, which, they argued, should be treated as a special case. They also pointed out that Chen Yun had been sent to Moscow to seek the Comintern's approval. Before they heard from Moscow, Chang Wen-tien suggested, the reshuffled Central leadership should carry on its duty in the interest of the party. But Chen Chang-hao had other ideas. He proposed to have another reshuffle and make Chang Kuo-tao the party's General Secretary instead of Chang Wen-tien. Meanwhile, Chang Kuo-tao unreservedly criticized the political line pursued by the Central leadership since the Sixth Party Congress held in Moscow in July 1928. He even questioned the wisdom of introducing the Soviet system to China. This was very foolish of him. By doing so, he virtually challenged the revolutionary guidelines laid down by the Comintern. He gave the others no alternative but to side with Chang Wen-tien and Mao Tse-tung. It would have been unthinkable for anyone to be so impudent to Moscow, even if he might secretly agree with Chang Kuo-tao's argument. In a way, he could have unwittingly helped improve Mao's standing with some Politburo members who had hitherto found this objectionable. Mao might be ambitious, but he did not try to rock the boat.

It was, however, possible that both Chang Kuo-tao and Chen Chang-hao did not take Mao seriously as a rival. Chang never regarded Mao as an equal, intellectually or ideologically. While in Chen's eyes, the country bumpkin from Hunan was not worth worrying about. Besides, Mao's disgrace in the Kiangsi Soviet had been an open secret. That he should have re-emerged as a contender for the leadership so rapidly was beyond their imagination. Chang was also an impatient man, often acting hastily and impulsively. Basically an intellectual by temperament, he lacked Mao's unrelenting ruthlessness and devious nature. Otherwise, he would not have been in the Comintern's disfavour.

In the Lianghoko meeting when it came to a deadlock, Chu Teh stepped in as a mediator. He appealed to both sides for tolerance and mutual understanding, and urged them to work out a compromise. It was then decided that the reshuffled Politburo should remain as it was, pending the final word from Moscow. But to pacify Chang Kuo-tao, the abolished post of Chief Political Commissar was restored for him to take on. As Chen Chang-hao insisted that the Fourth Front Army should have an adequate representation in the Central Committee, Hsu Hsiang-chien (originally an alternate member) and seven other high-ranking officers were made its new full members. Ironically, the compromise reached here was no more 'legal' than the Politburo reshuffle in Tsunyi, for, according to the party constitution, members of the Central Committee should be elected at the Party Congress.

Although these developments fell short of Chang Kuo-tao's expectations, he was, nonetheless, quite prepared to play a waiting game. With his Fourth Front Army now the backbone of the Communist forces, he was in an unassailable position. But the concession made by the Politburo regarding the additional Central Committee members sparked off the resentment of the First Front Army, down to every man. The bulk of its officers were of the opinion that the Fourth Front Army had held the Central leadership to ransom, mainly because they did not realize the illegal nature of the top level reorganization in Tsunyi. And, in spite of their present plight, they still considered themselves a part of the establishment in Juichin. In their thinking, the Fourth Front Army merely consisted of a bunch of outsiders who had no right to burst into the inner circle of power. Nor did the attitude of the Fourth Front Army, officers and men alike, help to ease the tension. They made no effort to conceal their contempt for the less fortunate First Front Army, especially as days went by. Furthermore, they never ceased talking about how the warriors from the Central Soviet Army were 'better at carrying wives of senior comrades on stretchers than fighting the enemy'. Since these remarks were not far from the truth, they were very hurtful.

As regards the future plan, no firm decision was reached in the Lianghoko meeting. Mao proposed to move the Red Army into Northern Shensi to join forces with Liu Chih-tan's local Communist units, with the ultimate aim of linking up with Outer Mongolia. He explained that such a move would shorten the geographical distance between the Chinese revolutionary base and Moscow, improving the prospects of obtaining material aid from the Soviet Union. According to him, moving northward also had its propaganda value, for the Red Army had been talking about 'advancing to the north to fight the Japanese' in the past few years. Even before the start of the Long March, he pointed out, the men were given to understand that they were marching northward to resist the Japanese invasion.

But Chang Kuo-tao disagreed with him. After analysing the current situation, he expressed the belief that the revolution was now at its lowest ebb. He regarded the northward move as an unsound strategy, involving unnecessary risks and unforeseen difficulties. Instead, he proposed to move southward and establish the revolutionary base along the Szechuan-Sikang border, with the immense territory of Sikang in the rear. He argued that this would spare the exhausted men the hardships of another difficult march. As he saw it, the Szechuan-Sikang border area would be more secure than Northern Shensi of which little was known. Naturally, he had the support of the military commanders of the Fourth Front Army who accepted him as their undisputed leader. Not to be outdone, Mao managed to sway the views of their counterparts in the First Front Army behind him. Again, Chu Teh had to offer his good offices.

In spite of their initial resistance, both Mao and Chang were persuaded to yield some ground. Not to make either of them lose face, it was agreed that the party should set the aim of establishing a revolutionary base in the border area between Szechuan, Shensi and Kansu—a mixture of both proposals. While making such preparations, the men of both the First Front Army and the Fourth Front Army were to remain in north-western Szechuan for some rest and recuperation. For the time being at least, the harmony within the party hierarchy was restored, no matter how precariously.

But in fact, neither Chang nor Mao was absolutely honest with his comrades regarding the future plan for the party. With a sizable army spreading out in the inaccessible areas of Szechuan, the former saw the advantage of extending his influence into the sparsely populated Sikang. Once he succeeded in doing so, he would, he thought, be in an unchallengeable position, either within his own party or for the National- ist forces. No favourite of the Comintern's, he would rather occupy an area to introduce his form of socialism, independent of Moscow. On the other hand, Mao had his personal considerations. After his success in regaining power in Tsunyi, he was not going to risk losing it again. He saw clearly that Chang Kuo-tao had a good chance of building up a revolutionary base along the Szechuan-Sikang border, which would leave himself in the unenviable role of having to play second fiddle. The disparity of strength between his depleted First Front Army and Chang's

Fourth Front Army was another worry. If the two armies fought side by side, it would not take Chang long, in all probability, to absorb a few units of the First Front Army into his Fourth Front Army, leaving Mao with even less military muscle to flex. A believer in the Chinese saying that large fish always swallow up small fish, he deemed it necessary to stay clear of Chang. Not that he was sure of the wisdom of dragging the battered troops across the grasslands and mountain ranges, he had to take the gamble when there was no hope of outmanoeuvring Chang by playing his game. As to the argument of moving nearer to the Soviet Union geographically, it was but his attempt to win the support of Chin Pang-hsien, Chang Wen-tien and the rest of the International Faction. He knew how they felt about Moscow.

For several weeks the Red Army remained inactive in north-western Szechuan. In the meantime, the Nationalists had been assembling their troops in three groups, obviously with the intention of closing in from three directions—north, south and east. To deal with the looming threat, the Communists held an urgent Politburo meeting in Maoerhkai on 5 August. Chang Kuo-tao again brought up the legality issue of the Tsunyi reshuffle for discussion, but he was overruled by Chang Wen-tien, who chaired the meeting. At such a moment, it was very unwise of the former to dwell on this sore point, for he merely antagonized the majority of the Politburo. When the future strategy was being discussed, Mao Tse-tung restated his proposal to march northward to join forces with Liu Chih-tan in Northern Shensi. He again stressed the need to open an international supply route to the Soviet Union through Mongolia and Sinkiang, apparently aware of the presence of several leading members of the International Faction in the meeting. But Chang Kuo-tao was equally adamant in advocating a contrary move. He argued that since the Nationalist forces were densely deployed along the Szechuan-Shensi-Kansu border, the Red Army would have to suffer heavy losses by crossing the grasslands to head for the North-west. He reiterated his conviction in the soundness of occupying the thinly defended area along the Szechuan-Sikang border, with Chengtu, the provincial capital of Szechuan, within easy reach. To strengthen his argument, he blamed the others for having previously rejected his idea in Lianghokou a few weeks earlier. Otherwise, he insisted, they would have already established a stronghold in Southern Szechuan, without having to be on the run again.

Not unexpectedly, he failed to convince the others who seemed more prepared to throw in their lot with Mao Tse-tung. It was then decided to continue marching northward along two routes, with Chang Kuo-tao directing the West Column. Assisted by Chou En-lai, Mao commanded the column which consisted of the bulk of the First Front Army, supplemented by some units transferred from the Fourth Front Army. The column under Chang Kuo-tao's command was his own Fourth Front Army, and he was joined by Chu Teh and Liu Po-cheng as a symbol of solidarity. But ahead of the East Column, Hsu Hsiang-chien and Chen Chang-hao led the advance unit consisting of the very best of the Fourth Front Army's main strength.

When the East Column moved towards the grasslands, it was intercepted by a Nationalist division. For reasons best known to Mao himself, he let an army unit of Chang Kuo-tao's do all the fighting. After a series of bloody battles for two nights and one day, the Nationalists lost more than 4,000 men while the Communists' casualties were equally heavy. As soon as the news reached Chang Kuo-tao at the head of the West Column, he was extremely upset. In his capacity as a Politburo member and the Chief Political Commissar of the Red Army, he suggested to Chang Wen-tien and Mao Tse-tung that both columns should turn back to march southward instead. Evidently, he wanted to revive his plan of occupying the area along the Sikang border. It was at this stage that the strangest thing happened. While discussions were still going on through the medium of emissaries, Mao secretly led the First and Third Army Corps of the First Front Army, as well as a part of the cadres column, to take the road. He did not even bother to inform Hsu Hsiang-chien and Chen Chang-hao, who were a part of the East Column, of his intentions. His outrageous act of deserting the other army units angered Chang Kuo-tao as much as Chu Teh and Liu Po-cheng, not to mention those senior cadres of the Fifth and Ninth Army Corps, the two original units of the First Front Army now attached to the West Column. The entire Fourth Front Army went into uproar. Both officers and men unreservedly denounced Mao as 'an escaping opportunist', and they were no less critical of the Central authorities headed by Chang Wen-tien. Even Chu Teh and Liu Po-cheng could not remain quiet. They openly deplored Mao's stealthy march to the north without waiting for the outcome of the discussions. Taking into account the prevailing mood. Chang Kuo-tao made his strike. He successfully persuaded the Fourth Front Army and the Fifth and Ninth Army Corps of the First Front Army to turn round and march southward, with Changtu as their target. Trapped, Chu Teh and Liu Po-cheng had to go along.

Unfathomable as Mao always was, it is almost impossible for one to analyse his motive in taking such an unusual step. But most probably, he might have sensed that Chang Kuo-tao would gain more support as the discussions went on. He was not a good loser, and the thought of losing out to Chang was too much for him to bear. Although he was quite aware of the imponderables lying ahead of him when he decided to go it alone, he would not shrink from playing against all odds. When I probed Yang I-chih, Chou En-lai's confidant, about this episode in Peking in early 1957, he refused to be too specific. But, however, he did say something quite interesting. 'If one wants to achieve an unusual feat', he said philosophically, 'one must have vision and courage. Chairman Mao is a revolutionary prophet; he often foresees new situations totally unthinkable to ordinary people. That is why in those years he did not always succeed in enlightening the majority. But since the Tsunyi Conference, many comrades have come round to see things his way. He has proved to them his insight and sound judgement. A great man is often misunderstood or even despised by his contemporaries, simply because he does not conform and has no respect for set rules.' Elusive though Yang's remarks sounded to me then, he definitely gave me the impression that Mao would have resorted to any means to defeat his opposition, rightly or wrongly.

To avoid further encounters with the Nationalist forces, Mao chose to cross the grasslands at full speed, ordering the men to discard heavier arms and more cumbersome objects before they started the forced march. Chou En-lai was then gravely ill, but it did not prevent him from being consulted by Mao at all hours. If what Yang Cheng-wu, the present Deputy Chief-of-Staff, wrote in the *Liberation Army Literature* in 1975 were reasonably accurate, it seemed that the six days across the grasslands sealed the close working relationship between Mao and Chou which was to last for many more decades to come. In the face of seemingly insurmountable difficulties created by nature, they really had to act closely together like twins, if not one person. Survival was their common concern. It was not enough for themselves to survive, they must bring the demoralized and shattered troops, their future political capital, to the other side of the endless and pathless grasslands which were sinking under them like quicksand. Having shaken off the enemy at their heels, they found the confrontation with nature far more daunting. They saw the men dropping dead, one after another like fallen leaves. Most commanders were fading away; they might have the will, but not the physical strength. Yet Mao continued to exude 'confidence and optimism', according to Yang Cheng-wu. To cheer up the men, he told them some episodes from *The Westward Journey*, a Chinese legendary novel about the adventures of the Monkey King. For on numerous occasions he described how the Monkey King went through all dangers to cross the Flaming Fire Mountain, encouraging them to emulate the legendary monkey. If the Monkey King could conquer the Flaming Fire Mountain, he would say, we should have no trouble in overcoming the grasslands, in fact a much easier task. Perhaps Mao was right not to bother quoting from Marx and Lenin to inspire the men. At a time like this, there was no room for dogmas or doctrines.

While crossing the grasslands, Mao only had over 7,000 men with him, as Liu Po-cheng recounted. To confuse the Nationalists, he renamed his unit the Shensi-Kansu Guerrilla Detachment of the Workers and Peasants Red Army, with Lin Piao and Peng Teh-huai respectively commanding the First and Second Column. He also appointed himself the political commissar of the whole detachment, for the sake of direct control. The change of name seemed to work, for after emerging from the grasslands, Mao reached a point in Southern Kansu without encountering any serious resistance from the Nationalist forces. It was also possible that the route across the grasslands defied the imagination of the Nationalist Supreme Command. Mao might have risked the total extinction of his military force, but he did take the Nationalists by surprise. The narrow escape had more to do with his courage, rather than his judgement.

Towards the end of October, however, Mao and his detachment eventually entered Northern Shensi, reputedly the poorest region in China at that time. In the presence of Chang Wen-tien, Chou En-lai and a few other top comrades, he met Liu Chih-tan, the key figure of the Shensi-Kansu Border Soviet Area, for the first time in a village called Wuchichen. Greetings were exchanged and Liu's welcome was sufficiently warm to make Mao and his associates feel at home. But behind the full display of comradeship and class love, all had not been going well in this Communist pocket for a considerable period. As Liu Chih-tan and his deputy, Kao Kang, were both natives of the province, they had been ruthlessly persecuted by Chu Li-chih, representative of the Chinese Communist Party Central Headquarters from Kiangsi, and Hsu Hai-tung, Commander of the Red Twenty-fifth Army which had recently moved into Northern Shensi. At the height of the struggle, both Liu and Kao had been thrown into jail, only to be released when the news of the impending arrival of the Central authorities reached this area. Nothing short of a full-scale war would have broken out between the Red Twenty-fifth Army and the local troops under Liu and Kao, known as the Red Twenty-sixth Army, if Mao and his detachment had not arrived at that crucial moment. Of course such a development had not been in Mao's reckoning, but it was most uncanny that he should appear on the scene just in time to handle the crisis. Had he agreed with Chang Kuo-tao to

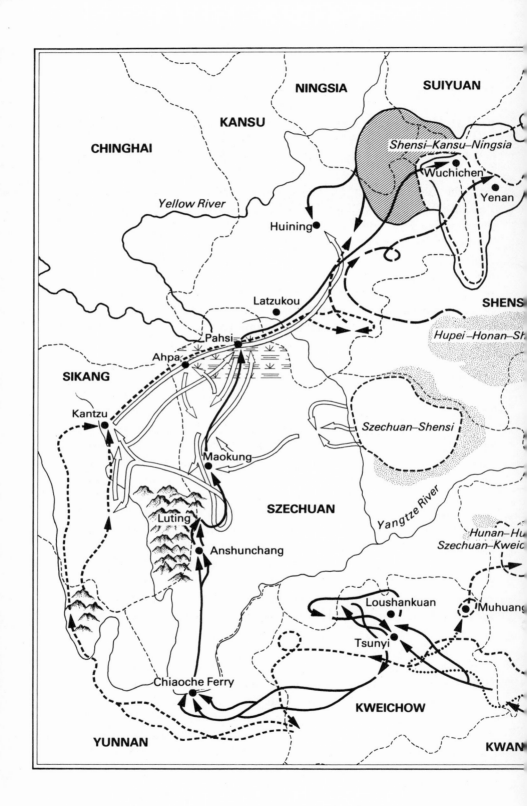

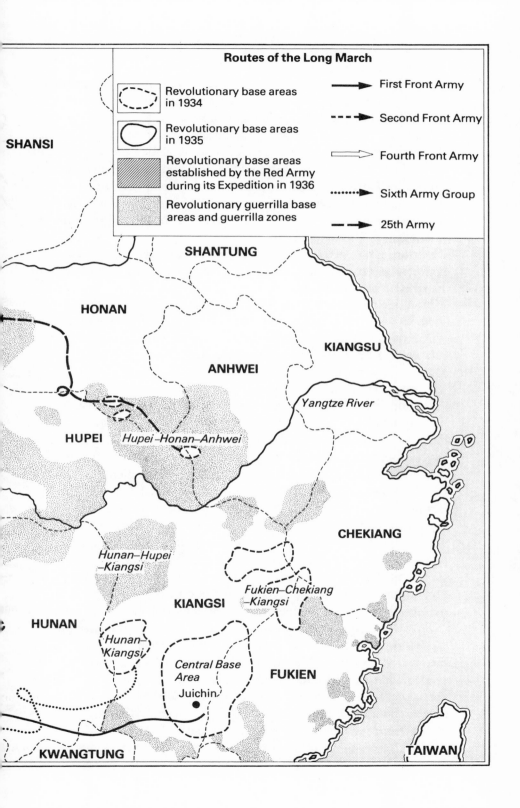

march towards Southern Szechuan, the Communist base in Northern Shensi would probably have ceased to exist. His rivals within the party might be more intelligent in many aspects, but none of them seemed to have the knack of landing in a favourable situation quite unintentionally.

With the party's Central Headquarters settled in Wayaopao near Anting county in Northern Shensi, Mao abolished the Kansi-Shensi Guerrilla Detachment and restored the First and Third Army Corps. In December Chang Hao was sent back by the Comintern from Moscow with a set of instructions. It appeared that the highest organ of the International Communist Movement had accepted the Tsunyi reshuffle as a *fait accompli*. Shrewd as usual, Mao had no intention of attracting undue attention on himself from the Comintern. He allowed Chang Wen-tien to continue as General Secretary of the party, and even supported Chin Pang-hsien as Chairman of the Council of People's Commissars. As for himself, he retained the post as Chairman of the Central Soviet Government. But his main interest lay in the Central Military Committee, of which he was head. Obviously, he fully appreciated the importance of establishing his power base in the Red Army before anything else. So long as he had the army behind him, he knew he could effectively control the party. He had learned it the hard way.

Having forced himself to be more cautious and less impulsive, he was no longer the person his comrades had known in the Chingkang Mountains or even during his political wilderness in Kiangsi. He played his cards closer to his chest than ever, taking absolutely no one into his confidence. But there was hardly any doubt that he had completely lost faith in the Comintern. Like most of the military commanders, he saw Otto Braun as the height of Moscow's folly. Still, he was realistic enough to know that the continuing patronage of the Comintern was an imperative need, which had to be solicited through the International Faction in his party. He must give Moscow the impression that he was prepared to toe the Comintern line and work in harmony with Chang Wen-tien and Chin Pang-hsien in spite of the recent conflicts during the Long March. In politics, deceptions and pretences are but a part of the game.

To strengthen his claim in the leadership stake, Mao realized that it was essential for him to be accepted as a theoretician and an ideologist. He started to study Marxist and Leninist writings, whatever was available in Chinese, more seriously, always trying to interpret them in the light of his own revolutionary experiences. With the benefit of a facile tongue and a facile pen, he involved himself a great deal in putting his ideas across to the cadres as a whole. He theorized, pontificated and tried to inspire them to the best of his ability. For it was clear to him that the morale of the party must be immediately lifted without further delay.

It was at this point that he and his top comrades, according to Tung Pi-wu, decided that 'the positive aspects of the Long March must be brought into focus'. In other words, this meant an orchestrated propaganda campaign to glorify the heroic deeds, the undaunted human courage in the face of impossible odds and the outstanding examples of revolutionary martyrdom. The strategic retreat might have cost no less than 90,000 human lives in some fifteen months, but the epic quality of the immense sacrifice, in the belief of Mao and his associates, would create an unprecedented impact on the Chinese people, regardless of their political affiliations, once the story was widely spread. To attain maximum effect, they deemed it necessary to saturate the Nationalist areas with anecdotes, episodes and tales about the Long March. In fact, since Japan's occupation of the North-eastern Provinces (Manchuria) after the Mukden Incident on 18 September 1931, the Communist underground workers had significantly penetrated the student movement in the Nationalist areas, particularly in big cities such as Peking, Tientsin and Shanghai. With Japan's aggressive designs to reduce China to a vassal state loud and clear, the students throughout the country were seized with the passion of patriotism and anti-Japanese fervour. They were disgusted with the protracted civil war, generally too naive to understand its ideological implications or visualize the shadows of the Comintern behind the scenes. For the majority of them, nothing was more important than to drive Japan's Imperial Army out of the occupied territories. In the past years, fellow travellers of the Chinese Communists had been publishing pamphlets and periodicals, under the protective shield of the International Settlement in Shanghai, with great success. These publications claimed a very big readership among the student population, and they naturally became the ideal vehicles of mass communication with the Nationalist Areas for the Communists cornered in the barren land of Northern Shensi, with their fate seemingly sealed.

Without any doubt, Mao's campaign to glorify the Long March turned out to be a most successful operation. Through these publications the heroic feats of the Communist marchers were presented to the students and other readers in the whole country with dramatic effect. The stories were avidly read and enthusiastically spread around. Since the Communists claimed that their sole aim was 'to march to the north to resist Japan's invasion', they suddenly emerged as the patriotic heroes in the eyes of most of the readers. Their advocacy of ending the civil war to fight Japan touched the core of many, many hearts. In Peking alone, the stories about the Long March caught on like wild fire as from the spring of 1936.

People kept talking about what they had read with ever-increasing interest and no little sympathy.

It seemed that Mao at this time began to recognize the value of international publicity as well, judging by what Mei Yi, then a spokesman of the Chinese Communist Delegation, told me in Nanking in 1947. He said that the party leadership after the Long March gave much attention to the international impression of the Chinese revolution, for 'our side of the story' must be told to the world. Knowing about my sympathy at that time for their cause, he was seeking my help in persuading some American correspondents to visit the Liberated Areas in Northern Kiangsu and Southern Shantung. He talked about Edgar Snow and Agnes Smedley with glowing praise, saying that 'their service to the Chinese people had been invaluable'. He emphatically told me that the party could do with 'more Snows and Smedleys', for they 'would help us to counter the Nationalist propaganda more effectively'. The future Director of China's National Broadcasting Administration minced no words when he revealed Mao's high esteem for Edgar Snow. 'Chairman Mao regarded Snow as a true friend', he said, 'for his book made the whole world suddenly aware of our just cause and heroic struggle. He was the one who put us on the international scene.'

But what Mei omitted to say was, of course, that Mao had other reasons to be grateful to the American journalist. In the summer of 1936, the Chinese Communist leader was still in the process of building himself up in the party hierarchy. While in the Nationalist-blockaded Northern Shensi he had to elbow his way cautiously in the midst of Chang Wentien, Chin Pang-hsien and their like, another Central Headquarters of the party, set up in Sikang by Chang Kuo-tao, posed an even more serious threat. Snow's timely arrival in Pao-an was a blessing for him. It not only fitted in perfectly with the party's new scheme of winning friends to form an International United Front, but also gave Mao the unique chance to expose himself to the American news media. In Mao's reckoning, if he could manage to convince the American journalist of his dedication to Communism as a means to save China, it would work well for both the revolutionary cause and his own standing. It was also possible that he saw his first contact with an American as a symbol of his independence of the masters in Moscow, in the hope of scoring some points over his nearest rivals who had the Comintern's backing. However, he certainly knew how to make full use of every available opportunity for his own advancement.

In a way, Chou En-lai seemed to be instrumental in effecting Mao's long interview with Edgar Snow. Since the Tsunyi Conference, a close link had been formed between the two leading Communists, according to Yang I-chih. Not really at ease while facing foreigners in those days, Mao at first, said Yang, thought of delegating Chou to brief Snow on the revolutionary situation. But it was upon Chou's insistence that Mao finally decided to do it himself, as Yang recalled in 1957. 'The Premier then told the Chairman that a full account by himself would stamp on it the authority of the leadership which is essential. In spite of his hectic working schedule, the Chairman concurred.' Knowing Mao as he did, Chou naturally would not want to steal the show from him. Even though the former might have indicated his wish to entrust him with the briefing job, it could have been a deliberate gesture designed to test his trustworthiness. In his dealings with Mao, he never ceased to take Mao's suspicious nature into account, always avoiding to outshine him.

It is often blatantly claimed by China's authorized historians that the party united as one under Mao's leadership after the Tsunyi Conference during the Long March, but then they have to sacrifice historical accuracy for political considerations. In fact, at the end of the Long March in Northern Shensi, even Mao's ambition of exerting his control of the army was only partly fulfilled. Apart from the several thousand men who had survived the march which he could count on, he had yet to extend his personal influence into the army units commanded by Hsu Hai-tung and Liu Chih-tan. Both had the advantage of having established themselves in this area first. Down in the south-west along the Sikang-Szechuan border, Chang Kuo-tao still had a military strength of 40,000 strong. Even the Second Front Army under Ho Lung was in better shape after marching along a different route to join up with Chang. Ho had more than 10,000 men with him.

Under these circumstances, Mao would have played up his loyalty to the Comintern by deferring to Wang Ming in Moscow. Since Chang Kuo-tao was constantly in the Comintern's disfavour, he realized that he stood a good chance of being regarded by Moscow as more reliable. Meanwhile, he could not have failed to draw some comfort from the nation-wide anti-civil war sentiment, sparked off by the student movement in Peking on 9 December 1935. For months, the students across the country had been demanding that the Nationalist Government turn its guns against the Japanese aggressors whose footprints had by now covered many parts of North China. And most important of all, there were signs that the efforts in promoting an anti-Japan United Front were beginning to reap their fruits. In the Nationalist camp, the North-eastern Army under Chang Hsueh-liang, the Young Marshal, became restless. Having lost the immense area of Manchuria to Japan in 1931, Chang was more anxious to recover his homeland than carry on the anti-Communist campaign. With his units forming an iron cordon around the Communist base in Northern Shensi, the Young Marshal refrained from applying pressures on Mao's much weakened Red Army. Influenced by some of his advisers with hidden Communist affiliations, he even established secret contacts with Mao and his top comrades in Pao-an. In his headquarters in Sian, the impulsive Chang frequently enjoyed the company of some eminent visitors from Northern Shensi. Unknowingly and unsuspectingly, he played into Mao's hands.

The new development gave Mao the much needed breathing space. With the friendly enemy's units surrounding it, Northern Shensi could not be safer. Systematically and gradually, he reorganized the Red Army. To squeeze Chu Teh out of the game, he moved Peng Teh-huai up in the structure of the military command, enabling himself to divide and rule. Recognizing the effectiveness and the scope of the United Front work, he entrusted it to Chou En-lai who had been steadily gaining his confidence. He sensed then that a war between Japan and China was about to break out very soon, according to what Tung Pi-wu said in Nanking eleven years later. But in 1936, however, most thinking men in China saw the inevitability of the Sino-Japanese War, simply because the Chinese people refused to be enslaved by any foreign aggressor. While Mao was not really a 'revolutionary prophet' as the Chinese Communists made him out to be, he must be given the credit for assessing the national mood fairly accurately.

Nor must it be forgotten that the future for the Chinese Communists looked very bleak in 1936. To rally the party, Mao would have to make optimistic forecasts and bold promises. But there is no doubt that Mao did have the ability to talk very convincingly. He also had the strength to face impossible situations with resourcefulness. Northern Shensi in 1936 might not be an ideal centre of Communist movement, but he had a helping hand stretched out to him from the unlikely direction of Chang Hsueh-liang. As regards the internal conflicts, his marriage of convenience with the International Faction seemed to be paying off. He could expect the Comintern's discreet backing in his struggle with Chang Kuotan. Calculatingly and hopefully, he waited for the tide to turn.

7 THE LAND OF PROMISE

If Japan always harassed Chiang Kai-shek in time to undermine his efforts in wiping out the Chinese Communists, Chang Hsueh-liang was entitled to earn more of Mao Tse-tung's gratitude when he and Yang Hu-cheng staged a military coup to kidnap the Generalissimo in Sian on 12 December 1936. Having become a convert to the Anti-Japanese United Front for some months, Chang intended to force Chiang Kai-shek into halting the civil strife in order to resist Japan as a united nation. Although the Sian incident ended farcically twelve days later with the Young Marshal escorting Chiang back to Nanking, the national capital, by plane, there was no denying that the authority and prestige of the Nationalists' supreme commander had been cruelly dented. As for Mao, the tide turned even sooner than he had expected. When Chang Hsueh-liang first informed him of Chiang's confinement and invited Chou En-lai over to Sian for consultation, the Chinese Communist leader reacted very emotionally. In an urgent meeting with the other Politburo members, he declared his wish to see Chiang summarily put to death by Chang Hsueh-liang and Yang Hu-cheng. It was his violent reaction that set off wild rumours in Pao-an, the then Communist nerve centre. The cadres started telling each other that Chiang would be flown to Pao-an for the 'People's Trial' while a landing strip was being hastily built, in fact, for the Young Marshal's plane to collect Chou En-lai. But Mao's desire to harm Chiang Kai-shek was never conveyed to Chang Hsueh-liang. In the meeting he was opposed by his comrades, notably Chou, who all thought that in the event of a war of resistance against Japan, Chiang would be the man to lead the whole nation. Still, Mao would not have been hushed up if Stalin had not immediately sent his instructions to the

139

Chinese Communist leadership, expecting them to work for the Generalissimo's release. Common sense prevailing, the Russian leader could not imagine a National United Front in China without Chiang. Naturally Mao was exasperated, but he was too realistic to incur the Big Brother's displeasure.

However, he soon had his reward from another direction. Shortly after the Young Marshal's departure with Chiang for Nanking, some units of the North-eastern Army abandoned Yenan, soon to become the Chinese Mecca of Communism, as a favour to the understrength Red Army. At the turn of 1937 Yenan might look just like any one-horse town in American Westerns, dusty and desolate in the midst of some loess hills, but it was far better situated than the remote Pao-an. With the Yen river girdling its walled city on one side, Yenan had another pride in the Pagoda Hill on which the lone pagoda pointed impudently towards the yellow sky. But it was the historical associations of this derelict ancient town that touched off Mao's fancy. In the eleventh century, the famous Sung general, Yang Yen-chao, made his headquarters here to repulse the Tartar invaders from the north, with great success. To inspire the men, Mao kept mentioning the coincidence in his pep talks, as if it were providence. It was very shrewd of him to do so, for General Yang, popularized through the medium of Peking opera, was a legendary name even with the illiterate and ignorant peasants on whose shoulders the future of the party rested.

When Japan's Imperial Army engineered the Marco Polo Bridge Incident near Peking on 7 July 1937 to impose the war on China, Chiang Kai-shek had no alternative but to forge another alliance with the Chinese Communists. By this time, Mao had consolidated his position in the party hierarchy to a further extent. Chang Kuo-tao had led his troops to Northern Shensi to return to the fold of the Central Headquarters, headed by Chang Wen-tien and Mao Tse-tung. The underground work in the Nationalist areas had flourished under the supervision and guidance of Liu Shao-chi, Mao's close associate since the Tsunyi Conference. Earlier in May, at the party congress first held in Yenan, Mao made his political report The Tasks of China's Anti-Japanese National United Front in the Present Period. The theme was developed from Wang Ming's proclamation on the United Front work made in Moscow on 1 August 1936, though Mao, for understandable reasons, claimed the full credit. In the report he explained that to resist Japan, the Chinese Communist Party must cease its hostilities against the Nationalists, for 'internal contradictions' should take a back seat in the intensification of 'external contradictions' between China and Japan. He proposed to rename the Soviet Area as the Special Region of the Republic of China, as a 'component part of the state, applying its democratic system under the new conditions'. He also advocated that the Red Army 'should immediately be reorganized into the National Revolutionary Army', the formal name of the Nationalist forces. In other words, what he meant was that hereafter the party should accept the authority of the Central Government of the Nationalists and place itself under the unified command of Chiang Kai-shek. He even assured his comrades of the 'correctness' for the Chinese Communists to agree with the Three People's Principles of Dr Sun Yat-sen—nationalism, democracy and people's welfare. Except for a few voices of dissent, the report was passed at the congress, more or less confirming Mao's position as a policy-maker. This was quite significant, for at the time the Politburo was still headed by Chang Wen-tien, in his capacity as the party's General Secretary. It was not until sometime later that the chairmanship of the party was created.

In August, the Red Army was formally reorganized as the Eighth Route Army of the National Revolutionary Army, consisting of three divisions with a total strength of 20,000. Chu Teh was its commander, with Peng Teh-huai as his deputy. As agreed between the Nationalists and the Communists, the main force of the Eighth Route Army moved into Northern Shensi to take part in the Anti-Japanese war about one month later. Theoretically speaking, Chu Teh should take orders from General Yen Hsi-shan who, as Commander-in-chief of the Second War Zone, was, in turn, responsible to the National Military Commission headed by Chiang Kai-shek himself. But it was not the case. Despite all the talk about national unification and the sacred war-of-resistance, the Eighth Route Army remained the same old Red Army, continuing to look to Yenan for guidance in both strategic and tactical moves. Having engaged in a prolonged civil war for a whole decade, neither the Nationalists nor the Communists were prepared to bury the hatchet overnight, regardless of Japan's invasion. Suspicions were deeply rooted and mutual distrust thinly veiled.

As far as Mao was concerned, the Sino-Japanese War should in no way retard China's 'progress to socialism'. Before the Eighth Route Army marched off from the Communist base in Northern Shensi, however, he minced no words when he briefed the cadres about their mission. Precisely and lucidly, he told them, according to the veteran Communist and eyewitness Li Fa-ching that 'The Sino-Japanese War offers our party excellent opportunity for further expansion'. He was very frank about what the cadres should aim to achieve. 'The policy we have decided on is a clear-cut one,' he said. 'We should use seventy per cent of our energy on our own expansion, twenty per cent on compromising with the Nationalists and ten per cent on fighting the Japanese. To carry out this policy successfully, we must divide it into three stages. In the first stage, we should compromise with the Nationalists, ostensibly obeying the National Government and supporting the Three People's Principles. But in reality, such a gesture is essential to our existence and expansion. Then comes the stage of competition in which we must build up our political and military strength within two or three years, enabling us to confront the Nationalists on equal terms. The third stage will be the one for launching the offensive. We must then penetrate Central China to establish more revolutionary bases, in order to cut off the links between various units of the Nationalist forces. Once the time is ripe, we shall replace the Nationalists to lead the nation.'

Since Li Fa-ching defected to the Nationalists in 1940, one tends to suspect that he might have deliberately misquoted Mao to please his new masters, which was not altogether impossible. But then, when Chang Hao, a Central Committee member in the Yenan days, gave a talk on the Strategy and Political Line of the Chinese Communist Party at the Red Army College (later renamed the Anti-Japanese Political and Military College) in the same September, the points he made were exactly like Mao's. This was certainly not a mere coincidence.

But while Mao articulately laid out the blueprint of the party's future struggle behind the United Front scenes, he had to handle another internal challenge to his position in the party hierarchy with no little finesse. In the latter part of October, Wang Ming was flown to Yenan from the Soviet Union via Sinkiang by the Comintern in a special plane. Now assuming the name of Chen Shao-yu, the Chinese chief delegate to the Third International did not come back alone. He was accompanied by Chen Yun, Kang Sheng and Tseng Shan, all of whom were not to Mao's liking. Moreover, they also brought with them the equipment for a radio station and some anti-aircraft guns, as if to remind him of Moscow's omnipresence. All of a sudden Yenan was overwhelmed with excitement, especially since no plane had landed in its vicinity before. The impact on Mao must have been considerable, yet he gave nothing away. In the welcoming meeting that very evening, he made a glowing speech full of praise about Wang Ming's past achievements and his present contributions to the party. As a master stroke, he told the gathering that the whole concept of the United Front owed its origin to Wang's famous 'August 1st Statement', urging everyone not to forget it lightly. If Wang Ming had had any doubt about Mao's sincerity, this open acknowledgement would have removed it at one stroke. A vain man, he was inclined to fall

The youthful-looking Mao Tse-tung. This picture was taken in North Shensi in 1936.

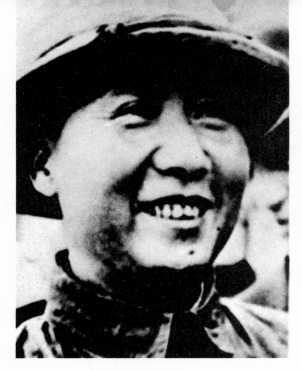

This picture taken by the author is of Mao at the peace talks.

Mao Tse-tung, second from the left flanked by Chou En-lai and American envoy Patrick Hurley, arrives in Chungking in August 1945 for peace talks. With him in this picture is also Chang Chih-chung.

In 1942 while Mao was in Yenan he paid particular attention to his theoretical teaching. These two pictures show him speech-making and instructing the 'Little Red Devils' – fore-runners of the Red Guards.

On V–J Day, 3rd September 1945, Mao toasts Chiang Kai-shek at a celebration dinner in Victory Mansions, Chungking.

Mao speaking at the seventh party congress in Yenan.

Mao Tse-tung and Chou En-lai together in Yenan in 1945.

In 1947 before the sudden evacuation of Yenan under Chiang Kai-shek's bombs of March this charming picture of Chiang Ching and Mao was taken. It shows them in their ninth year of marriage.

The 1st October 1949 was a momentous day for both Mao and China. From this rostrum Mao Tse-tung declared the establishment of the People's Republic of China.

Four years later Mao has become very much the head of state. Here he is seen reviewing a naval unit off Shanghai in 1953.

The pensive, rustic chairman stands amidst the harvest in Hanan just at the time he was planning the Great Leap Forward.

In November 1964 Chou En-lai returned from a visit to Moscow and was met at the airport by Mao.

Mao Tse-tung, Chou
En-lai and Chiang
Ching in informal
mood with a group
of Red Guards in
May 1967.

The official face of
Mao, together with
his signature.

for adulation and flattery, unable to think beyond them.

In the days that followed, Wang Ming busied himself in conveying Moscow's wishes to groups of senior cadres. He told them, in no uncertain terms, that Stalin regarded Mao as the most suitable man to lead the Chinese party. While weak in the field of ideology, Mao had, he said, ample experience in revolutionary struggles. It was up to the Russian-trained comrades, he quoted Stalin, to help Mao improve his knowledge of Marxism and Leninism, enabling him to avoid further errors. Conceivably, Stalin's approval must have put Mao in an unassailable position. After all, none of his rivals had the audacity to voice any dissent. But as for Mao, he certainly never ceased to be grateful to Stalin. This was why he stood firmly against Khruschev when the latter started the process of de-Stalinization in the Soviet Union after Stalin's death. Mao had a long memory. He could not forget what Stalin had done for him at a time when he needed all the help he could get.

To Mao's pleasant surprise Wang Ming picked Chang Wen-tien as his target. He claimed that the Comintern was opposed to Chang's present responsibility as the party's General Secretary, in view of his past connections with the Trotskyites. Although the accusation was not completely unfounded, Wang apparently had his own design. Before he went to Moscow in 1930, he was General Secretary himself. Realizing that Mao now had Stalin's blessing, he was prepared to settle for second best—taking over the General Secretaryship evacuated by Chang. Such a step, he hoped, would enable him to grasp the control of the party, virtually kicking Mao upstairs. Again he committed the error of underestimating Mao's shrewdness. He failed to see that Mao had the support of the army, with Peng Teh-huai and Lin Piao as his two chief lieutenants. Perhaps more unfortunately, his conflict with Chang Wen-tien registered the total collapse of the International Faction. With Chin Pang-hsien and Chang already at each other's throat, he would have fared better if he had set out to resolve their differences and work together with them as a team. In that way, their faction might have been able to regain its previous influence in the party. But by failing to do so, he unknowingly strengthened Mao's hand.

Through Wang Ming the Comintern also expressed its concern over the harsh treatment of Chang Kuo-tao by the Chinese comrades. Wang told his audience that during the Long March Chang had not been the only one at fault, and that for the sake of solidarity, he should be given another chance to prove his usefulness to the revolutionary cause. These words seemed to have their effect, for most of the senior cadres no longer treated the poor man with unconcealed disdain.

Not surprisingly, Mao still saw Wang Ming as a menace even though his own standing in the party had been enhanced by Stalin's approval. It did not take him long to test Wang's strength. In November 1937, shortly after the fall of Shanghai and Taiyuan (the capital of Shansi province), he bitterly attacked the Nationalist Government at the Party's Activists Conference in Yenan. But Wang Ming did not agree with him. At both the Secretariat meeting and another conference, he took Mao to task. Dismissing Mao's outburst as harmful to the National United Front, he advocated the need for the party to continue its support of the Nationalist Government, emphasizing the importance of national unity. While disapproving of the one-party-rule of the Nationalists, he said that it could form the basis of a 'Government of National Defence' to include other political parties. As regards the anti-Japanese war, he saw it as a protracted one, in terms of years instead of months. He criticized Mao for his apparent intention of splitting up the United Front to undermine the joint war efforts, as well as his undue pessimism about the future of the anti-Japanese war. His argument gained the support of the others, and this time Mao had to admit defeat.

But he soon had his revenge. In early December the Politburo met to discuss another reshuffle. Wang Ming formally related the Comintern's instruction regarding the replacement for Chang Wen-tien as General Secretary. Full of confidence, he expected a unanimous vote for himself to take over the post. He was not being presumptuous, for Mao had assured him of his support before the meeting, apparently in all earnestness. What he did not know was that in the past few days Mao had secretly seen the other members of the International Faction, convincing them that the post of General Secretary should be abolished in favour of the collective leadership of the Politburo. Fully aware of the conflicts between Wang Ming and Chin Pang-hsien and Chang Wen-tien, he knew he could drive them further apart. He was merely putting his 'unite and struggle' theory into practice. To struggle with Wang Ming, he united with Chin and Chang, making full use of their resentment against the new arrival from Moscow. The talk of 'collective leadership' was merely a bait, or rather a red herring. He must dangle something inviting in the air to tempt the latter two. At the meeting, however, he could afford to 'sit on the hilltop watching the tigers fight among themselves'. One after another, the Politburo members proposed to abolish the post of General Secretary and the motion was carried.

The victory, however, did not relax Mao's guard against Wang Ming. To prevent the latter from gaining more influence in Yenan, he sent him to Hankow as head of a three-man delegation to the Nationalist Government, the other two being Chou En-lai and Chin Pang-hsien. Naturally, he emphasized the utmost importance of the mission. He was effusive in praising Wang's grasp of the correct party line, his ability in handling the Nationalists, and also his connection with the Comintern. With his ego greatly satisfied, Wang Ming happily accepted the offer. Had he been more alert, he might have been less ready to take Mao's words at their face value. But in fairness to him, Mao was so good at saying things he did not mean that most people would have been trapped. Soft-spoken, full of smiles and tremendously patient, he looked like an honest peasant who had never lied in his whole life. When Tung Pi-wu talked with me about Mao's qualities as a leader, in 1946, he likened him to a world class chess player. 'Comrade Mao has an analytical mind', the future acting President of the State said, 'for he can foresee several moves ahead of his opponent. While on the other hand, his opponent can never tell what his next move will be. Like many great leaders in Chinese history, he is profound in thinking, resolute in taking action and perceptive about the weaknesses of human nature. Exceedingly tolerant, he even smiles when he is annoyed.' Of course, all these words were meant as compliments, but one could not help feeling that the wise old Tung did have some reservations.

That Mao should have sent Chou En-lai and Chin Pang-hsien along with Wang Ming to Hankow indicated his determination to keep all potential contenders for power out of his way. Both Chou and Chin had been over him at one time or another. It was true that the former had become increasingly reliable in his eyes, still he would not want to be too trusting. With the latter he had even more reason to be careful. If not for his conspiracy with Chang Wen-tien, Chin would not have been unsaddled. He only had to put himself in Chin's place to anticipate the worst from him. It was not in his nature to leave anything to chance. Of course there was the possibility that the three of them might gang up together, but then they would be too remote from the seat of power to matter much. Actually, the trick of 'making three horses share the same trough', learned by Mao from his favourite novel *The Water Margin*, seemed to work. For, instead of allying themselves with one another, the three rivals of Mao's went their separate ways in Hankow. Chou determinedly submitted himself to Mao's leadership, always keeping a watchful eye on Wang Ming and Chin Pang-hsien on his behalf. Though miles away in Yenan, Mao was extremely well informed. Wang devoted himself to the strengthening of the precarious Nationalist-Communist alliance, because he placed his faith in the National United Front, after recognizing that the anti-Japanese war could not be carried on without the

Nationalists at the helm. While doing so, he had no idea that Mao was equally busy in planning how to tackle his 'right-wing opportunism' in the not too distant future. Chin appeared to be less rigid than either Chou or Wang. He read and wrote a lot. He often met his Nationalist friends over a cup of coffee or a drink. Someone who saw him frequently in Hankow in that brief period later spoke of him quite favourably, describing him as a man 'in the mode of a radical professor, full of impractical ideas'.

But up north in Yenan, Mao had all the time and energy to afford some personal indulgence. Since the outbreak of the Sino-Japanese War in July 1937, university students and young intellectuals had started to pour into Yenan from Peking, Tientsin, Shanghai, Canton and other big cities. Stirred up by patriotic feelings and revolutionary fervour, these young people, in their thousands, were led to believe that the Chinese Mecca of Communism would be their answer. Having declared themselves as the true warriors against Japan's invasion, the Chinese Communists had to open the door to these pilgrims, especially with a view to recruiting new party members. While the unprecedented development took Yenan by storm, the survivors of the Long March had the greatest surprise of their lives. Among the newcomers were young females of all descriptions—high school girls, university students, nurses and even some entertainers and actresses. Suddenly there was spring in the air. For years, deprived of the pleasure of female company, the senior cadres were quick off the mark. They picked their objects of love and courted with the intensity of a seasoned revolutionary. Before long most of the desirable females found themselves sharing the loess caves with the legendary heroes they had heard about and admired, such as Peng Teh-huai, Lin Piao and a host of others.

Naturally, all these happy events did not escape Mao's notice. With his third wife, Ho Tzu-chen, away in Moscow for medical care, he had been leading the life of a grass widower for quite some time. At the age of forty-four, he was as highly sexed as ever. He often boasted of his virility with some of his close comrades at lighter moments, attributing it to his fondness for chili peppers. He was once quoted by Kuo Mo-jo, later to be President of China's Academy of Sciences after the Communist take-over in 1949, as saying, perhaps jokingly over a few drinks, that the constant diet of chili peppers was essential to the making of a revolutionary and a man. As Kuo was like a court jester to him, it was not unnatural for the Chinese leader to talk more freely to him.

In those days Yenan might suffer an acute food shortage, but like most poor regions in the North-west it produced abundant crops of chili peppers. Whether with or without the aid of them as a stimulant, Mao soon cast his eyes on a shapely female in his lectures at the Institute of Marxist Studies. She was none other than Chiang Ching, more widely known as Lan Ping to the outside world at that time. A not too successful film actress from Shanghai, she had, however, joined the Communist underground in Tsingtao. Still only twenty-three, she was extremely attractive. Sophisticated, articulate and smooth in manners, she struck Mao as someone very special. Compared with the women in his life, she was undoubtedly far more flirtatious, though less revolutionary.

But this obviously did not worry Mao. With Wang Ming and Chin Pang-hsien out of his way, he had won Kang Sheng's allegiance by making him the security chief. He entrusted Kang with the work of checking Chiang Ching's background. Within a matter of days, the latter reported back to Mao's satisfaction. As Chairman of the Central Committee, he immediately secured Chiang Ching as his personal secretary. Working and living in the same loess cave carved into two small chambers, it did not take them long to start sharing the same bed. The new arrangement seemed to work out well initially. Since in Yenan both men and women were supposed to adopt a more 'liberated' attitude towards sex, no eyebrows would be raised over liaisons or cohabitations. Besides, hidden behind the security screen, Mao seldom made public appearances. Except for a few top comrades and his personal guards, he and Chiang Ching were not even seen together. But as neither of them believed in birth control, he soon made her pregnant. Now that she had a hold over him, she demanded formal recognition as his 'lover' (wife). This put Mao on the spot. While life without her would become intolerable, he, as a party member, had to seek the Central Committee's approval before he could form a marital tie with her. The situation was made doubly difficult because he and Ho Tzu-chen were still 'lovers' (man and wife) as far as the others were concerned. One of the very few women who had gone through the Long March, Ho had the affection and sympathy of many comrades on her side. Her being away in Moscow did not alter this fact.

When it became clear that Chiang Ching would not settle for less, Mao had to resort to his resourcefulness. He presented his case to the Central Committee, claiming that Ho Tzu-chen's 'mental derangement' had forced him to abandon her for Chiang Ching. Then he requested the committee's permission for him to normalize his new relationship. To his surprise most members of the committee present were against his union with the actress from Shanghai. While some questioned her political credentials, others spoke up on Ho Tzu-chen's behalf. Liu Shao-chi was one of those who pointed out that Chiang Ching must have her own political ambition at heart to trap Mao into agreeing to marry her. Of course the accusation contained a grain of truth. But as his words eventually reached Chiang Ching's ears, she bore a grudge against him for many more years to come, until the Cultural Revolution in the 1960s gave her the chance to have her revenge.

At the Central Committee meeting in Yenan, however, Mao and his colleagues reached some form of compromise about his marital problem. Although he was allowed to marry Chiang Ching, it was decided that she must not seek political advancement in the party through him or his influence. As for Ho Tzu-chen, she would still be accorded all privileges in her own right, disregarding her separation from Mao. Whether he accepted these terms wholeheartedly is hard to tell, but the fact that Chiang Ching stayed out of the political scene until 1963 must be seen as his effort to keep his promise. But at the time, it would seem that his main concern was to have Chiang Ching constantly at his side, especially since she was carrying his child. Despite everything, his attitude towards women was not much different from that of his contemporaries. To him, Chiang Ching was a woman comrade whose contribution to the revolution could be made by giving him a happy and contented personal life. On the other hand, his male ego forbade him to think that she was more interested in his position than his manhood. Even with his reputed perceptiveness, he was still a middle-aged man dealing with a much younger woman who had had ample experience in amorous affairs. There was no way for him to see through her, even if he had set out to do so.

Anyway, life with Chiang Ching seemed to be a happy one. He no longer relied on his orderlies to look after him. Nor did he continue to work at all hours as before. Perhaps in view of the impending increase in the family, they moved to larger living quarters in the Orchard of Dates. It was still a loess cave, but with more rooms and a small vegetable garden in the front. The orchard used to belong to a landlord, and there was even a grey brick bungalow—a rare sight in that part of China—at the far end. For a variety of reasons, Mao chose to live in the newly-carved-out cave instead of the bungalow. Cool in summer and warm in winter, the cave was, in fact, an ideal dwelling in the North-west. Invisible from above, it was a natural air-raid shelter in the event of the sudden descent of Japanese bombers. But most important of all, he did not want to live differently from the other leaders who all had to settle for the caves. Anxious to achieve popularity, he had no intention of creating an unnecessarily unfavourable image.

To set himself up as a model for the food production drive, Mao from time to time would be seen bending over the tomato and potato plots in his vegetable garden, with Chiang Ching at his side carrying a watering can. But more often than not, the orderlies would take over the real work, insisting that the Chairman had to conserve his energy to handle the more important tasks of the revolution. Mao would tell them that he must do his share of physical labour like any other, before he was eventually persuaded to stop. The interesting thing was, his tomatoes and potatoes never ripened, though they were very much in the news. In Yenan, it soon became everyone's knowledge that the Chairman grew his own food, yet no one ever saw any of the produce.

Although Mao seldom saw other comrades in the Orchard of Dates, Kang Sheng was the exception. It seemed that the security chief was constantly there, almost like a fixture. Regardless of his past associations with Wang Ming and the International Faction, he became Mao's most trusted lieutenant. A native of Shantung like Chiang Ching, he must have seen something in Mao to desert the Comintern. While on Mao's part, he found in Kang Sheng as much a reliable henchman as a delightful companion. Though in many ways a more accomplished Chinese classical scholar than Mao himself, Kang deliberately played down his knowledge. Nor would he venture to be remotely assertive in the field of political ideology. As Mao saw it, he was the only Russian-trained comrade who remained Chinese in thinking and reasoning, according to Tung Pi-wu. This could be one of the reasons why Mao often asked Kang to read over his important statements before they were made public. On his suggestion, the Chairman would make some alterations or insertions, no matter how begrudgingly. But more important perhaps, Mao even asked him to polish up some of his poems. Although Kang was too discreet to admit it, Mao did, once or twice, refer to him, half-jokingly, as his 'one-word-teacher'—a Chinese allusion to someone who is good at polishing another person's writing. Since Mao was never known for his modesty, such an acknowledgement indicated his appreciation of Kang's discretion and self-effacement.

Undoubtedly, these endearing qualities of Kang's prompted Mao to entrust him with the massive task of screening the party cadres, with particular emphasis on the new arrivals from the Nationalist areas. The sudden emergence of Yenan on the national scene was of course a propaganda victory for the Communists, especially as it would give them the recognition they had been striving for. But the stream of new converts from all over China brought with it a very real threat. Mao had to guard against the infiltration of Nationalist agents and subversive elements. As an effective measure, he relied on Kang Sheng to train security workers and counter-espionage agents. A special training class was formed in the Orchard of Dates, with Kang as the director. Veiled in utmost secrecy, the class recruited its cadets very selectively. Before they were individually screened by Kang himself, with Mao in the background, they must be able to prove their unwavering loyalty and aptitude for the work. The course only lasted a few months, but it was a very demanding one. While Kang took care of the technical side of the training, Mao was responsible for political indoctrination. Between 1938 and 1942, the training class continued its function regularly, though most people in Yenan did not know a single thing about it. Since Mao did then declare that the party needed four to eight thousand dedicated workers for its security, those who had completed the training course in the Orchard of Dates must be a sizable number. The significant point was, having consolidated his influence in the army, Mao now could claim the loyal support of the newly-reshaped security service.

But meanwhile, he spared no less effort in mapping out the political line for the party to pursue. In the absence of Wang Ming and Chin Pang-hsien, he knew he must establish his authority as the party's foremost thinker and planner once and for all. Benefiting from the bitter experiences in the past, he realized the vital importance of such a step. Painstakingly and doggedly, he would spend many a sleepless night drafting his lectures or speeches, often forgetting to eat his meals. His serious writings in this period such as 'On Practice' and 'On Contradictions' were all first delivered as lectures at the Anti-Japanese Political and Military College, before they were circulated in the form of pamphlets for a wider audience. The way he wrote the article 'On New Democracy' fully indicated his appetite for hard work, judging by his bodyguard, Ho Ching-hua's recollections. For several days Mao did not have a wink of sleep, Ho vividly remembered, when he was in the process of writing that famous article. The bodyguard found him so absorbed in his writing that he could not tear himself away from the desk in a corner of the cave. Morning after morning, and night after night, he laboured away by the flickering oil lamp, completely oblivious to things around him. The faithful Ho brought him his meals at regular intervals as usual, but the food was hardly touched. Worried, he kept urging the Chairman to have a little rest. But Mao merely waved him away. Even Chiang Ching, whom Ho referred to as the 'secretary', did not succeed in persuading him to have a break. When this went on for a few more days, however, they had, according to the bodyguard, to take away the oil lamp and drag Mao to the *kang* (earthen bed), forcing him to sleep.

That Mao should have concentrated his energy on writing this particular piece was no surprise, for his theory on New Democracy later became the keynote of his United Front policy, instrumental to the ultimate victory of the Communist movement in China. To strive for broader popular support, he advocated the need for a coalition government, tactfully concealing the real political aim of his party. To confuse the people, he claimed to accept Dr Sun Yat-sen's Three People's Principles as the guideline for the new republic in his vision. He even coined the term 'national bourgeoisie' to pacify the fears of China's capitalists, giving them the impression that they would have their place in his type of 'democratic republic'. And, with a view to the rapid expansion of the Communist areas behind the Japanese lines, he deliberately ceased confiscating the land from landlords, as if the class struggle were no longer in existence. Nor did he hesitate to confer the title of 'enlightened landlord' on those landowners who chose to support New Democracy. It was, therefore, no coincidence that a number of political observers should have, at the time, gleefully lauded the Chinese Communists as 'agrarian reformers'. And for obvious reasons, Mao and his comrades did not bother to dispel such an illusion.

Apart from making his pronouncements and conferring with the other Communist leaders, Mao had another worry on his mind. With more and more intellectuals appearing on the Yenan scene, the image of China's Mecca began to tarnish a little. In spite of their pro-Communist sympathy, they emerged as the new critics of the hierarchy. With the aid of their waspish tongues and fluent pens, they criticized the bureaucratic practices, the inadequate ration system, the ignorance and incompetence of senior cadres and even the privileges enjoyed by the leaders. They also had harsh words for those women comrades who married important figures for the sake of prestige and comfort, questioning their motives in joining the revolution.

In a small town like Yenan, word got around quickly and these criticisms soon made their impact. The tide of resentment and discontent swept over hamlets and loess caves, gaining in volume. Fully aware of the possible consequences, Mao tried to intervene. He made a few speeches, in which he refuted these criticisms as vicious gossip circulated by irresponsible 'liberals' with their own design. In defence of the leaders, he pointed out that the concept of 'absolute egalitarianism' was entirely wrong. But despite his efforts, the tide showed no sign of receding.

Realizing the serious implications of such a situation, Mao decided that the most effective counter-measure would be the stepping up of political indoctrination. To achieve this end, he found it imperative to organize a massive campaign throughout the Communist areas, with Yenan as the focus. In February 1942, he launched the Rectification Campaign, known in Chinese as *Chen Feng*, in his speech to the Party School in Yenan. No one in the audience had the slightest inkling that the campaign was to last for more than three years, involving the loss of several thousand lives and leading to Mao's complete control of the party machine. Loosely named as a campaign to rectify the work style of the rank and file, it was, in fact, a purge of the severest kind, setting the pattern of thought control in China for many decades to come. In the campaign everyone was forced to reveal his family background, social contacts and every detail in his past life; he must also inform against his friends and relations, if only to prove his loyalty to the party. With Kang Sheng's assistance, Mao was able to draw some experience from the Russians and add to it some Chinese subtlety.

But as the campaign went on, Mao's real motive became crystal clear. After Chang Kuo-tao's desertion in 1938, the remaining thorn in his side was Wang Ming who, in a way, had become a national figure through his contribution to the United Front. In both Hankow and Chungking, as the chief spokesman of the Communist Party, he stole the show from Mao almost completely. Different from the latter, he regarded joint war efforts against Japan as the party's primary concern. As Mao saw it, this amounted to the betrayal of class struggle and 'capitulation to the bourgeoisie leadership' in the war of resistance. But what worried him more was that, should Wang Ming's ideas gain more support in the party, his own authority would be undermined. Having just reached the top rung of the ladder of power, he was not going to climb down. Previously, he sent Wang Ming away from Yenan to forestall his attempt to build up his influence. Now, he had to bring him back to Yenan to clip his wings. Since the rectification campaign requested the participation of all party members, he knew for sure that Wang Ming would not hesitate to come.

It must be admitted that for Mao the campaign was a complete success. With every step meticulously planned, he cast his net far and wide. Starting with the rank and file, he made them undergo the process of thought remoulding, gradually and systematically. When his rivals eventually realized what he was doing, it was already too late for them to extract themselves from the impossible situation. Of the International Faction, Chang Wen-tien was the first one to surrender. He accepted the responsibility for his past errors, and praised Mao's 'correct' leadership. Chin Pang-hsien was less forthcoming. But under the constant pressure of orchestrated criticisms, he had to give in. Chou En-lai was criticized, though he got off rather lightly.

Having subdued all the possible contenders, Mao turned to his main target, Wang Ming. He accused him of having abandoned the orthodox party line of promoting the class struggle at all costs, condemned his acceptance of Chiang Kai-shek's leadership in the anti-Japanese war as a form of 'capitulationism' and demanded his self-denunciation. Leaving no stone unturned, he quoted Wang Ming's past writings and statements at length, before he refuted them point by point. Ostensibly, he made all his verbal attacks along the ideological line, as if he merely wanted to save his rival's soul. But to everyone present, it was obvious that he meant to destroy Wang Ming completely, eliminating whatever chance the latter might have for a come-back. As usual, he was at his most articulate, despite his heavy Hunanese accent, when he set out to tear his opponent to pieces.

But in Wang Ming he found his toughest opponent. The protégé of the Comintern refused to yield an inch. Good at semantics and familiar with dialectics, he counter-attacked with equal eloquence. Dismissing Mao's charges as sheer fabrications, he reiterated his stand in the National United Front, citing Moscow's instructions to back himself up. For hours he went on arguing, with all intent to turn the tables on Mao. What he did not realize was that Mao had already outmanoeuvred him before the meeting took place. In the Politburo and the Secretariat, Mao had secured the support of everyone else, virtually isolating him at the top of the party machine. Even though some people might find Wang Ming's argument convincing and relevant, they were not in a position to tip the balance in his favour.

Still, Wang Ming was undaunted. No matter how Mao mobilized the other comrades to criticize, persuade and cajole him, he would not come round. But since he could not leave Yenan without the Politburo's approval, Mao decided to wear him down with other methods. He put the unrepentant Wang under house arrest in a remote loess cave, denying him any form of contact with other people. Except for his wife, Wang Ming was in the constant company of two secret agents detailed by Kang Sheng. Obviously, with the Comintern representative, Vladimirov, and a few Russian radio operators in town, Mao had to keep Wang Ming from them at a safe distance. Although he had given up hope of obtaining any substantial support from the Soviet Union since the German invasion of the Russian soil, the Chairman did not want to risk his superficial harmony with Big Brother yet. In private, he was often heard commenting on the desperate situation of the Soviet Red Army with a sprinkle of sarcastic remarks; but in public, he continued to expound the theme that the defence of Moscow meant to defend world peace. His loss

153

of faith in the Soviet victory could have influenced him to advance his plan to get rid of Wang Ming, as Tung Pi-wu later hinted to me in Nanking during the Nationalist-Communist peace negotiations. 'The outcome of the Leningrad campaign was a pleasant surprise for all of us', he said. 'It re-established Moscow's indisputable leadership in the socialist world. Before then, the Communist movement had more or less drifted along without the benefit of Moscow's guidance.' Of course Tung did not particularly refer to the Chinese Communist Party, but behind these vague words, one could sense that Mao would not have ventured to sort out Wang Ming if he had had to look to Moscow for guidance.

With Wang Ming languishing away in confinement, Mao involved himself in another aspect of the Rectification Campaign, the extension of thought control. Fully realizing that the intellectuals would be his primary hurdles, he took the battle to them. In a well-organized conference of writers and artists, he gave a lengthy talk on the 'correct path of development' for the revolutionary literature and art, stressing the urgent need for writers and artists to take 'the class stand, the stand of the proletariat and the masses'. It was in this talk that he laid down the principle that all forms of creative art must aim at 'serving the workers, peasants and soldiers'. In other words, writers and artists were forced to abandon all artistic considerations about their subject matter. They should only write or paint from the Marxist angle, setting out to glorify the revolutionary masses and denounce the class enemies. Human nature was completely disregarded, and the criterion of good and evil was to be class-oriented. Capitalists must be villians while heroes must only come from among the workers, peasants and soldiers.

Needless to say, these ideas of Mao's did not go down too well with many in the audience at first. Since this was not totally unexpected, the Chairman allowed them to state their views in the debate sessions which were dominated by his hand-picked speakers. When it came to the end, the dissenting voices were naturally subdued and silenced by the majority through the 'frank and democratic' discussions. After all, in Yenan Mao ruled.

It seemed that Mao really enjoyed his elevated status throughout the Rectification Campaign. While numerous cadres were being grilled and investigated from 1942 onward, he left the unpleasant decisions regarding executions and labour reforms in the capable hands of his henchman, Kang Sheng. In those days in Yenan, the mere mention of Kang's name, according to a classmate of mine who had spent three years there, was enough to send a chill down anyone's spine. But then not many people in the Communist nerve centre had the privilege of coming close to Mao. The Orchard of Dates was Yenan's Forbidden City, although it was only a couple of miles away from the town centre. Whenever the Chairman made a public appearance, which was rare, he was driven about in an ambulance donated by the Chinese residents in Singapore. Not that he was unwell, but the ambulance happened to be the newest motor transport they had. Besides, with the sign of the Red Cross distinctly painted on the top, it might have some protective value in the event of a Japanese bombing raid. If anyone felt strange about the association between the ambulance and the Chinese Communist leader, he had the good sense to make no comment. As for the hospitals, they could rely on the animal power of horses and mules, which were perhaps more economical.

Undeniably Mao had the rare gift of understanding the psychology of the ordinary people. He deliberately created the image of an inaccessible ruler for it was, he thought, the surest way to command popular support. For centuries, China has been governed by monarchs from the remoteness of the Imperial capital. Authority and power meant something mysterious and unpredictable. To the vast majority, their ruler must not be often seen in the flesh. They preferred to have him living in their imagination. This was particularly true with the populace of Yenan, mainly consisting of ignorant peasants who were like a flock of sheep. Apparently, Mao knew exactly what they would expect of him. He had to keep them at a distance, otherwise the mystery of authority and power would lose its appeal. He wanted his presence to be felt, intangible and yet imposing. Fully aware that familiarity breeds contempt, he chose to keep his private life within the confines of the Orchard of Dates. He liked to maintain the posture of a god-king, though clad in a Marxist robe. And in the name of security, he was able to conceal everything from the public.

Although Yenan might be only a town of 30,000, many people did not even know of the real relationship between Mao and Chiang Ching. The Chairman never talked about himself as a person, let alone the woman in his bed. As far as he was concerned, everything had to revolve around the cause of national liberation, and the rest was irrelevant. But this did not mean that he neglected his conjugal duties, for within three years he fathered two daughters by Chiang Ching at the height of the Rectification Campaign.

Knowing that the respect for age meant much in Chinese custom, Mao made good use of it. Once in a while, he would invite the elderly peasants to meet him in the Orchard of Dates, often in the form of a garden party. He chatted with them amicably, showing much concern about production and harvests. His dialect might sound strange to the natives, but his smiles were there for them all to see. For refreshment peanuts and dried persimmons were always in abundance, as well as endless mugs of tea and plenty of cigarettes. On these occasions Kang Sheng was close in attendance, hovering about like a shadow. Sometimes Mao would include Wu Yu-chang and Lin Tsu-han, the two old men of the party, showing his own respect for age. Such a gesture impressed the peasants greatly, for they saw it as a traditional virtue. In view of the conservatism of his guests, the Chairman never allowed Chiang Ching to appear. He understood that the old peasants had little regard for women and was unwilling to risk their disapproval. To the old-fashioned people, the intimate side of the ruler's life must not be known.

Even when he was by himself, Mao seemed intent on maintaining a facade. For according to accounts by several of his personal guards in this period, he emerged as someone who knew nothing but work. Without exception, they all remembered how he had stayed up night after night to ponder one important issue, write a historic statement or worry about a poor harvest, as if he shouldered the burdens of the whole world. To them he appeared to be void of emotions or personal desires, and as inscrutable as the ways of Heaven. Simple as these guards were, they naturally worshipped him and held him in awe. When their words spread around, Mao's image as a selfless revolutionary leader was greatly enhanced. But noticeably, none of these accounts even hinted at the existence of Chiang Ching. Nor was Mao's minor vice of chain-smoking vaguely mentioned. And yet in fact, the transport convoy from Chungking never failed to bring to Yenan, among other provisions, hundreds of tins of English cigarettes (State Express 555) in each overland journey, certainly not for popular consumption.

But apart from the luxury of smoking good cigarettes, Mao did not live any better than the rank and file. He made a point of sharing with his men the hardships that came their way, knowing that it was vital to morale. His office in the loess cave was spartanly furnished. Other than a coarse desk and two old straight-backed chairs, he had only a reclining chair to stretch himself out on after long hours of work. He ate very simply, his daily meal generally consisting of bowls of rice and a couple of vegetable dishes, always cooked with plenty of chili peppers. Once in a while, he might have eggs or a little meat, which were often presents from the visiting peasants. Still, he would share them with his personal guards, never forgetting to tell them that he really cared little for special treats when the poor people had nothing at all to eat. Apparently, this was one of his ways to imbue them with the rudiments of class consciousness.

It must be admitted that he did win the hearts of the Yenan peasants to some extent, for they genuinely felt drawn to him because of his endless displays of care and concern. Mass rallies and propaganda talks might be boring, but they were at least tolerable when compared with the peasants' previous experiences of living under the local warlords. To demonstrate their admiration for Mao, one of the peasants allegedly wrote the song 'The East Is Red' at this time, likening the Chairman to the sun and calling him 'the great saviour from the east'. It became an overnight success and soon was on everyone's lips in Yenan and beyond. Simple and easy to sing, it marked the beginning of the cult of Mao. Seen as the spontaneous expression of the peasantry's allegiance to the Communist Party, personified by Mao, the song was lauded as a musical masterpiece representative of the 'liberated genius of the masses'. If Mao always dis-approved of any form of personality cult, as many Chinese historians have claimed, he certainly made no attempt to stop the singing of 'The East Is Red' with religious fervour on every possible occasion.

Mao's total disregard for material comfort was another talking point in those days. With the anti-Japanese war dragging on and the Nationalist leaders living rather well, his patched coats and home-made slippers became a symbol of political virtue, especially since most people barely had the means of subsistence. But it was equally true that Mao sometimes overdid it. When his quilted jacket became soiled and beyond repair, his guards got together to have a new one made for him, putting it by his bed during his sleep. But to their amazement, as one of them later recalled, they found him a very angry man the following morning. No matter how they pleaded with him, the Chairman was adamant that the new jacket must be put away. He insisted on having his old one back, telling them not to treat him differently in spite of his position. It was not until the guards did as he asked that he was his smiling self again. Of course they could not understand that Mao considered his political image far more precious than a new warm jacket.

When the Comintern was dissolved in 1943, Mao greeted the news in Yenan with unconcealed delight. At long last, he did not have to pay lip service to the international organization on his back. More important perhaps, he could apply more pressure on Wang Ming without worrying about the consequences of Moscow's intervention. He started sending some senior comrades to see Wang in confinement, with the mission of persuading the latter to 'confess' his errors. But to his consternation, the intrepid captive showed no sign of repentance. Unfortunately, in spite of his moral courage, Wang Ming became seriously ill. Not entirely by coincidence, the doctor sent by Mao made the wrong diagnosis and prescribed the wrong medicine. As the patient's condition kept deteriorating, his wife approached Vladimirov, the Comintern agent, for help. It took the Russian a lot of time and effort to convince Mao that Wang Ming must be seen by the Soviet doctor in Yenan. If what Vladimirov recorded in his diaries was anything to go by, the Chinese doctor was suspected of having administered a slow poison on Wang Ming. However, probably realizing that his life was at risk, Wang finally admitted defeat. Although his self-criticism was half-hearted, it served Mao's purpose. Having extracted it from Wang Ming, the Chairman was able to declare his victory over the 'erroneous line of capitulationism' towards the Nationalists, or the 'Wang Ming line'.

But Mao's big day in Yenan did not come until the convening of the Seventh Party Congress in April 1945. By then he had firmly established himself as the indisputable leader of the party. Although he had not moved a step beyond the vicinity of the ancient town since 1937, he now could boast a military strength of 860,000, spreading behind the Japanese lines in North China and elsewhere. As 'power grows out of the barrel of a gun', he took full credit for the rapid expansion of the Communist forces, for it was he who had all along insisted on such a policy, putting himself in an unchallengeable position. He also had the foresight to cultivate Liu Shao-chi and Chou En-lai as his two chief lieutenants. While Liu helped him to consolidate his control of the party through the Rectification Campaign by reorganizing the party machine in the most thorough manner, Chou assumed the role of the executor of his United Front policy, as well as his chief spokesman to the outside world. Not usually generous at giving credit to people under him, Mao did, however, praise both of them for their 'contribution to the party' at the Yenan congress. In his eyes, Liu's greatest contribution must be the drafting of a new Party constitution in which the 'Thoughts of Mao Tse-tung' were stipulated as the 'banner' of the Chinese Communist Party, ranking him among Marx, Lenin and Stalin. Chou was invaluable in his capable handling of the intricate external relations of the party, outmanoeuvring the Nationalists, winning over the liberals and intellectuals in the Nationalist area and influencing the Western journalists in China to write favourably about the Chinese Communists.

Talking about the Yenan days with me in Peking in 1957, Yang I-chih was effusive in praising Mao's enlightened leadership. 'One of his qualities', the academician mused, 'was to employ the right people for the right jobs, to the best of their ability. In those days, nobody could have reorganized the party from top to bottom as Liu Shao-chi did, nor was there anyone remotely comparable to Chou En-lai in handling external relations. Without either of them, it would have taken us longer to liberate the whole country.' Almost as an afterthought, he added, 'Yenan was a lucky place for the party and the Chairman. It was the land of promise.'

8 THE DECISIVE CIVIL WAR

When the all-out civil war swept over China in 1947 after the complete breakdown of the Nationalist-Communist peace negotiations, Mao had already manoeuvred himself into an impregnable position. His policy of establishing Communist political and military bases behind the Japanese lines in the past years proved to be the decisive factor. It enabled the Communist forces to control vast rural areas whereas the Nationalists could only hold towns and communication lines such as highways and railroads. Mao had not the slightest doubt that the overall situation was in his favour. Speaking at a strategic conference in Yenan that spring, he was emphatic in expressing his conviction in the 'ultimate victory of the Liberation War'. To illuminate the military commanders and senior cadres, he analysed the situation in geometrical terms. He likened the rural areas to the 'plane', and the towns and communication lines to the 'points' and 'lines'. In his usually lucid words he told them that by controlling the plane (rural areas), they would have no trouble in isolating the points (towns) and cutting off the lines (highways and railroads), with the Nationalist troops at their mercy. He also said that the countryside was like the ocean while the towns were no different from some small islands, stressing the vulnerable position of the enemy. Simplistic though these expressions might sound, he was proved to be right as the whole picture began to unfold.

It was beyond any doubt that Mao was well prepared for this particular war. Even when he accepted the US mediation in the peace negotiations in 1945, the Communist forces continued to speed up their expansion scheme in the areas evacuated by the Japanese occupation army after its surrender. As Yang I-chih later, in 1957, commented on Mao's attitude towards the peace negotiations with the Nationalists, it seemed that the Chinese Communist leader never really put any faith in forming a coalition government with the Nationalist Party at any time. 'It was clear to Chairman Mao,' Yang said, 'that the peace negotiations were an integral part of our revolutionary struggle. If we could get what the Chinese people wanted at the negotiation table, that would be fine. But what could not be achieved through negotiations could always be obtained from the battlefield. This was in accordance with the Chairman's theory of 'Unite and struggle'. To negotiate was to unite and to fight was to struggle. The important point was, to unite and to struggle, under those circumstances, were complementary to each other. On the other hand, one must not forget that the peace negotiations, as far as we were concerned, were the revolutionary struggle brought to the conference table.'

With equal frankness Yang observed that at the time Mao had to show good faith in the Americans because the nation wanted peace. 'Although the Americans were bound to conspire with the Kuomingtang reactionaries,' he said, 'our leadership did not think it wise to reject the remotest chance of achieving peace. It would have been extremely harmful to our cause had we been held responsible for starting the civil war. Chairman Mao wanted the Chinese people to see how the Nationalists and the Americans had been colluding together to force an unacceptable peace on them. Otherwise, he would not have agreed to the intervention of any foreign power.'

His words, however, threw some light on Mao's decision to fly to Chungking in August 1945 after Japan's surrender. To demonstrate his sincere wishes for peace, he came to the wartime capital to see Chiang Kai-shek upon the American Special Envoy, Patrick Hurley's guarantee of his personal safety. But in fact, he had not made up his mind lightly. After discussing Hurley's suggestion with his top comrades carefully, he summoned Chou En-lai back from Chungking for consultation. Meanwhile, he also obtained a personal guarantee from Chang Chih-chung, one of the Nationalist negotiators who was then very close to Chiang Kai-shek. Chang even offered, as he later revealed in Nanking in the spring of 1949, to put him up in his own Chungking residence to ensure the Chinese Communist leader's safety throughout his brief stay. Judging by his suspicious nature, Mao would have been so cautious.

But once he was in Chungking, he put on an impeccable performance. Well briefed by Chou En-lai, he turned the whole trip into a publicity stunt. He had a couple of his old poems published in the *New China Daily News*, the party's mouthpiece in Chungking, winning himself the instant reputation of a classical poet. He received a stream of young liberals and writers, in between his sessions with the Nationalist leaders and the Americans. All he talked about was peace and democracy, articulately and enthusiastically, without giving away what he really had in mind. And he even excelled himself when he appeared at the V-J Day Celebration. (3 September 1945) in the Victory Mansions shortly after his arrival. Before the staring eyes of several hundred guests, he toasted Chiang Kai-shek wishing him every success in leading the post-war reconstruction of China. Not only that, when Chiang was cheered by the guests, he dramatically threw his arm in the air shouting 'Long Live the Generalissimo' at the top of his voice, loud and clear.

With all eyes fixed on him most of the time, his demonstration of good will created a great sensation. The assembly hall buzzed with excitement, for everyone present saw this gesture as Mao's spontaneous expression in accepting Chiang Kai-shek as the national leader. Even the hard-liners within the Kuomintang hierarchy were lost for words. They found it difficult to convince the others that Mao had no desire for peace. If one tended to read too much into Mao's raising of his arm on such an occasion, it was because of the anti-war feelings of the Chinese people as a whole. Having suffered immeasurably from the protracted war against Japan for eight years, they could not brace themselves to face the renewed hostilities between the Nationalists and the Communists. With the national mood high in his consideration, Mao would do anything to impress the public with his peace efforts. Like an actor, he used the wartime capital as the stage to reach a wider audience to his advantage.

But while he was posing as a peace-seeker in the glaring publicity of Chungking, he had the secret satisfaction that his expansion plan for the Communist bases had been carried out uninterruptedly behind the backs of the American mediators. To extend the Communist influence into the North-eastern Provinces (Manchuria), he had already quietly dispatched Kao Kang and Lin Piao to organize the Democratic United Army in that immense area. He instructed them to absorb both the resistance units and the Manchurian forces which had previously collaborated with the Japanese occupation army without any discrimination. For the sake of expediency, he chose to overlook the ignominious past of these collaborators so that his Democratic United Army could rapidly snowball into a sizable force. Equipped with the Japanese arms clandestinely passed on by the Soviet Red Army then occupying the leading cities in Manchuria, the Democratic United Army under Kao Kang and Lin Piao soon entrenched itself in the vast countryside of Manchuria, long before the

Nationalists were airlifted by the Americans to that part of China for the takeover.

Strategically speaking, this must be seen as Mao's brilliant move. With North China, except for the cities and communications lines, virtually under the control of the Communist guerrilla units, he regarded the occupation of Manchuria as a necessary step to consolidate the revolutionary rear, probably because of its adjacency to Siberia. Before he sent Kao Kang and Lin Piao into Manchuria, he analysed the situation to the Politburo in Yenan in a most convincing manner. Dismissing the chance of achieving a peaceful settlement with the Nationalists as extremely remote, he emphasized the vital importance of securing a vast territory to be 'the base of all bases in the Liberation War', according to a usually reliable source. In Mao's opinion, the source claimed, since the people in Manchuria had lived under Japanese occupation for fifteen years, they would be only too ready to return to Chinese rule, be it a Nationalist or Communist one. Having never come under the direct control of the Nationalist Government, they could be, he pointed out, easily educated to support the National United Front and New Democracy. He also hinted that the complicated international situation immediately after the Second World War would enable him to obtain some substantial aid from the Russians without causing any alarm. Full of optimism, he assured his colleagues that Manchuria in the party's possession could decide the future of China. Although he mentioned nothing about an understanding with the Soviet Union, the signs were all there. For one thing, Kao Kang and Lin Piao would not have been able to move so rapidly into Manchuria if the Russian troops there did not deliberately block the Nationalists' attempts to take over some strategic points.

In retrospect, one could see Mao's sound judgement regarding the importance of Manchuria in the outcome of the civil war. But his decision to carry on the peace negotiations with the Nationalists were equally significant. He saw very clearly, as the Chinese academician Yang I-chih told me in Peking in 1957, that the prolonged peace talks would sharpen the internal conflicts of the Kuomintang which was far from united about the prospects of a peaceful solution. Meanwhile, he predicted that the Americans were bound to lose their patience when the talks failed to yield quick results. 'Chairman Mao was of the opinion that while the Americans had their pre-conceived idea about the realization of peace in China', said Yang, 'they lacked the stamina to see it through. Since the Kuomintang reactionaries heavily relied on the Americans for everything, they had to try to please their benefactors before other considerations. As a result, the peace negotiations tended to exert more pressures on the Nationalists than on us.' What the academician omitted to say was that Mao really used the peace talks as an invisible weapon to create dissensions within the Kuomintang and to test the will of the American mediators. Perhaps it should be pointed out that whereas the people in the Nationalist areas fervently talked about the prospects for peace, the topic for discussion in the Communist areas was the liberation of the whole country. In other words, Mao saw that the hope for peace would not be encouraged in the areas under his control. As far as he was concerned, the strife for national liberation must take precedence over peace, and he wanted to prepare the people in the Communist areas for it.

It seemed that Mao's brief visit to Chungking, as he had hoped, did bring about some tension within the ruling Kuomintang. While its liberal wing spoke loudly about the desirability of achieving national unification through a peaceful settlement with the Communists, the conservatives were no less articulate in voicing their anti-Communist arguments. This not only split the party, but also put Chiang Kai-shek in an awkward position. And, perhaps more importantly, it gave people the impression that the Nationalists were not for peace. But as for Mao and his top comrades, they did not hesitate to accuse Chiang of attempting to undermine the peace negotiations by condoning the anti-Communist elements in his party. Actually, this was not the case. If Chiang had any fault in 1945, it was his implicit trust in the American role as the impartial mediator. He believed that a peaceful solution could be reached with a little bit of give and take. Unlike Mao, he really had no control of the opinions expressed by the Kuomintang members, especially as he was in the course of relaxing some restrictions on the freedom of speech after the war. Nor must it be forgotten that he did promise to introduce more democratic measures at the time.

Ironically, Mao would have found himself detained in Chungking throughout the duration of the peace negotiations if Chiang Kai-shek had listened to some of his advisers. Commenting on the failure of the peace negotiations in Nanking in 1949, General Yen Hsi-shan, the then Nationalist premier, revealed a most interesting episode about Mao's possible fate in Chungking. Shortly after his arrival, according to Yen, some advice was put to Chiang that he should keep the Chinese Communist leader as an 'honoured guest' in Chungking indefinitely, for such a step would speed up the peace negotiations. But Chiang rejected the idea straight away, Yen said with some regret. 'In dealing with Mao Tse-tung', he went on, 'one must not be too scrupulous. I'm sure the situation would have been completely different had President Chiang accepted that piece of sound advice. Even the Americans could not have complained, since it was the most effective way to ensure the realization of peace. After all, why should we worry about the American reaction?'

In fact, Mao faced no danger throughout his stay in Chungking. He knew that Chiang Kai-shek would not resort to any political tricks for a variety of reasons. To begin with, Chiang had his own reputation to consider. As the national leader, he could not afford to risk his credibility with the nation as a whole, in spite of the obvious advantage of holding Mao as a hostage for peace. Besides, he would not want to embarrass the American Special Envoy, Patrick Hurley, who had given Mao his guarantee. But as expected, Mao talked differently once he was back in Yenan after spending forty-four days in Chungking. The news of his safe return was widely circulated and a mass rally immediately organized. He got a hero's welcome from a crowd of some 10,000 people, amid the deafening sound of drums and cymbals. When he stepped onto the platform to address his audience, he portrayed, according to an eye-witness, his mission to Chungking as a victory of the people. Making no mention of the good offices of the Americans, he said that the Kuomintang reactionaries had no alternative but to comply with the people's wishes for peace, thus enabling him to extract a peace agreement from the Nationalists on their behalf. But towards the end of his speech, he suddenly shifted off the peace theme. He told the audience about the formidable manpower and military strength of the Liberated Areas (Communist region) assuring them that with 1,200,000 regular troops and more than 2,000,000 militia at his disposal, he could safeguard peace by securing a few more military victories.

With Chou En-lai posted in Nanking to continue discussing the technical side of the peace agreement, Mao involved himself in a totally different task in Yenan. In early 1946, he summoned his military commanders from most Communist areas in North China for a secret conference. For several days they were supposedly briefed by Mao on the prospects for peace though none of them would breathe a word afterwards. Since in Yenan everything was shrouded in secrecy, their reticence did not strike anyone as strange at the time. But if one associated the conference with the developments in the next few months, when armed clashes between the Nationalists and the Communists broke out in many parts of China, it would seem that Mao could not have merely talked about peace.

Whatever happened behind closed doors, Mao never ceased to maintain his superficial calm. In that autumn, he even allowed Chiang Ching to go to Shanghai for some dental treatment, despite the imminence of the outbreak of an all-out civil war. Apart from seeing her dentist, she indulged herself in a shopping spree. As the house guest of Chiao Kuan-hua and his wife Kung Peng, the two comrades high in Chou En-lai's confidence, the wife of the Communist leader managed to spend several weeks in Shanghai undetected. About the same time Mao had the pleasure of greeting his older son, An-ching, back from the Soviet Union, where the young man had spent the past fifteen years in completing his Marxist training. The reunion was a very happy event, according to one of Mao's guards, though the two of them talked about nothing but the revolutionary cause. After spending a few days together, Mao sent his son away to work with a peasant on his farm. He told An-ching that without the experience of manual labour, his education would be incomplete. With great thoroughness he explained about local customs and Chinese manners, making sure that the younger Mao would not forget to address the peasant as 'uncle'. Although An-ching had an escort with him, he had to carry his own luggage, as well as a food parcel in compliance with the ration system. However, the peasant felt extremely honoured to have the Chairman's son as his apprentice, though he was slightly uneasy at first.

Within a spell of several months An-ching learned all he was supposed to learn about the process of food production. He knew how to use a hand plough, feed pigs and mix manure with the right measure of water, in addition to sowing, weeding and thrashing. But the important thing was, his apprenticeship with the humble peasant became the talk of Yenan. The peasants were particularly excited, challenging one another for the title of 'Labour Hero' by producing more food. If the new wave of enthusiasm about agricultural production were what Mao had anticipated, he certainly did the right thing to win the hearts of the peasants, making his son one of them. When it came to the handling of the masses, he seldom put a foot wrong.

In the meantime, he managed to maintain daily contact with Chou En-lai in Nanking by coded telegrams, fully informed about every detail of the peace talks. Not that he could not trust Chou's skill and ability, but he wanted to conduct the talks in coordination with the latest military developments, of which he alone had full knowledge. For him a negotiated peace was desirable only when he encountered setbacks on the battlefield. But to impress the Chinese people with his peaceful intentions, he did not recall Chou En-lai to Yenan until that November, four months after small-scale fighting between the Nationalists and the Communists had begun. Even then, he ordered Tung Pi-wu to remain in Nanking for a few more months, indicating that the Communists did not completely abandon their hope for peace. By doing so, he scored a propaganda victory over the Nationalists. When the extensive civil war eventually broke out in 1947, most people in China were still under the illusion that the Communists could be brought round to the conference table.

In the spring of 1947, however, Mao made another vital decision after the fall of Yenan. When it became obvious that the objective of the Nationalist forces was to annihilate all the Communist units in Northern Shensi, a number of Politburo members and military commanders advised Mao to move the Central Headquarters across the Yellow River into the mountainous region of Shansi. Their argument was that Northern Shensi ceased to have its military value since larger bases had been established in other areas. They also tried to persuade Mao to leave Northern Shensi before the enemy closed in. But he disagreed with them completely. Stressing the political significance of holding out in the region around Yenan, he told them that the Communists must not be seen as abandoning their Mecca. In his opinion, to be able to draw a huge number of Nationalist troops into Northern Shensi would be militarily feasible, if only to confuse the enemy about the strategic aims of the Communists. As usual, he had the last say.

But for precaution's sake, he sent all non-combatant personnel and family dependents across the Yellow River into the areas occupied by Liu Po-cheng and Teng Hsiao-ping. Together with Chou En-lai, he remained behind to direct the operations in Northern Shensi. For several months, they played a hide-and-seek game with the advancing Nationalist units, staging ambushes but avoiding major encounters. Obviously, he wanted to wear the enemy down by means of these tactics. In this period, he and Chou became closer and closer. Out of necessity, they shared the same loess cave, doing everything together almost like twins. It was not infrequent, as one of Mao's guards recalled, that they would sit up all night to discuss their next military moves, with Mao smoking his endless cigarettes and Chou jotting down the important points in his notebook. Once in a while, they would step out of the cave to breathe some fresh air, before they sat down again at the desk. Both of them seemed so full of energy, said the guard admiringly.

As food was hard to come by in the barren area of Northern Shensi, Mao and his men often had to dig wild vegetables for their meals. To give him credit, he was very good at distinguishing the edible ones from the inedible, which impressed the men. When Mao kept on losing weight in this running and milling campaign, his guards became worried. Like most Chinese peasants, they believed in the nourishing value of a boiled hen. Somehow they managed to get one and cook it well. But Mao

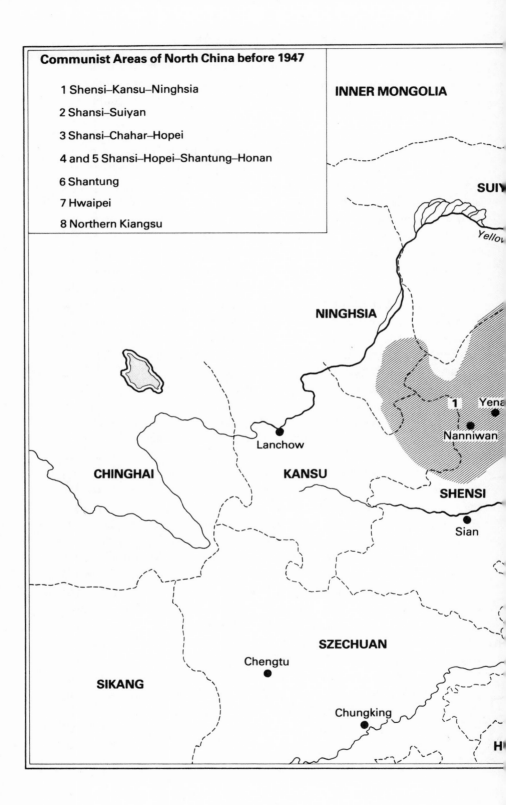

Communist Areas of North China before 1947

1 Shensi–Kansu–Ninghsia

2 Shansi–Suiyan

3 Shansi–Chahar–Hopei

4 and 5 Shansi–Hopei–Shantung–Honan

6 Shantung

7 Hwaipei

8 Northern Kiangsu

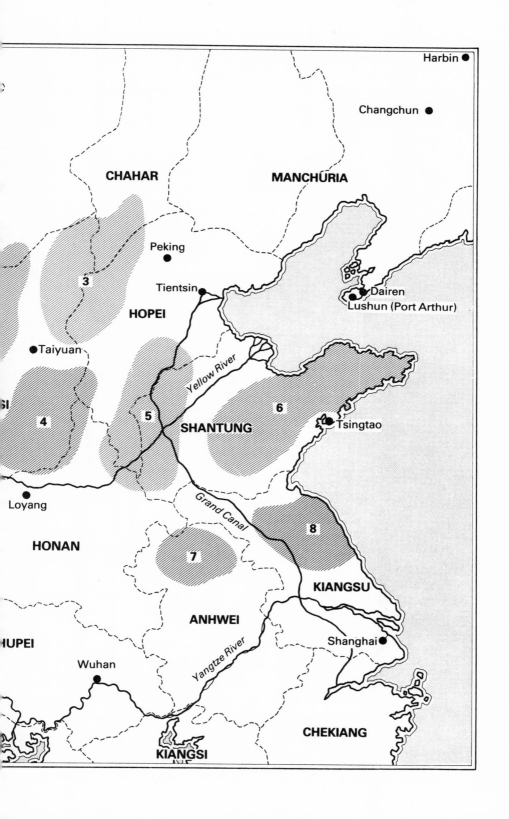

refused to eat the hen himself, insisting that Chou En-lai was in greater need of some nourishing food. Unable to persuade him any further, the guards brought the special dish to Chou. Touched by Mao's care for his second-in-command, they spread the story around, praising him as 'the selfless great leader'.

While Mao continued to tie down the Nationalist troops in Northern Shensi, his generals stepped up their offensives in Shansi, Shantung and Manchuria. As planned, each of them aimed at cutting the Nationalists up into isolated fighting units, forcing them to retreat into cities and towns. With the immense countryside in their possession, the Communist forces began to link up under Mao's orders, competent enough to fight positional warfare. In December 1947 he confidently declared that the revolutionary war was moving into the stage of offensive. The spring of 1948 saw the launching of an all-out Communist offensive in Manchuria. By now Lin Piao's Democratic United Army had a strength of 300,000, well positioned and much better equipped than any other Communist units. (According to the Chinese broadcast from Moscow on 4 September 1967, the Russians handed over to Lin Piao, between 1945 and 1947, the following military hardware: 700,000 rifles, 11,000 light machine-guns, 3,000 heavy machine-guns, 1,800 artillery pieces, 2,500 mortars, 700 tanks, 900 airplanes, 800 ammunition depots and abundant supplies of bullets, shells and petrol.) Confronting the Nationalist forces of roughly the same number, Lin had a slight edge over them because of the local support he had been able to muster. In November that year the Manchurian campaign ended with the complete Communist victory, dealing a heavy blow to the Nationalist forces across the country. This was understandable, for Chiang Kai-shek had sent two of his American-equipped armies into Manchuria, anticipating that their supreme firepower would reduce the Communists to pieces.

Encouraged by the Manchurian victory, Mao immediately moved his Central Headquarters into the southern part of Hopei province, with the occupation of North China as his next target. But at this point he was still quite cautious forecasting that it would take another three to five years to liberate the whole country. As his plan was then to establish a Communist regime north of the Yellow River, the North China People's Government was hastily formed in Shihchiachuan, with Tung Pi-wu as its Chairman. Meanwhile, he ordered Lin Piao to lead his victorious troops to lay siege to Peking and Tientsin, hoping to win international recognition by taking these two great cities.

To his advantage the Nationalists were then unable to persuade the Americans to provide them with the arms and ammunition for the defence of North China, since President Truman appeared to have decided not to interfere with China's civil war. Realizing that Fu Tso-yi, the then Nationalist commander-in-chief in North China, was less than a firm supporter of Chiang Kai-shek's, Mao resorted to his favourite United Front tactics. He sent Teng Pao-shan, a recently defected Nationalist general whose son was married to Fu's daughter, to approach Fu in secret, offering favourable terms for his surrender. At the same time, the liberal professors and leading businessmen in Peking were instigated by the Communist underground to launch a peace movement, urging Fu to give up fighting so that 'the culture and tradition of Peking would not be endangered'. This demonstration of public opinion made it easier for Fu to surrender Peking to the Communist forces without losing face. Of course not many people at the time knew about the secret bargain struck between him and Mao's emissary. Not surprisingly, Mao regarded the peaceful liberation of Peking as his master stroke, talking about it with his senior comrades on many occasions as an example of 'the flexible application of Marxist principles'. As Yang I-chih recalled, the Chinese Communist leader also attributed this success to his intimate knowledge of the ancient general Sun Tzu's strategic principles: 'To win without fighting is the best victory'.

But the capture of Peking gave Mao the chance to fulfil one of his secret dreams as well. Always likening himself to emperors and kings in Chinese history, he had the profound desire to enjoy the regal grandeur. Although there were many grand and splendid houses in Peking for him to choose, he surprised everyone by taking an unused Imperial lodge by the Chungnan Lake, the extension of the main palaces in the Forbidden City. The lodge was not particularly comfortable, but it had been used by many Manchu emperors as a study in summer months. If any of his comrades suspected his motive in choosing to live there, no one said anything. With the Gate of Heavenly Peace a couple of hundred yards to the left, he virtually installed himself in the very centre of Peking.

With both Manchuria and North China now under his control, he continued to press on with his military campaigns across the country. Having had his forces organized into four field armies rampaging in Central, Eastern and North-eastern China, he was in a position to crush the concentrated Nationalist troops in the Huaihai area, the main defence of the National Capital Nanking. And, after the fall of Hsuchow in January 1949, Chiang Kai-shek faced a split Kuomintang which challenged his leadership. He had no alternative but to step down from his presidential office, leaving Li Tsung-jen to take care of his collapsing regime. In his capacity as the acting President, Li sought to re-open peace negotiations with the Communists. Politically naive, he was hoping that Mao would allow the Nationalists to retain the areas south of the Yangtze river, dividing China into two parts in the pattern of Korea or Germany. He had no idea that nothing short of an unconditional surrender would be acceptable to the Chinese Communist leader.

But shrewd as he was, Mao agreed that Li Tsung-jen could send a peace delegation to Peking to present his terms. When the delegation headed by Chang Chih-chung flew to Peking in February, they were merely met by some insignificant Communist cadres at the airport. It was Mao's intention to humiliate them, as if they were his vassals coming to pay their tribute. While these delegates were being kept in their hotel on tenterhooks, Mao and his close associates were busily engaged in planning the military campaign to cross the Yangtze river, aiming at Nanking and Shanghai. When Chou En-lai eventually got round to receive these cowed Nationalists, he simply dictated the terms for an unconditional surrender. The terms were so unnerving that Li's delegates could not even summon their courage to return to Nanking. They betrayed poor Li's trust and defected to the Communist side.

As Mao had expected, the interlude of the so-called peace talks demoralized the Nationalists to a further extent. False hopes had been raised only to be dashed. Without Chiang Kai-shek at the helm, the Nationalists failed to rally their remaining troops to stage the last ditch defence. After crossing the Yangtze river, the Communist forces encountered no serious resistance. In April 1949 they occupied Nanking without fighting a battle. One month later, they marched into Shanghai almost casually after the Nationalist troops had evacuated it at the request of the local business community. Meanwhile, other cities fell into Communist hands like skittles. By that autumn, Mao's troops completed the occupation of the Chinese mainland.

With hindsight, one could see more clearly the Chinese Communist leader's unmatched brilliance in mapping out his whole scheme for the victorious civil war. Militarily, he was right in making the occupation of Manchuria his first objective. Remembering how the Manchus had swept away all resistance by their southward drive from their base, he saw the advantage of emulating them. He told Lin Piao that Manchuria must be taken at any cost, for victory in that area would mark the beginning of the end of Chiang's military superiority. What he did not say was that in his reckoning, he could at least establish a Communist state in Manchuria, even if he failed to conquer the other parts of China. The idea of forming the Democratic United Army indicated his realistic approach. Whereas Chiang Kai-shek refused to accept the Manchurian troops into his command, in view of their past collaboration with the Japanese, Mao welcomed them to join the Democratic United Army without any reservations. This enabled him to draw the local support which Chiang was sadly denied. His strategy of attacking the cities from the countryside proved to be a very sound one. By doing so, he effectively cut off all the supply lines to the Nationalist troops, which hastened the deterioration of their fighting will.

Although he never admitted it, Mao was really very good at psychological warfare. The proclaimed New Democracy and the much advertised United Front policy were adroitly used by him as the weapons to fight a psychological war against Chiang Kai-shek, with ever-increasing success. There is no denying that he assessed the situation correctly, far more perceptively than his enemy. He had the foresight of predicting the American withdrawal long before it happened. As early as the spring of 1946, he said in Yenan that the Americans were bound to wash their hands of Chiang Kai-shek 'once the Chinese people rise in unison to overthrow the reactionary Kuomintang regime'. He was quoted as saying, 'The Americans may have every wish to help the Nationalists obtain a peaceful settlement from us, but they are not going to fight a war for their protégés. Nor are they equipped to fight a people's war. Their lives are too precious to lose on our land. As for us, we can carry on fighting for another twenty or thirty years if necessary. Such a prospect will frighten the Americans off.' Conceivably, his words must have convinced his senior cadres of the invincibility of their cause.

It must also be mentioned that his success in infiltrating the Nationalist camp with some top agents was alarming. In Chiang Kai-shek's supreme command, he had planted Liu Fei who, as a deputy chief-of-staff, was consulted by the Nationalist leader practically on a daily basis. Liu kept the Communists well informed about Chiang's every military move even before the Nationalist generals received their orders. His contribution to the Communist military victory must have been invaluable. In the Nationalists' Central Bank another Communist agent, Chi Chao-ting, held one of the top posts, responsible for the issue of currency and advising Chiang on financial matters. Educated in the United States and with an American wife, he had worked in the Nationalists' financial nerve centre for more than twenty years. After the establishment of the People's Republic in 1949, he became the Deputy Governor-General of the People's Bank and Chairman of the International Trade Commission. The handsome reward undoubtedly proved his value as an undercover agent in the midst of the Nationalist bigwigs. Another less noticeable incident was the infiltration of the Generalissimo's personal office, through the daughter of Chiang's Secretary-General, Chen Pu-lei. As a Communist agent, she had access to the state secrets and confidential papers in her father's possession, transmitting them to her contacts undetected for a considerable period. When she was caught, the Nationalists hushed it up, but the harm had already been done. Of course these were but a few cases of Communist infiltration the extent of which defied one's imagination at the time. Extremely proud of his espionage network, Mao told some Nationalist defectors in 1950 that during the civil war, 'we knew every detail about your governmental and military units at all levels, due to the dedication of many selfless comrades'. He might have exaggerated a little, though he was not far off the mark.

Nevertheless, all these strategies and tactics would not have secured him victory in the civil war if he had not unleashed the peasant power. Familiar with China's history and social structure, he staunchly believed that without the support of the massive agricultural population, the revolutionary struggle could never succeed. It was this belief that inspired him to be so sure of the eventual outcome, in spite of internal conflicts within the party and endless setbacks. Basically, he drew more lessons from Li Tzu-cheng's uprising in the seventeenth century and the Taiping Rebellion in the late Manchu Dynasty than the revolutionary experiences of the Soviet Union. Marxism to him was just like Christian teachings to the Taiping rebels; it was to be revised and adapted to the needs of China at the given time. His flexibility and inventiveness might have appalled the ideologues and doctrinaires of the Communist world, but it was his triumph over the Nationalists that mattered.

9 THE MAN IN THE FORBIDDEN CITY

On 1 October 1949 Mao Tse-tung stood on the front porch of the gate-house over the Gate of Heavenly Peace, the main entrance to the Forbidden City. Flanked by Chu Teh, Liu Shao-chi, Chou En-lai, Kao Kang and hundreds of national figures, he proclaimed the founding of the People's Republic of China to more than a million people assembled in the marble square below. Three months short of his fifty-sixth birthday, he had arrived. The master of destiny for a population of 600 million, he had fulfilled his dream to surpass the past monarchs in power and glory. It was a far cry from the days in Juichin and Yenan. Two years earlier when he fought the advancing Nationalists around the Yenan area, the undernourished Mao weighed less than 130 pounds. But now, the same frame carried a weight of some 200 pounds, complete with a double chin and bursting waistline. Acknowledging the thunderous cheers from the crowds below with a waving hand, he grinned broadly in the Peking sunshine. After the ceremony he stepped down from the imperial gatehouse, immediately surrounded by a group of Chinese reporters most of whom had met him in Chungking during the abortive peace talks. Not yet accustomed to the regal posture, he stopped to exchange a few words with them. Laughing and joking, he teased some women journalists about their floral dresses. But when one of them remarked that he had gained much weight, the Chairman suddenly retorted. 'You must not think only capitalists and landlords are entitled to be fat. With the people now in charge, I feel so happy for them that I cannot help putting on weight.' Touchy though he was, his main concern was obviously to identify with the people as much as possible. Even his weight had political significance, and he was certain about it.

175

To consolidate the power base of his party, he decided to go about it in a cautious manner. Although there was not the slightest doubt in his mind that he must impose an absolute dictatorship on the Chinese people, he chose to tighten his hold gradually. Demonstrating his willingness to share power with the minor parties, he formed the Central People's Government on the basis of a National United Front, including three non-Communists as its Vice-chairmen. The generous gesture was out of necessity, since he had yet to broaden the foundation of his party. With a membership of around two million, mainly consisting of new recruits, the party was not quite ready for the mammoth task of upholding the dictatorship. Moreover, with victory coming much sooner than expected, he realized that the problems in front of him were far more complicated than those he had faced before. As the dose of Communism would be too strong for the people to swallow, he decided to precede it by the stage of New Democracy, in which the Communist Party could rely on the support of radicals, liberals and leftists of all descriptions, enlarging its influence indirectly. The Communists were still the masters, with the others following their lead and doing the work. Such a transitional period served to dispel the initial apprehensions of the people, for they, mistaking New Democracy for the whole extent of Mao's type of Communism, more or less came to terms with the new order.

Actually, Mao was right in this respect. The majority of his cadres might be competent enough in handling peasants and village affairs, but they could hardly be expected to understand the complexities of governing a country of the size of China. To cope with the new situation, he had to rely on experts, specialists and people with better education. Since the introduction of New Democracy would permit the party to draw support from a far wider spectrum of the society, it conformed with the United Front policy. Mao even had the way of making full use of the capitalists in this period. Bestowing on them the title of 'national bourgeoisie', he either employed them as managers of state enterprises or encouraged them to form joint enterprises with the state. To assure them of their status in the new society, he specified that they should be symbolized by a small yellow star on the national flag—the other three denoting workers, peasants and soldiers. The gesture proved to be very useful, for the capitalists in China played a big part in revitalizing the economy.

In the initial years, Mao's comparatively moderate approach seemed to work. Judging from what outsiders were allowed to catch a glimpse of, workers and peasants in and around main cities such as Peking,

Shanghai, Hangchow and Canton appeared to have improved their lot. Whenever interviewed by China's 'foreign guests' or some selected Overseas Chinese leaders, they never failed to tell the visitors how much better off they had been since the Liberation, expressing their gratitude to Chairman Mao and the Communist Party in no uncertain terms. As to the standard of living enjoyed by workers and peasants throughout the whole country, those eyewitnesses could only rely on the official briefings and reports thoughtfully and assiduously provided for them from all directions. But one thing was certain—after living through eight years of the Anti-Japanese War and three years of an all-out civil war, the majority of the Chinese people were glad to be alive, prepared to live under any regime and hoping for the best in the future. More important perhaps, Mao did succeed in restoring their national pride, especially since the presence of foreign powers in China had been abruptly brushed away. This was particularly true with most Chinese living abroad. For years the Overseas Chinese had been treated as second-rate human beings by their host countries; Mao's emergence as the leader of the most populous nation and a potentially great power enabled them to hold their heads up, full of confidence. Many of them tended to worship the Great Helmsman from a safe distance.

Meanwhile, to consolidate the foundation of the socialist society, Mao launched the nation-wide land reform, mobilizing millions of 'positive elements' (young hotheads) to organize the 'struggle meetings' in every village square. Landlords and wealthy peasants were brought shivering before the hysterical mobs, completely at their mercy. They were denounced, spat on, beaten up and stoned to death by the poor peasants who claimed to have been tortured or ruthlessly exploited by them before the liberation. As a rule the accused were not allowed to defend themselves, no matter how they had been wronged. The whole country was thrown into tumult, and the summer of 1950 registered the liquidation of landlords as a class. Millions of them were massacred, including those who had been named as 'enlightened landlords' by the Communists themselves during the Sino-Japanese War. Those who were spared from death lost everything they had, apart from being branded as 'black elements' and deprived of their basic rights. But the loss of human lives did not seem to bother Mao, for a few years later he casually admitted that the land reform had been carried out with 'some unavoidable errors like any other mass movement'. He put the number of deaths between six and seven million, as if it were nothing unusual. The figure was confirmed to me by Yang I-chih in 1957 when we discussed the achievements of the land reform, though not in so many words. He argued that the land reform had to be carried out in such a drastic and sweeping manner, for 'the landlords formed the backbone of the reactionaries and counter-revolutionaries who were plotting to overthrow the people's regime'. In defending the Chinese leader, he said that Mao had the unenviable task of seeking to establish the revolutionary order in China in the most effective way. 'Not that the Chairman meant to exterminate the landlords as individuals,' he said, 'but as a class they must be severely dealt with. Besides, the wishes of the masses ought to be respected.'

To put things in perspective, one could more easily understand Mao's callousness about the fate of several million human lives. Safely installed in the Forbidden City, he was no longer in touch with the ordinary people. Like an emperor in ancient times, he enjoyed the absolute power of being able to dictate to the whole country. His orders were accepted as imperial decrees, and his wishes were carried out to the letter. All of a sudden, his words were law. He only had to say that the landlords must be suppressed for vast numbers of people to lose their lives. Remote from the scene, he found the number of deaths no more than a set of figures. Cruel by nature, he had no trouble in dismissing massacres and human tragedies as something trivial in the light of the revolutionary cause. As far as he was concerned, since 'revolution was not a banquet', the loss of a few million lives, in his eyes, was a fair price.

But if Mao encountered no opposition in handling domestic issues as he saw fit, the same could not be said of his foreign policy. Before he announced his decision of 'leaning to the side of the Soviet Union' in his public statement after the establishment of the People's Republic, serious discussions at the top level had been carried out behind closed doors for several weeks. The main issue under discussion was the shaping of China's foreign policy. Headed by Liu Shao-chi and Chou En-lai, most of the comrades were of the opinion that formal relations with all foreign powers should be established as soon as possible. They empha-sized the importance of international recognition to China's prestige in the world, seeing it as the surest way to deal the Nationalists on Taiwan the final blow. With the American Ambassador Dr John Leighton Stuart then hanging around in Nanking, the intention of the United States was not hard to guess. Undoubtedly, both Liu and Chou must have con-templated the early possibility of winning American recognition. But Mao thought differently. He insisted that China did not have to rely on the good will of the West to carry out its socialist reconstruction. For the first time he advanced his theory on the world situation, dividing the world into the socialist camp, the imperialist camp and the neutral camp. He stated that China must stand firmly in the socialist camp and look to Moscow for guidance and leadership, for he had no doubt that the close cooperation of the two great Communist powers would change the world. Conceivably, the 'correct' political line taken up by him would have been unchallengeable, especially since he had led the party to power.

Although Mao's decision to consolidate the Sino-Soviet relationship came as no surprise to the people on the Chinese mainland, his uncompromising Anti-American stand constantly raised doubts in many minds. To begin with, his denunciation of the 'American support of the reactionary Chiang Kai-shek regime' lacked substance. If the Americans had interfered in Chiang's favour, Mao and his military commanders would have found the civil war a different proposition. Despite all the anti-American propaganda launched by the Communists during the recent civil war, the ordinary people never took it seriously. Of all foreign powers whose presence counted in China, the United States had always been favourably accepted. This had much to do with the extensive involvement of American missionaries in China's universities, schools and hospitals, which was generally regarded as an expression of friendship and good will.

But from Mao's point of view, the pro-American sentiment among the Chinese people constituted a grave danger to his regime. He believed that he must do everything to wipe out the lingering American influence in the country, lest his effort to build a totalitarian state be hindered. Outweighed by such consideration, he adopted the anti-American line as the cornerstone of his foreign policy. To convince the people, he had to single out the United States as the foremost enemy of the People's Republic, mainly for domestic consumption. Whether he realized that his move really drove the United States to continue its support of the Nationalist regime in Taiwan is hard to tell. Even if he did, his obstinacy would have stopped him from admitting it.

On the other hand, his pronounced allegiance to the Soviet Union was not as natural as it seemed. Behind all the talks about Communist solidarity and political ideology, Mao was realistic enough to see the need for accepting Moscow's leadership in the Communist world. With the industrial installations in Manchuria stripped and taken away by the Russians, he had to find some way of getting them back. Nor could he afford to be ungrateful to the Russians who had helped him secure the victory in Manchuria, the turning point of the civil war. But most important of all, he knew that without the seal of approval from Moscow, he could not hope to control the whole party. Apart from the dormant International Faction, there was a dominant Pro-Soviet force in the party machine. Having not always been high in Moscow's favour, he realized that the Russians might be tempted to influence China through his rivals if he were less than convincing in his pro-Soviet gesture. Although it was not in his nature to play a submissive part, he had no alternative but to defer to Moscow. Fortunately for him, Stalin seemed quite prepared to accept him more or less as his equal. During his eight-week visit to Moscow between December 1949 and January 1950, Mao was accorded the honour no other Communist leader had ever received. This not only satisfied his vanity but also won Stalin his unwavering admiration. After his return to Peking with the signed Sino-Soviet Treaty of Friendship and Alliance, he was most explicit in expressing his gratitude. On a number of occasions, he praised Stalin as 'the greatest leader of human-kind', firmly declaring that the 'Sino-Soviet friendship will last thousands of years'. Under his instructions, the Sino-Soviet Friendship Associations were rapidly formed throughout the country, down to the county level. 'Learn from the Soviet Union' became a watchword on every lip and Russian was stipulated as the first foreign language.

His display of total loyalty to the Soviet Union was duly rewarded for Stalin extended him a loan of 200 million US dollars to launch China's 'socialist reconstruction', in addition to the sending of a huge number of engineers, technicians and experts for the 'selfless assistance' to the Chinese people. Inconsequential though the aid later turned out to be, at the time it did signify Stalin's seal of approval which mattered a great deal to Mao. For once he could claim to have the Kremlin's blessing as the undisputed leader of China, rising above the heads of all his rivals.

It was at the height of his pro-Soviet fervour that the Korean War broke out in June 1950. Determined to demonstrate China's firm stand in the Communist world, he planned to intervene long before the UN forces began to gain some ground. As early as July, he already alerted his top comrades that China must be prepared to assist 'the Korean people to liberate their country' in case the tide turned against them. He only waited for the UN forces to push near the Yalu river to justify his claim that China's security was under threat to send in the 'Chinese volunteers', several hundred thousand of regular troops with their emblems concealed. Before the Chinese troops were sent, however, he found out that the idea of intervention was not entertained by his ministers unanimously. As a democratic gesture, he ordered Chou En-lai to summon the State Council for consultation before he declared his decision to plunge into the Korean War. When he explained to the council about the aggressive designs of the United States on China, the reaction was a mixture of disbelief and surprise. Although no one had the courage to disagree with him, the Chairman was still offended. He insisted that everyone present must speak up for the benefit of 'reaching a democratic decision'. Naturally, they all harped on the same tune, since it was obvious that Mao had already made up his mind. But Lo Lung-chi, a non-Communist minister, took Mao's words too literally. An expert on international affairs trained in the United States, he bluntly expressed his doubt about the possibility of an American invasion. He pointed out that if the Americans had had such a design, they would have stayed on in China to help Chiang Kai-shek out. It was unthinkable, he said, that they could have chosen to invade China through the Korean route.

This was too much and Mao exploded. He went into a long harangue. Accusing Lo of being poisoned by his American education, he said that the non-Communist minister failed to understand the world situation from the socialist angle. The Americans were definitely going to invade Manchuria, he insisted, for the occupation of that area would cut off the Soviet supplies for China's industrialization. Even if the United States forces stopped short of crossing the Korean border, he went on, their presence in an anti-Communist Korea must not be tolerated. Embarrassed, Lo hastily apologized for his incorrect assumption. But Mao was still not satisfied. Looking around, he told the others that Lo was not alone in fearing the military might of American imperialism. He challenged them to name one reason why he should not send troops to aid North Korea. Not surprisingly, he won their unanimous support instead.

At the time, Mao's decision to intervene in the Korean War might seem risky in the eyes of his associates. But it was a risk he must take. To use his words, he needed some 'external conflicts' to unify the Chinese people who had been divided by 'internal conflicts' such as land reform and reclassification of social status. Whether he believed that the US forces would invade Manchuria was immaterial. He had to find a common target for the Chinese people to let off their steam. Most important of all, he wanted to root out whatever friendly feelings the Chinese people might still cherish for the Americans, a danger very alive in his mind. As to the cost of human lives in an unimposed war, it was the least of his concern. He felt that he owned the country.

But in spite of his stubborn belief in himself, Mao was not unaware of the gravity of the task at hand. To seek popular support for his military intervention, he launched a full-scale anti-American propaganda campaign throughout the country. The Resist US and Aid Korea Associations were formed in every city and town, responsible for mobilizing supplies and churning out pamphlets and broadsides. To instil confidence into the minds of the people, he called the Americans 'paper tigers' in one of his public utterances. The expression was immediately picked up, and it soon became closely associated with American imperialism on every Chinese tongue. In fact, when Mao used the expression 'paper tigers', he merely meant to achieve a dramatic effect for his statement. As Ku Mu, the then Party Chief of Shanghai, told a group of journalists (myself included) in 1952, 'Chairman Mao is the last one to underestimate the real strength of American imperialism. But since we are at war with them, he had to boost the people's morale by calling them "paper tigers". When it comes to propaganda, the Chairman always knows how to use it to the best of our advantage. We all know that the Americans are no paper tigers; otherwise we would not have sent our best troops into Korea.'

If Mao did not really care about the huge number of casualties suffered by the 'Chinese Volunteers' in the Korean War, the loss of his older son, An-ching, in a battle near the 38th parallel certainly shocked him. When An-ching volunteered to join the Chinese forces in the spring of 1951, he could not find any reason to stop him. Meanwhile, he expected the military commanders to look after his son as well as they could. In the first few months, nothing happened for An-ching was safely installed in one of the division headquarters. But towards the end of 1951, in a ferocious battle the whole division was wiped out and An-ching shared the same fate. Not knowing how to break the bad news to Mao himself, Peng Teh-huai (commander-in-chief of the Chinese forces in Korea) informed Liu Shao-chi and Chou En-lai instead, leaving it to their discretion. For some time Liu and Chou did not say anything. They were worried that Mao might not be able to take it. It was not until Mao became suspicious that they told him in a meeting. Unexpectedly the Chairman showed no emotion at all. Without raising his voice, he merely said that they should have told him earlier. When Liu and Chou tried to console him, Mao told them that it was quite unnecessary. He went on to say that he was not the only father who had lost his son in the Korean War. If they felt sorry for him, he said, they should extend their condolences to the fathers of all revolutionary martyrs who had sacrificed their lives to defend Korea and world peace. Then he told everyone at the meeting not to reveal An-ching's death.

But actually, he broke down after the others were gone. He refused to show any sign of weakness in front of his colleagues for fear that his image as a selfless leader of the people might be spoiled. Like ancient emperors, he was anxious to maintain his inscrutability and unpredictability, even at the cost of appearing inhuman and heartless. As the grief of bereavement lingered on, he took off to the Huangshan (Yellow Mountain) resorts in Chekiang province for a prolonged rest. The mountain air and quiet atmosphere seemed to have done him a lot of good. He even met some of the patients in the same sanatorium, exchanging a few brief remarks with them. Before he left, he felt cheerful enough to write a few lines in the visitors' book as advice to the other patients:

> 'To recuperate one must be patient.
> Nor should one have any fear.
> Still much effort must be made before one can
> restore one's health.'

Since whatever he said was regarded as the gospel truth, these few lines were soon circulated in most hospitals and sanatoriums across the country.

However, Mao's reckless intervention in the Korean War did reap some unexpected reward for him in an indirect way. The fact that 'the Chinese Volunteers' were able to hold the United States and United Nations forces at bay shocked many countries in South-east Asia. Too near to China for comfort, they bent like slender bamboos in the 'prevailing east wind', to borrow Mao's favourite expression. In Manila, Kuala Lumpur, Rangoon, Bangkok and New Delhi Mao was suddenly spoken of with awe; while in Vietnam, the Vietminh guerrillas under Ho Chi Minh could not but feel inspired and encouraged. Most South-east Asian leaders, already acutely aware of the delicate situation created by their traditional policies towards the ethnic Chinese in the whole area, started to look over their shoulders. It became obvious to them that with China forcing its way into the international arena of power, they were sitting on a political volcano. They realized that the discontent of the politically underprivileged Chinese residents in their countries would sooner or later erupt. Although Mao did magnanimously declare that China would not 'export revolution', they had no effective means of stopping the ethnic Chinese under their feet from identifying themselves with Peking. To make the situation worse, rival politicians in their midst wasted no time in sidling up to the new master of the Forbidden City, dancing attendance and angling for support. The new development would have emboldened Mao to take a further step of 'vying with Heaven in stature', setting China on the path to 'lead' the Third World.

It seemed that the death of An-ching could have prompted Mao to think about finding Chiang Ching, his fourth wife, a political role. In the spring of 1952, after his return to Peking from the Huangshan retreat, he brought it up at a Central Committee meeting. He told the committee that Chiang Ching would like to contribute more to the cause of socialist revolution, especially at a time when the Korean War kept so many of the leading comrades fully occupied. Since he had previously promised in Yenan not to use his personal influence to advance Chiang Ching's political career, the suggestion took the committee by surprise. But Liu Shao-chi was both quick and tactful. Without reminding Mao of his previous assurance, he calmly pointed out that Comrade Chiang Ching had been contributing much to the party and the people. By taking good care of the great leader, he said, she really commanded the gratitude of the whole nation. What else could be more important than the health and well-being of the Chairman himself, he asked. The other members of the committee agreed with him and Mao's suggestion was shelved. Although Mao could see through Liu's real intentions, he was unable to reverse the situation.

The setback in the Central Committee, however, must have been hard for Mao to swallow. For he was even more determined to emulate Stalin in encouraging the cult for himself. Before the Korean War, on the walls of assembly halls in China, Mao's portrait was displayed together with those of Chu Teh, Liu Shao-chi and Chou En-lai. At the outset of the war, the Chairman's portrait began to appear in a much larger size. It was flanked by two national flags on the main wall while the portraits of the other three leaders, reduced in size, were demoted to the side walls. Then in 1952, they disappeared altogether, leaving the smiling Mao alone. Even though no one in China could tell the reasons for the change, it was pretty obvious that the order must have come from high above. Actually, in promoting the personality cult for himself, Mao had been very patient and careful. As early as 1949, when someone, believed to be his personal secretary, Chen Po-ta, suggested that Peking should be renamed after him, the Chairman dismissed the idea completely. Naturally, Chen was not slow in praising his modesty and humility. But what Mao next said shook him up. 'Comrade Po-ta', he smiled, 'there are so many big cities in our country. If one of them is named after me, how about the others? I don't want to start the trend. If Peking is renamed after me, then there will have to be Chu Teh City, Liu Shao-chi City, Chou En-lai City and Heaven knows how many more.... In that case, Mao Tse-tung City is but one of many. I'm sure that one can achieve immortality in many other ways, without lending one's name to one particular city. You should know me better.'

But when it came to his public image as the sole ideologue of the party,

Mao tended to be extremely assertive and overbearing. In 1952, when the nation-wide Thought-Remoulding Movement was launched to consolidate the anti-American stand of the Chinese people, Hsu Ying, a colleague of mine who was later appointed Director of Religious Affairs under the State Council, went to interview Chou En-lai about the significance of the campaign. Stressing the need for political education, Chou said that to err was human and even Chairman Mao was no exception. A first-rate reporter, Hsu had the story published in the Shanghai edition of the *Ta Kung Pao*, the newspaper he wrote for. Within hours he was summoned by a very angry Chou En-lai who insisted that he had been misquoted. The premier demanded that Hsu retract his story and insert a full apology for having cast some doubt on the correct and enlightened leadership of Chairman Mao who was totally free of any errors. Though absolutely sure of the authenticity of his report, the poor Hsu had to do as he was told. But this was not all. The *Ta Kung Pao* was suspended from publication for three days, paying the penalty for having shown 'disrespect for the great leader'. Perhaps to ease his own conscience, Chou En-lai subsequently appointed the perplexed Hsu Ying Director of Religious Affairs, a very responsible post for a journalist who was supposed to have committed a 'political error'.

In a way, Mao's obsession with his own ideological authority was not that strange. Familiar with Chinese history, he knew how the past rulers had succeeded or failed in consolidating their imperial powers. For centuries taught to accept authority and obey orders, the Chinese people, in Mao's eyes, could be easily ruled. But meanwhile, he realized what they would expect of their ruler. In the past, Chinese monarchs could claim the mandate from heaven, keeping themselves above the heads of the ordinary people, inaccessible and unimpeachable. Since Mao claimed to have the mandate from the people, the only way for him to rise above them was to create the myth of his infallibility. He must appear to be the one who was always right. It was not enough for him to be the people's leader; he must also be the prophet, the philosopher and the teacher. He could not afford to have any competition in the intellectual field, or his omnipotence would be challenged. An admirer of Chin Shih Huang (the First Emperor of Chin) who burned the books and buried scholars alive to maintain his intellectual supremacy, he deemed it necessary to impose the strictest thought control on the largest population in the world so that his own immortality could be assured. Such an impossible ambition would not have been entertained by any other ruler with more understanding of human nature. But then Mao was both a fanatic and a dreamer, bred by the arrogance of power.

As Mao had expected, the Korean War gave him the pretext to tighten the internal security of China to a further extent. To root out corruption and bribery, two successive campaigns were launched against cadres and businessmen on a national scale. But for political purposes, these mal-practices were condemned as 'the ills of capitalism'. Like all mass move-ments in China, the campaigns resulted in excesses and caused numerous deaths. Mao might not have intended to go this far, but neither did he seem to show any concern. It was only towards the last phase of these campaigns in 1953 that he was reported to criticize some of the extreme measures and urge moderation. Still, he made no attempt to right the wrongs or discourage unfounded persecutions. Almost indifferently, he admitted that some people were bound to be wronged in any form of mass movement. But in order not to dampen the enthusiasm of the masses, he pointed out, it would be a mistake to demand too much caution from them in making accusations. Obviously, as far as he was concerned, the victimization of a comparatively small number of people for the sake of revolution was nothing if not acceptable.

But before these two campaigns were officially wound up, Mao ordered the extensive suppression of counter-revolutionaries throughout the country. With the Ministry of Public Security taking the overall responsibility, the campaign was turned into a massive witch-hunt. On the basis of Mao's interpretation of the class struggle, it was directed against no less than five per cent of the 600 million population, taking into account these people's family background, past connections and political sympathies. The so-called counter-revolutionaries did not have to be saboteurs, provocators or subversive elements; a few words of dis-content or scepticism about the new order would qualify one to become 'the people's enemy'. Since Mao believed that the masses must be mobilized to assist the cadres and activists, the campaign was incor-porated with all the political study groups which had been organized in every factory, farm, school, office, street and lane. In these groups, every member had to talk about his personal history, social contacts and poli-tical views. This done, he would be encouraged or forced to expose his relations and friends who seemed to be 'politically unreliable', telling what he knew about their activities and private thoughts. He must write all this down, so that it could be handed over to the public security authorities for their use. In other words, most people were converted into informants, informing against one another. It did not matter whether they merely picked up some gossip or had some wrong ideas, they had to pass them on to the party functionaries who were assigned to the study groups. The frightening aspect of the whole process was that the innocent could be incriminated without a shred of evidence.

From 1953 onward, the campaign for the suppression of counter-revolutionaries spread to every corner of the country. Numerous people were arrested and imprisoned, but never charged or tried. They were methodically held incommunicado, investigated by secret police and forced to make 'confessions'. Millions of them were sent to labour camps for re-education, whether the cases against them were established or not. According to Mao's theory, hard labour would reform the character of most counter-revolutionaries, for the majority of them had been under the unhealthy influence of the old society. Unlike in the land reform period, he decided that humiliations and mental tortures would work better than mass executions. He defined his policy on the suppression of counter-revolutionaries as the method 'to cure the illness and save the patients', promising leniency to those who 'voluntarily confessed their crimes' and threatening severe punishment for those who 'resisted the government's way of helping them', by which he meant prolonged detentions and endless investigations. Obviously, he believed that it was more advisable for him to root out the 'reactionary' thought in the Chinese mind than to follow Stalin's footsteps in exterminating the opposition forces physically.

But unlike other campaigns, the suppression of counter-revolutionaries was carried out as a long-term measure, forming a part of the security routine. It also became the central issue for all mass movements, for Mao repeatedly said that 'the enemy of the people would never give up the attempt to restore the reactionary regime', always waiting in the wings to stage a comeback. To forestall such possibilities, he saw the tightening of thought control as the answer. He convinced himself that to achieve this aim he must tame the intellectuals first. As early as 1942 in Yenan, he had already laid down the guidelines for the cultural workers and creative artists regarding their approach to revolutionary tasks, with ideological purity as the sole criterion. Now he demanded that the intellectuals in the whole country must accept the same restrictions, thinking in uniformity and expressing themselves along the correct line. That he should have taken so much trouble in dealing with the intellectuals is understandable. In Chinese history, although peasant uprisings brought about the downfall of several imperial dynasties such as the Han, the Tang and the Ming, there were always those intellectuals who planned and masterminded the rebellions behind the scene. Having successfully mobilized the peasantry to obtain political power himself, Mao knew very well that he must guard against the same possibilities.

As the intellectuals were traditionally respected in Chinese society,

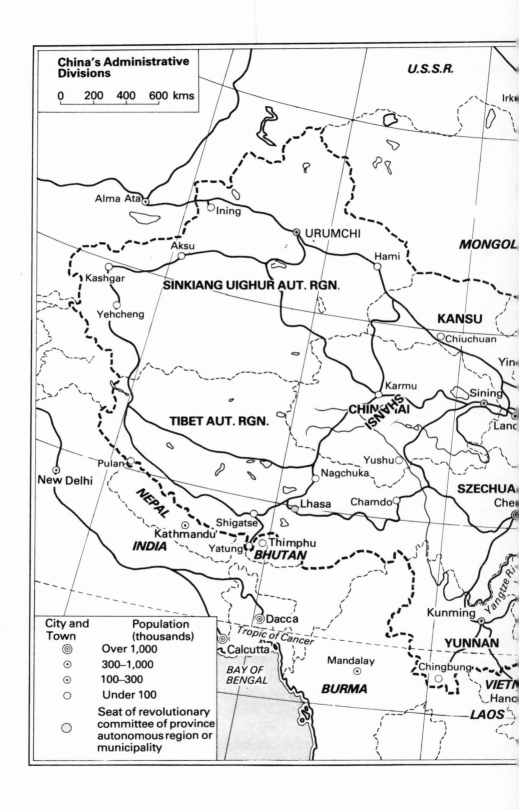

China's Administrative Divisions

0   200   400   600 kms

U.S.S.R.

Irk•

Alma Ata

Ining

URUMCHI

Aksu

Hami

MONGOL

SINKIANG UIGHUR AUT. RGN.

KANSU

Kashgar

Chiuchuan

Yin•

Yehcheng

Yushu

Karmu

Sining

CHINGHAI

SHENSI

Land

TIBET AUT. RGN.

Yushu

Pulan

Nagchuka

SZECHUA

New Delhi

Chamdo

Che•

Lhasa

NEPAL

Shigatse

Kathmandu

Yatung

Thimphu

INDIA

BHUTAN

Kunming

Yangtze River

Dacca

Tropic of Cancer

YUNNAN

Calcutta

Mandalay

Chingbung

VIETN

BAY OF
BENGAL

BURMA

Hano

LAOS

City and Town	Population (thousands)
◎	Over 1,000
⊙	300–1,000
⊙	100–300
○	Under 100
○	Seat of revolutionary committee of province autonomous region or municipality

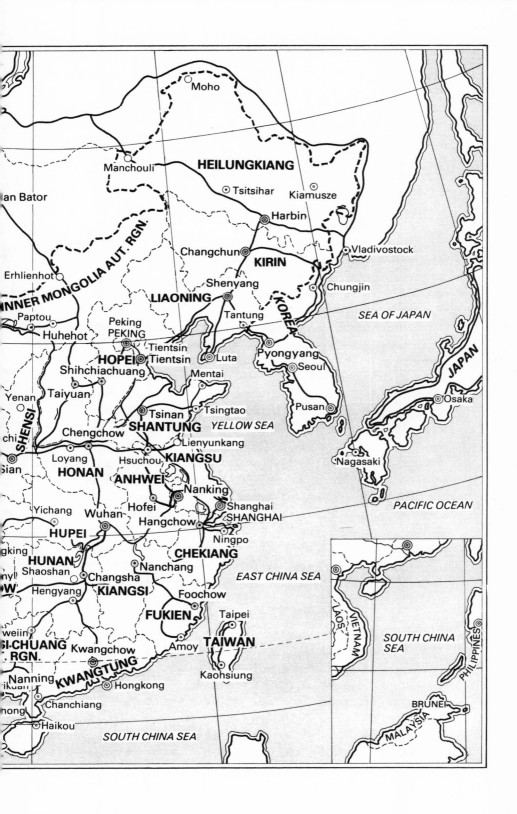

Mao found it necessary to destroy their self-confidence and integrity. He made his four volumes of selected works compulsive reading material for everyone in the country. Classics were banned and historical studies discontinued. Even popular novels such as *The Dream of the Red Chamber* and *The Water Margin* were not to be reprinted until annotations from the Marxist angle were added and deletions made. By doing so, he hoped to establish his intellectual supremacy as the 'Great Teacher' for the whole nation. It was clear to him that he could not afford to allow others to think independently or differently. He must be the one who provided all the answers for humankind.

In schools and universities, the authority of teachers used to be a strong feature. But Mao had other thoughts. By his order, the 'new teacher-student relationship' was introduced in 1952. In political study groups, the teachers had to make self-criticisms in front of their students who, in turn, were encouraged to criticize their teachers. As a result, the traditional authority of teachers was greatly reduced. At the time, the new relationship was widely applauded as 'revolutionary' and 'progressive'. Apparently, no one dared to interpret it as a move to downgrade the intellectuals. It was not until later during the Cultural Revolution in the 1960s that Mao's obsessive hatred for intellectuals was publicly revealed, when he condemned them as 'the stinking ninth-rate beings', ranked more lowly than thieves, beggars and prostitutes and other curses of society.

If one takes into account Mao's egocentricity and megalomania, one would be better able to understand his comparatively patient approach in handling the intellectuals in the 1950s. He genuinely believed that he could remould them into all shapes to his liking on the strength of his own intellectual supremacy. He was under the illusion that political indoctrination and the destruction of their self-respect would transform the intellectuals completely. All he had to do, he thought, was to keep them away from 'the harmful influence' of other schools of thought. Ridiculous though it might seem, he set out to impose the censorship of mind on the Chinese people as a whole. More ambitious than his hero the First Emperor of Chin, he wanted to turn the intellectuals into his faithful disciples, propagating his philosophy and preaching his ideology.

With this as his ultimate aim, he launched a nation-wide thought-remoulding movement in the autumn of 1952, bearing down upon professors, writers, artists and journalists for they were his prime objects. Apart from his fervent wish to transform the intellectuals, he intended to expose the ideological foes in their fold. More important perhaps, he also regarded the campaign as an extension of the suppressive measures against the counter-revolutionaries. From his point of view, the three-month-long intensive campaign was a success. Many renowned professors were pulled down from their pedestals, many literary idols summarily destroyed, and many prominent figures disgraced and silenced. No matter what people might think in private, they forced themselves to pay lip service to Maoism with seeming enthusiasm and sincerity, if only for the sake of self-preservation. Although Mao was not so naive as to believe that he had won the war, he was, nonetheless, convinced of his ability to exert authority over the intellectuals. He was prepared to 'accumulate small victories to attain a major triumph in the long run', for he declared that there would be many more thought-remoulding processes for the intellectuals to go through.

Meanwhile, he turned his attention to the historians and ideologues within the party, ordering them to rewrite history books and interpret Marxist theories to conform to his views. For justification, he asserted that since historical works in the past had been written by official historians to glorify the rulers, they were full of distortions and inaccuracies. With the people now in power, he pointed out, it was only sensible to redress the balance. The moment the word got around, historians and ideologues flocked to produce works to his order. For obvious reasons, ancient statesmen and heroes associated with the ruling class had to be vilified while rebels and outlaws were canonized. To comply with Mao's request to 'reverse the historical verdicts', truths and facts were sacrificed for political considerations. The man who excelled himself at this kind of work turned out to be Kuo Mo-jo, the then president of the Chinese Academy of Sciences. Having known Mao for a long time, Kuo was fully aware of the Chairman's real wishes. It was clear to him that Mao aimed at building up his own image as a man of destiny, to be projected as 'the great saviour of the Chinese people'. For a start, Kuo wrote a series of articles to eulogize Tsao Tsao, a controversial and ruthless political figure in the Period of Three Kingdoms (A.D. 221–265) who commanded Mao's admiration since his childhood. In these historical dissertations he advanced new arguments to justify the ancient politician's usurpation of the Han throne, reassessing his feats and achievements. Making an allusion between the past and the present, he subtly drew a parallel between Tsao Tsao and Mao. Not unexpectedly, the Chairman was delighted and did not hesitate to tell his wife Chiang Ching that Kuo was a 'true scholar', as she later revealed. To show his appreciation, Mao showered Kuo with favours and honours, including a party card and the privilege of private audiences at the latter's request. He even went so far as to dedicate one or two of his poems to Kuo—an honour denied to many other far more important comrades of his.

But as for those scholars who refused to abandon integrity for political expediency, Mao was ruthless in punishing them. Their books were banned and they were forced to write self-criticisms over and over again, much maligned by the official publications as the 'diehards of reactionary philosophy' until they came round to confess their 'political errors'. Outstanding historians and philosophers such as Li Ta, Hou Wai-lu, Chien Po-chan and Liang Su-ming were submitted to constant criticisms and attacks made by newspapers and magazines at Mao's pleasure. Apparently, the Chairman not only wanted to humiliate these intellectuals publicly, he was also convinced that the reading public would accept his thought as the guiding light.

Among the victims of Mao's thought-remoulding processes, the case of Professor Feng Yu-lan merits a special mention. For more than twenty-five years, until Mao's death in 1976, the Columbia-educated philosopher had to rewrite his *History of Chinese Philosophy* along Mao's political line three times to demonstrate his loyalty to the Chairman. Each time it took him seven or eight years to finish his manuscript which was then submitted to Mao for his approval. The poor man had to live on tenterhooks for months before Mao would instruct his literary henchmen to sound the bugle of an all-out attack on him in some official publication, to be followed by an avalanche of criticism from all quarters carefully organized. It was hard to understand why the Chairman never bothered to indicate his disapproval to Feng directly instead of taking so much trouble. But according to Yang I-chih, this was evidently Mao's way of 'helping the philosopher to rectify his mistakes in the public eye, and educating the masses at the same time'. However, humbled and scared, Feng had no alternative but to condemn himself in his own articles, expressing his remorse as if he had committed some unforgivable crime. Then he would be permitted to embark on the rewriting task once more. After another seven or eight years, he again submitted his revised manuscript to Mao, only to receive the same treatment as before. And when he eventually rewrote his book for a third time, the Chairman had just gone to the other world 'to see Marx', leaving the octogenarian philosopher wondering whether he would have met with his approval at long last. In any case, a quarter of a century is a long time in a man's life, and it is frightening to think that one of the foremost Chinese philosophers has had to spend all these years trying to satisfy Mao's flippancies.

Ironically, after enforcing the thought-remoulding processes at all levels for three or four years, Mao seemed to believe in the invincibility of his philosophy and ideology. In the spring of 1957, he confidently launched the 'Let a Hundred Flowers Bloom Movement', encouraging the intellectuals to speak out their mind for the party's benefit. He asked them for suggestions and criticisms. His liberal gesture took the country by surprise. At first, most people held back for they were not sure of the real motive behind it. But when the party organizations continued the campaign for some time, the more courageous or more naive ones began to speak up. To Mao's amazement, the majority of them criticized the cadres, the government and even the party, pointedly and bitterly. Undoubtedly, discontent and dissatisfaction were widely spread. This was not what Mao had expected. All along, he had been waiting for praise and eulogia when he invited criticisms. Having built new railroads, big bridges and completed the land reform, he genuinely believed that he had earned the people's gratitude. What angered him more was that the intellectuals were far from being tamed. Immediately he ordered the ending of the Hundred Flowers Movement and succeeded it with an Anti-Rightist Campaign, with dissenters and outspoken critics as the main targets.

Probably a little embarrassed with his own misjudgement of the situation, as well as the need for the turnabout, he contrived to give the impression that the Hundred Flowers Movement was merely called to a halt. In one of his statements, he proclaimed that the Anti-Rightist Campaign was the sequel to the previous movement, with the important aim of sorting out the 'poisonous weeds' from the 'fragrant flowers'. In other words, he meant to get rid of the dissenters and critics and reward the faithful. Since it was always his belief that he would rather 'kill the innocent than let the guilty escape', a policy pursued by his hero, Tsao, Tsao, many centuries ago, the Anti-Rightist Campaign cast its nets far and wide. One could be judged as a rightist not just because of one's writings or public utterances, casual remarks in private were equally incriminating. Almost without exception, anonymous letters were held as strong evidence and secret informants hailed as 'progressive elements'. Towards the end of 1957, the campaign reached its peak. Thousands and thousands of rightists had by now been dragged out to be humiliated in public. They were brought to mass meetings to condemn themselves 'to educate the people', often having to withstand verbal or even physical assaults from the agitated mobs. At the end of the day, they would still be branded as 'rightists', expected to redeem themselves through their efforts in 'raising their political level' under the people's supervision. Like prisoners on probation, they had no chance of recovering their personal pride, especially since another mishap would land them in an abyss. The most frustrating aspect was that rational arguments in the act of self-defence would only aggravate the already untenable situation.

But for the leading rightists, they did not get away so lightly. In the instance of Ting Ling, the first Chinese winner of the Stalin Literary Prize, she possibly suffered the worst fate. A favourite of Mao's in the Yenan days during the civil war, she was made an editor of the *Literary Gazette*. Together with Feng Hsueh-feng and Chou Yang, two other writers reputed to have maintained the close association between the party and the late Lu Hsun, who was regarded as the Chinese Gorki, she was responsible for Mao's literary policy. During the Anti-Rightist Movement, she was accused of having deliberately deviated from the guidelines laid down by Mao at the Yenan Forum on Literature and Art in 1942. Submitted to months of fierce attacks and criticisms organized by the national newspapers, she went to great lengths to make her self-criticisms to indicate her repentance. But this did not save her from the final disgrace. She was sent to the Peitahuang farm in Manchuria for labour reform which was to last no less than twenty years. However, Mao's death meant her liberation. Another two years later, in June 1979, she was eventually rehabilitated by Senior Vice-Premier Teng Hsiao-ping, attending the National Political Consultative Conference as a representative.

Both Feng Hsueh-feng and Chou Yang got into trouble as well. But they were less harshly treated. Feng's self-criticisms eventually met with Mao's approval, though he did not live long enough to be restored to his previous position. Chou was the luckier of the two. An opportunist by nature, he readily admitted his errors and denounced himself like a reformed character. He regained Mao's favour after a few years' intensive re-education, only to be disgraced again during the Cultural Revolution, frog-marched by the Red Guards in the Peking streets complete with a dunce cap on his head and ropes around his body. Fortunately, he still managed to survive the unpredictable Chairman.

Of course, there were countless writers and artists who suffered various degrees of humiliation throughout the Anti-Rightist Movement. Even Mao Tun, the then Minister of Culture and an outstanding novelist, was publicly denounced as a rightist by the official publications. However, he was allowed to retain his post after he had confessed his deviations from the correct line. He was later quoted as saying that the intellectuals must cease to be a thinking reed if they wanted to survive.

Actually, the novelist was only partly right in his advice. In Mao's China, it was not good enough to cease to think. Frivolous as the Great Helmsman was, he often changed course very abruptly. To strike a balance between the right and the left, he considered it his privilege to sway from one side to the other. Sometimes he talked like a rightist, but some other times he became a leftist. To curry favour with him, the intellectuals would have to shift their views as frequently as the Chairman did. What he approved one day could be disapproved by himself the day after. Worse still, he always expressed his ideas in such an ambiguous manner that it was almost impossible to pin him down. Perhaps this was intentional, for it enabled him to shift blame on others more conveniently when the need arose. Not that he could be held for what he had said; he would rather appear to have been misinterpreted or distorted.

When the Anti-Rightist Movement was wound up in early 1958, however, Mao did not bother to revive the 'Hundred Flowers' campaign, as he had promised. With the intellectuals not likely to voice their candid opinions, he had more urgent matters to attend to. Since the autumn of 1956, the Chairman had been anticipating the inevitability of the Sino-Soviet split. After the death of Stalin, he began to regard himself as the sole custodian of the orthodox Marxism-Leninism. He had little esteem for Khrushchev, especially after the latter had started the de-Stalinization process in the Soviet Union. In Mao's opinion, Stalin might have his defects, but his contribution to the Soviet Union and the World Communist Movement had been so great that he should not have been defamed after his death. At first, the Chinese leader merely hinted at his disagreement with Khrushchev about the issue. While the Eastern European countries applauded Moscow's bold measures of de-Stalinization and followed suit, China stayed clear of the tide. Stalin was never criticized and his giant-sized portrait continued to adorn the Tienanmen Square in Peking, in the company of Marx, Engels and Lenin. Not known for his admiration for Stalin, Mao even surprised some of his top comrades by taking such a stand. But if one tried to see things through Mao's eyes, one would have found no irrelevancy in his defence of Stalin. In many ways, his position in the Chinese hierarchy was similar to the Russian leader's in his lifetime. To achieve monolithic power, they had both ruthlessly mown down rivals and opponents. To rule with fear and suspicion, they had both found it necessary to take precautions against all eventualities. What Khrushchev did to Stalin made Mao realize that it could happen to him after his death. Seeing himself as the creator of Communist China, he could not bear the thought that his revolutionary philosophy would not survive him. It was not enough for him to rule the country unopposed when he was alive, he wanted to make sure that his influence would last for centuries to come. By upholding Stalin's position in the Communist Movement, he hoped to forestall the possibility of sharing his fate in the future. With this in mind, he set out to challenge Khrushchev and his 'revisionism', concealing the true nature of the conflict under an ideological cloak for the sake of respectability.

Actually, to be fair to Khrushchev, Mao would still be at odds with him even without de-Stalinization. In the Eighth Party Congress in 1956, the Chinese leader stated clearly that China and the Soviet Union were 'the two pillars of world peace', emphasizing the revolutionary role played by China in Asia and Africa. According to sources close to Mao, the Chairman had always insisted that the Soviet Union should confine their revolutionary activities to Europe and the two Americas, since China could adequately take care of Asia and Africa, as well as Australasia. Though Mao did not use the term 'sphere of influence', this was exactly what he had in mind. He believed that in the course of world revolution, China should be the Soviet Union's equal, not its junior partner. He saw no reason why Peking should not join Moscow in becoming 'the fortress of socialism and world peace', held in esteem by revolutionary forces throughout the world. When Stalin was alive, 'Mao deferred to him for the need of uniting the different factions in his own party. But this did not mean that he respected and trusted the Soviet dictator without reservations.

Being no fool, Mao knew all along that Stalin had been encouraging his old rival Kao Kang to build up an 'independent kingdom' in Manchuria, hoping to control the Chinese party through him. Between 1949 and 1953, when Kao served as the overlord of Manchuria, he had frequent contacts with Moscow behind Mao's back, as it was later revealed in a Chinese document (the unexpurgated version of a Decision Concerning the Anti-Party Alliance of Kao Kang and Jao Ju-shih). But Mao deliberately played down Kao's Moscow connection when his attempt to seize party and political power was exposed in 1954. As China then heavily relied on the Soviet Union for economic and technical aid in its projected industrialization, Mao obviously did not want to embarrass the Russians unnecessarily. Besides, he could not very well hold the new masters of the Kremlin responsible for what Stalin had done. These considerations, however, decided him to shelve his grudge against the Soviet Union for the time being.

Perhaps more surprisingly, the Korean War turned out to be another sore point. When Mao rushed the 'Chinese volunteers' into Korea to fight the UN forces, he was under the impression that the Russians would foot the bill and supply arms and ammunitions. He was, therefore, shocked to find out, after the Korean truce, that China had to repay the Soviet Union an enormous sum for the military expenditure in Korea. Although he was 'too angry for words' at a top level meeting, according to an eyewitness, he decided that the Russians should have every penny they asked for.

Nor did the much-heralded 'selfless assistance of the Soviet Union' to China's industrialization work. The industrial equipment and machines supplied by the Russians were either obsolete or sub-standard while the Soviet engineers and technicians were far from competent. In the case of the Wuhan Railway Bridge across the Yangtze river, the men from Moscow blundered and bungled, only to be rescued by the Chinese engineers previously trained in the United States and Europe. Though for political reasons incidents such as these were never publicized, they were widely known to the people. As for Mao, he would have seen the whole thing as another trick played by the Kremlin against him. Meanwhile, he could not but begin to doubt whether the Chinese people still needed the aid of science and technology for their socialist reconstruction.

Impulsive as well as stubborn, he suddenly came to the conclusion that China could carry out industrialization on its own. No doubt, his realization of the unavoidable Sino-Soviet split must have also affected his thinking. In February 1958, he confidently launched the Great Leap Forward drive, plunging the whole nation into frenetic activities to increase industrial and agricultural production. As far as he was concerned, he had spent quite some time in conceiving the ambitious but unrealistic plan. In the winter of 1957, he started to put his ideas together, relying more on his own imagination rather than expert advice. Then at the National People's Congress in the following February, he produced the outline of the Great Leap Forward movement for endorsement. Needless to say, the congress voiced its unanimous support, though some of the delegates must have had their doubts and fears.

On all accounts, the Great Leap Forward was doomed to failure before it even took off. With self-reliance as the keynote, the campaign, as Mao conceived it, was based on the successful mobilization of human power. Without any scientific and technical knowledge, the Chairman believed that all obstacles could be overcome by numerous pairs of hands with the aid of revolutionary enthusiasm. In his usual sweeping manner, he promised the nation to 'overtake Britain in fifteen years and the United States in thirty, as if it were a foregone conclusion. He urged the peasants to resort to their ingenuity in producing more crops, and encouraged the workers to take over industrial production from the engineers and specialists, in the belief that 'to be red is more important than to be experts'.

But ignorant and limited though Mao might be, he had no trouble in driving the Chinese people to leap forward. In the spirit of self-reliance, backyard furnaces were raised to make steel and antiquated refining processes were brought back into use. To make up for the shortage of iron ore, pans, knives, bolts and latches of every household were collected to feed these furnaces. And when there was not enough coal, firewood was used instead. Frankly, most people could not tell the difference between steel and iron, let alone the furnace temperature required. The enthusiasm was not matched by the products, despite all the exaltations and newspaper headlines.

On the agricultural front the leap was not as impressive as it was made out to be. True, there were individual cases of good crops in some places, but they were far from universal. In order to please the Chairman, the cadres undertook to falsify the figures and exaggerate the harvests as a usual practice. Consequently, Mao was led to believe that all was going well while in reality nothing went right. The picture before his eyes in the Forbidden City was most heartening, though many of his comrades were not unaware of the true state of the Great Leap Forward. But they did not have the courage to tell him.

Convinced of his success, however, Mao went further to lay down the guidelines for the Great Leap Forward. Known as the General Line for Socialist Construction, the plan dealt with the correct balance between the industrial and agricultural development. It also stipulated the coordination of national and local industries and encouraged the employment of both modern and indigenous production methods. To popularize such a concept, Mao used the vivid expression of 'walking on two legs' in many of his utterances up and down the country. In this period he travelled a lot, often appearing at the most unexpected places to inspire, he thought, the people. Doubtlessly, having been saturated in the atmosphere of adulation and worship as he was, it was only natural for him to overestimate his personal influence.

But as usual, Mao was too impatient to wait for the Great Leap Forward to produce any tangible results before he took another step. In March 1958, it suddenly occurred to him that the existing agricultural cooperatives should be reorganized and incorporated into the people's communes to spur the Great Leap. To be fair to him, he had been toying with the idea since the completion of land reform in the early 1950s. The trouble was, he obviously chose the wrong time to impose such a radical change on the basically conservative peasants. In any case, his proposal was dutifully accepted by the Politburo. In June the people's commune came into being, and within two months, more than 740,000 advanced agricultural cooperatives were absorbed into some 24,000 people's communes.

Extremely pleased with his master stroke, Mao proclaimed it to be a part of his Three Red Banners policy — the other two being the Great Leap Forward and the General Line for Socialist Construction. Perhaps it is worth noting that Mao's obsession with the people's commune system was partly caused by his firm belief in the inevitability of a Sino-Soviet military clash. In his concept, each commune was not just a production unit. It was organized along the lines of a local government, complete with its own military arm in the form of a militia. He intended each commune to be a separate fighting command in the event of war, self-sufficient and capable of harassing the enemy with guerrilla tactics. To project this very aspect of the people's commune, he called for 'militarization of the organization, combatization of action and collectivization of life'. In a sense, he was trying to revive the military system of the Han Dynasty in the second century, combining soldiers and peasants into one entity in the hope that national defence and agricultural production would complement each other. What he did not take into account was the change of time. Nor did he seem to realize the complexities of adapting an ancient system to a modern society.

Worse still, he totally ignored the customs and traditions cherished by the Chinese people when he enforced the 'collectivization of life'. With public ownership as the basis, he took away the private lots of the peasants after they were forced to join people's communes. And to break up the family ties, he made them eat in the same mess halls and send their children to the day nurseries. Of course this was done in the name of efficiency and organization but the peasants were no fools. After a hard day's labour, they would like to relax over a family meal surrounded by wives and children. Not that they would have had better food at home, but they felt entitled to some form of private life. Between the farm work and the evening classes for political studies, they needed some moments which they could call their own.

The discontent did not seem serious at first; but it soon spread far and wide. This was not helped by the mismanagement of most people's communes, not to mention the lack of leadership at this level. Production went down and morale became the central issue. The peasants lost their interest in work, since they had been deprived of all material incentives.

But Mao was not in the mood to concede defeat despite the gathering storm. Instead he pushed even harder. He simply could not see how his Three Red Banners should fail to arouse the Chinese people to work for the early realization of his type of socialist society. It was possible that he overestimated the political consciousness of the peasants who had, after all, been subjected to ceaseless thought-remoulding processes since the land reform. More important perhaps, having established himself as the absolute ruler who could do no wrong, he had to maintain his authority by refusing to face the realities. Besides, he really believed in the 'correctness' of his political philosophy. It was inconceivable to him that his ideas could be unworkable. He could not understand human nature.

Perhaps he should have listened to Liu Shao-chi before he plunged into the whirl of economic adventurism crystallized by his Three Red Banners policy. In his political report to the Eighth Party Congress in September 1956, Liu criticized the agricultural cooperatives for their 'overemphasis of collective interest and collective management, erroneously overlooking the individual interests and individual liberties of their members'. He concluded that 'such errors must be quickly rectified' for the common good. What Mao did with the people's communes was to repeat the same errors committed by the agricultural cooperatives, and to a greater degree.

However, towards the end of 1958, even Mao had to admit that the Great Leap Forward had been a flop. At a Central Committee meeting in December, it was decided that the movement should be modified and readjusted for necessary reasons. The peasants were allowed to keep small private lots and to engage in sideline production, provided they did their share of work for the communes. Public mess halls were disbanded and the land reverted to collective ownership, with the production team as the basic unit responsible for gains or losses. In other words, this was a retreat from the Great Leap Forward and Mao's dream was crushed.

Ostensibly to devote more time to the study of ideology, he resigned as chairman of the People's Republic of China, to be succeeded by Liu Shao-chi who was to salvage the people's commune system by introducing material incentives and encouraging diversified production methods. This could hardly have met Mao's approval. But he chose to remain quiet. Although he had to stay out of the limelight for the time being, he knew he would come back. As chairman of the Chinese Communist Party, he was still regarded as the supreme leader of the whole country. Waiting in the wings, he lost none of his appetite for another power struggle.

10 THE ADDICTION TO POWER

For any other man in Mao's position, the price he paid for the ill-fated Great Leap Forward would have seemed acceptable. He might have been forced to surrender some authority, yet it had been so carefully worked out that his prestige remained intact. In the eyes of the ordinary people, his image as the national leader was as firm as ever. The personality cult continued to flourish, and he was still at the head of the collective leadership in every sense.

But obviously Mao thought otherwise. For him power must be monopolized, not shared. Having assumed full control of the party since 1945, he was not prepared to let it slip out of his hands despite everything. Unable to see his own errors, he refused to accept the responsibility for the failure of the Great Leap Forward. In his mind, it could have worked if his ideas had been correctly carried out by the cadres at all levels. It was unimaginable to him that the whole task could have met with the strong opposition from the peasants, knowing them as he had before. He felt that he had been let down, though he had yet to point an accusing finger in some direction.

He spent most of 1959 out of the public eye, which was nothing unusual since he had never shown much interest in ceremonial matters. Dividing his time between Peking and Hangchow, he seemed to take things in his stride. Except for his wife, Chiang Ching, and a few confidants, he generally kept his own company.

In July he appeared at Lushan, the summer resort near Kiukiang, to preside over the Central Committee meeting with the Great Leap Forward as the focus of discussion. At this point, he was still convinced that the Great Leap Forward, in spite of its minor setbacks, had been an

201

unprecedented success. Armed with falsified production figures and highly unreliable progress reports, he began to talk about the possibility of 'catching up with Britain in industrial production within four years'. At this rate, he enthused, there was every chance 'for us to overtake Britain much sooner than fifteen years'.

While most people at the conference refrained from openly disagreeing with him, the Defence Minister, Peng Teh-huai, spoke up. He first expressed his doubts about the success stories of the Great Leap Forward at a sub-committee meeting. Then he wrote Mao a long letter stating his views on the movement, listing both its merits and faults. The letter was actually frank and sincere, without any trace of the malice Peng was later accused of during the Cultural Revolution. Peng began his letter by praising the correctness of Mao's Three Red Banners policy and the 'great achievement' in 1958, full of enthusiasm and euphemism. He went on to suggest that errors had been committed in the execution of the General Line of Socialist Construction, caused by 'overhastiness and the lack of experience'. As a result, he said, capital had been frittered away and some targets unreached. He also pointed out that even in 1959 no effective measures had been taken to rectify these errors so that the policy could be set on an even keel.

Perhaps unwittingly, the Defence Minister criticized the 'confusion and chaos' in the running of the people's communes which had created serious problems. But meanwhile, he hastened to add that since the successive work conferences held in Wuchang, Chengchow and Shanghai, 'the defects and errors of the system had been basically rectified and the chaotic state was largely over'.

As for the Great Leap Forward, he saw it as the Chairman's master stroke in solving the serious problem of unemployment, quite warm in his praise. But he was at his most sarcastic when he commented on the backyard steel furnaces. He dismissed the idea of 'making steel by the whole people' (Mao's famous slogan) as absurd, though not in these exact words. After pointing out the waste of raw material, money and human power in carrying out the programme, he estimated that 'it has cost the nation 2,000,000,000 RMP dollars (about 1,320,000,000 US dollars) to improve the technical knowledge of the cadres'.

Finally, he told Mao in no uncertain terms that most of the production figures had either been 'exaggerated or falsified, thus creating the illusion of having solved the food shortage'. He criticized the official newspapers for their part in reporting 'incredible miracles' in both argicultural and industrial production, making it impossible for people 'to come to grips with the real situation for a considerable length of time'. This must have, he said, damaged the prestige and credibility of the party, which should not be allowed to continue. And, to make it even harder for Mao to swallow, he summed up the Great Leap Forward as the product of 'petit bourgeois fervour, liable to give rise to a series of leftist errors'. Once the party line inclined to the left, he argued, 'most comrades are bound to think we can step into Communism at one stride, abandoning the mass line and pragmatism which have been the features of our party'. He appealed to Mao to place greater emphasis on party solidarity, stressing the importance of 'democracy within the party'. While agreeing that the Great Leap Forward should be carried on, he reminded the Chairman of the need to overcome the unavoidable difficulties with patience and care.

Mao exploded after reading the letter. He saw it as Peng's plot to undermine his leadership in an indirect manner. Although the Defence Minister did not criticize the Three Red Banners policy sweepingly, the Chairman was not in the habit of accepting criticisms with grace. He hated to be questioned about the soundness of his decisions, for he considered himself as the man who had every right to charter the course for the new China he had created. Subconsciously, he likened himself to the imperial rulers in the past dynasties who could do whatever they desired with their humble subjects. He was to be obeyed, not to be challenged. Having had to resign as Chairman of the State was already too much for him; he could not help associating Peng's opposition to his policy with the disgrace he had just experienced. He suspected that the Defence Minister was among a group of conspirators who had been planning his downfall.

For three days the Chairman was ominously reticent, sitting through the meeting with his inscrutable smile. On the fourth day he took action. With copies of Peng's letter distributed to everyone at the meeting beforehand, he summed up the achievements of the Lushan conference in his capacity as the chairman. Suddenly he directed everybody's attention to Peng's letter, stating that it merited a thorough discussion from the ideological angle. Immediately he launched a forty-minute tirade against the confounded Peng, who had not had the slightest inkling that Mao would deal with his letter in such a manner.

Telling the meeting that Peng's criticisms of the people's communes were completely unfounded, the Chairman denounced him as a malicious objector to his General Line of Socialist Construction. He insisted that Peng had planned his campaign very carefully. 'Superficially Peng Teh-huai may have voiced his support of the people's commune system', he said, 'but you only have to read between the lines to spot his objection. Most people would have mentioned the merits of people's communes before criticizing the mistakes. But Peng dwelt on their defects and errors alone.' Then he went on to deny the existence of falsified production figures and exaggerated success stories, accusing Peng of having failed to keep in touch with the real developments. As regards Peng's remark about the 'petit bourgeois fervour', Mao was extremely bitter. He attributed these words to the Defence Minister's deep-rooted antagonism to the socialist system. 'If the People's Libera-tion Army decided to follow the lead of Peng Teh-huai', he said furiously, 'I would have to step down to fight another guerrilla war.'

His outburst made it difficult for anyone to speak up on Peng's behalf, since it was obvious that the Chairman wanted to get rid of him, with or without the letter. Since his appointment to the defence post, Peng had been taking measures to modernize the army on the Soviet pattern. This was regarded by Mao as his design to undercut the party's control of the army. Unable to understand the complexities of modern warfare, he still believed that the outcome of a war would be decided by the human factor rather than fire-power. He saw no reason why the Chinese Army could not carry on the revolutionary tradition of concentrating on political indoctrination and adhering to his concept of the people's war. And at the back of his mind, he was suspicious of the possible connection between the Soviet Union and Peng in modernizing the army. A man with a long memory, he could hardly have forgotten about the rivalries within the party inspired by the Russians in the recent past, especially after the exposure of Kao Kang's conspiracy in 1954.

Unfortunately for Peng, at the Eighth Party Congress in 1956, he was the one who proposed to eliminate the clause about Mao Tse-tung's Thought from the preamble of the new party statutes. At the time Mao could not do anything about it, since he himself stressed the importance of discouraging any form of personality cult. But this did not stop him from bearing a grudge against Peng. He merely bided his time to take revenge.

At the end of the Lushan conference, however, Mao told the Central Committee to dismiss Peng from his defence post, giving him the opportunity 'to improve himself through political studies and self-criticisms'. His order was duly carried out and Peng was summarily sent to a remote place in Szechuan province under surveillance. Although he was allowed to take his wife, Pu An-hsiu, with him, she had the unenviable job of having to write reports about his 'ideological progress'.

Understandably, Peng resented the treatment very much. He continued to criticize Mao in front of his occasional visitors who were actually sent by the Chairman to spy on him. But as these people were mostly his old comrades, they did not have the heart to carry out their assignment faithfully. Instead they would report back that Peng had been showing signs of remorse, though he was rather slow in consolidating his political consciousness. Probably due to these reports, Mao did not take further action against the man he had previously praised as 'my greatest general' in one of his poems.

For several years Peng lived in oblivion, with gardening and fishing as his pastimes. Then the Cultural Revolution broke out in the autumn of 1965. Since the historical play *The Dismissal of Hai Jui* by Wu Han, a deputy mayor of Peking, was interpreted by Mao himself as the author's attempt to insinuate at his wrongful treatment of the former Defence Minister, Peng immediately became one of the main targets for the rampaging Red Guards. He was dragged out by the young hotheads for 'open trial', submitted to physical tortures and verbal abuses. Removed to another place in solitary confinement, he died a few years later under a cloud of suspicion.

It goes without saying that Peng was but one of the countless victims who had, knowingly or unknowingly, incurred Mao's displeasure. But at the Lushan conference in 1959, the Chairman looked over his shoulder all the time. He might have been adamant about the correctness of his Three Red Banners policy, but there must have been moments of doubt in his mind. Fully aware of the fact that power produces authority, he was much worried by the political alliance formed by Liu Shao-chi and Teng Hsiao-ping. With Liu steadily gaining in popularity and Teng controlling the party machine, he was often left out of some important matters. As he later complained during the Cultural Revolution, his two rivals seemed to have deliberately kept him in the dark about many things. According to him, he could not even afford to talk freely in private, for 'his residence was bugged' on the two's instructions. Under these circumstances, perhaps it was not unnatural for him to read conspiracy in everything. He was determined to regain his monolithic power at any cost.

But to avoid the risk of beating the grass and disturbing the hidden snake, as the Chinese saying goes, he went about it with enormous patience and great caution. By appointing Lin Piao as Defence Minister to succeed Peng, he was not just trying to restore the emphasis on political orientation of the army. Knowing all about Lin's political ambition, he intended to cultivate the new army chief as his 'closest comrade-in-arms' on whose shoulders he could place the responsibility of launching his contemplated counter-attack on the Liu-Teng alliance.

Having lost effective control of the party, he had to build his power base in the army, gradually and inconspicuously.

In this respect Lin certainly did not let him down. With Mao's approval, he set out to build up the Chairman's ideological influence in the army. He compiled his sayings in a condensed version, aptly called 'Quotations from Chairman Mao', to be distributed to all the men as reading matter. The pocket-sized book, later to be known as *The Little Red Book*, was to be carried by every soldier day and night, as essential as his weapon and ammunition. Between drills and brief spells of rest, both officers and men must read Mao's quotations until they could remember them by heart. Lin also had small badges with the Chairman's image made, to be worn by the men on their uniforms. In his speeches and writings, he described Mao as the Father of the Red Army, conveniently omitting to mention the part played by Marshal Chu Teh and others. These intensive efforts proved to be very effective, and the Mao cult was firmly established in the army.

Quietly keeping abreast of the new development, Mao was delighted. But it did not make him relax his guard. Without anyone he could really trust, he relied on his wife, Chiang Ching, to maintain secret contacts with Lin. Because of her involvement in the production of revolutionary films and stage plays, she was able to make frequent trips between Peking and other places without arousing undesirable curiosity. Incidentally, Mao seemed to have taken pains to get her the job she needed for her cover. In 1962, he suddenly pontificated to the Central Committee on the importance of 'Grasping Class Struggle in the Ideological Field'. In this speech he advanced the view that the party should impose a tighter control on the performing arts, apart from reiterating what he had always said about art and literature. At the end he proposed to create a supervisory post and nominated Chiang Ching. As no one seemed to have any reason to oppose him, the resolution was carried.

In retrospect, this must be seen as one of Mao's shrewdest moves to outwit his rivals. Having failed to install Chiang Ching in the party organization at a higher level as he had tried before, he now managed to find her a seemingly inconsequential position which appeared to be a temporary arrangement. An ex-actress not known for her political astuteness, she impressed most of Mao's associates with her flippancy rather than her brain. To them it would have seemed harmless enough for her to meddle with the performing arts which they tended to dismiss as something insignificant. Some even regarded her new assignment as the Chairman's way of appeasing a nagging wife whose vanity had always been the talking point among the top comrades. Little did they realize that Mao had been planning to attack the party from outside with a series of unprecedented measures, and that Chiang Ching's new responsibility was but a part of his scheme.

As Mao later admitted, with the party entrenched in 'bureaucracy and revisionism', he had no alternative but to 'rely on the masses to make revolution'. To mobilize the masses, he decided that nothing could be more effective than revolutionary plays and films. He wanted to stir up their emotions for quick action, without the slightest intention of appealing to their reasoning power. Although in 1962 he had not yet conceived the idea of the Cultural Revolution, he had, however, made up his mind 'to create chaos in order to achieve great harmony'. Obviously, with his wife responsible for revolutionizing plays and films, he had no trouble in directing her to use the newly acquired medium to pave the way for mass agitation. Ironically, his rivals might have disapproved of the universally monotonous themes and stereotyped characters in Chiang Ching's productions; they did not seem to be perceptive enough to see the hidden motive behind them.

With Peking under the firm control of Liu Shao-chi and Teng Hsiao-chi, Chiang Ching encountered considerable opposition when she tried her hand at revolutionizing ballets, orchestras and dramas. In a way, this was a blessing in disguise. She immediately left for Shanghai where she enlisted the help of Ke Ching-shih, the local party chief high in Mao's confidence. It also enabled her to recruit Chang Chun-chiao and Yao Wen-yuan, two subsequent members of the Gang of Four directing the Cultural Revolution, into her camp. Benefiting from the favourable situation, she launched ferocious attacks on some of the current stage plays in a glare of publicity. The *Liberation Daily* controlled by Ke gave her full support, and was soon to be joined by the *Liberation Army Daily* with Lin Piao's tacit approval. All of a sudden, she assumed the role of a literary supremo unopposed. Away in Peking, the Central Committee could not do anything without having a showdown with Mao himself. Encouraged by her initial success, Chiang Ching moved on to direct and produce two revolutionary ballets, *The White-haired Girl* and *The Red Detachment of Women*. Predictably, the former dealt with the landlord's inhuman torture of his farm-hands while the latter eulogized a group of women's heroic deeds in supporting the Liberation Army during the civil war. They were first staged in Shanghai, and then in Peking. By this time, the voice of opposition was hushed.

In September 1964, she collected her first political reward. She was 'elected' to the National People's Congress representing her native province of Shantung, presumably for her contribution to the raising of the ideological level of the performing arts. But without a shadow of doubt, this new honour was engineered by Mao to gradually move her up the political ladder.

It was not until one year later that Mao staged the Cultural Revolution, plunging the whole country into great turmoil which was to last for more than ten years. In the summer of 1965, he was finally assured of Lin Piao's unflinching support, after having worked on him for several years. But with a view to the extensive influence exerted by Liu Shao-chi and Teng Hsiao-ping on a national scale, he decided to sound the first trumpet of the Cultural Revolution on a low key. That October he sent Chiang Ching to Shanghai to instruct Yao Wen-yuan to write an article attacking Wu Han's historical play *The Dismissal of Hai Jui*, which he saw as the author's effort to vindicate Peng Teh-huai, the former Defence Minister whom he sacked in 1959 for his criticisms of the Great Leap Forward. Hai Jui, the central character of the play, was a Ming official in the sixteenth century who was wrongfully dismissed by the emperor because of his concern for the peasants' welfare. The strange thing was, Wu Han would not have ventured to write the play had Mao not encouraged him to do so in 1962 during an interview. The suggestion that the author intended to malign Mao by likening Peng to the Ming official, as Mao himself insisted, was even more unthinkable. Hardly knowing the former Defence Minister, there were no grounds for Wu to stick his neck out for such an undertaking. A historian by training, he accurately presented the historical facts in his work. That the Chairman should have drawn a parallel between an unpopular Ming emperor and himself was his misfortune. But like all dictators, Mao constantly lived in fear and suspicion. Once he suspected something or someone, he would never admit that he might possibly be wrong.

On the other hand, since his main target was Liu Shao-chi, he would have considered it wise to direct his attack against one of Liu's less prominent protégés such as Wu. It conformed with his struggle strategy of 'digging the wall corner before pushing the wall down'. He was even more shrewd in unleashing Yao Wen-yuan to lead the probing attack. A stage critic without much distinction, Yao was not yet known for his association with Chiang Ching. If his criticism of Wu Han's play failed to spark off the Cultural Revolution, as Mao had expected, he was expendable. It would be most unlikely that Mao's role behind the scenes would be discovered. In that case, the Chairman could plan another assault with a different strategy.

But to Mao's great satisfaction Yao succeeded in taking the country by storm with his article. After its appearance in a Shanghai newspaper, the article drew both favourable and unfavourable comments. While some writers agreed with the young critic, others deplored his transparently vicious attitude in attacking a well-received play. With great enthusiasm both sides locked themselves in the ensuing debate, refuting each other in a flood of newspaper articles. This was exactly what Mao wanted, for he needed such an atmosphere to 'raise the discussions to the ideological level', his code words for the launching of the Cultural Revolution.

Without indicating his wish to destroy the party machine at this point, he called for 'ideological purity' and 'correct attitude towards class struggle'. On his instructions, the official publications rushed out articles to condemn Wu Han for his attempts 'to revive reactionary and feudal rule in China'. His other writings, including those published before the Communists came to power, were re-examined and attacked with equal venom. Meanwhile, more and more academics and writers were singled out as advocates for 'reactionary bourgeois ideology' to be subjected to criticism and verbal attack before they were publicly humiliated and physically tortured to death by the Red Guards when the Cultural Revolution reached its height.

When the Cultural Revolution or rather its prelude actually commenced in the autumn of 1965, Mao appeared to be able to conduct himself with some restraint. There were signs that he was quite prepared to rely on his supporters within the party to struggle with the Liu-Teng elements till he gained the upper hand. With Lin Piao and the army on his side, he did not expect Liu Shao-chi and Teng Hsiao-ping to put up the resistance they did. But when frustrations continued to pile up in the next few months, he began to realize the futility of pursuing the conventional approach. He found his directives concerning the Cultural Revolution constantly altered, distorted or, at the best, watered down. He could not even count on the Central Cultural Revolution Group, which was formed under his order, to function properly to give the country a lead.

In May 1966, he forcibly reorganized the Central Cultural Revolution Group, bringing in his personal secretary, Chen Po-ta, and his wife, Chiang Ching, to head it. The stage was now set for the introduction of militancy and other radical means. In June the first group of Red Guards appeared on the campus of Peking's Tsinghua University, chanting slogans and putting up wall posters in support of Mao's guidelines for the Cultural Revolution. There were only scores of them, and the school authorities benignly tolerated their extra-curriculum activities by turning a blind eye. But the Chairman was not slow in showing his approval of the budding movement. Within days he wrote words of encouragement for these students to use in their wall posters. He praised their revolutionary enthusiasm and urged them on. The unusual gesture shocked the bureaucracy but sparked off the fanatic fervour of the student population in the whole country. Almost overnight the Red Guards began to appear in every school and their number shot up at an amazing pace. Now in their millions, they exuded 'boundless vitality', as Mao put it, and became a formidable force full of 'proletarian revolutionary rebel spirit'.

To signify his personal link with the Red Guard movement, the Chairman took another unusual step. He allowed these youths, mostly in their teens, to abandon their studies and converge on Peking 'to make revolution'. By that August, more than a million Red Guards poured into the capital for the pilgrimage. On the 18th Mao made his dramatic appearance on the rostrum in the Tienanmen Square when a mass rally of the Red Guards was suddenly called. Flanked by Lin Piao and Chou En-lai, the Chairman in his military uniform waved and smiled to the hysterical crowd below. He received an armband with the inscription of the Red Guards which was presented to him by the representatives of the rally. To thunderous cheers he immediately wore it around his left arm as a gesture to identify with them. The act of public approval created an immense impact for it was now clear to the whole country who was behind these young rebels. Since that day Mao continued to review the Red Guards in their tens of thousands, until 13,000,000 of them had marched past before his eyes. His message for them was extremely simple: make revolution and rebel against any form of authority. In other words, he ordered them to destroy everything.

If Mao's employment of such a strategy to regain power appeared to be totally irresponsible, it reflected his state of mind. Like ancient rulers in Chinese history, he felt that he owned the country, and was entitled to do whatever he liked with it. As far as he was concerned, to oust Liu Shao-chi and Teng Hsiao-ping he must resort to surprise moves, lest he should stand very little chance of success. Not that he failed to foresee that the unleashing of the Red Guards would throw the whole country into turmoil and chaos; he simply did not care. Having controlled the army through Lin Piao, he knew he could always use it to hold the Red Guards in line when the need arose.

But he was most unforgivable when he called upon the Red Guards to destroy the 'old ideas, old culture, old customs and old habits of the bourgeoisie' in order to bring about a new society. Acting under this slogan, millions of Red Guards rampaged the country, demolishing historical monuments, ransacking museums and public libraries, burning Buddhist temples and destroying countless works of art. With equal ignorance and viciousness, they caused incalculable losses to the nation's culture and heritage.

This would have been too much for any rational man, but Mao had no intention of dampening the revolutionary zeal of his 'little generals'. Instead of curbing the mass hooliganism and indiscriminate destruction, he encouraged the Red Guards to carry on their mission with greater determination. He assured them that 'there is no construction without destruction, and destruction means revolution'. Inspired or rather possessed, the young hotheads turned to their new targets. They criticized and attacked the authorities, accusing them of having betrayed Mao's trust. Professors, scientists, scholars and writers of note were all dragged out to be physically assaulted and publicly humiliated. At first these cases looked a result of the outbursts of youthful fanaticism. But in reality, they were the preliminaries of the much more ambitious onslaught on the party hierarchy soon to follow. With his wife, Chiang Ching, and her Gang of Four taking charge of the Red Guards, Mao had been designing to undermine the power base of his rivals from the very bottom. To chop down a big tree, he deemed it necessary to lop the branches off first. Since Liu Shao-chi had the support of the party organization and the intellectuals, he was forced to employ the strategy of 'converging our attacks against the enemy from the exterior'.

Meanwhile, to consolidate his alliance with Lin Piao, he made Chiang Ching responsible for the cultural and literary work in the army. And, to control the army's propaganda line, he had his daughter Li Na, still in her twenties, made chief editor of the *Liberation Army Daily*. Discreetly but determinedly, he took steps to lay the foundation for the Mao dynasty. Marxism or no Marxism, he obviously showed more interest in passing at least some part of his power to his wife and daughter. The bargain he had struck with Lin Piao may never be known, but it would not be too dogmatic for one to presume that some provisions could have been made for Chiang Ching when he eventually named Lin as his future successor in the 1969 Constitution.

Actually, he came to terms with Lin Piao about the succession issue as early as August 1966. At a Central Committee meeting in that month, he nominated the then Defence Minister as his heir-apparent before he started to criticize Liu Shao-chi. As revealed in later documents, the Chairman did not then plan to submit Liu to public humiliation. He hoped that his main rival would admit his errors and show signs of repentance to plead for leniency. But to everyone's surprise Liu put up a strong resistance, defending himself vigorously against all charges. His uncompromising attitude made Mao realize that he had no alternative but to smash the party machine into pieces with the aid of the Red Guards. Although he had been prepared to go to extremes all the time, he would have settled for a less drastic solution if Liu had not been so unco-operative. For his own benefit, he still wanted to use a repentant Liu to check Lin Piao. An old hand in the power game, he thrived on playing one off against the other. Despite Lin Piao's sworn allegiance, he would not like to relax his guard.

When it became clear that Liu would rather die than give in, in January 1967 Mao ordered the Red Guards to attack 'the supreme command of the black gang within the party' and seize power. Thus the big witch-hunt began like a conflagration. It went on for months before the name of Liu Shao-chi was formally mentioned. This did not mean that Mao still hoped for Liu's surrender under the intolerable pressure; he merely created the tense atmosphere to scare many more of Liu's followers into making confessions or breaking down. He counted on the mob violence exerted by the Red Guards to produce results which were otherwise unobtainable. He derived much satisfaction from the humiliation suffered by his old comrades at the hands of hordes of young fanatics knowing nothing better than waving the *Little Red Book* of his quotations. His talk about perpetual revolution and his emphasis on the wisdom of the masses were but the rhetoric he used to conceal the true nature of the relentless power struggle.

After removing Liu Shao-chi, Teng Hsiao-ping and the important members of their clique from the key posts either in the party or in the government, Mao started talking about winding up the Cultural Revolu-tion within the next year for 'its aims have basically been achieved'. But it was not to be. By this time the Red Guards ran out of control. With millions of them continuing to rampage the country 'to make revolution', both industrial and agricultural production was seriously disrupted. Workers were restless and peasants voiced their protests. To make matters worse, in spite of Mao's directive to the People's Liberation Army to 'support the left', the clashes between the army and the Red Guards became more and more frequent.

As Mao realized that it was impossible for him to do without the army, he decided to get rid of the Red Guards by sending them to the country-side to assist agricultural production. With exaltations and sublime messages, they were bundled off to devote themselves to 'constructive work after the great destruction'. Unhappy though the Red Guards were, they had to obey the Great Helmsman who could always rely on the army to chase them away from the cities.

If the treatment Mao dealt to the 'little red generals' of the Cultural

Revolution appeared to be harsh, it certainly did not give him a sleepless night since the usefulness of these Red Guards had expired. As the rules governing the Chinese game of chess dictate, once you succeed in moving other pieces across the river, the pawns are to be sacrificed. When Mao first mobilized the Red Guards, his main aim was to take his rivals by surprise. Now that the party machine had been broken up, he had to concern himself with the redistribution of power and reorganization, neither of which would require the continuing dominance of the young hotheads.

To effect a radical change of the power structure, Mao introduced the policy of organizing revolutionary committees at all levels to replace the existing party and governmental organizations. In conformity with this theory about solidarity through struggle, he stipulated that the revolutionary committee should be formed on the basis of a 'three-way alliance', consisting of representatives from the army, the revolutionary masses (the Red Guards) and the reformed party cadres. He had to bring the army into the arena of political power for he was dependent on Lin Piao's support when the country was still beset with confusion and disorder. Nor could he afford to exclude the Red Guard leaders although he had clipped their wings by sending the bulk of their followers to the countryside. Besides, it was also his wish to cultivate a new generation of revolutionaries who would never cease to carry out the more radical side of his political line such as perpetual revolution and endless class struggle. As to the inclusion of the party cadres who had previously sided with the Liu Shao-chi clique, it was out of necessity since they had the experience and the expertise. Then of course, it must have been clear to Mao that he could not completely dismantle the party.

But despite Mao's endeavour to restore order through the setting up of revolutionary committees, things did not turn out as smoothly as he had expected. To him the sharing of power between the army, the revolutionary masses and the party cadres seemed to be an ideal solution, especially since it would enable him to control all of them through the common channel of revolutionary committees. But even with his political shrewdness, he failed to take into account the conflict of interest between the three totally different power groups. Having played its part as the guardian of the Cultural Revolution, the army felt entitled to a rich reward. The idea of having to share power with the others was hard to accept, if not totally unacceptable. With their role already reduced, the Red Guard leaders saw the revolutionary committees as the vehicle for them to recoup some of their political influence. They resented the army's dominance and refused to play second fiddle. As for the party cadres, to be given back some of their former power was indeed quite welcome. Yet it was hard for them to defer to the other two factions of the revolutionary committees without feeling aggrieved.

Because of these conflicts, the forming of revolutionary committees led to numerous rounds of power struggles at all levels, though less publicized. It took months for one revolutionary committee to come into being. Even when it was finally formed, the conflicts within continued to exist. The "three-way alliance' conceived by Mao never worked, in spite of all the praise piled on him. But this did not seem to bother the Chairman. Isolated at the top, he had no way of finding out everything. Moreover, obstinate and self-opinionated as usual, he could not believe that his ideas were less than perfect.

Meanwhile, it seemed that his relationship with Lin Piao began to sour during the process of forging the 'three-way alliance'. Understandably, Lin would like to grab as many revolutionary committees as possible. To expand his influence in the army to a further extent, he wanted to turn all revolutionary committees into power bases for the military. Although Mao had publicly proclaimed him to be his successor, he was not unaware of the Chairman's efforts to build up Chiang Ching in the leadership's stake. Familiar with Mao's political intrigues in the past, he found it necessary to take precautions against all eventualities. As he saw it, the 'three-way alliance' was a ploy to weaken the army's virtual control of the political situation. But since Mao was devious enough to conceal his real intention, he had to go along with it. While never failing to voice his support, he took positive measures to ensure the army's domination in the set-up of revolutionary committees. This naturally caused much resentment among the Red Guard leaders, who continued to rally around Chiang Ching and her associates who were known as the Cultural Revolution Clique.

It did not take Mao long to see through Lin. But he chose to bide his time. Realistic as he was, he did not want to confront his 'closest comrade-in-arms' prematurely. Moreover, it was difficult for him to turn abruptly against Lin without shaking up the army. Gradually and carefully, he started working on the other military leaders through the aid of Chou En-lai. He knew he must win over Lin's rivals in the army before he could contemplate his next move. As Chou was always prepared to defer to his wishes, he had no hesitation in relying on him to carry out the delicate operation. He seemed to have the gift of choosing the right man for the right job. Perhaps this was why he generally succeeded in beating his opponents.

Mao's waiting game, from his own angle, paid off. When time dragged on, Lin Piao lost his patience. As from 1970, he could not help noticing the rapid rise of Chiang Ching's political status. With Mao seldom seen or heard in public, she became the Chairman's voice. Whatever she said or did, she claimed to represent her husband. Since it was impossible for anyone to challenge her, she began to wield more and more power. Obviously with Mao's approval, official publications started to play up her 'contributions to the Cultural Revolution and ideological purity', clearly a part of an orchestrated campaign to increase her stake in the succession ring. As though by coincidence, Mao was quoted as saying that the woman's role in revolution was as important as the man's. While the saying could be interpreted as the Chairman's belief in the political equality between the sexes when the drive to recruit more women cadres was under way, the timing would have raised a few doubts in Lin Piao's mind.

But what worried Lin most was the steady corrosion of his influence in the army as Chou En-lai had been successful in persuading some military commanders to reaffirm their support of the central leadership with Mao and himself at the helm. The development seemed to have swayed Lin towards the decision to stage a military coup to overthrow Mao before it was too late. If the official version of 'Lin Piao's Incident' belatedly issued at the Tenth Party Congress in 1973 was anything to go by, Lin was alleged to have embarked on the road to rebellion against Mao as early as the summer of 1970. Then at a Central Committee meeting, he supposedly planned some moves to undermine Mao's authority without success. In the spring of 1971, however, he went further by making plans for the 8 August military coup. The plot was to kill Mao by setting a time bomb in the special train which was scheduled to take him from Shanghai to Peking. It was exposed by Lin Tou-tou, the Defence Minister's daughter from his first marriage, who secretly alerted Chou En-lai in the nick of time. The strange thing was, Lin was allowed to flee to the Soviet Union about a month later in a British Trident, according to Chou's report, though the plane crashed over Mongolia. Between the exposure of Lin's unsuccessful attempt on Mao's life and the fatal air crash, why Mao and Chou refrained from taking any action against the confirmed conspirator remains a riddle, particularly since the Chairman was never indecisive in seeking his revenge. Stranger still, apart from Lin's wife, Yeh Chun, aboard the crashed airliner were also supposedly his fellow conspirators including the then Chief of Staff, the Air Force Commander, the Navy's Political Commissar and the Commander of Logistic Supplies as Chou claimed. How they could still manage to get together to take off in the same plane seemed incredible, if one considered carefully the tightened security measures since the abortive coup in August.

After Lin Piao's death, Mao tried to put the army under the party's control once again. To clean up Lin's remaining influence, he purged more than sixty military commanders who were known for their past connections with the dead man. In the meantime, be began to make preparations for Chiang Ching to strengthen her ties with the army. He promoted Li Teh-sheng, Commander of the Anhwei Military Region, to the post of Director of the General Political Department of the People's Liberation Army, entrusting him with the work of upholding his political line in the army. With proven loyalty to Mao by supporting Chiang Ching during the Cultural Revolution, Li was regarded by the Chairman as the ideal person to assist Chiang Ching in military matters when the time was ripe. His design became even clearer later on. In 1973, he made Li one of the five Vice-Chairmen of the Central Committee, rubbing shoulders with Chou En-lai, Wang Hung-wen, Kang Sheng and Yeh Chien-ying, before sending him to take over the all-important Military Region of Shenyang (Mukden) a few months later. It was, therefore, not surprising that Li quickly had Mao Yuan-hsin, the Chairman's nephew and a university drop-out, as his political commissar, in return for the special favour.

But even with all intentions to hand over power to Chiang Ching, Mao must have had doubts about her ability and political credentials. He only had to look around to see the odds against her. In spite of her seat in the Politburo and the Central Committee, she was far from being securely established in the reorganized party hierarchy. Her active role during the Cultural Revolution had won her more foes than friends. And as the executor of Mao's radical political line, she would have to face the consequences once the Chairman was no longer around. These considerations seemed to have affected Mao's decision on the succession issue. He chose to help install a leftist collective leadership including Chiang Ching which would, he hoped, carry on his rigid policies regarding socialist reconstruction, reviving the Great Leap Forward spirit. In spite of all the disastrous effects, he was still adamant that his Three Red Banners — the Great Leap Forward, the People's Communes and the General Line for Socialist Construction — would work well in China.

As the collective leadership could not be formed without solidarity, he laid down the guidelines by forging another kind of 'Three-way Alliance' — the alliance of the old, the middle-aged and the young at all levels of the party machine. This meant the even distribution of responsible posts among all age groups, in the hope that conflicts arising from the generation gap and the internal rivalry could be resolved. It was also Mao's idea to maintain continuity without blocking the way of new talents. But being a revolutionary romantic, he tended to underestimate the difficulties of introducing radical reforms to a party which had become the sole ruling class and the establishment. It was not surprising that the preconceived alliance merely served to sharpen the conflicts within the party. Those who had the power refused to share it, and those who wanted to obtain it had to fight.

Naturally, at the top Mao encountered no open opposition in the process of enforcing his new 'Three-way Alliance'. At the Tenth Party Congress in 1973, he undertook to elevate Chiang Ching's three associates Chang Chun-chiao, Yao Wen-yuan and Wang Hung-wen to the power centre at one stroke. Together with Chiang Ching, they were all made members of the Politburo. In the eyes of the top comrades, this was already too much. But Mao did not stop here. On the basis of his 'Three-way Alliance' theory, he picked Wang Hung-wen, the thirty-six-year-old Shanghai factory worker, as Vice-Chairman of the Central Committee, with only Chou En-lai taking precedence over him in the power structure. By according Wang the highest honour, Mao made a very shrewd move. He was in fact making him hold the seat for Chiang Ching, since it would be scandalous for her to become a Vice-Chairman at this early stage. Without much intelligence or political experience, Wang could be, Mao thought, easily manipulated by Chiang Ching with the aid of Chang and Yao. Furthermore, such an arrangement would make his design to build the Mao dynasty less conspicious even though it required more time. Before everything was under control, he did not think it wise to let his wife take unnecessary risks by attracting too much attention.

Fully realizing the importance of military muscle in the power game, Mao tried to lay the foundation for the working relationship between Chiang Ching's Gang of Four and the army. He appointed Chang Chun-chiao Director of the General Political Department of the People's Liberation Army to succeed Li Teh-sheng who moved on to command the Shenyang Military Region. To complement Chang's task of establishing the 'politics takes command' principle, he also detailed Wang Hung-wen, in his capacity as a Vice-Chairman of the Central Military Council, to work on the second echelon of military commanders, doubtlessly with the aim of weakening the position of the top generals. Under the pretext of forming the 'Three-way Alliance' in the army, Wang was able to carry out his mission with qualified success.

Meanwhile, the Chairman did not slacken his usual effort to consolidate the supremacy of his political philosophy. Now reaching the eightieth year of his life, he was increasingly obsessed with the idea of achieving immortality as the greatest thinker in Chinese history. It was no coincidence that he freely admitted that he would like to be remembered as the 'Great Teacher of the Chinese people'. For him, to rule the people was not enough. He wanted to control their minds for generations and generations. This was why he found the intellectuals most undesirable. He could not bear the thought that he did not have the monopoly of knowledge despite his dictatorial power. But as he had never really succeeded in controlling the minds of the Chinese people, he decided that he must launch an all-out attack on Confucius as well as Confucian philosophy which had survived all the political and social changes. Actually, the new attempt indicated his frustration as well as an admission of defeat. He had had high hopes that his philosophy and ideology would prevail over the wisdom of Confucius to become the guiding light for the Chinese people. It had been his belief that his ideals would withstand the challenge from other schools of thought. But after having encountered setbacks in a series of thought-remoulding campaigns since the Hundred Flowers Movement in 1957, he could not but realize that the extensive and profound influence of Confucian philosophy on the Chinese mind must be wiped out before his political ideology could take root and survive.

If the anti-Confucius campaign appeared to have sprung up from nowhere, it did not mean that Mao came to a sudden decision. When the Cultural Revolution formally took off in 1966, the attack on old ideas, old culture, old customs and old habits was, in fact, directed at Confucian philosophy as a whole. At that time, Mao refrained from naming Confucius for fear that the people would not accept it. It was also possible that he saw no need to go to such an extent. But in 1973 he could not afford to be patient and subtle any longer. Knowing that his days were numbered, he had to deal Confucius a final blow. Since he wanted Chiang Ching and her Gang of Four to uphold his political line after his death, this move was essential.

With a view to expanding the campaign on a nation-wide scale, he dragged in Lin Piao as the ancient sage's accomplice. He condemned Lin for his plot of 'restoring the feudal society in the Confucian pattern'. Ridiculous though the charge was, neither Confucius nor Lin Piao was there to refute it. By branding both of them as 'reactionaries', the Chairman obviously believed that he could dissuade the people from resorting to Confucian philosophy for guidance. Since Lin had turned out to be a 'traitor', he might as well establish the cause of his 'treason' as being a Confucian disciple. In his reasoning, this should enlighten the

Chinese people on the harmful nature of Confucius's lasting influence. If the idea bordered on the absurd, Mao put his whole weight behind the Anti-Confucius and Anti-Lin Piao Campaigns in all seriousness. For months to come, official publications were inundated with articles of denunciation along the same line. In Mao's China, one did not even have the freedom of remaining silent.

In the midst of the war of words against Confucius and Lin Piao, however, some articles were evidently written with Chiang Ching's interest in mind. Both Empress Lu of the Han Dynasty (206 B.C. – A.D. 221) and Empress Wu of the Tang Dynasty (A.D. 618 – 907) were enthusiastically discussed from the allegedly Marxist angle. While the political achievements of the two women rulers in the feudal age were affirmed and lauded, the records of their misdemeanors and sexual indulgence were conveniently discarded as historical distortions without a grain of truth. Since in those days 'alluding the past to the present' was a usual practice, anyone could see that these dissertations were intended to promote Chiang Ching's interests. With the propaganda machine firmly under their control, she and her radical associates were anxious to manoeuvre themselves into a more favourable position while they could use Mao as a shield. Although Mao had previously warned his wife of the danger of 'falling heavily down the peak after the hasty climb', he seemed no longer able to impress on her the importance of exercising caution and restraint. When it came to the power game, he could not expect Chiang Ching to handle all the intricacies and assess the situation with his insight and skill.

Perhaps the irony was that her political appetite would have been less insatiable had he not set his mind on the continuity of his political influence after his death. It was for this purpose that he flung the whole country into the destructive and disastrous Cultural Revolution which produced the Red Guards and kindled Chiang Ching's ambition. He might be forgiven for his decision to purge Liu Shao-chi and those leading comrades who were against his radical political line, but his total disregard for the nation's fortunes and the loss of human lives was unforgivable. Being a man of limited intellect and yet intoxicated with power, he simply had to have his way whatever the consequences might be. His ruthlessness sprang from his self-righteousness as much as from his sense of infallibility. But most important of all, he had the mentality of an absolute monarch in spite of his Marxist robe.

But his continuing trust in Chou En-lai proved to be the saving grace for the Cultural Revolution. Throughout that period of great uncertainty Chou did his level best to preserve some sanity. Behind Mao's back he sheltered scores of leading comrades from the humiliation and physical tortures indiscriminately dispensed by the Red Guards under Chiang Ching's orders. He frequently confronted the angry mobs at the risk of his personal safety, managing to exercise his authority and save the day. Without his ceaseless efforts and timely interventions, the Cultural Revolution would have destroyed the Chinese Communist Party completely. Nobody else could have picked up the broken pieces and healed the wounds in the way that Chou managed to do.

Whether Mao had in mind securing Chou's support for Chiang Ching was unclear. But there was no doubt that he did seek to bring them closer through some form of working relationship. On many occasions Chiang Ching spoke of herself as one of the Premier's admirers, stressing that she benefited from his advice and suggestions. It seemed that she would like to create the impression of having obtained Chou's cooperation. She even told the Red Guards to obey Chou for he represented the Chairman, as she was quoted in their wall posters at the height of the Cultural Revolution. From the practical point of view, she would have tried to consolidate her position by such an approach. After Lin Piao's death and with Mao's health rapidly declining, Chou was the man who ran the show and commanded popular support.

That Mao should have suddenly decided to abandon the policy of self-imposed isolation regarding China's international relations was not out of character. It conformed with his theory on the interrelation between the external and internal contradictions. Having solved the internal contradictions, he thought, through the Cultural Revolution, it was time for him to tackle the external contradictions originating from the Soviet Union. In other words, he was ready to take steps to outmanoeuvre the Kremlin leaders on the international scene. With his approval, Chou En-lai probed the possibility by launching the ping-pong diplomacy in 1971. While the American table-tennis players sweated over the friendly games with their Chinese counterparts, secret negotiations were conducted in preparation for Peking's most unlikely visitor, Henry Kissinger, to descend from the sky via Pakistan.

Despite Mao's professed indifference to the international recognition of China's role in world politics, he believed that the conflicts in the capitalist West could be utilized to the advantage of his country, particularly in its confrontation with the Soviet Union. He saw the distinct possibility of playing the Americans off against the Russians for he was of the opinion that the Kremlin had embarked on the road to 'Socialist Imperialism' while 'American Imperialism' had been considerably weakened by the Vietnam War. He found the situation extremely favourable for China to have a stake in the superpower politics since it was quite obvious that the United States would like to harass Moscow by exploiting the Sino-Soviet conflicts. He knew that China only had to show the slightest sign of flexibility for the United States to come forward.

In the spring of 1972 Mao scored his major diplomatic success. President Nixon made his first pilgrimage to Peking, almost like a vassal in the old days of the Chinese Empire. Mao merely granted the American President a visit at his own request, as the Chinese official press succinctly worded it. The intention was clear. It was Mao's way of humbling the leader of the strongest nation before he would be received with due honour. The Chairman did not even indicate his wish to meet the American president till the very last moment when he suddenly summoned Nixon and his aides for an audience. The total disregard for diplomatic courtesy was not just due to Mao's impudence. It had been planned well ahead to emphasize his unpredictability if only to keep the state visitor in prolonged suspense. No doubt this gave Mao the psychological advantage when they met. While Nixon was secretly relieved that Mao eventually accorded him the rare honour, the Chairman had the satisfaction of playing the role of a world statesman according to his own rules.

It was Nixon's visit that whetted Mao's appetite for pontificating on world affairs with a stream of visiting Western politicians, some of whom even likened him to Sir Winston Churchill afterwards. If the flattery did not go down well with the leader of the Chinese Revolution, he had the good grace to put up with the incongruous comparison. After all, his vanity must have been well satisfied by finding himself admired by politicians from the West. It suited his plan to counter the expansionist designs of the Soviet Union when he could obtain some sympathetic Western politicians to share his view to a certain extent. Unfortunately, he never understood the functioning of democracy, nor the limitations of power enjoyed by political leaders in the West. This explained his continuing interest in Nixon and Edward Heath even after they were out of office.

Mao's involvement in world politics did not, however, help much in solving the internal conflicts brought to the fore by the Cultural Revolution. Surrounded by the Gang of Four headed by Chiang Ching, Mao seemed unable to assess the situation realistically. Whether he was then being manipulated by Chiang Ching (as the present Chinese leadership claims) or had begun to lose his mental grip of things, did not alter the fact that he was no less suspicious than before. He even ceased to trust Chou En-lai when he allowed Chiang Ching to insinuate and launch veiled attacks against the Premier in the last stage of the Anti-Confucius Campaign. It was possible that having survived so many power struggles he could not but feel insecure all the time. Since he had ruthlessly got rid of his political rivals, he must have been living with his conscience which would bother him more in his dotage.

After Chou's death in January 1976, Mao lost the only comrade who could sometimes tactfully influence him. The next few months found him in a state of complete inactivity, with two nurses constantly at his side. It is believed that he was himself for only a few hours each day. But despite his mental deterioration, he still exercised his power in sacking Teng Hsiao-ping and promoting the more junior Hua Kuo-feng to the position evacuated by Chou En-lai, both in the party and in the government. Obviously his strange decision must have been resented by quite a few senior comrades at the time, though no open protest was registered. Perhaps they realized that Mao did not have many more years to live, choosing to sit it out. But the irony was, when Mao took the unusual step of making Hua his successor, he could not have foreseen that his wife, Chiang Ching, would be arrested and imprisoned by the very man he picked to protect her stakes in the power game.

On 9 September 1976 Mao died. It happened to coincide with the Moon Festival, a day for reunion and rejoicing in the Chinese lunar calendar. But the most powerful man in China died quite alone. Not even his wife, Chiang Ching, was at his bedside.

11 MAO AS AN INDIVIDUAL

Like most Chinese rulers in the past, Mao spared no effort in maintaining his remoteness, inaccessibility and unpredictability. He wanted to be seen as a great leader without the slightest human weakness, a father-figure who was above reproach and a dedicated revolutionary too busy to have any private life. To enhance his infallibility as the Great Helmsman guiding the destiny of 800 million people, it was essential that he appear to be completely selfless and devoid of worldly desires. It suited him better to conceal his personal feelings, remain elusive about his family ties and clamp down on the vaguest reference to his private activities. As he told Chou En-lai and other leading comrades as early as the spring of 1950, 'We Communists must not drift into the Kuomintang path of self-glorification through publicity exercises. To serve the people, there is no need for them to know who we are or what we are. It does not matter whom we are married to or what we eat for breakfast. All these are totally irrelevant to our tasks of socialist construction. If there are newspaper reports on our private life or personal activities, they will trivialize our image as revolutionaries, which is very harmful. On the other hand, public exposure is bound to encourage the growth of hero worship and personality cults against our policy.'

But behind these words Mao hid his real purposes. Already starting to build up his own public image after controlling the country, he hated to share the limelight with any of his top comrades. It was obvious to him that any publicity enjoyed by them would distract some of the nation's attention from him. Always regarding newspapers as a political weapon, he was not about to see them used to the advantage of his political rivals. Even though some of the leading Communists were too familiar with

Mao's tricks to believe what he said, they could not challenge his seemingly faultless argument. Perhaps Tung Pi-wu, one of Mao's oldest comrades, was right when he told me in 1956 about the Chairman in his role as the national leader. 'Chairman Mao does not want to encourage the comrades to exaggerate their importance when they come face to face with the masses. As revolutionaries, we must strive to remain faceless figures in order not to be elevated over the heads of the people. It is his firm belief that some comrades might entertain a delusion of grandeur if they were exposed to endless praises or other forms of adulation'. What the wily Tung did not say was that since Mao had his portrait hung in every household, there was hardly any need for him to seek further publicity.

Of course, even if the Great Helmsman might have been utterly sincere in voicing his abhorrence and disdain of self-glorification, he certainly had no intention of setting himself up as a model. Such mentality can perhaps be expressed with an old Chinese saying: 'It is permissible for the county official to set houses alight, but ordinary folk must not be permitted to light their oil lamps.'

It is true that Mao seldom made public appearances. But once he did, he would go for maximum dramatic effects. His master stroke must be that 'historic swimming feat' in the full blast of massive world-wide publicity. On 16 July 1966, during his inspection tour of Wuhan, he found the atmosphere and climate congenial enough for him to take a plunge in the Yangtze river. The moment he stepped into the water that afternoon, hundreds of strong swimmers from the Liberation Army immediately formed a human raft around him. Hustling and bustling, they escorted the seventy-three-year-old Chairman down the stream. With the strong current behind them, Mao and his escorts covered a commendable distance in an hour or so, and 'the world record was broken', as the Chinese media put it.

Clearly, what people failed to realize then was the political motive behind this sporting scene. Having identified himself with the Red Guards, Mao was anxious to project his 'youthfulness and vigour', as well as to impress the Chinese people with his 'robust health'. With the Cultural Revolution about to be switched into a higher gear, he wanted to convince the world that he would be around for a long time. And as usual, he had his way.

In the eyes of most people, Mao was as unfathomable as he was enigmatic. The constant smile on his face, the heavy Hunanese accent and the occasional jokes slipping from his mouth gave nothing away about his inner thoughts. Even when he was extremely angry, he could still smile amicably. Obstinate like most of his fellow natives from Hunan, he lacked their frankness. By no means a good speaker, he often droned away for hours until his audience inevitably became drowsy. But he wrote well and enjoyed writing. He had a very lucid style, remarkably fluent and forceful. Words and ideas seemed to come to him easily, for none of his writings bears the traces of labouring or chiselling. He mixed historical allusions with current events to advance his arguments, never forgetting to insert a few witty remarks. This gift for writing contributed much to his political success, for China had been ruled by decrees since the days of the First Empire of Chin. In the past, emperors and kings did not have to be seen; public notices and statements bearing the seals of their approval were good enough for the subjects to bow to their wishes. Knowing Chinese history as he did, Mao naturally chose to emulate the imperial rulers along the same path.

But unlike them Mao did not have to rely on court officials to do the writing. Fully confident of his own writing ability, he preferred to push the persuasive pen himself whenever he had the time. In the early 1950s he showed great interest in the *People's Daily*, the party's mouthpiece. Once in a while he would undertake to write an editorial for the paper. It was he who first wrote a short comment under the name of 'A Commentator', and it later became the fashion for other top comrades to hide their identity behind the same pseudonym. As he placed so much importance on the editorial policy of the *People's Daily*, the editor often had to await his last-minute instructions before the paper went to bed, especially when there were political movements going on. Not infrequently, the paper would be held up several hours for the Chairman to indicate his final approval, since no one in his right mind would have the audacity to remind him of the deadline.

Mao seemed equally proud of his own calligraphy which is, in fact, appalling. He broke all the rules governing good Chinese calligraphy, an art harder to excel in than painting. If one examines the Chairman's handwriting with an open mind, one can see that he did not even hold his brush at the right angle. First of all, he wrote the characters slantingly and unevenly, disregarding the rudimentary requirements of Chinese calligraphy. It was also his habit to miss out some strokes in a character — the equivalent of misspelling in any European language. And when he wrote a few characters together, they fell all over the place, never in a straight line. But because of his political status, his particular style of calligraphy was slavishly copied and imitated on the Chinese mainland, which is really an offence to the traditional art. If Mao had not succumbed to his own conceit, he would have discouraged such a trend.

Instead he allowed the Maoist calligraphy to catch on. No public building was spared the adornment of those sprawling and unattractive samples of Chinese ideographs, and least of all the Great Hall of the People in Peking.

Compared with his calligraphy, Mao's poems are certainly not without some merit. He wrote in the classical style, a poetic form which originated in the Tang Dynasty (A.D. 618 − 907). With strict rules about cadence, rhyme and rhythm, as well as length and tonal pattern, the Chinese classical form of poetry is exceedingly difficult to write. It is not enough to observe these rules to the letter, for an accomplished poet must be able to convey his thoughts through the medium of imageries and allusions despite the restrictions. Like many political figures in Chinese history, Mao mainly wrote poems for his own amusement or as a diversion from his serious writings. Understandably, sometimes he would overlook or ignore the rules when he found himself unable to handle particular tonal patterns or rhyme schemes.

By no means a prolific poet, Mao left less than forty published poems behind. The most widely read one could be the long poem on snow which was first shown to the distinguished poet, Liu Ya-tzu, in Chungking when he went there for peace talks with Chiang Kai-shek in 1945. It reads as follows:

North country scene:
A hundred leagues locked in ice,
A thousand leagues of whirling snow.
Both sides of the Great Wall
One single white immensity.
The Yellow River's swift current
Is stilled from end to end.

The mountains dance like silver snakes
And the highlands charge like wax-hued elephants,
Vying with heaven in stature.
On a fine day, the land,
Clad in white, adorned in red,
Grows more enchanting.

This land so rich in beauty
Has made countless heroes bow in homage.
But alas! Chin Shih-huang and Han Wu-ti

> Were lacking in literary grace,
> And Tang Tai-tsung and Sung Tai-tsu
> Had little poetry in their souls;
> And Genghis Khan,
> Proud Son of Heaven for a day,
> Knew only shooting eagles, bow outstretched.
> All are past and gone!
> For truly great men
> Look to this age alone.

Perhaps it should be pointed out that the poem reads much better in its Chinese version. Written in the style of verse called tzu, it follows a standardized tonal pattern and rhyme scheme, with a fixed number of lines and words. It is hard to fault Mao as far as poetic skill is concerned, for he strictly adheres to all the requirements without losing spontaneity and fluency. But the most interesting thing is that the poem reflects much of his inner thought, both as a man and a political leader. He speaks of several famous emperors from the past centuries with no little contempt, hinting that he will surpass them all. This indicates that he really regards himself as an emperor in this age, in spite of his ideology and Marxist faith. Throughout the whole poem, one can detect his imperial aspirations and 'individual heroism' which he has frequently condemned.

During the Long March (1934 – 5) Mao wrote a few short poems to inspire himself. They are full of vigour, defiant and unyeilding. The one about crossing the Loushan Pass typifies such spirit:

> Fierce the west wind,
> Wild geese cry under the frosty morning moon.
> Under the frosty morning moon
> Horses' hooves clattering,
> Bugles sobbing low.

> Idle boast the strong pass is a wall of iron,
> With firm strides we are crossing its summit.
> We are crossing its summit,
> The rolling hills sea-blue,
> The dying sun blood-red.

But he seems to be at his most forceful in the following little poem:

Mountains!
I whip my swift horse, glued to my saddle.
I turned my head startled.
The sky is three foot three above me!

With a few simple words he describes the steepness of the mountains
vividly, as well as the tense atmosphere during the climb. By rhetorically
lowering the sky within the reach of his arm, he conveys the impression of
having reached the peak. Again one can sense his arrogance and
confidence.

Like many statesmen-poets before him, Mao does not express personal
feelings in his poems. The only exception is perhaps the poem he sent to
Li Shu-yi, the wife of an old comrade, in May 1957. In this poem he
laments the loss of his second wife Yang Kai-hui, the woman who shared
his early revolutionary aspirations. It reads as follows:

I lost my proud Poplar and you your Willow,
Poplar and Willow soar to the Ninth Heaven.
Wu Kang, asked what he can give,
Serves them a laurel brew.

The lonely moon goddess spreads her ample sleeves
To dance for these loyal souls in infinite space.
Earth suddenly reports the tiger subdued,
Tears of joy pour forth falling as mighty rain.

In one of his rare moments Mao confesses how he feels about the woman
in his heart, allowing himself the luxury of alluding to the legendary
woodcutter Wu Kang in the moon and the moon goddess. As his wife's
Chinese surname means 'poplar', he simply refers to her as 'proud
Poplar' to indicate his pride in her. The poem may not be his best, yet it
does at least give us a glimpse of his inner self.

By contrast Mao's poem for Chiang Ching does not contain such
tender feelings. In September 1961 they were together at the summer
resort of Lushan (the Lu Mountains) in Kiangsi province. He wrote four
lines for the inscription on a picture of the Fairy Cave taken by her:

Amid the growing shades of dusk stand sturdy pines,
Riotous clouds sweep past, swift and tranquil,
Nature has excelled herself in the Fairy Cave,
On perilous peaks dwells beauty in her infinite variety.

Although the poem describes the views quite well, it lacks his usual fluency. But if one is inclined to read some premonitions in these few lines, one may find 'riotous clouds' and 'perilous peaks' very apt descriptions of Chiang Ching's political career during the Cultural Revolution.

There is hardly any doubt that his worst poem is the one entitled 'Two Birds': a Dialogue, written in the autumn of 1965. Obviously intended as an attack on 'Soviet Revisionism', he likens China to a roc and the Soviet Union to a sparrow, contrasting one's great ambition with the other's shortsightedness. To score his political points, he used a lot of vulgar expressions which no poet worthy of his name would have dreamed of doing. In Chinese it reads more like a badly worded slogan than a poem. It must have given his translator some nightmares to render this particular poem into English:

> The roc wings fanwise,
> Soaring ninety thousand *li*
> And rousing a raging cyclone.
> The blue sky on his back, he looks down
> To survey Man's world with its towns and cities.
> Gunfire licks the heavens,
> Shells pit the earth.
> A sparrow in his bush is scared stiff.
> 'This is one hell of a mess!
> O I want to flit and fly away.'
>
> 'Where, may I ask?'
> The sparrow replies,
> 'To a jewelled palace in elfland's hill.
> Don't you know a triple pack was signed
> Under the bright autumn moon two years ago?
> There'll be plenty to eat,
> Potatoes piping hot,
> Beef-filled goulash.'
> 'Stop your windy nonsense!
> Look, the world is being turned upside down.'

However, Mao's occasional dallying with rhymes and rhythms did not stop him from discouraging young people to write poetry in classical form. He told them that they should devote all their time and energy to more useful things than the writing of poetry. Sensible though he might sound, it is equally undeniable that he always treated himself as a special case. For a man in his position, he thought, should be able to do anything he liked. On the other hand, he would not have liked to see his poems compared unfavourably with those by other poets once many people flocked to write poetry in its classical form.

In the West Mao is freely praised for his success in adapting Marxism to the specific circumstances in China. He is admired for his 'Chineseness'. But in fact, he was very unChinese in many aspects, none more than his relationship with his father. It is unthinkable for a Chinese son to speak ill of his father in the way he did to the American journalist, Edgar Snow. He might have every reason to rebel against his harsh and mean father, but that he should have hated the old man like an enemy went beyond the Chinese code of ethics. His hatred for him was so profound that he did not even bother to visit his father's tomb in Shaoshan when he returned to his native village in the 1950s, which must have shocked the villagers. Although as a revolutionary he could easily dismiss filial duty as a 'feudal concept', it was unforgivable that he should continue to bear a grudge against his dead father in such a hideous manner. No wonder his old comrade, Chen Yi, found it necessary to cover up for him. Sometime later, when Chen talked about the Chairman's trip to his native village, he made a point of mentioning his visit to his mother's tomb, probably to give the impression that he had also visited his father's.

Even for his mother Mao did not seem to show much of the affection he claimed to have. After her death he indeed wrote her obituary, but that was about all he did for her. In 1955 when Hua Kuo-feng served as the local party chief in Mao's home county, Hsiangtan, he won the Chairman's favour after he had built a new tomb for the remains of Yang Kai-hui. But strangely enough, Hua the opportunist did not take the trouble to have the tomb of Mao's mother repaired, although it was in a very bad state. Had the Chairman shown as much care for his late mother as he had for his dead wife, Hua would not have been so negligent. Like most bureaucrats he knew what he had to do to please his master.

But Mao certainly was very close to his two younger brothers, Tse-min and Tse-tan. In a sense, this conformed with his character. Quite a few years older than either of them, he enjoyed the privilege traditionally reserved for the eldest son in a Chinese family. While he had to obey his parents no matter how much he disliked it, he was entitled to some form of authority over the two younger boys. He could order them around or make them follow his lead. Anxious to challenge his father, he set his mind on forming a United Front in the family against the older man. As he later admitted, to isolate his father he had his mother and two brothers on his side. They were his 'masses' in the revolutionary terminology.

Later when Mao decided to become a Communist, he realized it would be to the party's advantage to recruit his two brothers. He knew he could count on their loyalty and dedication, since they always looked to him for guidance. It also satisfied his quest for leadership in the family. By turning them into Communists, he could exert his political influence on them both as a big brother and a comrade. He could also be sure of his personal safety, for the two brothers would shield him from the slightest sign of danger.

In fairness to Mao, when he first absorbed his two brothers into the party, he could hardly have expected that they would become useful to him in the subsequent power struggles. At that time, he was very much an idealist about Communism, not yet familiar with its dogmas and fallacies. But as he went along, it did not take him long to strive for power and position. Taking to intrigues and schemes like a fish to water, he was good at the power game and always emerged victorious. The loss of his two brothers, one in Kiangsi and one in Sinkiang, along the path to the top might have saddened him a little bit, but he would not let it spoil his appetite for power. As one of his official historians wrote succinctly, the Chairman 'brought his whole family to join the revolution, accepting the loss of his dear ones with great courage'. What the historians could not say was that the two brothers were actually Mao's pawns in a series of power struggles.

As to Mao's attitude towards women, it is hard to define. In his early days he did write some articles about women's emancipation and equal status, but he never pursued it in his later works. Though not a male chauvinist by intention, he seemed to have some reservations about women's role in politics. It was all very well for him to say that in the Chinese Communist party women were as important as men, yet he did nothing to advance the careers of women comrades. There is no denying that most women leaders in the Chinese hierarchy were either the wives of top comrades or related to them in some other way. It must be seen as a form of petticoat politics, to say the least. If Mao were really prepared to give women an equal role in Chinese politics, many, many women activists would have made their mark without having to be married to the leading Communists.

But it was the way he treated his wives that shed a better light on his attitude towards women as a whole. Mao's first marriage to a village girl, according to him, was never consummated. But he preferred to leave her with his parents, helping and working in the farmhouse for free. From time to time, he would receive gifts of clothes and cloth slippers that she had made, as if it were a husband's privilege. Throughout his school days in Changsha, he did not bother or venture to tell his parents how he felt about the arranged marriage. Either he did not care about his nominal wife's future, or he dared not risk his father's anger which might mean the cutting off of his subsidies. As a revolutionary, he could have been more compassionate and less practical.

He courted his second wife, Yang Kai-hui, when she was still in her teens. Quite a few years older himself, he found her easy to handle. Far from intellectually mature, she readily accepted his domination. This seemed to be the quality in a woman that Mao looked for. After their marriage they were quite happy, and he lost no time in making her join the Communist Youth Corps. He was so pleased with her conversion that he called their marriage a model of 'revolutionary romance'. Because of his underground activities, he often had to make quick escapes by a hair's breadth. On these occasions he just left her behind to fend for herself. In his reasoning, the party could do without her, but not without him. Of course he did not hesitate to justify his decisions as political considerations, though as a husband he was undoubtedly selfish, if nothing more.

Although their married life was quite an unsettled one, she produced three sons for him in the space of six years in spite of their frequent separations. When they were together she actually worked harder than he did. She cooked, laundered, looked after the children and ran errands for him. Apart from these chores, she also acted as his secretary, organizing clandestine meetings and speaking at women's gatherings. And, to improve herself, she also had to read Marxist literature under Mao's guidance. It would not be unfair to say that what he got out of her was almost as much as a Chinese peasant could demand from his wife. But in the name of the revolution, Mao naturally got away with it.

When Mao took part in the Autumn Harvest Uprising in 1927, however, he had no alternative but to send Yang Kai-hui and their young boys to stay with her mother. He never saw her again, for she was arrested and executed shortly after he had established the first Communist military base in the Chingkang Mountains. The sad news did not reach him until much later. But it mattered little. For while she was wasting away in prison, he met Ho Tzu-chen, a young schoolgirl of eighteen who swept him off his feet. He took her as his wife, without bothering to find out Yang's fate. Leaving other points aside, he knowingly committed bigamy. Since he professed to love Yang profoundly, his hasty marital tie with Ho looked even more remarkable. Granted that he, as a revolutionary, had the courage to disregard law and convention, his attitude towards women was nothing if not reactionary. He treated both Yang and

Ho as sex objects, as long as it suited him. Later in Yenan he showed his streak of male chauvinism to a further extent. He stipulated that it was 'legal' for Communist cadres to remain married to two wives at the same time, on the grounds that the Sino-Japanese War had made it impossible for a man to stay faithful to one wife when they could not be physically together due to the circumstances.

Nevertheless, Mao was lucky to have Ho Tzu-chen during the Kiangsi Soviet period. Between 1928 and 1936, she was as much his faithful wife as his loyal comrade. When Mao was out of power, she consoled and encouraged him. When Mao was seriously ill, she nursed him back to health. More and more isolated, he clung to her as his contact with those comrades who secretly sympathized with him. Under very difficult conditions, she made his personal life as comfortable as possible. Their sex life seemed to be none the worse despite Mao's political frustrations. She bore him four or five children who either died or got lost during the Long March. But she steeled herself to brave these losses, as Tung Pi-wu later recalled.

Among scores of women who made the Long March, Ho Tzu-chen showed tremendous courage. In her early stage of pregnancy, she refused to be treated differently. While Mao had a horse at his disposal, she was on foot most of the time. Even after Mao took over the command, she continued to march with the rank and file. It was only after her mis-carriage that she had to be carried on a stretcher. Apparently, for the sake of discipline and morale, Mao would not have wanted his wife to enjoy special treatment. Still, he could have let her have his horse.

But of course Mao was even harsher when he decided to jilt the unfor-tunate woman. After reaching Yenan at the end of the Long March, Ho was a very sick woman. The after-effects of physical exhaustion and mental strain wore her down to a mere shadow of herself. Still only twenty-seven years old, she had lost all her looks and vigour. No longer able to offer Mao wifely comfort, she gradually became his mental burden. In 1937 she was sent to Moscow for medical treatment, much to Mao's relief. During her absence he had one or two casual affairs, though his comrades chose to be discreetly quiet about them. Then Chiang Ching came into his life. He first met her at one of his lectures to the party school. In the midst of grey and blue uniforms, she looked conspicuously attractive with a touch of sophistication. To catch his attention, she rose to ask questions during the lecture, feigning revolutionary fervour.

She might be just a small-time actress from Shanghai, but in the back-water of Yenan no other woman could hope to match her in flirtations or charm. Since Mao always had an eye for the women, he was immediately attracted to her. At the time Chiang Ching was living with Hsu I-hsin, registrar of the party school later to become China's ambassador to Albania, so Mao resorted to one of his favourite tricks. After consulting his security chief Kang Sheng about her background, he transferred Chiang Ching to work in the Central Military Council as a secretary. But as he headed the council himself and the office was also his living quarters in the same cave, she moved in to work under him and they commenced their cohabitation behind the screen of military security. For quite some time, she was merely known as his secretary.

It was not until she became pregnant that Mao conceded to her demand for the status of a wife. With the two sons by Yang Kai-hui now studying in the Soviet Union, he thought that Chiang Ching might give him another son. At first he had no intention of divorcing Ho Tzu-chen, for he did not find it necessary to conform with the bourgeois practice, according to Tung Pi-wu. But Chiang Ching would not hear of it. Obsessed with political ambition, she refused to forego her claim as the Chairman's sole 'lover', the Chinese Communist term for wife. With no other alternative, Mao went to seek the Central Committee's approval and encountered stiff opposition from most of its members, notably Liu Shao-chi. The conditions laid down by the committee to restrict Chiang Ching's political career did not really bother Mao, for he probably believed that she just wanted to be his wife. Like most older men, he chose to think that the much younger Chiang Ching loved him unconditionally.

If the accounts by his bodyguard Chiang Tai-feng are to be believed, Mao in those Yenan days seemed to prefer leaving Chiang Ching in the background. He seldom appeared in public with her, and she was never included in any of the important meetings. It was only when he received the Russian advisers or other foreigners that she would be at his side, more or less as a hostess. She would then serve tea and pass around cigarettes and sweets, amiable and quiet. On these occasions, she hardly said anything. Perhaps she did enjoy being Mao's wife because she was treated with deference. She had a horse and a cook as well as a woman to mind her two little daughters. In Yenan these must have been seen as the height of luxury. Then, with Chou En-lai in Chungking periodically sending truckloads of provisions to the Red Capital, she did not have to worry about the strictly observed ration system in the Communist areas.

Either because of his promise to the Central Committee or his own image, Mao seemed quite happy to keep Chiang Ching out of the political scene permanently until the Cultural Revolution. He might not have admitted it, but the suspicion that he held a conventional view about a woman's role in politics is hard to dispel. If he had treated Chiang Ching's political ambitions more seriously, he would not have waited so long to launch her career until the Cultural Revolution when he had little choice in view of his increasingly isolated position. And in his last years, he was even more explicit about what he thought of a wife's role. He praised the relationship between Chou En-lai and his wife Teng Ying-chao, commenting that 'the two of them have never exchanged a harsh word throughout their long married life'. As Teng always deferred to Chou, one can safely deduce that Mao began to find Chiang Ching's reluctance to obey him less than tolerable.

Without being unfair to Mao, one may also assume that he was simply unable to accept people as his equals, men or women. Judging by what Tung Pi-wu and some other veteran Communists said of him, the Chairman had no friends in the ordinary sense. 'Comrade Mao is a most unusual man,' Tung once said in Peking, 'for he has discarded all the unhealthy considerations of the old society. He has the party as his family and the comrades as his friends. This enables him to be objective and unemotional. With the party's interest at heart, he has to remain detached and, to some extent, aloof.'

But it was Yang I-chih the party historian who came closer to giving Mao away as a person when he chatted with me on a winter night in Peking. While enthusing about Mao's greatness as a leader, Yang remarked that 'the Chairman, like some of the imperial rulers in the past, does not have private feelings or personal considerations'. Pausing a few minutes to search for the appropriate words, he then went on: 'Chairman Mao is the personification of the party; he must be seen as just, impartial and always right. He cannot afford to cloud his judgement with human weaknesses, and therefore he only has good or bad comrades, but not friends. As a true Marxist, he is devoid of the emotional ties formed in the conventional way. Otherwise, he would not have been able to uphold the correct political line to which the party owes its complete success.' While he was saying these words, I could not help thinking about how Mao had survived the power struggles since the 1920s. Because he never had personal considerations, he could afford to be as ruthless as he wished.

However, with the underlings, Mao could not have been nicer. He was particularly good to his boydguards. Those who had served him seemed to remember him with affection. Chai Cho-chun, one of them, recounted how Mao had taken the trouble to teach him to read in Yenan when they were together. Through Mao's help, he eventually entered the training school for junior cadres and then won his promotion. In 1952, when he went to see Mao in Nanking, thirteen years had passed since their last meeting. He was thrilled that the Chairman could still remember the name of the small village where he came from. And, despite his busy schedule, Mao made him stay for lunch during which his children were the centre of their discussion. The former bodyguard also made a point of mentioning that the Chairman ordered two extra dishes to celebrate their reunion. 'Between us, we had five delicious dishes and a soup — instead of the usual three when the Chairman eats alone.'

Chiang Tai-feng, another bodyguard, recalled the Yenan days vividly. In his book, *Around Chairman Mao*, he described how he and his colleagues tried unsuccessfully to feed the Chairman with better food. Mao simply refused to eat differently from them. Once they managed to prepare him a pot of stewed lamb's offals, but Mao insisted on sharing it with all of them. These small gestures, however, did win the Chairman the unwavering loyalty of his bodyguards. Being of peasant stock, they felt as if they had been bestowed with some form of imperial honour. In their minds, the Chairman was their emperor. As far as Chinese peasants in those days were concerned, the man who led them still had the Mandate from Heaven, be it as a president, a chairman or whatever title the leader might use.

Although Mao was absolutely merciless to his rivals, he could appear to be kind and thoughtful to those senior comrades who no longer mattered in the balance of power. Throughout the Yenan period, he demonstrated sufficient respect for veteran Communists such as Wu Yu-chang, Lin Tsu-han and Tung Pi-wu. He never failed to consult them on various problems from time to time. Not that he valued their opinions or listened to them, but he merely observed the formality in view of their age and seniority. To be correct, he would walk miles to go to these people instead of sending for them. When Tung Pi-wu talked about these episodes years later in Peking, he attributed them to Mao's 'humility and democratic attitude'. But in fact, it suited Mao to put on the appearance of respecting age and experience. It must not be forgotten that after the Long March the party was sorely in need of solidarity and stability. For these aims, he would have found it feasible to use these veteran Communists as the figureheads to symbolize continuity. Since he knew very well that they would not disagree with him on anything, there was no harm in enlisting them as his dutiful audience. Besides, assertive and confident though he was, to be able to receive more praise and verbal support would still make him feel good.

But on the other hand, Mao's ruthless nature defied the imagination of many people, not least his comrades. Shortly after the War of Liberation in 1949, he casually talked about the elimination of 700,000 opponents on his way to power, as though they were but ants. This figure was given by him at a top level conference when he summed up the victory of the Liberation, sometime before the introduction of land reform which was to cost a few more million lives, not to mention the Cultural Revolution which was even worse in terms of human sacrifice. To seize power and to consolidate his control at the top, Mao must have killed millions of people, not to be outdone by Hitler or Stalin in any sense. Behind his benign smile and mild manner, he was as hard as the two other dictators, if not more so.

Of his earlier rivals, Chang Kuo-tao was the one who managed to get away. He was most emphatic in pointing out Mao's imperial aspirations. He said the Chinese leader merely used Communism to veil his personal ambitions and thirst for power. To achieve personal victory, Chang said, he would resort to any means. 'He was hardly satisfied even when I deferred to him all the time. He would not stop short of grasping the full power of a dictator . . . . He modelled himself on Stalin in order to establish his dictatorship.' In summing up his criticisms of Mao, Chang went on to say, 'Mao Tse-tung cherished the reactionary thoughts of an emperor, which has nothing in common with modern Communism. Under the camouflage of Communism, he was a mixture of guerrilla concepts, peasant mentality and political intrigues.'

Perhaps it was Liu Shao-chi, the disgraced Head of State during the Cultural Revolution, who understood Mao better than the other comrades did. Under house arrest in 1967 after his disgrace, he refused to submit himself to the further political degradation of writing self-criticisms for Mao's approval. He told some visitors sent by Mao that their master should not bother to reform him. Since the party came to power, he reportedly said, only one man made decisions and remained immune to criticism. While no other comrade could hope, he pointed out, to be perfect, what was the use of admitting some errors not of his own doing? What Liu hinted at was that Mao shifted the blame on to others whenever things went wrong. Knowing the Chairman as he did, he realized that his usefulness to him had long expired. As Mao obviously set out to humiliate his one time 'comrade-in-arms', Liu did not want to give him the additional pleasure of being able to extract some 'confessions'.

No less familiar with Mao's untrustworthiness as an ally was Lin Piao, the 'closest comrade-in-arms' who restored the Chairman to his power throne during the Cultural Revolution. He denounced the Great Helmsman as 'the greatest feudal tyrant in China's history, executing the laws of the First Emperor of Chin under the skin of a Marxist'. Unflatteringly accusing Mao of being 'a pen-wielding Trotkyist', he claimed that the Chairman had turned 'the state machine into a meat grinder to effect mutual slaughter and mutual annihilation', enabling him to impose on the Chinese people 'the feudal, dictatorial and partriarchal system'. About Mao's conceit the one time heir-apparent also had a few sharp words. He pointed out that his mentor allowed 'a handful of half-baked intellectuals [meaning the Gang of Four headed by Chiang Ching] to run amok and grasp military power, creating enemies on all sides while he himself, with a swollen head, overestimated his own ability'. But it was Mao's political intrigues which seemed to bother Lin most. He stated that the Chairman had created inner conflicts within the party, playing one faction off against another to suit his own purposes. Yet once the job was done, he said, Mao would not hesitate to liquidate those who had carried out his orders. 'Looking back at the past decades,' he went on to ask, 'has there been a single person initially in his favour not submitted to the sentence of political death at last?'

Like Liu Shao-chi, Lin was affirmative about Mao's trick of shifting blame to others. 'He is a maniac of suspicion and persecution. When he decides to sort someone out, he will not stop short of putting him to death. Once you are in his bad books, you are there forever. He can do no wrong for he makes others responsible for all the bad things. He has even driven his own son into insanity.' The 'son' Lin Piao referred to could be An-ching who, according to the party historian Yang I-chih, had never been 'mentally sound since his adolescence, much to Chairman Mao's regret'. This was as much as Yang would permit himself to say when I probed him about Mao's private life, in 1957. Far from being critical of Mao, he meant to impress me with the Chairman's 'selflessness and dedication to the revolutionary cause' at the sacrifice of everything else. For on that occasion he also mentioned how Mao had borne the loss of An-ying, the elder son by Yang Kai-hui, in the Korean War with equanimity.

However, drawn on the aforesaid people's experiences or impressions, Mao emerged as a man who was incapable of love and care. He built the universe around himself, indulging in self-importance and believing in his own infallibility. To him everyone was dispensable, including his nearest and dearest — if he ever felt that way towards any living soul. He was a stranger to forgiveness and betrayal was his second nature. As an ardent admirer of Tsao Tsao, the great master of political intrigues in the Three Kingdoms period (A.D. 221 − 265), as he frequently expressed, he had no compunction in betraying the whole world in order not to be betrayed himself. It was not just a question of survival; he was intent on destroying all opposition. Driven by blind ambition as well as fanaticism, he drew his strength, strangely enough, from his ignorance and limitations. As Chou En-lai once remarked to one of his confidants, 'When the odds are against you, being ignorant can be a blessing. It does not matter whether you have made the right or wrong decisions, so long as you have the courage to carry them through. Sometimes, careful calculations have to give way to impulsive urges and hasty conclusions. If you are limited, it is far less painful for you to commit blunders. Since you do not know that you are wrong, you don't have to live with your conscience.' Although the cunning Chou did not mention any name, the hint was pretty clear, if only because he said these words when the Cultural Revolution swept over China like a storm in 1967.

But if self-denial and stoicism can be considered the virtues of a political leader, Mao had every claim to them. To him material comforts meant nothing. Even after he had conquered the whole country, he did not live much better than in the Yenan days. He avoided all the state banquets and was happy to have his simple meals, mostly alone, in his Chungnan Lake residence within the confines of the Forbidden City. Except that the food must be hot and spicy, he had no demand for delicacies. In 1952 and 1953 he observed a vegetarian diet on medical advice. He was also advised to cut down his smoking, the most difficult thing for him to do. Before then, he used to smoke seventy to eighty cigarettes a day, jokingly telling others that he merely tried to economize on matches. His favourite brand was *Chung Hua* (China), a Chinese imitation of the British State Express 555 which he had enjoyed smoking during the Sino-Japanese War. And according to Yang I-chih, he only cared for canned cigarettes because of their freshness and stronger aroma.

About the same time he gave up drinking, although he had never been an excessive drinker. Obviously becoming more health conscious after his political success, he wanted to live longer. In 1956 and 1957, rumours in Peking had it that Chiang Ching had ordered several medical experts to study the possibility of prolonging one's life expectancy. To inspire these experts, it was said, she quoted one line from an early poem by Mao stating that a man can live 200 years. For those who are familiar with the ancient history of China, they will remember that the First Emperor of Chin sent the Taoist Hsu Fu abroad to Fusang (Japan) to seek 'the medicine of longevity'. Since Mao often compared himself with the Chin emperor, he might have entertained the same illusion that there were ways to prolong one's life.

If Chiang Ching's words were to be believed, Mao seemed to have lost interest in women, and her in particular, as early as the 1950s. But this did not affect his appetite for some sexual jokes in the company of such as Kuo Mo-jo, president of the Chinese Academy of Sciences. Once when Kuo presented a poem to him, the two of them fell into a long chat. While praising Kuo's literary proficiency, the Chairman suddenly embarked on a lighter note. 'Comrade Mo-jo,' he allegedly said, 'it occurs to me that you are productive in more ways than one. You do not restrict yourself to having a prolific pen — but something else.' As Kuo's third wife Yu Li-chun was a former chorus girl from Shanghai thirty years his junior and had produced many children for him, he understood the Chairman perfectly. Smiling, he quietly replied, 'Under your enlightened leadership, I strive to do my best, creative at the desk as well as elsewhere.' Mao roared with laughter, probably thinking of the ten children he himself had fathered with three different women.

Kuo must have been one of the very few people with whom the Chairman could share a joke or two. Talkative but rather amusing, the pseudo-academic was every inch a political clown. He excelled at the art of flattery, always coming up with the right words at the right moment. With him Mao could afford to feel relaxed, indulging in frivolous talks for a change. Since their relationship was like that between a patron and his old family retainer, the Chairman did not mind letting his hair down, even though Kuo was not particularly known for his discretion.

Among the Chinese Communist leaders, Mao's obsession with personal safety was taken very seriously. But at the same time, they had to pretend to admire his courage and disdain for danger. When he went to Chungking in the autumn of 1945 for the peace negotiations with the Nationalists, his constant worry was about possible attempts on his life from the most unexpected sources. Apparently, aware of his mental burden, Chou En-lai took pains to make life more tolerable for him. At each meal he would taste all the dishes first, ostensibly for culinary appreciation. But in fact, he was trying to assure Mao that the food was not poisoned. He put the Chairman up in the most secure room in his residence-cum-office, with access only to the bodyguards whom Mao had brought from Yenan. Before his house guest went to bed, he would personally search the room with fastidious care, night after night. And when Mao went out, he would check the engine, the tyres and the undercarriage of the car until he was satisfied that everything was all right. One day Mao happened to be indisposed. After obtaining the medicine prescribed by the physician himself, the tactful Chou suddenly claimed that he seemed to be suffering from the same ailment and swallowed a couple of pills before he gave the rest to the Chairman.

Apart from Chou En-lai, Lo Jui-ching, Minister of Public Security in the 1950s, appeared to know how to allay Mao's fears for his own life with equal adroitness. In 1955, the Chairman once casually mentioned that he missed the Sian speciality beef stewed with *momo* (the North-western variety of Chinese pancakes), wondering whether it was obtainable in Peking. Lo immediately suggested sending for a cook from Sian to join the kitchen staff at the Chungnan Lake residence. But Mao told him that one could only enjoy this dish in the hustling and bustling atmosphere of a restaurant.

Resourceful as he was, the Minister of Public Security knew what to do. After the audience, he lost no time in fetching a couple of cooks and some kitchen hands from Sian to start a new 'restaurant' in Peking. In a matter of days, the Sian Eating House was set up in one of the ministry's 'safe houses' in the western part of Peking. Both the customers and waiters were security agents in disguise handpicked by Lo himself. Then he went to report to the Chairman that he had spotted a typical Sianese restaurant by chance, raving about the quality of the beef stew.

Mao was evidently very pleased. He asked Lo to take him to the Sian Eating House without delay. When they got there, the Chairman was in for a greater surprise. The beef stewed with *momo* tasted exactly like that he had eaten before in the North-west, with pickled garlic as the side dish and the special brand of Hunanese tea to follow at the end. More important perhaps, the place was packed with people as a good restaurant should be. Whether Mao realized that they were but a bunch of security agents even Lo was not sure. However, the Chairman moved about in a very relaxed manner, stopping at a couple of tables to chat with other diners about the wholesome food. In 1959 he promoted the Minister of Public Security to the post of Chief of Staff. It was only then that he praised Lo for his ability to organize security measures in the most unobtrusive manner. If he thought of the Sian Eating House at that moment, he did not say it.

In spite of the laboured official publicity about his 'robust health', Mao had been suffering from some form of illness which was guarded as a state secret. In the 1950s his personal physician was known to be Dr Shen Ke-fei, a lung specialist trained in the United States. Since the late 1960s the Chinese leader had appeared to have difficulty in moving his limbs and was seldom seen without two nurses close in attendance. But the signs of senility did not surface until 1970 or 1971. By then he seemed, according to an impeccable source, unable to concentrate for more than a few hours each day. It was not unusual for him to let his mind wander, talking incoherently or incomprehensibly. Sometimes he managed to remain clear in thinking and speaking in the morning, sometimes in the afternoon. Perhaps this was why he often had to receive foreign dignitaries on the spur of the moment. On these occasions Chou En-lai was usually there, looking at his watch every now and then. Presumably the premier could detect the early signals of Mao's mental relapse, making sure that the guest would take his leave in good time.

Judging by the recent denunciations of Chiang Ching made in China, Mao had been ruthlessly manipulated by her in his last years. Sadly for him, he might have succeeded in becoming the most powerful individual China has ever seen, yet in the face of old age and death, he was as powerless as any other mortal.

12 THE FUTURE OF MAOISM

It was the belief of ancient Chinese historians that a man should be judged only after the last nail had been driven into his coffin. But in the case of the Great Helmsman, it would be a folly for anyone to make such an attempt. Ever since his death, his successors have virtually been carrying out an extensive, if veiled, de-Mao-ification campaign. It started with the arrest of the Gang of Four headed by his widow, Chiang Ching, and the purge of the Cultural Revolution diehards, to be followed by the systematic rehabilitation of his old rivals and unfaithfuls including Chang Wen-tien and Peng Teh-huai, even posthumously, and the glorification of his comrades-in-arms, Chou En-lai and Chu Teh, for their part in the revolution that led to the unification of China in 1949. While Chou has been elevated to the status of Mao's co-helmsman, Chu has regained his title as the Founder of the People's Liberation Army and its predecessor the Red Army. Chen Yi, the Foreign Minister who was mercilessly victimized during the Cultural Revolution, has also been posthumously eulogized as 'an eminent proletarian strategist, diplomat, as well as a poet'. Behind Peking's terminology such as 'reappraisals of historical facts', 'reversals of verdicts' and 'the seeking of truth', the message is clear. It looks as though what used to be accepted as Mao's achievements are becoming extremely questionable.

Furthermore, the illusion that Mao has at least succeeded in feeding and clothing the millions of Chinese has now burst like a bubble, when beggars and peasants in vintage rags began to appear in Peking of all places, not to mention the fact that in recent years China has been purchasing huge quantities of wheat from Australia, Canada and the United States. No wonder US Congressman Norman F. Lent, after his August

243

1979 trip to China, sadly revealed that he had found Chinese agriculture remaining in the eighteenth-century stage. And as China undertakes to launch Four Modernizations — of agriculture, industry, science and technology, and defence, it suddenly dawns on the outside world, through the eyes of unbiased experts and scientists, that the New China of Mao's creation is virtually lagging behind in every aspect of between thirty and fifty years. With Mao assuming control of the whole country from 1949 to 1976 until his last breath, it is obvious who should have shouldered the blame. Undeniably, as the head of a totalitarian state, he had every chance to translate his vision into reality, if he had the vision for the building of a modern state at all.

But on the other hand, one must admit that Mao did shake the world and upset the balance of power between the East and the West. He intruded onto the scene of world politics like a seasoned poker-player, keeping his cards very close to his chest. On the strength of persistent and intensive propaganda, with the aid of self-imposed isolation for China, he had little or no trouble in convincing the appeasement-oriented demo-cracies that he could unleash 800 million Chinese people to launch a massive war anytime and anywhere. His image as the historic cult figure seemingly worshipped like a god by the multitude of revolutionaries strengthened his hand to a further extent. Unable to see through him behind the bamboo curtain, political leaders of other countries opted for caution and restraint, which was again to his advantage. It is, therefore, fair to say that Mao's impact on the outside world far exceeded his contri-bution to the Chinese people. In his lifetime, he was sustained by his myth.

Mao Tse-tung would have died a much happier man if he had been assured that his political philosophy would continue to dominate the Chinese mind for many centuries to come. Of all his ambitions, none was more important to him than the propagation of his revolutionary theories which he claimed to be the gist of Marxism-Leninism. After examining his writings and studying his policies during his long reign of power, one cannot but conclude that the cornerstone of his philosophy was hatred. He firmly believed in perpetual revolution and unceasing class struggle, regarding both as the indispensable means to stimulate social progress and achieve world Communist domination. To him a man's family back-ground determined his right to exist in a Communist state. Under his rule, the children and dependents of landlords, rich peasants, reactionary scholars, counter-revolutionaries and rightists in China were deprived of their educational as well as other rights. They had to be content with their status as second-class citizens, looked down upon and sneered at by the offspring of workers, peasants and soldiers. In Mao's reasoning, men cannot be born equal, for they must be made to carry the marks of class struggle around their necks like an albatross. He asserted that 'contradictions among the people' would never cease to exist, though in nature they 'are different from the contradictions between ourselves and the enemy', for 'we are always in the right'. He advocated 'the correct handling of contradictions among the people', for he did not believe that these contradictions could ever be resolved.

By coining the term 'the people's democratic dictatorship', he strove to conceal the true nature of his type of imperial communism. Since he was the party, the state and the people, he became the sole dictator. Arming himself with absolute power, he ruled China like an emperor. He could do no wrong and was above criticism; he must be obeyed for 'his wishes are the wishes of the people'. The party Politburo to him was no more than the privy council to an absolute monarch.

To consolidate his control of the party, he designed the two-line struggle policy on the assumption that he must steer the course between leftist adventurism and rightist opportunism both of which had hindered and would continue to affect the 'correct direction of the party'. But since he actually changed course from time to time, either out of necessity or due to his impulse, the 'correct direction' was hard to define. The past developments in China have fully indicated that Mao himself was responsible for both the leftist and rightist deviations within the party. Sometimes he would lean towards the left while other times he would opt for the rightist approach. The Hundred Flowers Movement and the subsequent Anti-Rightist Campaign in 1957 must be seen as the typical examples of his sudden shifts of position. Within a matter of months, no sooner had he encouraged free expression and candid opinions than he condemned them as 'poisonous weeds' and clamped down. To defend him, some party historians have argued, though unconvincingly, that Mao never really abandoned his stand on the Hundred Flowers. He had to root out, they insisted, 'poisonous weeds' so that 'fragrant flowers [desirable opinions] may bloom more luxuriantly'. But the fact remains that Mao did go from one extreme to another, no matter how one looks at it.

However, there is no doubt that Mao employed the two-line struggle policy in order to keep the contradictions within the party alive. It enabled him to play one faction off against the other, whenever necessary. He sought to divide and rule, mainly to strengthen his personal power. But in spite of his occasionally moderate approaches, he was basically in favour of the radical line. In the case of the Great Leap Forward, he backed down only when it turned out to be a great disaster. Even then, he refused to admit that the policy was wrong.

Unlike most revolutionaries, he did not mellow with age. The older he grew, the more radical and reckless he became. This was proved by his launching of the Cultural Revolution in 1966 as a final fling. For any other political leader at the age of seventy, to destroy the party machine completely and throw the whole country into unprecedented chaos would have been unthinkable. But Mao did just that. In the process he turned the party and the army against each other, creating more contradictions than he was able to handle. As always it was the Chinese people who paid the price. When the Red Guards were unleashed to 'make revolution' historical monuments were destroyed, national treasures were looted, and millions of lives were struck down. It was not until after Mao's death that his successor, Hua Kuo-feng, formally declared the end of the Cultural Revolution, when Chiang Ching and her Gang of Four were jailed and their followers purged. Due to one man's sudden madness, ten years were wasted, to say the least.

But ironically, despite its fallacies and faults, Maoism has every likelihood of surviving, although not in its entirety. Since 1945 the Chinese Communist Party has been put under the ideological leadership of Mao, for it was in that year the authority of his political line was confirmed by a special clause in the party constitution which was drafted by Liu Shao-chi, his ally at the time. Since then, the *Thoughts of Mao Tse-tung* has become the bible of the Chinese Communist Party, applauded as the 'orthodox and creative interpretation of Marxism and Leninism'. Party historians and ideologues have been conditioned to walk a tightrope in expounding Mao's dogmas and theories. For years they have laboured away to establish the 'ideological purity of Mao Tse-tung Thought', providing dissertations and explanatory notes within the rigid framework of Maoism. They have had to retrace Mao's thinking process, carefully and hopefully. Despite its simplistic and dogmatic approaches, Maoism has, however, become the sole ideological foundation of the Chinese Communist Party. Even after Mao's death, there is no way for his successors to get rid of the straight jacket without which the ideological bits and pieces cannot hold together.

But as Mao's political theories are permeated with ambiguities and inconsistencies, they are open to interpretation. At present, the rival factions in the Chinese party, the products of his two-line policy, have been busily engaged in offering different interpretations of the guiding principles left by the late Chairman. Hua Kuo-feng, the self-asserted 'true heir', set the tune by publishing the fifth volume of the *Selected*

Works of Mao Tse-tung in March 1977. This posthumous anthology consists of Mao's speeches and articles between 1949 and 1957, which represent the moderate phase of his thinking, quite some time before he launched the Great Leap Forward, let alone the Cultural Revolution. Though previously a supporter of Chiang Ching and her radical line during the Cultural Revolution, Hua had a change of heart after Mao's death and arrested Chiang Ching and her Gang of Four to side with the pragmatic faction, consisting of the old guard such as Yeh Chien-ying, Li Hsien-nien and later Teng Hsiao-ping. To give himself the authority to pursue a more moderate line, Hua was obliged to draw ideological strength from Mao's utterances and writings hitherto unpublished. Otherwise, he would not have been able to subdue the unavoidable opposition of the radicals whose sympathy with Chiang Ching is far from diminished. What he has done is to use Maoism in part to justify his political stand.

Teng Hsiao-ping, the one time 'capitalist-roader' twice banished by Mao, went further. Since his comeback in 1977, he has cautiously taken on the unenviable task of the de-deification of Mao. While proclaiming that 'there can be no New China without Chairman Mao', he has continually employed all available arguments to impress the party cadres and the people that Mao was no god. He once quoted Chou En-lai's past criticisms of the Chairman for his errors and superstitions, pointing out that Mao had not always been right. Fully aware of the dangers of completely destroying the late leader's image which had been built up through the most intensive personality cult over the years, Teng has merely been trying to modify and rectify some of Mao's rigid dogmas. He has given the workers their first wage increase in more than ten years; he has re-introduced material incentives in the form of bonuses and pay differentials. To heal the national wounds inflicted by the Cultural Revolution, he and his pragmatic associates have restored most of Chiang Ching's victims — in fact, Mao's — to their former positions, including senior cadres, military leaders, scientists, experts and professors.

Between Hua and Teng an uneasy alliance has been formed, mainly because neither of them can hope to live up to Mao's mythical height. While the former has risen to his present position through some flippant decisions made by the Chairman in his dotage, the latter has twice been banished to political oblivion which leaves a permanent scar on his credibility and respectability as the supreme leader. For different reasons they have to content themselves with the sharing of power, though the conflicts between them will continue to develop.

At present the Four Modernizations (agriculture, industry, defence and science and technology) offer them the basis for cooperation, since they both agree that China must strive to catch up with the advanced nations by the end of this century. But as the ambitious programme still requires Mao's blessing to be 'ideologically correct', the diminutive Teng, as its main architect, has managed to dig out some of the late leader's favourable remarks about the urgent need for modernization. He has repeatedly quoted one of Mao's political reports to the Central Committee in 1958, saying that the Chairman was then forced to defer his modernization plan because of the 'more urgent task to forestall the aggressive designs of Soviet revisionism'. Realistic as he is, Teng has chosen to strengthen his own authority by inferring that Mao would have no hesitation in approving the mammoth venture had he been alive. It is clear to him that his radical rivals in the party may have been temporarily silenced, but they are still a force to be reckoned with. Despite his grievance against the Great Helmsman, he has no alternative but to pretend to be the faithful executor of his wishes. A pragmatist, he knows very well that any attempt to exorcise Mao's ghost in the foreseeable future will not succeed. For too long the party has been subjected to the ideological saturation administered by the late Chairman. It will take some time for the influence to wear out. Meanwhile, the 'red banners of Mao Tse-tung Thought' must be dutifully hoisted to bind the party together, especially since the Four Modernizations have not been accepted by the doctrinaires as the correct answer to 'socialist reconstruction'.

As regards the de-deification of Mao, Teng has, thus far, handled it with caution and subtlety. He has confirmed his contribution to the revolutionary cause, but emphasized the importance of the collective leadership including Chu Teh and Chou En-lai. He has denounced the commonly held notion in the party that Mao was a revolutionary prophet, infallible and always right. Taking care not to destroy Mao's image completely, he has stated that the Chairman, in spite of his 'minor defects', was an outstanding leader. In recent months, the official publications have taken up this line. The importance of Mao Tse-tung's ideology has been expounded and reaffirmed, but no longer with the usual adulations and exaggerations. To project him as a moderate with sound judgement, his more sensible policies concerning national heritage, art and literature and historical studies have been reactivated. Intellectuals are no longer regarded as the potential threat to the socialist society; most of the scholars, scientists, writers and artists victimized during the lengthy Cultural Revolution have been rehabilitated. They are encouraged to pick up the broken pieces, resuming their work where it was abruptly disrupted. In their fields they can now again have the limited freedom granted by Mao in the 1950s, without having to recite his quotations slavishly.

But in the meantime Teng Hsiao-ping and his pragmatic associates have virtually repudiated Mao's theory of the unceasing class struggle. Without much ado, they have reversed the Chairman's policy that the children and dependents of landlords, rich peasants and other undesirable elements should be deprived of equal rights. It is no longer mandatory for these people to have their identity cards marked as such, and they are allowed to sit for the entrance examinations of universities and colleges — a right which they have hitherto been denied. Apart from the need to seek a broader popular support for the party and its current policies, Teng does not believe that the class conflicts will exist forever. Unlike Mao and the radicals, he cannot see why one should be punished for one's family background.

Naturally, Teng would not stop short of reshaping Maoism to its fullest extent. His boldest touch is to present Mao as an admirer, though with some reservations, of Confucius. Under his guidance, party historians and ideologues have begun to reassess the dominating influence of Confucian philosophy on Chinese history. Mao's saying that the Chinese people 'should take over the valuable legacy from Confucius' has been quoted and re-emphasized. Not surprisingly, the Anti-Confucius and Anti-Lin Piao Campaign launched by him in 1974 is now conveniently dismissed as the Gang of Four's plot to distort 'the Chairman's critical approach to history'. Chiang Ching and her fellow radicals are accused of 'criticizing Confucius for their political ends . . . and disgracing Confucius to serve their sinister attempt to topple a number of the leaders of the revolution inside the Party'.

In the arduous work of restoring Confucius to his shrine the party historian Pang Pu has played his part well. His article 'A Reappraisal of Confucius and His Philosophy' was published in the official periodical *Historical Studies* (No. 8, 1978) to set the trend. Since then, more articles in a similar vein have been published, reflecting the official line of modifying Maoism to suit the needs of the present leadership. Confucius is again described as a man of great learning, an educationalist, a thinker and a political figure. He is even praised for his 'aim of improving the rulers' relations with the people', as well as his stress on 'the need for people to love each other'. But what the ancient sage himself would have found most puzzling is that these Communist scholars have credited him with the 'application of some dialectical methods in teaching' and the 'materialistic nature of some of his theses in practice'.

Actually, the effort to reconcile Confucian philosophy with Maoism is not as ridiculous as it seems. With Teng and his assorted group of pragmatists now in power, it is essential that an established order be upheld to carry out their modernization programme. Since Confucius was a conservative wishing to preserve the unified rule of the Chou Dynasty, his teachings about the significance of political stability and economic prosperity, in the eyes of Teng and his associates, can be utilized to subdue the opposition and motivate the people. But as Maoism still remains the 'red banner of correct ideology', it is absolutely necessary for the pragmatists to bring the ancient sage in line with the late Chairman, giving him a Marxist cloak.

If Teng and his assortment of associates succeed in modernizing China, as they have promised, by the end of this century or slightly later, the moderate aspects of Maoism will continue to dominate Chinese thinking. Even though there may be some mass movements periodically, they are bound to be more restrained and less destructive. It is hard to imagine the repeat of the Great Leap Forward or the Cultural Revolution. By that time the bureaucracy will have been firmly entrenched and the new ruling class would hardly have the appetite to indulge in Mao's belief that periodic upheavals are the stimulants to progress. The movements, if any, will be controlled from above with fixed aims, as a form of general mobilization to rally more popular support. Nominally, they will conform with Mao's line of 'relying on the masses', but in essence they will be totally different.

On the other hand, if the pragmatists fail to achieve the goals of modernization or encounter some insurmountable obstacles in the process, the radicals waiting in the wings will strive to gain control. Staunch supporters of the Cultural Revolution, they believe in the feasibility of perpetual revolution and unceasing class struggle. Attacked by the present leadership as the 'elements of whateverism', they are known to have such blind faith in Mao that whatever he said is accepted as the gospel truth. They prefer self-reliance to the importation of science and technology from the West; they insist that Mao's ideology holds the solutions to all problems. As for them, the 'purity of Mao Tse-tung's Thought' must be maintained disregarding the change of time and circumstances. Rigid and unyielding, they represent the hard-liners of Mao's legacy produced by the execution of the two-line struggle policy. If they succeed in grasping political power from the pragmatists, the moderate side of Maoism will be rolled back to make room for policies more in keeping with perpetual revolution and unceasing class struggle. Mao will then be projected as an uncompromising militant instead of a moderate as conjured by the present leadership. One way or the other, the hard core of Maoism will survive with its dogmas and aphorisms.

But if the pragmatists and the radicals will not cease to interpret Mao differently as far as domestic policy is concerned, both sides appear to be firmly behind his guidelines for China's foreign policy. On the basis of his understanding of the 'international contradictions', the Great Helmsman has established his 'Three Worlds' theory, dividing the world into three groupings of power. The First World, according to him, consists of the two superpowers the United States and the Soviet Union, both of which are engaged in the practice of 'hegemony', seeking world domination. He has thus designed the strategy of aligning China with the Third World of Asian and African nations while striving to improve its relations with the Second World (Western Europe and Japan). It is his belief that once a united front of the Second and the Third World is formed, neither of the two superpowers will be able to pursue its aggressive designs. This line of thinking obviously has something to do with his conviction that deficiency in strength can be compensated with numerical superiority.

To break up the First World, he has observed the conflicts between the United States and the Soviet Union with great interest, and come to the conclusion that these conflicts should be fully exploited. Always considering the Soviet Union as the main threat to China, he eventually decided to play the American card when President Nixon gave him the opening in 1973. In his reasoning, he was merely reviving the ancient Chinese political strategy of 'controlling barbarians with barbarians'. And from a practical point of view he was also glad to be able to advance China's international status by involving it in superpower politics, in spite of its poverty and backwardness.

Since his death there have been no signs that the present leadership is about to abandon his theories on the 'Three Worlds' and 'superpower hegemony' which have become the ideological foundation of China's foreign policy. In the foreseeable future, the Chinese leaders will not be anxious to seek a *rapprochement* with their Russian comrades at the cost of being seen as renegades of Maoism. Besides, the confrontation with the Soviet Union, so long as it remains at the present level, serves to improve the chance of maintaining internal unity. As Mao has frequently stated, 'internal contradictions can be resolved in the face of external contradictions'.

However, while Maoism will survive in one form or another in China, the ideological confusion can hardly be avoided. It is conceivable that there will be different schools of Maoism, not dissimilar to different denominations of the Church. Without Mao there to play the role of an adjudicator, contentions and debates cannot be put under control. Ironically, although the Chairman did everything within his power to ensure the supremacy of his political philosophy after his death, he could not have expected that it would be modified, revised and given a new slant by the different factions within the party. Perhaps the only comfort he could draw is that pragmatists such as Teng Hsiao-ping and the others have no alternative but to accept his continuing ideological leadership. In the April 1979 issue of the *Red Flag*, the theoretical magazine of the Chinese Communist Party, four guiding principles are reaffirmed as inviolable: the socialist line, the proletariat dictatorship, the Communist Party leadership and the supremacy of Marxism, Leninism and Mao Tse-tung's Thought.

Even if Maoism may lose its militant element or develop into some form of revisionism against Mao's wishes, to be ranked among Marx and Lenin would have gratified him immensely, for what it is worth. After all, this was his idea of achieving immortality.

CHRONOLOGY

1893 — 26 December — Mao Tse-tung was born in the village of Shaoshan Chung, Hsiangtan county, Hunan; his father Mao Shun-sheng was a smallholder.

1901 — Mao started his Chinese classical education with a village teacher and worked on his father's small farm as a child labourer.

1908 Mao married a village girl named Li, six years his senior, through the arrangement of his parents.

1910 Mao entered Tungshan Primary School in Hsianghsiang county.

1911 Mao went to Changsha, the provincial capital of Hunan, and enrolled at Hsianghsiang Middle School.
10 October — National Revolution led by Dr Sun Yat-sen broke out in Wuchang and spread nation-wide. Mao joined the revolutionary army in Hunan in the same month.

1912 Mao left the army and entered Hunan First Middle School in Changsha.

1913 Mao transferred to Hunan First Normal School for teacher's training.

1918 Mao graduated and went to Peking that September. Worked as a junior assistant in the Peking University library. Met Chen Tu-hsiu and Li-Ta-chao, who were to be the founders of the Chinese Communist Movement.

1919 Mao returned to Changsha via Shanghai in the spring and became politically active in local affairs.
December — Mao went to Peking again, petitioning against the governor of Hunan.

1920   April — Mao had talks with Chen Tu-hsiu in Shanghai and became a confirmed Marxist.

July — Mao returned to Changsha to become headmaster of the primary school attached to Hunan First Normal School.

August — Mao married Yang Kai-hui, daughter of his former teacher.

1921   July — The Chinese Communist Party was founded in Shanghai. Mao was one of the thirteen participants in the meeting.

October — Mao established the Party branch in Hunan.

1922   July — The Second Chinese Communist Party Congress was held in Shanghai and Mao failed to attend.

1923   January — Dr Sun Yat-sen agreed to cooperate with the Chinese Communists through some form of alliance.

June — The Third Chinese Communist Party Congress was held in Canton to forge cooperation with the Kuomintang (the Nationalist Party). Mao was elected to the Central Committee.

July — Mao left Canton for Shanghai to work out the cooperation between the two parties.

December — Mao went to Canton to attend the First Kuomintang Congress.

1924   January — Mao was elected alternate member of the Central Executive Committee of the Kuomintang.

November — Mao returned to Hunan from Shanghai after some disagreement with his Communist comrades.

1925   January — The Fourth Chinese Communist Party Congress was held in Canton and Mao was dropped from the Central Committee.

12 March — Dr Sun Yat-sen died in Peking.

July — Mao went to Canton from Hunan.

August — Mao was made director of the Kuomintang's Training Institute for the Peasant Movement in Canton. He also became secretary of the Kuomintang's Central Propaganda Department.

1926   January — The Second Kuomintang Congress met in Canton and Mao was re-elected alternate member of the Central Executive Committee.

July — Mao left Canton for Shanghai to become secretary of the Chinese Communist Party's Advisory Committee for the Peasant Movement.

1927   January — Mao went to Wuchang via Hunan to set up another training institute for the peasant movement.

April — The Kuomintang started the purge of Communists in Shanghai. Chiang Kai-shek formed the Nanking Government.

May — The Fifth Chinese Communist Party Congress met at Wuhan. Mao became alternate member of the Politburo.

1 August — The Chinese Communists launched the Nanchang Uprising.

September — The Chinese Communists organized the Autumn Harvest Uprising in Hunan and other provinces and failed.

October — Mao led the Communist survivors to escape to the Chingkang Mountains on the Hunan-Kiangsi border.

November — The Party Politburo met in Shanghai. Mao was dismissed as alternate member of the Politburo. He also lost his post as member of the Hunan Provincial Party Committee.

1928   April — Chu Teh and Mao Tse-tung joined forces in the Chingkang Mountains, with Mao as second in command.

July — Mao married his third wife, Ho Tzu-chen, a student of eighteen.

December — Chu and Mao were forced to abandon the Ching-kang base to seek a foothold in Western Fukien and Southern Kiangsi.

1929   January — The Red Fourth Army under Chu and Mao entered Southern Kiangsi and established the Kiangsi Soviet.

May — The conflicts between Chu and Mao sharpened. Mao left the army to organize local Party units in Western Fukien.

December — Mao organized the Kutien conference to criticize Chu Teh's military strategy.

1930   January — Mao's plan of occupying Kiangsi province within one year was rejected by the Party leadership in Shanghai. The Red Army commanders launched concerted attacks on Mao.

April — The Party leadership repeatedly summoned Mao to Shanghai for consultation but he refused to go.

June — The Party Politburo adopted Li Li-san's line of attacking the cities to bring forth urban uprisings.

July — Peng Teh-huai (under Chu Teh's command) occupied Changsha for ten days and then withdrew.

September — Chu Teh and Mao Tse-tung attacked Changsha but they were defeated by the Nationalists.

November — Li Li-san was reprimanded by the Comintern

and summoned to Moscow. The International Faction (those who had been trained in Russia) headed by Wang Ming (Chen Shao-yu) and Chin Pang-hsien (Po Ku) took control of the party.

December — Mao persecuted and killed Li Li-san's sympathizers in the Soviet Region indiscriminately — known as the Futien Incident.

1931   January — Hsiang Ying arrived in Kiangsi to set up the Soviet Region Politburo. Mao was not included as a member.

18 September — The outbreak of the Mukden Incident forced Chiang Kai-shek to slow down his military campaign against the Kiangsi Soviet.

7 November — The First All-China Soviet Congress was convened in Juichin, the Red Capital. Mao was elected Chairman of the Soviet Central Government, but lost his influence in the party and the army.

December — Chou En-lai arrived in Juichin from Shanghai. Mao's power was further curbed and his political decline commenced.

1932   June — Mao left Juichin to live in the countryside, under a cloud of criticism.

August — Mao was forced to admit errors at the enlarged meeting of the Central Politburo in Ningtu.

October — Mao was relieved of his post as political commissar in the army and sent to Changting in Fukien province for 'recuperation'.

December — The Party leadership in Shanghai moved into the Soviet Region in Kiangsi.

1933   January – September — Mao condescended to involve himself in the land investigation movement, completely out of touch with the power centre in Juichin.

October — Chiang Kai-shek launched his Fifth Annihilation Campaign against the Soviet Region in Kiangsi.

1934   January — The Second All-China Soviet Congress was held in Juichin. Mao was re-elected Chairman of the Soviet Central Government.

May — The Party Politburo started preparations to abandon the base in Kiangsi without Mao's knowledge. (He was not a member of the Politburo).

October — The Chinese Communist forces broke through the Nationalist blockade. The Long March commenced.

1935   January — The Tsunyi Conference studied the Communist defeat. Chou En-lai was removed from military command. Mao was elected Chairman of the Party's Military Committee.

June — Mao and Chang Kuo-tao's Red Fourth Front Army joined up at Maokung in Szechuan.

August — Mao and Chang disagreed on the future base and military strategy. The Maoerhkai Conference marked the split. Mao secretly led his troops to march towards Shensi in the North-west.

October — Mao arrived at Wayaopao in Northern Shensi. The Long March ended.

1936   December — Chiang Kai-shek was kidnapped by his subordinates in Sian. Chou En-lai secretly approached Chiang for resumption of Nationalist-Communist cooperation against Japan's invasion.

1937   January — Mao moved his headquarters to Yenan after the Nationalist forces had abandoned it.

May — The Chinese Communist Party Congress was held in Yenan. Mao reported on the United Front policy. Chang Kuo-tao was criticized.

7 July — Japan attacked Peking and hence the Marco Polo Bridge Incident. The war between China and Japan broke out.

September — The Chinese Communists resumed cooperation with the Nationalists. The Red Army was reorganized as the Eighth Route Army under the Nationalist Command. North Shensi Soviet was renamed Shensi-Kansu-Ninghsia Border Region.

October — Wang Ming (Chen Shao-yu) flew to Yenan from Moscow.

November — Mao started cohabiting with Chiang Ching who eventually became his fourth wife.

1938   The Red Army unit under Hsiang Ying was reorganized as the New Fourth Army in Southern Anhwei and Northern Kiangsu in the spring.

Mao consolidated his power base in Yenan. Chang Kuo-tao fled to Hankow to avoid persecution.

1940   January — Mao proclaimed his theory 'On New Democracy'.

March — Mao expanded local governments in North Shensi to include non-Communist elements.

1941   January — The New Fourth Army clashed with the Nationalist forces and Hsiang Ying was killed.

1942   February — Mao launched the Cheng Feng Movement (Rectification of Work Style) to purge opposition. The movement lasted more than three years, enabling Mao to exert full control of the party.

1944   November — American Ambassador Patrick Hurley flew to Yenan from Chungking to promote peace negotiations between the Communists and the Nationalists.

1945   April — The Seventh Chinese Communist Party Congress opened in Yenan. Mao was elected Chairman of the Central Committee. His political thoughts were written into the constitution as the guiding principles for the party.

June — Mao denounced the US Government at the closing session of the Party Congress.

July — Mao repeatedly condemned Ambassador Hurley for 'his collusion with the Nationalists to create civil war'.

18 August — Japan surrendered.

28 August — Mao flew with Hurley to Chungking for peace talks with Chiang Kai-shek.

10 October — Mao and Chiang signed the peace agreement.

1946   January — Chiang Kai-shek summoned the Political Consultative Conference in Chungking to discuss the forming of a coalition government. Meanwhile, clashes between the Communist and Nationalist troops were reported.

April — Chou En-lai moved to Nanking to continue negotiations with the Nationalists.

July — Large scale fighting between the Communists and Nationalists broke out.

November — Chou En-lai left Nanking for Yenan on Mao's orders. Tung Pi-wu succeeded him as peace delegate in Nanking.

1947   March — Mao abandoned Yenan.

September — Mao launched an all-out counter-offensive.

December — Mao declared the beginning of the offensive war.

1948   April — The Communists commenced the spring offensive in Manchuria.

November — The Communists occupied the whole of Manchuria.

1949   January — Peking and Tientsin fell to the Communists. The Hsuchow campaign led to another Communist victory.

April — The Communists captured Nanking, the national capital.

May — The Communists crossed the Yangtze river at all points and went on to occupy the whole mainland.

1 October — Mao proclaimed in Peking the establishment of the People's Republic of China.

December — Mao flew to Moscow to negotiate the Sino-Soviet Friendship Treaty.

1950 October — Mao sent in Chinese troops to intervene in the Korean War. He also ordered the launching of the most extensive anti-US movement throughout China.

1951 – 3 Mao introduced a series of 'thought-remoulding' movements, tightened political control and encouraged the development of the Mao cult.

1954 September — The First National People's Congress was convened in Peking. The constitution was passed. Mao was elected as Chairman of the State.

1956 September — At the Eighth Chinese Communist Party Congress Mao proclaimed China and the Soviet Union the 'two pillars of world peace'.

1957 February — Mao launched the 'Let a Hundred Flowers Bloom' Movement to promote 'democratic practices'.

June — The Anti-Rightist campaign commenced.
November — Mao went to Moscow to attend the International Conference of All Communist Parties.

1958 May — Mao launched the Great Leap Forward Movement.

December — The Central Committee decided to retreat from the Great Leap Forward Movement. Mao resigned as the State Chairman.

1959 July — At the Lushan meeting of the Central Committee Peng Teh-huai attacked Mao's Great Leap Forward policy. Peng was sacked as Defence Minister. His successor, Lin Piao, in the following years intensified the cult of Mao, issuing *The Little Red Book* in its millions.

1961 The Sino-Soviet conflict surfaced.

1962 Peking began to denounce the Soviet 'revisionism'.

1963 – 5 Mao and Liu Shao-chi were engaged in a prolonged power struggle.

1966 May — Mao launched the Great Proletarian Cultural Revolution with Liu as his main target.

June — Mao mobilized the Red Guards for 'great destruction'.

259

In the subsequent months and years the chaos persisted.

1967 — January — Mao ordered the Red Guards to seize power. He then directed the Liberation Army 'to support the left'.

1968 — September — Revolutionary Committees began to be set up to replace provincial, municipal and county governments throughout the country.

1969 — March — Border incidents broke out between China and the Soviet Union.

— April — The Ninth Chinese Communist Party Congress was held. Lin Piao was named Mao's successor.

1970 — Mao took measures to promote his wife, Chiang Ching's political career.

1971 — September — Mao ordered Chou En-lai to purge Lin Piao.

1972 — February — President Nixon visited China. The Shanghai Communiqué marked the thaw in Sino-American relationships.

1973 — April — Mao restored Teng Hsiao-ping's political position.

— August — The Anti-Confucius campaign was launched. The Tenth Chinese Communist Party Congress led to the rise of Chiang Ching and her fellow radicals.

1974 — The Anti-Lin Piao drive was intensified in conjunction with the Anti-Confucius campaign.
Mao's health was visibly deteriorating.

1975 — Chiang Ching built up her succession stake. She made efforts to woo some military leaders.

1976 — 8 January — Chou En-lai died. Mao did not attend the funeral.

— April — The masses demonstrated in Peking in memory of Chou En-lai. Teng Hsiao-ping was again dismissed from office.

— 9 September — Mao Tse-tung died.

SOURCE NOTES

With a work primarily intended for the general reader, the usual way of lacing the text with footnotes and numerous tiny figures can be an irritant to the eyes in the course of reading. What the author endeavours to do is to give indications of his sources, chapter by chapter, in a separate sequence. To facilitate the checking process, reference to key words in the relevant passages is hereby made.

Introduction: The Making of the Myth

1 Mao's sense of insecurity. In 1945 I saw Mao several times in Chungking. He struck me as someone who smiled too readily. While speaking, he never ceased to cast suspicious glances at the faces around him, his high-pitched voice sometimes faltering. Then in subsequent years I had the chance to talk about him with a host of leading Communists. Although they refrained from making candid remarks on their leader's characteristics, I could still sense their fears and worries.

2 The Taiping Rebellion. See *The Taiping Rebellion* by Wolfgang Franke, included in *Imperial China* by Franz Schurmann and Orville Schell (Penguin Books, 1967). But written in Chinese, *A Comprehensive History of the Taiping Kingdom* by Chien Yu-wen (Hong Kong) represents the most exhaustive study of the subject.

3 Li Hung-chang and Chang Chih-tung. See *Imperial China*, pp 195 – 233.

4 *The Water Margin* has been translated into English by Pearl Buck, under the title of *All Men Are Brothers*.

5 *Romance of the Three Kingdoms* is not known to have been translated into any foreign language. Both this and *The Water Margin* were allowed to circulate during the Cultural Revolution.

6   Tsao Tsao. To please Mao, Kuo Mo-jo, the late president of the Chinese Academy of Sciences, wrote a series of articles in the 1950s to build the historical figure up as a hero of his time.

7   Li Tzu-cheng. Mao's admiration for the Ming rebel is fully expressed in many of his writings. In 1958 he encouraged the Chinese novelist, Yao Hsueh-yin, to write the historical novel *Li Tzu-cheng* (China Youth Publishing House, Peking, 1976) which took the author seventeen years to churn out some 1,300,000 words to Mao's specifications.

8   Chang Kuo-tao makes his accusation of Mao in his autobiography *My Recollections* (serialized by *Ming Pao Monthly*, Hong Kong, 1966 – 71).

9   Lin Piao denounces Mao in his secret document 'An Outline for Number 571 Engineering Work' (his secret plans to overthrow Mao), reissued for internal consumption by the Central Committee of the Chinese Communist Party in January, 1972 during the Anti-Lin Piao campaign.

10   Mao's enthusiasm for hard work. In his *The Early Life of Comrade Mao Tse-tung*, Hsiao San (Emi Siao) writes about it in glowing terms.

11   Mao's remark about the killing of 46,000 scholars was made in 1957 at the height of the Anti-Rightist Campaign.

12   The propaganda line about the myth. In their article, 'The Spring in Western Fukien' (*The Liberation Army Literature*, April issue, 1977), Teng Tzu-hui and Chang Ting-cheng, both members of the Central Committee, recall how Mao tried to motivate the peasants by telling them anecdotes about legendary heroes and historical figures.

Chapter 1   Early Years and School Days

1   Mao's family background. His long talk with Edgar Snow about himself in 1936 (*Red Star over China*, Victor Gollancz, 1937) can be seen as his autobiography. *The Early Life of Comrade Mao Tse-tung* by Hsiao San (Shanghai, 1945) is based on the author's intimate knowledge of Mao during their school days at Tungshan Primary School and then in Changsha. *The Stories about Chairman Mao's Youth* by Chou Shih-chao (Peking, 1962) has been authorized by Mao himself.

2   Mao's arranged marriage with the village girl, Li. Mao reluctantly talked about it with some of his schoolmates at Hunan First Normal School for it was nothing unusual in those days. But later on, he chose to keep quiet about the whole episode.

3   Mao's experience at Tungshan Primary School. Hsiao San's account about it is vividly written, portraying Mao as a stubborn village boy.

4   Mao's first school in Changsha and his signing up with the revolutionary army. Both Chou Shih-chao and Hsiao San describe this episode in their books. And so does Li Jui in his *The Early Revolutionary Activities of Comrade Mao Tse-tung* (Peking, 1957).

5   The self-education period at the provincial library. In *The Stories about Chairman Mao's Youth*, Chou Shih-chao writes about it in great detail.

6   Mao's life at the First Normal School. In *Mao Tse-tung and I Were Beggars* (Syracuse University Press, 1959), Hsiao Yu describes it quite vividly, though not without a touch of sarcasm. His brother Hsiao San's account in *The Early Life of Comrade Mao Tse-tung* is very favourable to Mao.

7   Yang Chang-chi and Hsu Teh-li. According to Hsiao Yu, Yang considered Mao as his second best student. But later on, Mao would not have gone to Peking if Yang had not promised to help him find a job there. Mao's trip to Peking actually decided his future involvement with the Communist Movement in China. Hsu proved very useful to Mao in the Yenan days for he was always willing to be a figurehead.

8   Tsai Ho-shen. His influence on Mao seems to have been deliberately played down by the Chinese official historians. Actually, in those days, Mao generally followed his lead.

9   New People Study Society. Accounts by Hsiao Yu, Hsiao San, Li Jui and Chou Shih-chao do not vary too much, though dates and minor details are slightly different sometimes. In 1937, I met Hsu Teh-li during his brief stay in Sian. He regarded the organizing of the society as the initial success of the Chinese Communist Movement.

10   Mao's demonstration of military talent in defending the First Normal School. Hsiao San writes a colourful account about it in *The Early Life of Comrade Mao Tse-tung*.

11   The poem entitled 'Changsha'. See *Mao Tse-tung Poems* (Foreign Language Press, Peking, 1976).

Chapter 2   The Road to Marxism

1   The Worker-Student Programme. It later proved to benefit the Chinese Communists most. Chou En-lai, Chen Yi, Nieh Jung-chen and Teng Hsiao-ping, to name a few, all went to France under the programme.

2   Mao's assistant librarianship at the Peking University Library. In those days, qualifications were not as important as recommendations. Besides, Mao's job was a fairly menial one.

3   The visit to the Confucius Temple in Chufu. Mao later mentioned it

in his interview with Edgar Snow (*Red Star over China*.) At that time, he was still a traditionalist.

4   The failure to go to France. It was a great disappointment to Mao, though he never openly admitted it. However, it also explains his immense dislike for those comrades who had been trained abroad.

5   Mao's marriage with Yang Kai-hui. According to Hsiao Yu, the author of *Mao Tse-tung and I Were Beggars*, Yang's father had had the plan to marry her off to him. He believed that Mao and Yang fell in love in Changsha. But Hsiao San in *The Early Life of Comrade Mao Tse-tung* asserts that Mao fell for Yang during his first trip to Peking.

6   Great Hunan mentality. The development of provincialism within the Chinese Communist Party owes much to Mao's favouritism to his fellow natives.

7   Tsai Ho-shen's letter from Paris. In *The Stories about Chairman Mao's Youth*, Chou Shih-chao states that Mao, at that time, compiled his personal correspondence as a bulletin of the New People Study Society.

8   Mao's role at the First Party Congress. Tung Pi-wu, one of the thirteen delegates, told me in Nanking in 1946 that Mao 'kept the records of the meetings very competently'.

9   Self-Study University. In those days, there was no educational system to speak of. Anyone could form a university, a college or any kind of educational institution.

10   The financial aid from the Comintern. In his *Analytical History of the Chinese Communist Party* (Taipei, 1973), Warren Kuo gives a well-documented account of the relations between the Comintern and the Chinese Communist Party.

11   The organizing of the trade unions. Actually, Mao's involvement with the trade unions has been exaggerated by his official biographers. Both Li Li-san and Liu Shao-chi, his two rivals, played a greater part in organizing the workers.

Chapter 3   Between Collaboration and Subversion

1   Dr Sun Yat-sen's policy of cooperating with the Communists. Before he took this step, Sun had repeatedly appealed to Britain and the United States for aid without success, according to all available historical records.

2   The United Front Line. Warren Kuo writes comprehensively about it in his *Analytical History of the Chinese Communist Party*, with first-hand knowledge and the aid of primary sources.

3   The First National Congress of the Kuomintang. Dr Sun Yat-sen's attitude towards the Communists reflected his sincerity regarding the

United Front principle, though it led to the split within his own party.

4   Mao's return to his native town, Hsiangtang. In his interview with Edgar Snow (*Red Star over China*), Mao admitted his difference with Chen Tu-hsiu at that time.

5   The use of his native village, Shaoshan, as a base. A full description can be found in a special article on the Shaoshan Museum, included in the book *In Memory of Chairman Mao* (Peking, 1977), a collection of commemorative articles.

6   Mao's narrow escape from Shaoshan. In *The Early Revolutionary Activities of Comrade Mao Tse-tung*, Li Jui writes about it fully.

7   Mao as Deputy Director of the Kuomintang's Central Propaganda Department. A detailed account is made by Warren Kuo in his Analytical History of the Chinese Communist Party. Most Kuomintang veterans I have met remember this episode very well, though not without resentment.

8   The Peasant Movement Training Institute in Canton. In an article entitled 'The Cradle of Revolution', Wang Shou-tao, a member of the Chinese Communist Party's Central Committee, writes about it most comprehensively. (The article is included in the book *In Memory of Chairman Mao*.)

9   Failure to impress Borodin. The story was told to me in Nanking in the 1940s by several politicians including Shao Li-tze, one-time Nationalist ambassador to the Soviet Union.

10   The Wuchang Institute for the Peasant Movement Training. Liu Chen's account can be found in the book *In Memory of Chairman Mao*.

11   'Hairy barbarians' and 'hunchback foreign devil'. See Warren Kuo's *Analytical History of the Chinese Communist Party*, (Taipei) Chapter 10.

Chapter 4   The Plunge into Civil War

1   Madame Sun Yat-sen. She is better known as Soong Ching-ling, now vice-chairman of China's National People's Congress.

2   The Nanchang Uprising on 1 August. China has made it Army Day since 1949.

3   The Autumn Harvest Uprising. In Warren Kuo's *Analytical History of the Chinese Communist Party*, the account of the uprising is fairly comprehensive. Lo Jung-huan, sometime Chief-of-Staff of the Liberation Army, gives the Communist version in his article 'The Autumn Harvest Uprising and the Red Army' (Peking, 1954).

4   The Chingkang Mountains. The Hunan Institute of Philosophy and Social Sciences published a study report about this period in 1977. An article by Lai Yi, a veteran Red Army warrior, appears in *The Liberation*

Army Literature (January 1976). Another veteran, Chen Po-chun, also writes about this episode in his article 'Chairman Mao led Us to the Chingkang Mountains', included in the collection of articles under the title *The Red Flags Are Flying* (Peking, 1957).

5 Ho Chang-kung. He became one of Mao's most trusted aides since the Chingkang days, rising to the position of member of the Central Committee after 1949.

6 Chu Teh joining forces with Mao. It was of greater importance to Mao, though Chinese official historians such as Ho Kan-chih and Wang Li describe this episode in their works in a different light.

7 For Chu Teh's background, see Agnes Smedley's *The Great Road — The Life and Times of Chu Teh* (American Review Press, 1956).

8 Kung Chu. The author of *The Red Army and I* (Hong Kong, 1954) seems to be fairly objective in writing about Mao and other Communist leaders.

9 Mao's third wife, Ho Tzu-chen. She has recently been made a member of the National Committee of the People's Political Consultative Conference — after a silence of more than forty years since Mao jilted her in Yenan. (Peking Review, 22 June 1979.)

Chapter 5   The First Taste of Power Struggle

1 The Li Li-san line. Within the Chinese Communist Party, many thought that Li was then merely carrying out Moscow's instructions. In 1956, the Party historian, Yang I-chih, confirmed this view for me.

2 Mao's conflict with Chu Teh. During the Cultural Revolution in the 1960s, charges were made by the Red Guards against Chu Teh in regard to 'his plot against Chairman Mao in the Chingkangshan period' in their publications, obviously with Mao's blessing.

3 Moscow's support for Wang Ming. This must be seen as one of the key factors which has caused the endless power struggles within the Chinese Communist Party. Chang Kuo-tao's *My Recollections* and Warren Kuo's *Analytical History of the Chinese Communist Party* provide all the details.

4 Mao's limitations. In 1956, I met many senior Communists in Peking. They spoke highly of both Liu Shao-chi and Chou En-lai, regarding their insight and abilities. But when it came to Mao, they merely talked about his 'enlightened leadership' in a rather vague way.

5 Lai Chuang-chu's account about Western Fukien. His article 'Before and After the Kutien Conference' appears in *The Liberation Army Literature* (January 1977).

6 The purge of the Li Li-san line and the Futien Incident. A well-

researched account appears in Warren Kuo's *Analytical History of the Chinese Communist Party*, including many of the original documents.

7   Chou En-lai's arrival at Juichin. It marked the beginning of Mao's political decline in that period. The accounts by Chang Kuo-tao (*My Recollections*) and Kung Chu (*The Red Army and I*) may vary in details, but they do corroborate it. My conversation with Tung Pi-wu, later acting Head of the State, in Nanking in 1946, further strengthens the credibility of the story.

8   The Ningtu Military Conference. Mao's critics at the conference, with the exception of Chou En-lai, later all became the targets for the Red Guards during the Cultural Revolution between 1966 and 1969.

9   Problems of Strategy in China's Revolutionary War. See *Selected Works of Mao Tse-tung*, Volume I, pp 179 – 254 (Foreign Language Press, Peking, 1975).

10   The Fifth Encirclement Campaign by Chiang Kai-shek. In a sense, it saved Mao from being further persecuted by his comrades, in view of the timing.

Chapter 6   The Long March and After

1   Otto Braun and his tactics. The Chinese Communist historians have all been evasive in writing about it. Chen Hsiao-wei, the late Nationalist military expert, was very knowledgeable about these campaigns, discussing them with me in Hong Kong in 1958. In *My Recollections*, Chang Kuo-tao is very critical of the Comintern agent.

2   Emergency meeting in Juichin. Warren Kuo's *Analytical History of the Chinese Communist Party* gives a full account. His source Chen Jan (Kuo Chien) was at the meeting.

3   The great exodus. In his article 'The Long March in Retrospective' (*The August 1st Magazine*, 20th issue, 1959, Peking), Liu Po-cheng, the then Chief-of-Staff of the Red Army, gives a fairly detailed account.

4   Chen Chang-feng. His book *With Chairman Mao during The Long March* (Shanghai, 1959) provides some minor details of The Long March, though it is full of Communist jargon.

5   Tsunyi Conference. The account in *Analytical History of the Chinese Communist Party* is based on the recollections of Kuo Chien who actually took part in it. The Chinese Communist historians give their version of the conference rather succinctly.

6   Mao as chairman of the Central Military Committee. It has often been confused with the Revolutionary Military Commission which was headed by Chu Teh.

7   The Lianghokou meeting of Mao and Chang Kuo-tao. Both Kuo Chien and Chang Kuo-tao provide a detailed account of it.

8   The Maoerhkai meeting of the Politburo on 5 August. Chang Kuo-tao writes comprehensively about it in his autobiography *My Recollections*.

9   The crossing of the grasslands. Yang Cheng-wu, sometime Chief-of-Staff of the People's Liberation Army, writes concisely about it in his article 'Chairman Mao Guided Us across the Grasslands' (*The Liberation Army Literature*, December 1975).

10   The Westward Journey. The novel has been translated into English by Arthur Waley under the title *Monkey* (The Penguin Classics, 1961).

Chapter 7   The Land of Promise

1   The kidnapping of the Generalissimo in Sian. I was then a student at the Peking Normal University, feeling as shocked as most people in China. Then between 1937 and 1949, I was given different versions of the story by both Nationalist and Communist sources. Fan Chang-chiang, later a minister in the Peking regime, gave me the fullest account in Nanking in the spring of 1946.

2   The Tasks of China's Anti-Japanese National United Front in the Present Period. This political report has since been slightly revised. It now appears in *Selected Works of Mao Tse-tung*, Volume I, under the title 'The Tasks of the Chinese Communist Party in the Period of Resistance to Japan'.

3   Wang Ming's arrival in Yenan. As several of my classmates spent some years in Yenan during that period, I was able to draw from their first-hand knowledge to form a mental picture when we met in Nanking and Hong Kong in the 1940s and 1950s. And their accounts tally with one another.

4   Mao and his fourth wife, Chiang Ching. The story told to me by several sources is roughly the same, though varying a little in minor details. In a tiny place like Yenan, one saw and heard everything.

5   Mao's private life in the Orchard of Dates. In *Around Chairman Mao* (Peking, 1963), Chai Cho-chun writes about the daily occurrences in great detail. He was Mao's bodyguard in the Yenan period.

6   On New Democracy. See *Selected Works of Mao Tse-tung*, Volume II, page 339.

7   The Rectification Campaign known as Chen Feng in Chinese. According to Yang I-chih, the Party historian, the campaign was master-minded by Kang Sheng who had learned all the methods in the Soviet Union.

8   Mao turned to his main target Wang Ming. In *The Vladimirov Diaries* (Doubleday, New York, 1975), Peter Vladimirov records Mao's persecution of Wang Ming most vividly.

Chapter 8   *The Decisive Civil War*

1   Speaking at a strategic conference in Yenan that spring. After the conference, Mao sent a telegram to commanders of various units of the North-west Field Army. See 'The Concept of Operations for the North-west War Theatre' (*Selected Works of Mao Tse-tung*, Volume IV, page 133).

2   He received a stream of young liberals and writers. I was among them, listening to him with great interest.

3   Shouting 'Long live the Generalissimo', I stood a few feet away from him, very surprised.

4   According to a usually reliable source. The source is Yang I-chih, the Party historian and Chou En-lai's confidant.

5   He got a hero's welcome from a crowd of some 10,000 people. In Chairman Mao's Chungking Trip, an article by his bodyguard, Tung Hsiao-peng, gives a full description of the scene. (*In Memory of Chairman Mao*, Peking, 1977.)

6   He even allowed Chiang Ching to go to Shanghai. I learned about her Shanghai trip from Chiao Kuan-hua himself.

7   An-ching back from the Soviet Union. Hao Kuang-hua, a Yenan peasant, writes about his experience with the Chairman's son as his apprentice in a newspaper article (*Shensi Daily News*, 29 June 1961).

8   He scored a propaganda victory over the Nationalists. As a working journalist at that time covering the peace talks, I found the Communists most willing to provide the newspaper men with information while the Nationalists simply refused to talk.

9   After the fall of Yenan. I flew there with a group of Chinese and American journalists. After nightfall, we could hear sporadic outbursts of rifle shots in the vicinity from time to time. It seemed to me that the Communist forces did not abandon Yenan completely.

10   Together with Chou En-lai, he remained behind to direct operations. In a lengthy article, Mao's bodyguard Yen Chang-lin, writes about this short period fully. (*The Liberation Army Literature*, June 1977.)

11   Mao told some Nationalist defectors in 1950. He was later quoted by Fu Tso-yi and Cheng Chien, two defected Nationalist generals in their conversations with my uncle, Chou Shih-kuan, for many years an adviser of the State Council under Chou En-lai.

Chapter 9   The Man in the Forbidden City

1   A population of 600 million. At present, China's population has risen to 900 million.

2   The Chairman suddenly retorted. The woman journalist concerned is my former colleague, Kao Feng, who later told me this episode herself.

3   The shaping of China's foreign policy. I learned from Lo Lung-chi, a member of the Democratic League and a government minister, about the discussions at the top level at that time.

4   He ordered Chou En-lai to summon the State Council. Lo Lung-chi later on told me about this meeting in full.

5   The loss of his older son, An-ying. This episode was told to me by Yang I-chih, Chou En-lai's confidant, in Peking in 1956.

6   He felt cheerful enough to write a few lines in the visitors' book. In 1953, during my stay at the Hungchiao Sanatorium in Shanghai, my ward-mate Wang Hao, a cadre from the Ministry of Public Security, showed me these lines which he had copied down during his Huangshan assignment.

7   The death of An-ching could have prompted Mao. I learned about the whole episode from Yang I-chih in Peking in 1956.

8   No less than five per cent of the 600 million population. The figure of 'counter-revolutionaries' was given by Mao himself at The Eighth Party Congress in September 1956.

9   A nation-wide thought-remoulding movement in the autumn of 1952. I was then caught in the movement in Shanghai, going through the process of criticisms and self-criticisms in a 'study group' for four months without a break.

10   To dedicate his poems to Kuo. See 'Reply to Comrade Kuo Mo-jo' (*Mao Tse-tung Poems*, page 41).

11   Let a Hundred Flowers Bloom Movement. My writer friends Tuangmu Hung-liang and Wu Chu-kuang fell victims to the movement because of their outspokenness. And so did some of my journalist friends.

12   Ting Ling, the first Chinese winner of the Stalin Literary Prize. In June 1979, she suddenly appeared in public, a very old and frail woman in her seventies.

13   The Eighth Party Congress in 1956. I attended the congress as an observer.

14   Sources close to Mao. This refers to his personal secretary, Chen Po-ta.

15   'Too angry for words' at a top level meeting. My informant was Yang I-chih, and his story corroborates that from other sources.

Chapter 10   *The Addiction to Power*

1 Peng Teh-huai's doubts about the Great Leap Forward. The whole incident is fully reported in a pamphlet entitled 'The Criminal History of the Great Conspirator, Adventurist and Warlord Peng Teh-huai'. It was published by the Red Guard Unit of Tsinghua University, Peking in November 1967. The Central Committee's resolution on Peng's dismissal and Mao's speech can be found in *Long Live the Thought of Mao Tse-tung* (Peking, 1966 and 1969 editions).

2 'Grasping Class Struggle in the Ideological Field'. Mao made this speech at the tenth session of the Central Committee of the Eighth Party Congress in 1962.

3 Wu Han's historical play *The Dismissal of Hai Jui*. I knew Wu Han quite well when we both taught at the South-west Associated University, Kunming in the 1940s.

4 When the Cultural Revolution actually commenced in the autumn of 1965. Yao Wen-yuan's attack on Wu Han in a Shanghai newspaper on 10 November, 1965 marked the beginning.

5 Mao's remarks on the woman's role in revolution. He has been constantly quoted as saying so by the *People's Daily* during that period.

6 Lin Piao incident. See 'The Investigation Report on the Counter-revolutionary Crimes of Lin Piao's Anti-Party Clique' (The Chinese Communist Party's Central Committee, Peking, 1973).

7 Chiang Ching was not at his bedside. This bit of information came out during the purge of the Gang of Four in 1977.

Chapter 11   *Mao as an Individual*

1 He told Chou En-lai as early as 1950. Yang I-chih, Chou's confidant, told me the story.

2 Mao was unfathomable. My interview with him in October 1956 confirmed such an impression.

3 Mao's calligraphy. No renowned Chinese calligrapher thinks very highly of Mao's calligraphy.

4 The English version of Mao's poems. See *Mao Tse-tung Poems* (Foreign Language Press, Peking, 1976).

5 'Stop your windy nonsense!' In Mao's original poem, he uses the expression: 'Don't break wind!'

6 When he received the Russians. According to Peter Vladimirov (*The Vladimirov Diaries*), he always saw Chiang Ching at Mao's side.

7 Lin Piao denounced the Great Helmsman. See 'The Investigative Report on the Counter-revolutionary Crimes of Lin Piao's Anti-Party Clique' (Peking, 1973).

8   His appetite for sexual jokes. Kuo Mo-jo talked about this episode with Yang I-chih who recounted it to me in 1956.

9   The Sian Eating House. I learned about this episode from Director Li of the Ministry of Public Security in Peking in 1956.

Chapter 12   The Future of Maoism

1   Contradictions among the people. See Mao's *On the Correct Handling of Contradictions among the People* (Foreign Language Press, Peking, 1967).

2   Chou En-lai's past criticisms of the Chairman. They are taken from a 1948 document, hitherto uncirculated.

3   The collective leadership including Chu Teh and Chou En-lai. In his recent public utterances, Teng Hsiao-ping has always mentioned Chou together with Mao. See China's official publications such as the *People's Daily* and *Peking Review*.

BIOGRAPHICAL NOTES

(In alphabetical order, names in Chinese Pinyin system in parentheses)

Chang Chun-chiao (Zhang Chunqiao). One of the Gang of Four. He rose to fame and power during the Cultural Revolution (1966 – 76). Became a vice-premier and the political chief of the Liberation Army before Mao's death. Together with Chiang Ching, Mao's widow, he was arrested by the present premier, Hua Kuo-feng, (Hua Guofeng) in 1976, pending public trial.

Chang Hsueh-liang (Zhang Xueliang). Known in the West as the Young Marshal. Son of the Manchurian warlord Chang Tso-lin, he kidnapped Chiang Kai-shek in Sian in 1936 when the Chinese Communists were on the verge of extinction. His act enabled Mao and his comrades to regroup and reorganize and damaged Chiang's reputation and prestige. He is now in his seventies living in Taiwan under house arrest.

Chang Kuo-tao (Zhang Guotao). One of the leaders of the Chinese Communist Party who was more important than Mao at the early stage of the movement. He split with Mao during the Long March (1934 – 5) over strategy and deserted the party in 1938 to live under the Nationalist Government. He spent many years in Hong Kong after Mao gained power in 1949. Recently living in retirement in Canada and converted to the Christian faith, he died in December, 1979.

Chang Ting-cheng (Zhang Dingcheng). Mao's staunch supporter in the Kiangsi Soviet days. Since 1949, he has been Governor of Fukien, the State Prosecutor-general as well as Commander of Fukien Military Region. He has been a member of the Central Committee of the Chinese Communist Party since the early 1950s.

273

Chang Wen-tien (Zhang Wentian). Educated in the Soviet Union in the 1920s. A leading member of the International Faction of the Chinese Communist Party. His cooperation with Mao at the Tsunyi Conference (1935) enabled the latter to gain military control. Communist China's first ambassador to the Soviet Union. He fell out of grace in 1959, though Mao allowed him to do some research work. He was persecuted by the Gang of Four during the Cultural Revolution. He died in 1976 and was posthumously rehabilitated in 1979.

Chen Po-ta (Chen Boda). Mao's confidant and ghost writer for over thirty years. He played a prominent role in launching the Cultural Revolution. He was closely associated with Chiang Ching from 1966 to 1970, and instrumental to her rise in the Party hierarchy. But in 1971, he was condemned by Mao for his involvement in Lin Piao's plot to seize power.

Chen Shao-yu (Chen Shaoyu). Also known as Wang Ming. Educated in the Soviet Union, he was the leader of the International Faction, always looking to Moscow for guidance. Before Mao gained firm control of the Party in 1945, he had been cultivated by Stalin to lead the Chinese Communists. His political line, the Wang Ming Line, was branded by Mao as a mixture of leftist adventurism and rightist capitulationism. He was allegedly almost poisoned to death in Yenan in the 1940s. He went to live in Moscow before the Sino-Soviet split became open in 1961, and died there.

Chen Tu-hsiu (Chen Duxiu). A professor of the famed Peking University, he was one of the two founders of the Chinese Communist Party. In the late 1920s, he fell out with the Third International and was subsequently expelled by the Party. Then in the 1940s, he was constantly denounced by his former comrades for 'being a Trotskyist'. He died after the Second World War.

Chen Yi (Chen Yi). Joined the Chinese Communist Party in France while a student there in the 1920s. One of Mao's ablest generals during the 1947 – 9 civil war, he was first Communist Mayor of Shanghai. He rose to be Foreign Minister and a Vice-Premier in the 1950s, generally seen as Chou En-lai's right-hand man. He was disgraced during the Cultural Revolution. He died in 1972.

Chen Yun (Chen Yun). A printer by trade, he joined the Party in the early 1920s. In the Yenan days (1937 – 47), he was the overlord of finance and economy. He became a Vice-Premier after 1949, responsible for the first two Five-Year Plans. Out of favour since the 1959 Great Leap Forward he was further disgraced during the Cultural Revolution. He was restored to be a Vice-Chairman of the Party in 1978, as well as a Politburo member in charge of the newly established Commission of Discipline and Investigation.

Chiang Ching (Jiang Qing). Mao's fourth wife. Her real name is Li Yunho, also known as Lan Ping and Li Chin. A small-time actress, she married Mao in Yenan in 1937 and has borne him two daughters, Li Na and Li Min. She shot up in the Party hierarchy after the launching of the Cultural Revolution in 1966, reaching the top by becoming a member of the Politburo's Standing Committee. Shortly after Mao's death, she was condemned as one of the Gang of Four with the design to seize power and put under arrest, pending public trial.

Chiao Kuan-hua (Qiao Guanhua). Educated in Germany in the early 1930s. For many years he was Chou En-lai's trusted adviser on foreign affairs. He rose to the position of Foreign Minister in 1975, but after Mao's death in 1976, he was summarily dismissed for his alleged association with Chiang Ching and her Gang of Four.

Chin Pang-hsien (Qin Bangxian). Moscow educated, he was a leader of the International Faction of the Chinese Communist Party. He held the post of General Secretary during the Kiangsi Soviet period, but was held responsible for the massive defeat which led to the Long March. He lost his leadership at the Tsunyi Conference. He died in a plane crash in 1945. He was also known as Po Ku (Bo Gu).

Chou En-lai (Zhou Enlai). China's premier from 1949 to 1976. He was educated in France in the early 1920s when he organized the branch of the Chinese Communist Party there. Superior to Mao in the party hierarchy until the Tsunyi Conference (1935) during the Long March. He was the only Chinese leader who had survived Mao's countless purges scot-free. Without him, the damage done by the Cultural Revolution would have been even greater. He died in 1976, eight months before Mao.

Chu Teh (Zhu De). A warlord turned Communist. He joined the Party while touring Germany in the early 1920s, with Chou En-lai as his sponsor. One of the founders of the People's Liberation Army, he had been its Commander-in-Chief, Chairman of the National People's Congress and Member of the Politburo's Standing Committee. Though bitterly attacked by the Red Guards during the Cultural Revolution, he survived. He died in 1976.

Ho Lung (He Long). A bandit turned Communist, he joined the Party after the Nanchang Uprising in 1927. Since 1949, he had been Member of the Politburo and a Vice-Premier. He was hounded to death by the Gang of Four in 1969 at the height of the Cultural Revolution. Posthumously rehabilitated in 1979.

Ho Tzu-chen (He Zizhen). Mao's third wife. While a high school student of eighteen, she married Mao in 1928 when his second wife was still alive. She went through the Long March with Mao in 1935 but was jilted two years later by him for the sake of Chiang Ching. Out of public view since 1937, she suddenly reappeared in 1979, as member of the National Committee of the People's Political Consultative Conference.

Hsiang Ying (Xiang Ying). The only factory worker among the Chinese Communist leaders in the 1920s and 1930s, he and Mao never got along. He was killed in 1941 when his New Fourth Army clashed with the Nationalist Forces, much to Mao's secret delight.

Hsiao Ching-kuan (Xiao Jingguan). Mao's protégé and supporter before and after the Long March. A native of Hunan, he went to the same school as Mao, though later. Since 1949, he has been Commander of Hunan Military Region, Commander of the Chinese Navy and Vice-Minister of Defence. He has also been Member of the Central Committee since 1959.

Hsu Hsiang-chien (Xu Xiangqian). A graduate of the Nationalists' Whampoa Military Academy, he joined the Chinese Communist Party in 1927. He associated himself with Mao's rival, Chang Kuo-tao for a long period. Since 1949 he has held a variety of military posts including Chief-of-Staff of the People's Liberation Army and Vice-Chairman of the National Military Council. After Mao's death, he came out of retirement to be Chief-of-Staff once again. He is now Member of the Central Committee, and the Politburo.

Kang Sheng (Kang Sheng). Trained with the Soviet Secret Service in 1932. But when he eventually returned to Yenan in 1937, he succeeded in winning Mao's confidence and became his security chief. He assisted Mao to launch the Cultural Revolution in 1966, as the head of a Five-man Group directly responsible to the Chairman. In 1973, he became a Vice-Chairman of the Party and Member of the Politburo's Standing Committee, ranked below Mao and Chou En-lai. He died in 1975.

Kao Kang (Gao Gang). One of the two founders of North Shensi Communist Base which became Mao's refuge at the end of the Long March in 1935. He and Lin Piao (Lin Biao) completed the occupation of

Manchuria in 1948 to ensure the Communist victory. Purged by Mao in 1954 for his alleged contacts with Moscow, he killed himself during imprisonment.

Ku Mu (Gu Mu). Member of the Central Committee and a Vice-Premier, responsible for some projects of the modernization programme.

Li Li-san (Li Lisan). Moscow trained, he led the Party before Mao did. His slavish adherence to the Comintern guidance produced the Li Li-san Line, emphasizing urban uprisings and all-out military attacks. He was subdued by Mao and became his whipping boy.

Li Ta-chao (Li Dazhao). One of the two founders of the Chinese Communist Party. Instrumental in Mao's conversion to Communism. He was executed by the Peking Warlord Government in the early 1920s.

Li Teh-sheng (Li Desheng). Member of the Politburo and Commander of Mukden (Shenyang) Military Region. Registered meteoric rise in the party hierarchy during the Cultural Revolution for his support of Chiang Ching (Jiang Qing). But he turned against her and her Gang of Four in time to consolidate his own position.

Lin Piao (Lin Biao). Played a major part in defeating the Nationalists during the 1947–9 Civil War. Commanded 'the Chinese Volunteers' in Korea initially until his illness. He had held a variety of high military posts including a spell as Defence Minister from 1959 to 1971. He gave Mao full military support during the Cultural Revolution and became his designated successor, written into the 1969 constitution. But in the spring of 1971, he was discovered to have been preparing for a military *coup*. That September, he and his fellow conspirators died in a crashed Trident while trying to escape to the Soviet Union.

Liu Po-cheng (Liu Bocheng). Member of the Politburo. He was Chief-of-Staff of the Red Army during the Long March (1934–5). Since 1949 he has not been particularly active in spite of successive important posts. Now in his eighties, he is also a Vice-Chairman of the National Military Council.

Liu Shao-chi (Liu Shaoqi). For a long time China's Number two leader, deferring to Mao only. He had been of great help to Mao in his consolidation of power. He was the main target of the Cultural Revolution, humiliated and tormented by the Red Guards. Dismissed by Mao from his post as Chairman of the State, he died during his prolonged confinement. However, his widow, Wang Kuang-mei (Wang Guangmei), was rehabilitated in June 1979, becoming Member of the National Committee of the Chinese People's Political Consultative Conference.

Mao An-ching (Mao Anqing). Mao's second son. Studied in the Soviet Union in the 1930s. He has had mental trouble for years. His name was seen on a wreath at the Chairman's funeral.

Mao An-ying (Mao Anying). Mao's eldest son. He studied in the Soviet Union with his younger brother in the 1930s. He was killed in the Korean War (1950 – 3).

Mao Shun-sheng (Mao Shunsheng). Deceased. Mao's father.

Mao Tse-min (Mao Zemin). Mao's younger brother. In the Kiangsi Soviet he was its financial expert. Killed in Sinkiang by the local warlord in the early 1940s.

Mao Tse-tan (Mao Zetan). Mao's youngest brother. Killed during the Long March while trying to break through the Nationalist siege.

Nieh Jung-chen (Nie Rongzhen). He trained in France as an engineer in the early 1920s. Joined the Party then and there. He played an important part in capturing Peking during the 1947 – 9 Civil War. He was very close to Chou En-lai. For years he has been in charge of China's nuclear development. He is Member of the Politburo.

Peng Teh-huai (Peng Dehuai). For many years Mao's man to rally the support of the military. He was China's Defence Minister until 1959 when he was sacked by Mao due to his frank criticisms of the Great Leap Forward. An able soldier, he directed the military campaigns during the 1947 – 9 Civil War and then commanded 'the Chinese Volunteers' in the Korean War. He was persecuted and tortured to death during the Cultural Revolution. But recently, he has been posthumously rehabilitated and acclaimed.

Sun Yat-sen, alias Sun Wen (1866 – 1925). The founder of the Nationalist Party (Kuomintang) who staged the 1911 Revolution to overthrow the monarchy in China. His policy of uniting with the Soviet Union and accommodating the Communists changed the course of history. He died in 1925. Regarded as the pioneer of Chinese Revolution, he has been accorded due honour by the Chinese Communist leaders.

Teng Hsiao-ping (Deng Ziaoping). The greatest survivor of the power struggles in China. Educated in France in the early 1920s and joined the Party there. Until 1959, he was trusted and elevated to the all-important post of General Secretary of the Party. Then, his collaboration with Liu

Shao-chi (Liu Shaoqi) incurred Mao's fury. Persecuted and disgraced during the Cultural Revolution, he was merely permitted to retain his Party card. He was restored as Vice-Premier in 1974, only to be sacked by Mao in 1976 once again. He staged his second come-back after Mao's death and now holds the real power in China, though without the title to go with it. He is the motivating force behind the Four Modernizations — of agriculture, industry, science and technology, and defence.

Tsai Ho-shen (Cai Heshen). Mao's best friend at the Changsha Normal School as well as in the Party. Gave Mao much help in finding his footing within the Party set-up. He died in Hong Kong in 1931.

Tung Pi-wu (Dong Biwu). Veteran Communist leader, one of the thirteen delegates to the first Communist Congress in Shanghai in 1921. Highly respected by Mao, he was made Deputy Chairman of the State as from 1959 until his death in 1975. After the dismissal of Liu Shao-chi (Liu Shaoqi), he acted as Head of State for many years.

Wang Chia-hsiang (Wang Jiaxiang). A leading figure of the International Faction in the Chinese Communist Party. Very close to Wang Ming and Chin Pang-hsien until Mao seized control of the Party in 1945. Since 1949, he had been China's Ambassador in Moscow and a Vice-Minister of Foreign Affairs. He died in 1974.

Wang Hung-wen (Wang Hongwen). One of the Gang of Four now under imprisonment. His association with Chiang Ching during the Cultural Revolution caused Mao to promote him to the position of Number three leader in the hierarchy when he was a mere factory worker of thirty-eight in Shanghai.

Wen Chi-mei (Wen Qimei). Mao's late mother who gave him the chance to receive modern education.

Yang Chang-chi (Yang Changji). Father of Mao's second wife, Yang Kai-hui. At the Changsha Normal School he was Mao's teacher and mentor. He found Mao the post of librarian at Peking University. He died in Peking in the 1920s.

Yang Kai-hui (Yang Kaihui). Mao's second wife who bore him three sons: An-ying, An-ching and An-lung. She was executed by the Nationalists in 1930.

Yao Wen-yuan (Yao Wenyuan). One of the Gang of Four. Originally a drama critic, he was promoted by Mao to be a member of the Politburo during the Cultural Revolution. After Mao's death, he was arrested together with Chiang Ching, Chang Chun-chiao and Wang Hung-wen, pending public trial.

Yeh Chien-ying (Ye Jianying). China's nominal Number two leader. First Vice-Chairman of the Party. For decades he was Mao's political general, often a compromise choice for many posts. Humiliated and hounded during the Cultural Revolution, he survived owing to Chou En-lai's protection. He is a conciliator in the present hierarchy.

INDEX

All China Soviet Congress, 110, 111
An Ching, 182, 183, 238
Anti-Imperialism League, 102
Anti-Japan United Front, 137, 138, 139
Anti-Japanese Political and Military College, 150
Anti-Lin Piao Campaigns, 219 *see also* Lin Piao
Anti-Rightist Campaign, 193, 194, 195, 245
Army Day, 69
Around Chairman Mao, 236
August Incident, 87
Autumn Harvest Uprising, 70, 71, 82, 85, 232

Borodin, M.M., 54, 60, 61, 62, 63, 67
Boxer Rising, 2, 9
Braun, Otto, 113, 114, 115, 118, 119, 120, 121, 134
Brief History of the Red Army's Development, A, 87
Bukharin N.I., 90 *see also* Third International

Canton, 46, 53, 57, 58, 60, 62, 63, 66, 70, 78
Central Army, 123
Central Bureau, 46, 48
Central Column, 116

Central Committee (Shanghai), 51, 53, 54, 60, 61, 62, 63, 64, 65, 66, 69, 70, 71, 72, 82, 87, 90, 91, 92, 93, 95, 96, 97, 98, 99, 101, 110, 114, 117, 120, 126, 142, 148, 184, 200, 201, 204, 206, 215, 216, 217, 234, 248
Central Cultural Revolution Group, 209
Central Executive Committee, 98, 111
Central Military Committee, 99, 103, 115, 116, 120, 121, 122, 125, 134
Central People's Government, 176
Central Political Bureau, 67, 72, 82
Central Propaganda Department, 58 *see also* Dr Sun Yat-sen
Central Soviet Army, 126
Central Soviet Government, 107, 114, 122
Chang Chih-chung, 172
Chang Chih-tung, 2
Chang Ching-yao, 36, 37, 38, 39
Chang Chun-chiao, 207, 217
Chang Hao, 134, 142
Chang Hsueh-liang, 137, 138, 139
Chang Kuo-tang, 66
Chang Kuo-tao, 4, 5, 45, 46, 48, 53, 54, 56, 64, 66, 67, 68, 90, 98, 99, 123, 124, 125, 126, 127, 128, 129, 130, 131, 136, 137, 138, 140, 152, 237
Chang Ting-cheng, 94, 102, 105
Chang Tse-min, 102

Chang Wen-tien, 99, 110, 115, 117, 120, 121, 123, 124, 125, 128, 129, 131, 134, 136, 140, 141, 143, 144, 243

Changsha, 17, 22, 23, 24, 26, 27, 28, 29, 30, 31, 33, 34, 36, 37, 39, 40, 41, 42, 43, 45, 46, 48, 50, 53, 56, 64, 70, 71, 78, 85, 101, 106, 232

Changting, 92

Chao Heng-ti, 47, 48, 49, 50, 56, 57

Chekiang, 105, 115, 183

Chen Chang-hao, 124, 125, 126, 129

Chen Po-chun, 73

Chen Po-ta, 6, 184, 209

Chen Pu-lei, 174

Chen Shao-yu, 6, 142 see also Wang Ming

Chen Tu-hsiu, 5, 24, 31, 33, 34, 35, 38, 39, 43, 44, 45, 46, 48, 50, 51, 52, 53, 54, 55, 57, 60, 61, 62, 63, 64, 65, 66, 68, 69, 70, 119

Chen Yi, 79, 83, 87, 92, 93, 103, 116, 230, 243

Chen Yun, 99, 117, 119, 120, 125

Chenchow, 37

Cheng Feng Movement, 12

Chentu, 128

Chi Chao-ting, 173

Chiang Ching, 5, 147, 148, 149, 150, 155, 156, 161, 165, 183, 184, 191, 201, 206, 207, 208, 209, 211, 214, 215, 216, 217, 218, 219, 220, 221, 222, 228, 229, 233, 234, 235, 238, 239, 242, 243, 246, 247, 249

Chiang Kai-shek, 32, 33, 54, 58, 60, 62, 65, 72, 95, 100, 103, 105, 110, 111, 113, 114, 123, 139, 140, 141, 153, 161, 162, 164, 165, 170, 171, 172, 173, 179, 181, 226

Chaing Tai-feng, 236

Chaio Kuan-hua, 166

Chien Po-chan, 192

Chienning, 114

Chin Pang-hsien, 98, 99, 104, 107, 110, 113, 114, 115, 117, 119, 120, 121, 122, 124, 125, 134, 136, 143, 144, 147, 150, 152

Chin Shih Huang, 185

China's National Broadcasting Administration, 136

Chinese Academy of Sciences, 61

Chinese Communist Party, see Communist Party

Chinese Soviet Republic, 98

Ching Shih-huang, 6

Chingkang mountains, 72, 73, 74, 75, 77, 78, 79, 82, 84, 85, 86, 88, 89, 93, 98, 101, 106, 134, 232

Chingkangshan, 76, 78, 82, 83, 84, 85, 86, 87, 88, 89, 90, 91, 93, 101, 103, 117

Chinsha river, 123

Chou En-lai, 61, 68, 69, 91, 93, 96, 99, 100, 103, 104, 106, 107, 111, 112, 113, 114, 115, 117, 118, 120, 121, 122, 124, 125, 128, 130, 131, 136, 137, 138, 144, 145, 146, 152, 158, 161, 165, 166, 167, 170, 172, 175, 178, 182, 184, 185, 210, 214, 215, 216, 219, 220, 221, 222, 234, 235, 239, 240, 242, 243, 247, 248

Chou Kuni, 116

Chou Yang, 194

Chu Chiu-pai, 54, 61, 66, 69, 70, 72, 74, 90, 93

Chu Hsi, 32

Chu Liang-tsai, 83

Chu Li-chih, 131

Chu Teh, 69, 78, 79, 82, 83, 84, 85, 86, 87, 88, 89, 90, 91, 92, 93, 95, 96, 99, 103, 110, 114, 117, 121, 122, 126, 127, 129, 138, 141, 175, 184, 206, 243, 268

Chu Yuan, 28, 29

Chu-ke Liang, General, 27, 95, 106

Chung Chen, Emperor, 4

Chung Hsin Study Group, 41

Chungking, 161, 162, 164, 165, 175

Chungshan Gunboat Incident, 60, 62

Civil War, 160–74

Comintern, 51, 53, 56, 65, 66, 67, 68, 70, 74, 88, 90, 92, 98, 105, 113, 115, 119, 120, 121, 122, 124, 125, 127, 134, 135, 136, 137, 138, 142, 143, 145, 149, 153, 157, 158

Communist, The, 45

Communist Manifesto, 33

Communist Party, 24, 25, 28, 31, 38, 45, 46, 48, 49, 51, 52, 53, 54, 55, 56, 57, 58, 59, 61, 62, 63, 65, 66, 67, 68, 69, 70, 71, 72, 89, 97, 114, 116, 119, 122, 123, 128, 129, 131, 134, 135, 136, 137, 138, 139, 140, 141, 146, 149, 151, 152, 154, 155, 158, 160, 161, 162, 163; 164, 165, 166, 167, 170, 171, 172, 174, 176, 177, 179, 195, 200, 203, 220, 223, 231, 236, 237, 240, 244, 246, 252
  Hunan Branch, 45, 46, 49
  Party Congress,
    Third, 53, 54, 56
    Fourth, 60, 61
    Fifth, 65
    Sixth, 90
    Seventh, 158
    Eighth, 200, 204
    Tenth, 215, 217
Communist Youth International, 51, 232
Confucius, 21, 34, 218, 219, 222, 249, 50
  Anti-, 219, 222
  Temple, 34
Council of People's Commissars, 98, 110, 114, 134
Cultural Bookstore, 40, 42, 43, 44, 45, 49
Cultural Revolution, 6, 13, 18, 47, 57, 148, 190, 194, 202, 205, 207, 208, 209, 212, 213, 214, 215, 216, 218, 219, 220, 221, 224, 229, 234, 235, 237, 239, 243, 246, 247, 248, 250

Dalin, A.S., 51
Das Kapital, 43 see also Marx
Democratic United Army, 162, 170, 172, 173
Dismissal of Hai Jui, The, 205, 208
Dream of the Red Chamber, The, 190

East is Red, The, 157
Eighth Route Army, 141

Fan Shih-sheng, 78, 79
Feng Hsueh-feng, 194
Feng Yu-hsiang, 95

Feng Yu-Lan, Professor, 192
First All China Soviet Congress, 98, 99
First Campaign of Encirclement, 97
First Emperor of Chin, 5
First Middle School of Hunan, 19
First Normal School of Hunan, 20, 21, 23, 24, 26, 30, 34, 39, 41, 106
First Party Congress of Soviet Area, 99
Forbidden City, 175, 178, 183, 198, 239
Four Modernizations, 244, 247, 248
French Revolution, 35
Fu Lien-chang, Dr, 101
Fu Tso-yi, 171
Fukien, 88, 91, 92, 94, 95, 102, 105, 106, 110, 114, 115, 124
  Military Region, 106
Futien, 96, 97, 98

Gang of Four, 5, 207, 211, 217, 218, 221, 238, 243, 246, 247, see also Chiang Ching
General Line for Socialist Construction, 198, 199, 202, 203, 216 see also Great Leap Forward
Generalissimo, 139, 140, 173
Gettysburg Address, 52
Geat Leap Forward, 197, 198, 199, 200, 201, 202, 203, 208, 216, 245, 247, 250
Guide Weekly, 64 see also Peasant Movement Training Institute

Health Bookstore, 40
Hengyang, 37, 39
History of Chinese Philosophy, 192
Ho Chang-kung, 74, 76, 78, 79, 82
Ho Chi Minh, 183
Ho Lung, 69, 116, 117, 137
Ho Shu-heng, 46, 110
Ho Tsu-chen, 86, 100, 101, 111, 116, 117, 146, 147, 148, 232, 233, 234
Ho Yi, 102
Hou Wai-lu, 192
Hsia Hsi, 50
Hsiang Chung-fa, 91
Hsiang Ying, 96, 97, 98, 99, 100, 101, 103, 104, 110–11, 115, 116, 120

Hsiangchiang Ping Lun, see Hsiang-chiang Review
Hsiangchiang Review, 35, 36, 39
Hsianghsiang, 16, 18, 28
    Middle School, 18, 19, 20
Hsiangtang, 16, 57, 64, 230
Hsiangya Medical College, 36
Hsiao Ching-kuan, 106
Hsiao San, 14, 16, 22, 23, 32
Hsiao Yu, 22, 23, 24, 25, 26, 43
Hsin Ching Nien, *see New Youth Magazine*
Hsin Min Hsueh Hui, *see* New People Study Society
Hsiu Yeh Primary School, 34
Hsu Fu, 239
Hsu Hai-tung, 131, 137
Hsu Hsiang-chien, 124, 126, 129
Hsu I-hsin, 234
Hsu Teh-li, 21
Hsu Ying, 185
Hu Han-Min, 55
Hu Shao-hai, 84
Hua Kuo-feng, 222, 230, 246
Huang Hsing, 28
Hunan, 9, 17, 18, 28, 31, 33, 34, 35, 36, 38, 39, 40, 41, 45, 48, 53, 59, 60, 62, 64, 68, 69, 70, 92, 94, 105, 115, 116
    Labour Union, 40, 41
    Peasants Assembly, 62
    Provincial Party Committee, 70, 71, 82, 86, 87, 88, 93
Hundred Days Reform, 16
Hundred Flowers Bloom Movement, *see* Let a Hundred Flowers Bloom Movement
Hung Hsiu-chuan, 4, 10
Hupei, 46, 69, 70

I Shun-ting, 39
International Faction, 92, 99, 102, 105, 107, 110, 112, 122, 128, 134, 138, 143, 149, 152, 179
International Settlement in Shanghai, 135
International United Front, 136

Jao Ju-shih, 196

Japan-Resisting Vanguards, 115
Japan's Imperial Army, 135, 140
Joffe, A.A., 51
Juichin, 100, 101, 104, 105, 106, 107, 111, 114, 121, 126, 175

Kanchu, 114
Kang Sheng, 147, 149, 150, 152, 153, 156, 216, 234
Kang Yu-wei, 16, 17, 18
Kansu, 127
Kao Chun-yu, 48
Kao Kang, 131, 162, 163, 175, 196, 204
Kao Tsu, Emperor, 23
Ke Ching-shih, 207
Khruschev, N.S., 143, 195, 196
Kiangsi Military Region, 107
Kiangsi Soviet, 3, 61, 69, 92, 94, 96, 97, 98, 100, 105, 107, 111, 112, 115, 125, 131, 134, 136, 231
    Provincial Soviet, 101, 102, 107·
    Provincial Party Committee, 107
Korean War, 180, 181, 182, 183, 184, 186, 196, 238
Ku Mu, 182
Kuang Hsu, Emperor, 16
Kung Chu, 84, 86, 88, 89, 93, 101, 111
    see also The Red Army and I
Kung Peng, 166
Kuo Mo-jo, 61, 146, 191, 240
Kuomintang, 48, 51, 52, 53, 54, 55, 57, 58, 59, 60, 61, 62, 63, 65, 66, 67, 68, 69, 78, 79, 82, 102, 106, 119, 161, 162, 163, 164, 171, 173, 223
    Army, 87
    Central Executive Committee, 54, 60
    Executive Headquarters, 55, 62
    First National Congress of, 54
    Revolutionary Committee, 69
Kutien, 92
Kwangchang, 114, 115
Kwangsi Army, 26
Kwangtung, 59, 62, 69, 70, 78, 92, 117
    Trade Union, 70
    Engineering Union, 70
Kweichow, 117, 121, 123

Lai Chuang-chu, 94
Lai Yi, 76, 77
Lan Ping, 11, 147
Lenin, V.I., 5, 12, 33, 38, 45, 78, 92, 112, 130, 134, 143, 158, 195, 244, 246, 252
Let a Hundred Flowers Bloom Movement, 193, 195, 218, 245
Li Chih-lung, 60
Li Fa-ching, 141, 142
Li Han-chun, 45, 46
Li Hsien-nien, 247
Li Hsiu-Cheng, 4
Li Huang, 32
Li Hung-chang, 2
Li Li-san, 25, 48, 68, 91, 92, 93, 95, 96, 97, 98, 119
Li Piao, 4, 6
Li Shih-tseng, 30
Li Shu-yi, 228
Li Ta, 46, 192
Li Ta-chao, 5, 31, 32, 33, 34, 35, 38, 39, 43, 45, 46, 48, 54
Li Teh, see Otto Braun
Li Teh-sheng, 216
Li Tsung-jen, 95, 171, 172
Li Tzu-cheng, 4
Li Wei-Han, 117
Liang Chi-chao, 16, 17, 18
Liang Su-ming, 192
Lianghoko Meeting, 125, 126, 128
Liberation Army, see People's Liberation Army
Liberation Army Daily, 207, 211
Liberation Army Literature, 130
Liberation Daily, The, 207
Lin Piao, 83, 106, 116, 118, 123, 131, 143, 146, 162, 163, 170, 205, 208, 209, 210, 211, 212, 213, 214, 215, 216, 218, 219, 220, 238, 249
Lin Tsu-Han, 54, 60, 61, 62, 156, 236
Linghsien, 74
Literary Gazette, 194
Little Red Book, The, 206, 212
Liu Chen, 63
Liu Chih-tan, 126, 128, 131, 137
Liu Fei, 173
Liu Po-cheng, 85, 103, 104, 114, 118, 121, 122, 129, 131, 167

Liu Shao-chi, 6, 48, 101, 117, 118 – 19, 120, 140, 147 – 8, 158, 175, 178, 182, 184, 200, 205, 207, 208, 210, 211, 212, 219, 237, 238
Liu-teng, 205, 209
Liu Ya-tzu, 226
Lo Chia-lun, 33
Lo Fu, see Chang Wen-tien
Lo Jui-ching, 240, 241
Lo Lung-chi, 181
Lo Ping-hui, 116
Lominadze, Besso, 68, 69
Long March, 60, 100, 102, 104, 107, 113, 116, 118, 121, 123, 127, 134, 135, 136, 137, 143, 146, 147, 227, 233
Lu, Empress, 219
Lu Hsun, 194
Luhsien, 123
Lungyen, 92
Lushan, 204, 205

Manchu Court, 1, 2, 10, 18, 52 Dynasty, 19
Manchuria, 162, 163, 170, 171, 172, 179, 181, 194, 196
Mao An-ching, 5, 101, 166
Mao An-ying, 5, 101
Mao Lu-chung, 15
Mao Shun-sheng, 10, 11, 13, 14, 15, 16
Mao Tse-min, 14, 47, 59, 73, 230
Mao Tse-tan, 14, 47, 78, 107, 116, 230
Mao Tun, 194
Mao Yuan-Hsin, 216
Maokung, 123
Marco Polo Bridge Incident, 140
Marin, G., 51
Maring, 46
Marx, Karl, 3, 4, 5, 12, 13, 21, 31, 33, 34, 38, 39, 40, 41, 42, 43, 45, 47, 49, 53, 57, 61, 66, 74, 75, 78, 94, 100, 106, 112, 120, 131, 134, 143, 154, 158, 166, 171, 190, 191, 195, 211, 219, 235, 244, 246, 252
Marxist Communism School, 106
Marxist Study Group, 32, 33, 34, 40, 41, 44, 45
May the Fourth Movement, 34, 35, 38
Mei Chou Ping Lun, see The Weekly Review

Mei Yi, 136
Meihsien, 92
Miao Tribe, 10
Mienyang, 27
Military Strategy of Sun Wu, 100
Ming Empire, 4
Moon Festival, 222
Moslem Rebellion, 1
Mukden Incident, 135

Nanchang Uprising, 69, 78, 83
Nanking, 65, 90, 138, 139, 140, 164, 165, 166, 172
Government, 65, 90
National Military Commission, 141
National People's Congress, 197, 207
National Political Consultative Conference, 194
National Revolutionary Army, 62, 65, 141
National United Front, 140, 144, 145, 163, 176
Nationalist Supreme Command, 131
Nationalists, 63, 68, 69, 70, 72, 75, 76, 78, 79, 82, 84, 86, 87, 88, 91, 92, 95, 97, 101, 102, 103, 106, 113, 114, 115, 116, 117, 119, 121, 123, 128, 129, 130, 131, 135, 136, 139, 140, 141, 142, 143, 145, 146, 149, 158, 160, 161, 162, 163, 164, 165, 166, 167, 170, 171, 172, 173, 174, 175, 179, 240
Fourth Encirclement Campaign, 102, 105
Fifth Encirclement Campaign, 110, 113, 119, 120
Nineteenth Route Army, 110
Neumann, Heinz, 68, 69
New China Daily News, 161
New Democracy, 163, 173, 176
New Era, 69 *see also* Communist Party, Hunan Branch
New Fourth Army, 96
New Hunan, 36
New People Study Society, 24, 25, 26, 27, 34, 35, 36, 39, 40, 41, 42, 43, 44, 45, 50
New Youth Magazine, 24, 30, 31, 33
Nieh Jung-chen, 118, 120

Nien People, 10
Nikonsky, 46
Ningkang, 74
Ningtu Military Conference, 102, 103
Nixon, R.M., 221, 251
Northward Expedition, 79

October Revolution, 98
Opium War, 1, 10
Orchard of Dates, 149, 150, 155

Pan Han-nien, 120
Pang Pu, 249
Pao-an, 104, 138, 139, 140
Party Congress, *see* Communist Party
Peasant Movement Training Institute, 58, 59, 60, 62, 63, 64, 94
Advisory Committee, 62
Peking, 30, 31, 33, 35, 38, 46, 52
University, 30, 31, 33, 38
Warlord Government, 35
Peng Kung-ta, 70
Peng Pai, 58
Peng Te-huai, 87, 88, 95, 96, 103, 106, 110, 114, 116, 118, 121, 131, 138, 141, 143, 146, 182, 202, 203, 204, 205, 208, 243 *see also* Red Fifth Army
People's Communes, 216
People's Daily, 225
People's Liberation Army, 204, 207, 212, 216, 224, 243
People's Republic, 105, 175, 178
People's Trial, 139
Po Ku *see* Chin Pang-hsien
Politburo, 68, 90, 91, 92, 96, 97, 98, 99, 102, 103, 104, 105, 106, 107, 110, 111, 113, 115, 117, 118, 119, 120, 121, 122, 123, 124, 125, 126, 128, 129, 139, 141, 144, 153, 163, 167, 198, 216, 217, 245
Political Weekly, 58
Problems of Strategy in China's Revolutionary War, 104
Provincial Association of Hunan Students, 35, 36, 42
Provincial Party Committee, 78, 79, 107
Provincial Soviet, 107

Provisional Central Committee of the Chinese Communist Party, 39, 45
Provisional Political Bureau, 69, 71
Pu An-hsiu, 204

Quotations from Chairman Mao, see *The Little Red Book*

Reappraisal of Confucius and his Philosophy, A, 249
Rectification Campaign, 16, 152, 154, 158
Red Army, 84, 85, 89, 99, 100, 103, 104, 106, 113, 114, 115, 116, 117, 118, 119, 123, 126, 128, 134, 138, 140, 141, 153, 206, 243
  Third, 95
  Fourth, 79, 82, 83, 86, 87, 88, 91, 94, 95, 123, 124, 126, 127, 128, 129
  Fifth, 87, 88
  Seventh, 106 – 7
  Twenty-fifth, 131
  Twenty-sixth, 131
Red Army and I, The, 84, 88, 101, 111
Red Army Corps, 114, 115, 116, 117, 118, 121, 129, 134
  First, 114, 116, 129, 134
  Second, 116, 117, 118, 121
  Third, 106, 114, 116, 121, 129, 134
  Fifth, 114, 116, 118, 129
  Sixth, 115, 118, 121
  Seventh, 115
  Eighth, 116, 121
  Ninth, 114, 116, 129
  Tenth, 115
Red China Magazine, 106, 107
Red Detachment of Women, The, 207
Red First Front Army, 95, 116, 123, 124, 126, 127, 128, 129
Red Flag, 252
Red Guards, 209, 210, 212, 213, 214, 219, 220, 224, 246
Red Labour Union International, 45
Red Second Front Army, 137
Resolutions on Some Historical Issues, 97

Revolution and War, 103
Romance of the Three Kingdoms, 3, 4, 12, 13, 17, 27, 56, 85, 94, 100, 103, 104, 106, 107
Roy, M.R., 67
Russian Red Army, 103
Russian Revolution, 44

Sanwan Men, 73
Selected Works of Mao Tse-tung, 247
Self-study University, 46, 47, 49
Shanghai, 2, 34, 38, 39, 43, 45, 46, 50, 51, 55, 62, 64, 68, 90, 91, 93, 97, 98, 101, 107, 120, 207, 208
Shanghang, 92
Shansi, 170
Shangtung, 136, 170
Shaokuan, 78
Shaoshan, 3, 16, 19, 47, 57, 230
Shaoshan Chung, 9, 10, 13
Shen Ke-fei, Dr, 241
Shensi, 126, 127, 128, 134, 137, 138, 167, 170
Shensi-kansu Guerilla Detachment of the Workers and Peasants Red Army, 131, 134
Shih Nai-an, 12 see also *The Water Margin*
Sian, 138, 139
Sikang, 136
Sinkiang, 231
Sino-French War, 2
Sino-Japanese War, 2, 177, 233
Sino-Soviet Friendship Associations, 180
Sino-Soviet Treaty of Friendship and Alliance, 180
Socialist Youth Corps, 40, 41, 44, 45, 47
Society for the Study of Russia, 43, 44
Special Committee of Southern Hunan, 93 see also Hunan
Ssu-ma Yi, 27
Stalin J.V., 6, 65, 140, 143, 158, 180, 184, 187, 195, 196, 237
Stuart, Dr John Leighton, 178
Student Self-government, 24, 26
Suichuan, 74, 76, 77
Sun Tzu, 171

Sun Wu, General, 100, 103
Sun Yat-sen, Dr, 18, 51, 52, 54, 55, 58, 59, 72, 141, 151
Sunday Club, 41
Sung Dynasty, 3
Szechuan, 123, 127, 128, 134

Ta Kung Pao, 185
Tai Tsu, Emperor, 23
Taiping Rebellion, 1, 4, 9, 10, 28, 100, 104, 174
Taiwan, 179
Tan Chen-lin, 105, 106
Tan Ping-shan, 54, 55, 60, 61, 62
Tan Ssu-tung, 28
Tan Wu-peng, 23
Tan Yen-kai, General, 37, 39, 41, 42
Tao Ssu-yung, 43
Tasks of China's Anti-Japanese National United Front in the Present Period, The, 140
Tatu river, 123
Teng Chung-hsia, 38
Teng Hsiao-chi, 207
Teng Hsiao-ping, 100, 101, 102, 105, 107, 111, 167, 194, 205, 208, 209, 210, 212, 222, 247, 248, 249, 250, 252
Teng Pao-shan, 171
Teng Tzu-hui, 110
Teng Ying-chao, 235
Third International, 54, 66, 90, 91, 98, 142
Thought Remoulding Movement, 185
Thoughts of Mao Tse-tung, 246
Three People's Principles, 52, 141, 142, 151 *see also* Dr Sun Yat-sen
Three Red Banners, 199, 200, 202, 203, 205, 216
Three-way Alliance, 216, 217
Tin Tou-tou, 215
Ting Ling, 194
Tokyo, 46
Tsai Ho-shen, 22, 23, 25, 30, 31, 33, 44, 48, 53, 65
Tsai Yuan-pei, 30
Tsao Tsao, 70, 88, 191, 193, 238
Tseng Kuo-fan, General, 28, 100, 103, 104

Tse-tan, 102
Tsinan, 46
Tsoan, 77
Tsunyi, 117, 118, 121, 122, 123, 124, 125, 126, 130, 134, 136, 137, 140
Conference, 117, 118, 130
Tuan Hsi-peng, 33
Tung Chen-tang, 116
Tung Pi-wu, 135, 138, 145, 149, 154, 166, 170, 224, 233, 234, 235, 236
Tung Ping-wu, 72, 90, 106
Tungshan (East Hill) Primary School, 16, 17, 22
Tungtao, 117
Twenty-eight Bolsheviks, *see* International Faction

United Front, 48, 51, 52, 53, 140, 142, 151, 152, 171, 173, 176, 230

V-J Day celebration, 162
Vladimirov, P.N., 158

Wang Chi-fan, 17
Wang Chia-hsiang, 122
Wang Ching-wei, 55, 58, 59, 60, 62, 63, 64
Wang Hung-wen, 216, 217
Wang Kai, 79 *see also* Chu Teh
Wang Ming, 92, 96, 97, 98, 99, 105, 124, 137, 140, 142, 143, 144, 146, 147, 149, 150, 152, 153, 154, 157, 158 *see also* Chen Shao-yu
Wang Shou-tao, 59, 63
Wang Tso, 73, 74, 88
War of Liberation, 236
Warlord Government (Peking), 36, 38, 52, 62
Water Margin, The, 3, 4, 12, 13, 17, 56, 72, 76, 78, 85, 100, 103, 104, 145, 190
Weekly Review, The, 35, 36
Wei troops, 27
Wen Chi-mei, 10
Westward Journey, The, 130
Whampoa Military Academy, 55, 61, 83
White-haired Girl, The, 207

Worker-student Mutual Aid Group, 32

Worker-student programme, 31, 32

Workers and Peasants Revolutionary Army, 75, 76, 79, 82, 84

World Communist Movement, 195

Wu, Empress, 219

Wu Han, 207, 208, 209

Wu Kang, 228

Wu Pei-fu, General, 37, 39

Wu river, 123

Wu Yu-chang, 156, 236

Wuchang Institute, 63

Wuchung, 92

Wuhan, 63, 64, 65, 66, 67, 69
  National Government, 63, 65, 67, 69

Yang Chang-chi, 20, 21, 22, 24, 30, 31, 33, 37, 43

Yang Cheng-wu, 130

Yang Hsiu-ching, 4

Yang Hu-cheng, 139

Yang I-chih, 100, 101, 111, 113, 130, 137, 160, 161, 163, 171, 177, 192, 235, 238

Yang Kai-hui, 3, 7, 39, 40, 43, 45, 47, 49, 56, 57, 85, 101, 228, 230, 232, 234, 238

Yang Yen-chao, 140

Yao Wen-yuan, 207, 208, 217

Yeh Chien-ying, 216, 247

Yeh Chun, 215

Yeh Ting, 69

Yen Hsi-shan, 95, 141, 164

Yenan, 99, 102, 106, 140, 142 – 58, 163, 165, 173, 175, 184, 187, 233, 235, 236, 239

Yipin, 123

Young China Society, 31, 32, 39

Young Marshal, 137, 138, 139, 140

Yu Shu-teh, 54

Yuan Shih-kai, 22

Yuan Wen-tsai, 73, 74, 88

Yuchiang, 114

Yungshin, 74, 86

Yungting, 92, 94

Yunnan Army, 79

Yutu, 101